T0317647

Basic Income: A History

Basic Income
A History

Malcolm Torry

Visiting Fellow, Institute for Policy Research, University of Bath, Senior Visiting Fellow, London School of Economics, Treasurer, Basic Income Earth Network (BIEN), former Director, Citizen's Basic Income Trust. He is a Priest in the Church of England and Priest in Charge of St Mary Abchurch, City of London, UK

Edward Elgar
PUBLISHING

Cheltenham, UK • Northampton, MA, USA

© Malcolm Torry 2021

All rights reserved. No part of this publication may be reproduced, stored in a retrieval system or transmitted in any form or by any means, electronic, mechanical or photocopying, recording, or otherwise without the prior permission of the publisher.

Published by
Edward Elgar Publishing Limited
The Lypiatts
15 Lansdown Road
Cheltenham
Glos GL50 2JA
UK

Edward Elgar Publishing, Inc.
William Pratt House
9 Dewey Court
Northampton
Massachusetts 01060
USA

Paperback edition 2023

A catalogue record for this book
is available from the British Library

Library of Congress Control Number: 2021939465

This book is available electronically in the **Elgar**online
Sociology, Social Policy and Education subject collection
http://dx.doi.org/10.4337/9781839102417

ISBN 978 1 83910 240 0 (cased)
ISBN 978 1 83910 241 7 (eBook)
ISBN 978 1 0353 1344 0 (paperback)

Printed and bound by CPI Group (UK) Ltd, Croydon, CR0 4YY

Contents

Figures

Preface

In January 2019, members of Cambridge University's Department of Politics and International Studies and Faculty of History, and of the Universitè Libre de Bruxelles, held a gathering of academics to discuss the history of Basic Income. During the day the absence and need of a comprehensive history of Basic Income was noted, and during the dinner at the end of the event a discussion took place as to who was going to write it. A number of scholars who would have been eminently qualified to do so declined the opportunity for various reasons, and I was left as the only one not to have refused the opportunity, even though I was far less qualified for the task than all of the obvious candidates.

Writing a history of such an important and increasingly influential idea has been both daunting and a privilege. The indefinite article in the subtitle is important. Any history of a period, a place, or an idea, is *a* history, rather than *the* history. Many different histories could have been written: and the same is true in relation to Basic Income. This is definitely *a* history of Basic Income, and should not be regarded as in any sense definitive.

The history that I have written is first of all a history of Basic Income—of a regular unconditional income paid without means test or work test—and only of such 'cousins' as Negative Income Tax and Minimum Income Guarantee when their histories relate to the history of Basic Income. Similarly, historic and current social security and taxation systems are only mentioned to the extent that they relate directly to the Basic Income debate.

The history is comprehensive in the sense that it is about both the idea of Basic Income and a variety of relevant pilot projects and experiments, and in the sense that it begins at the beginning of the modern debate at the end of the eighteenth century and ends as close as possible to the present day. An additional intention has been to be geographically comprehensive. This has been a more difficult criterion to meet, for two reasons: first of all, I know far more about Basic Income's history in the UK than anywhere else because I have been intimately involved in that history since 1984; and secondly, and connectedly, because a high proportion of the Basic Income debate before the 1980s occurred in the UK, and a substantial proportion of it since then. Comprehensiveness in relation to events, discussions and publications has been relatively easy to achieve for the earlier part of the debate, but comprehensiveness in relation to more recent debate has been quite impossible to achieve simply because there has been so much of it. About fifteen years ago there was a significant step change in the character of the debate. Pilot projects took place, the debate became worldwide (in the sense of widespread around the planet) and then global (in the sense that a single debate was happening globally), and the number of publications about Basic Income exploded. Until about fifteen years ago I could honestly claim to have read most of what was published in English on Basic Income, and occasional literature in other languages, as could a number of other people involved in the debate. Now nobody could claim that. It is generally true of any history-writing that a different author would have chosen different material to include and would have ordered it differently. That would certainly be true of this history, and particularly in relation to the more recent period.

Acknowledgements

Being aware of my lack of qualification for the task of writing a history of Basic Income, I have relied to a considerable extent on books written by Timothée Duverger, Peter Sloman, Karl Widerquist, Philippe Van Parijs, Walter Van Trier, and Yannick Vanderborght; on chapters containing historical material in collections edited by Richard Caputo and Larry Liu; John Cunliffe and Guido Erreygers; Karl Widerquist, José Noguera, Yannick Vanderborght and Jurgen De Wispelaere; and Robert van der Veen and Loek Groot; on a number of the chapters in *The Palgrave International Handbook of Basic Income*; and on a wide variety of other books, chapters and articles. Wherever possible, and particularly for the earlier period, I have consulted original sources, and I have been grateful for assistance with this from librarians at the British Library and at the British Library of Political and Economic Science at the London School of Economics. I am particularly grateful to a significant number of individuals who have assisted me with historical material and with useful advice, and particularly to Peter Sloman, Philippe Van Parijs, Walter Van Trier and Karl Widerquist, who have read and commented on all or most of a first draft; and to Gabriela Cabaña, Marc de Basquiat, Sarath Davala, Loek Groot, Louise Haagh, Claudia and Dirk Haarmann, Seán Healy, Barb Jacobson, Julio Linares, Rubén Lo Vuolo, Leire Rincón, Ulrich Schachtschneider, Enno Schmidt, Lena Stark, Hamid Tabatabai, Enkeleida Tahiraj and Gunmin Yi, who have provided useful comment on those parts of the history that they know most about. Statements made and opinions expressed are of course entirely the responsibility of the author and should not be taken to be statements by or to represent the views of any other individual or organization.

In relation to this and the other books that I have been able to write on Basic Income I am grateful to the Social Policy Department at the London School of Economics for granting me Visiting Senior Fellowships between 2011 and 2020, and to Professor Hartley Dean for supervising my work; to the publishers of my previous books on Basic Income—Policy Press, Palgrave Macmillan, Edward Elgar Publishing, and Darton, Longman and Todd—and, in relation to this history, Edward Elgar; to the trustees of the Citizen's Basic Income Trust, which it was my privilege to serve as secretary and then honorary Director for a total of twenty years; to the Executive Committee and members of the Basic Income Earth Network (BIEN), of which I am currently honorary General Manager; to staff at the Institute for Social and Economic

Research for assistance with microsimulation research; and to successive Bishops of Woolwich and the officers of the South London parishes that I have served in a stipendiary capacity from 1980 to 2014 for permission to spend some of my time researching and debating Basic Income.

A little while ago, I held a discussion with Guy Standing, author of numerous books on Basic Income and related subjects, on the current state of Basic Income literature. We came to the view that the literature was substantially saturated, and we could identify few gaps. My most recent publication on the subject, *A Modern Guide to Citizen's Basic Income: A Multidisciplinary Approach*, published by Edward Elgar Publishing in 2020, filled one of those gaps, as there was until then no single author multidisciplinary study of Basic Income. Another gap was a comprehensive history. I hope that this history will fill that gap until a better one is written.

Any royalties due on this book will be donated to the Basic Income Earth Network (BIEN).

Malcolm Torry
London, February 2021

A note on *A Modern Guide to Citizen's Basic Income*

The writing of this history overlapped to some extent with the writing of a multidisciplinary study of Basic Income: *A Modern Guide to Citizen's Basic Income: A multidisciplinary approach*, which was published by Edward Elgar Publishing in 2020. The publisher describes the book like this:

> Debate on the desirability, feasibility and implementation of a Citizen's Basic Income – an unconditional, nonwithdrawable and regular income for every individual – is increasingly widespread among academics, policymakers, and the general public. There are now numerous introductory books on the subject, and others on particular aspects of it. This book provides something new: It studies the Citizen's Basic Income proposal from a variety of different disciplinary perspectives: the economics of Citizen's Basic Income, the sociology of Citizen's Basic Income, the politics of Citizen's Basic Income, and so on. Each chapter discusses the academic discipline, and relevant aspects of the debate, and asks how the discipline enhances our understanding, and how the Citizen's Basic Income debate might contribute to the academic discipline.

Of particular interest to readers of this book might be Chapter 3, which studies the history of history-writing, from political history, through social history, to economic history, and concludes that history-writing is the construction of narratives influenced by contemporary agendas and backed up by evidence. Questions are then set: Is the history of Basic Income a subdiscipline of history, or of social history, or of economic history? What are the agendas that historians bring to their history-writing? What are the data that they seek to back up their arguments? Should a history of Basic Income be a history of the idea of a Basic Income, of policy debates, or of practical experiments? To what extent should the history be located in the broader history of existing tax and benefits systems? To what extent should 'close cousins', such as Negative Income Tax, be included? Five histories of Citizen's Basic Income are then evaluated against these questions, and conclusions are drawn.

Readers of this history might find it interesting to evaluate it in relation to the questions asked in Chapter 3 of *A Modern Guide to Citizen's Basic Income: A multidisciplinary approach*.

Abbreviations

AFDC	Aid to Families with Dependent Children
AIRE	Association pour l'Instauration du Revenu d'Existence (Association for the Implementation of an Existence Income)
ANC	African National Congress
BBC	British Broadcasting Corporation
BCE	Before the Common Era
BI	Basic Income
BIEN	Basic Income European Network (until 2004); Basic Income Earth Network (after 2004)
BIG	Basic Income Grant (in Namibia); Basic Income Guarantee (in the USA)
BIKN	Basic Income Korean Network
BIRG	Basic Income Research Group
B-MINCOME	Barcelona Minimum Income [Experiment]
CBI	Citizen's Basic Income
CBINS	Citizen's Basic Income Network Scotland
CBIT	Citizen's Basic Income Trust
CI	Citizen's Income
CIEPP	Centro Interdisiplinario para el Estudio de Políticas Públicas (Interdisciplinary Centre for the Study of Public Policy)
CIT	Citizen's Income Trust
CNBC	Canadian National Broadcasting Corporation
CORI	Conference of Religious of Ireland
COSATU	Congress of South African Trade Unions
CPAG	Child Poverty Action Group
DWP	Department for Work and Pensions (UK)

EITC	Earned Income Tax Credit
EU	European Union
EUROMOD	[Tax-benefit microsimulation programme for the European Union]
FAP	Family Assistance Plan
GAI	Guaranteed Adequate Income; Guaranteed Annual Income
GDP	Gross Domestic Product
HMRC	Her Majesty's Revenue and Customs (UK)
ILO	International Labour Office; International Labour Organization
IMF	International Monetary Fund
INBI	India Network for Basic Income
IPPR	Institute for Public Policy Research (UK)
LBU	Landelijk Beraad Uitkeringsgerechtigden (Netherlands) (National Claimants Council)
LSE	London School of Economics
MEP	Member of the European Parliament
MFRB	Mouvement Français pour un Revenu de Base (French Movement for a Basic Income)
MIG	Minimum Income Guarantee
MINCOME	Minimum Income [Experiment]
MP	Member of Parliament
NAMTAX	[Namibian Tax Commission]
NBLSS	National Basic Living Security System (Republic of Korea)
NCVO	National Council for Voluntary Organisations
NGO	Nongovernmental Organization
NIT	Negative Income Tax
OECD	Organisation for Economic Co-operation and Development
PBI	Personal Basic Income
POLIMOD	[Early tax-benefit microsimulation programme for the UK]

PT	Partido dos Trabalhadores (Workers' Party)
RMI	Revenu Minimum D'Insertion (Minimum Insertion Income)
RSA	Revenu de Solidarité Active (in France); Royal Society of Arts (in the UK)
RUA	Revenu Universel d'Activité (Universal Activity Income)
SEWA	Self-Employed Women's Association
SIME/DIME	Seattle/Denver Income Maintenance Experiment
SOAS	School of Oriental and African Studies
SSA	Sub-Saharan Africa
TAXMOD	[Early tax-benefit microsimulation programme for the UK]
UBI	Universal Basic Income; Unconditional Basic Income
UBIE	Universal Basic Income Europe
UCT	Unconditional Cash Transfer
UK	United Kingdom [of Great Britain and Northern Ireland]
UKMOD	[Tax-benefit microsimulation programme for the United Kingdom]
UNICEF	United Nations International Children's Emergency Fund
US	United States [of America]
USA	United States of America
USBIG	United States Basic Income Guarantee [Network]

1.   A history of Basic Income

INTRODUCTION

The writing of history requires boundaries to be set: chronological boundaries; geographical boundaries; and a set of boundaries around the particular
aspects of the vast diversity of human activity with which the history will
be concerned. This history has no geographical boundaries: it intends to be
a worldwide history, in the sense that it is about the Basic Income debate
around the world: and it also intends to be a history of the global debate, in the
sense that it is a history of a debate that is now a single debate happening in
many parts of the world. So this history's subject-matter will be the worldwide
and global debate about Basic Income, which is defined as an unconditional
income for every individual; and the period with which it will be concerned
will be any period of human history in which thought or activity in relation to
Basic Income has occurred.

The main tasks of this introductory chapter will therefore be to discuss the
definition of Basic Income, and to set some boundaries around what the history
will be about. As well as discussing the meaning of 'Basic Income', it will also
explore the meanings of three other words significant for an understanding of
the Basic Income debate: 'guarantee', 'unconditional' and 'universal'; and in
order to decide on some important boundaries for the subject matter, it will
discuss a variety of alternative reform proposals. Finally, the structure of the
book will be described.

BASIC INCOME

A Citizen's Basic Income is an unconditional, automatic and nonwithdrawable
income for each individual as a right of citizenship. A Citizen's Basic Income (CBI)
is sometimes called a Basic Income (BI) or a Citizen's Income (CI). (Citizen's Basic
Income Trust, 2018a: 3)

As this is a history about Basic Income, we need to know what we mean by
that combination of words, because only then shall we know what should be
included in the history.

1

Defining Basic Income

When we ask about the meaning of words, we are asking how they are used. As Wittgenstein put it, 'we see a complicated network of similarities overlapping and criss-crossing; sometimes overall similarities, sometimes similarities of detail ... Now I know how to go on ... *This is how these words are used*' (Wittgenstein, [1953] 2001: §66, 27; §180, 62; §179, 62: italics in the original. Cf. Grayling, 1988: 90). This is how dictionaries work. Compilers collect a wide variety of usages of a word or phrase, and then attempt to capture the general meaning—the 'definition'—by using other words, which then themselves require definition, and so on (Bambrough, 1969: 94). Whilst meanings will be different in different contexts, there might be similarities in the ways in which words and phrases are used across a variety of contexts: what Wittgenstein called 'Familienähnlichkeiten', 'family resemblances' (Wittgenstein, [1953] 2001: §67, 27): and it is on these resemblances that dictionary compilers rely. This means that if we are to know what 'Basic Income' means, then we shall have to know how it is used in a wide variety of contexts, and we shall have to look for similarities between those uses.

There is no entry for 'Basic Income', 'Citizen's Income' or 'Citizen's Basic Income' in the *Oxford English Dictionary* (which is interesting), but we do of course find both 'basic' and 'income'. 'Basic' used as an adjective is given a wide variety of definitions, the first two of which are as follows:

> a. Of, pertaining to, or forming a base; fundamental, essential: ... b. That is or constitutes a standard minimum amount in a scale of remuneration or the like.

The dictionary also offers the following definition:

> Providing or having few or no amenities, accessories, functions, etc., beyond the ordinary or essential; of or designating the lowest standard acceptable or available; rudimentary.

An example is given: 'Pastries and other sweets in the north can be pretty basic'. English as spoken in the United States of America exhibits similar meanings:

> a. being the main or most important part of something ... b. very simple, with nothing special added: 'The software is very basic.' (*Cambridge Essential American English Dictionary*)

The somewhat derogatory undertones of the word 'Basic' in English were one of the reasons for the shift in the United Kingdom (UK) from 'Basic Income' to 'Citizen's Income' during the early 1990s. The meaning was the same, but the latter term was believed to escape the problem of unfortunate undertones: which of course it did not, because 'citizen' does not necessarily apply to everyone living within a jurisdiction, and so can be exclusionary. It is because the word 'Basic' was retained across most of the global debate, and 'Grundeinkommen' and 'Basiseinkommen' were the words used in the German-speaking debate, and 'revenu de base' in the French, that the UK turned to the rather more complex 'Citizen's Basic Income' terminology, and sometimes to 'Universal Basic Income' (on the word 'universal' see later in this chapter) (Torry, 2017b; 2020a: 7–27).

It is all very well deciding that the uses to which a word or phrase is put decide its meaning: but precisely whose uses of the term 'Basic Income' should we choose? Even if we decide to leave to one side the uses made of the phrase by thousands of individuals and choose to ask about the term's use by organizations, we face a substantial diversity of usage among the growing number of organizations in the field. Any organization can decide to use 'Basic Income' in whatever way it wishes, of course, but by studying what organizations say about those uses we can discover some family resemblances. For instance, most of the organizations affiliated to BIEN—the Basic Income Earth Network—would say that a Basic Income is 'unconditional' and 'individual'; and they all make identical or similar assumptions: for instance, that the payments will be regular; that they will not vary from week to week or from month to month, apart from being uprated each year; and that the levels of Basic Income might vary with people's ages.

Because BIEN is a global membership organization with affiliated organizations, its definition of 'Basic Income' is likely to reflect current usage, and in particular current usage among its affiliated organizations. The wording on BIEN's website runs as follows:

A basic income is a periodic cash payment unconditionally delivered to all on an individual basis, without means test or work requirement.

That is, basic income has the following five characteristics:
1. Periodic: it is paid at regular intervals (for example every month), not as a one-off grant.
2. Cash payment: it is paid in an appropriate medium of exchange, allowing those who receive it to decide what they spend it on. It is not, therefore, paid either in kind (such as food or services) or in vouchers dedicated to a specific use.
3. Individual: it is paid on an individual basis—and not, for instance, to households.
4. Universal: it is paid to all, without means test.
5. Unconditional: it is paid without a requirement to work or to demonstrate willingness-to-work. (Basic Income Earth Network, 2021)

And a shorter form, last amended at BIEN's 2016 General Assembly in Seoul, reads like this:

> A periodic cash payment unconditionally delivered to all on an individual basis, without means test or work requirement. (Basic Income Earth Network, 2021)

Both of these definitions represent a consensus among affiliated organizations (Torry, 2017b), and they reflect common usage of the term 'Basic Income' (although note that 'without means test' is thought to be implied by 'universal' rather than by 'unconditional', which would be a more natural connection).

The longest standing organization related to the modern Basic Income debate is the UK's Citizen's Basic Income Trust, established in 1984 as the Basic Income Research Group. It defines a (Citizen's) Basic Income as

> an unconditional, automatic and nonwithdrawable income for each individual as a right of citizenship.
> (A Citizen's Basic Income (CBI) is sometimes called a Basic Income (BI) or a Citizen's Income (CI))
> • 'Unconditional': A CBI would vary with age, but there would be no other conditions: so everyone of the same age would receive the same CBI, whatever their gender, employment status, family structure, contribution to society, housing costs, or anything else.
> • 'Automatic': Someone's CBI would be paid weekly or monthly, automatically.
> • 'Nonwithdrawable': CBIs would not be means-tested. Whether someone's earnings or wealth increased, decreased, or stayed the same, their Citizen's Basic Income would not change.
> • 'Individual': CBIs would be paid on an individual basis, and not on the basis of a couple or household.
> • 'As a right': Everybody legally resident in the UK would receive a CBI, subject to a minimum period of legal residency in the UK, and continuing residency for most of the year. (Citizen's Basic Income Trust, 2018a: 3)

In some ways this is clearer than the BIEN definition, because it makes it explicit that although the amount of Basic Income paid might vary with someone's age, no other conditionality would apply: and so, in practical terms, everyone of the same age would receive the same amount of Basic Income. For the purposes of this book, I shall employ this simpler expression, and define a Basic Income as

> an equal and regular payment of the same amount, varying only by an annual uprating, to every individual of the same age legally resident in the jurisdiction in question.

A significant definitional outlier is the way in which Ontario called an income-tested benefit a 'Basic Income' (Ontario, no date). This clearly contradicts the definitions listed above. Some uses of 'Basic Income' fall between 'an equal and regular payment of the same amount, varying only by an annual uprating, to every individual of the same age legally resident in the jurisdiction in question' and Ontario's usage. For instance, in 2019 the Green Party in the UK suggested supplements for lone parents and pensioners living alone (Green Party, 2019); and a general case has been made for making slight variations and still calling the income a Basic Income (Smith-Carrier and Green, 2017). For the avoidance of doubt: no variation in the definition will be permitted throughout this history. If something is not an equal and regular payment of the same amount, varying only by an annual uprating, to every individual of the same age legally resident in the jurisdiction in question, then it is not a Basic Income.

What *will* be permitted will be different terminology for Basic Income, on condition that the terminology means the same as 'Basic Income'. So texts, discussions, ideas, activities, and anything else relevant, might say that they are about 'Basic Income', 'Citizen's Income', 'Citizen's Basic Income', 'Universal Basic Income', or 'Social Dividend', and if what those terms express is a genuine Basic Income—that is, an equal and regular payment of the same amount, varying only by an annual uprating, to every individual of the same age legally resident in the jurisdiction in question—then those texts, discussions, ideas, activities, and anything else relevant, belong in this history. However, this history will employ 'Basic Income' terminology throughout. The reason for this is that what is intended is a global history, and it is 'Basic Income' that functions as the default terminology globally. 'Citizen's Income' and 'Citizen's Basic Income' are mainly found in the UK; 'Universal Basic Income' is global, but less common than simply 'Basic Income'; and 'Social Dividend' is now mainly restricted to debates about sovereign and social wealth funds, and to discussion of a Eurodividend for the European Union or the Eurozone, although during much of the twentieth century it was a common term for Basic Income. The confusingly ambiguous 'Basic Income Guarantee' is common only in the United States and Canada, and we shall not be using it. 'Basic Income' will be our default terminology, although readers might find other terminology in quotations. The reader can be secure in the knowledge that 'Basic Income' and any of the terms listed above will all be used with the same meaning: that is, they will mean an equal and regular payment of the same amount, varying only by an annual uprating, to every individual of the same age legally resident in the jurisdiction in question. If any instances of the terminology mean something else, then that will be made clear.

How Much?

The only significant disagreement among BIEN's affiliated organizations relates to whether the definition of Basic Income should include a statement of the level at which it would be paid. A survey conducted in 2017 found that for some national organizations only an unconditional individual income at 'subsistence level', or 'sufficient to satisfy basic needs', could qualify as a Basic Income, whereas for other organizations an unconditional, regular and individual income of any amount could count as one (Torry, 2017b: 9–17). A similar division of opinion can be found in the literature on Basic Income, in which some authors assume that the level of the Basic Income should lie above a poverty line, somehow defined (Pereira, 2017: 2), whereas others do not (Torry, 2017b; 2018c; Reed and Lansley, 2016; Lansley and Reed, 2019; Martinelli, 2017a; 2017b; 2017c). This book will assume that an equal and regular payment of the same amount for every individual of the same age will be a Basic Income, whatever the level at which it is paid for each age group. This is for several reasons. 'Subsistence level' is difficult to define, with Governments often defining it in relation to political imperatives, and think tanks and social policy academics attempting more evidence-based approaches (Davis et al., 2018); social policy tends to be path-dependent—that is, policy change is more likely to be incremental than radical, even if some of the small steps might be radical—so Governments are more likely to pay attention to proposals for a Basic Income of modest size than to proposals for more substantial payments; and, most importantly, almost every individual and organization active in this policy field can agree that a Basic Income is an equal and regular payment of the same amount, varying only by an annual uprating, to every individual of the same age legally resident in the jurisdiction in question, even if they might disagree over how much should be paid. Where the amount to be paid becomes an issue in this history, the reader might find reference to terminology developed by Hermione Parker, for whom a 'Full Basic Income' meant a Basic Income at subsistence level (somehow defined), and a 'Partial Basic Income' meant a Basic Income at a lower level (Parker, 1989: 4).

Basic Income Schemes

An essential distinction is that between Basic Income and Basic Income scheme. A Basic Income is always an unconditional income for every individual; a Basic Income scheme is a Basic Income with the different levels for different age groups specified, with the funding method fully specified, and with accompanying changes to existing tax and benefits systems also fully specified. There is of course an infinite number of different schemes, and different schemes will exhibit different effects from each other and also different feasibilities (De Wispelaere and Stirton, 2004).

'Guarantee', 'Unconditional' and 'Universal'

Whilst the most important definition to discuss in relation to the global Basic Income debate is that of 'Basic Income', there are three other words that will often be found in any account of a history of the debate: 'guarantee', 'unconditional' and 'universal'.

'Guarantee'
In 1982, Brandon Rhys Williams, a UK Member of Parliament, proposed a Basic Income scheme to a House of Commons committee. Both he and his research assistant Hermione Parker called the Basic Income a 'Basic Income Guarantee', meaning by that that 'every citizen would be entitled to a personal basic income ... These guaranteed basic incomes would replace virtually all existing benefits and allowances ...' (House of Commons Treasury and Civil Service Committee Sub-committee, 1982: 425. Cf. House of Commons Treasury and Civil Service Committee Sub-committee, 1983; Parker, 1989). What was guaranteed was the Basic Income: an unconditional income for every individual; but 'Basic Income Guarantee' was ambiguous because it could mean either that the Basic Income was guaranteed, or that the Government guaranteed that an income of a certain level would be reached by each individual or household, which could imply a means-tested benefit. Largely because of this ambiguity, the word 'guarantee' was quickly dropped from the UK debate (Parker, 1985: 5), and 'Basic Income Guarantee' was replaced by 'Basic Income', 'Universal Basic Income', 'Citizen's Income' and 'Citizen's Basic Income', as they emerged one after the other and then remained as a diverse common currency.

However, for reasons that readers of Chapter 6 will understand, 'guarantee' lingered on in North America. The USBIG (United States Basic Income Guarantee) Network defines a 'Basic Income Guarantee' as a 'Government ensured guarantee that no one's income will fall below the level necessary to meet their most basic needs for any reason' (USBIG Network). 'Basic Income Guarantee' can mean Basic Income, Negative Income Tax, and similar mechanisms, all of which are understood as mechanisms for ensuring that no household incomes should fall below specified levels. As Sheahen puts it, 'Basic Income Guarantee' can encompass all of

Alaska Permanent fund, Basic Income (BI), Basic Income Grant (BIG), Citizen's Dividend, Citizen's Income, Daily Bread, Demogrant, Dividends for All, Guarantee Annual Income (GAI), Guarantee Adequate Income (GAI), Guaranteed Basic

Income, Guaranteed Income (GI), Guaranteed Minimum Income, Guaranteed Minimum, Income Guarantee, Minimum Income Guarantee, Minimum Income, National Minimum, National Tax Rebate, Negative Income Tax (NIT), Refundable Income Tax Credit, Share the Wealth, Social Credit, Social Dividend, Social Income, Social Wage, State Bonus, Territorial Dividend, Unconditional Basic Income (UBI), Universal Allocation, Universal Basic Income (UBI), Universal Benefit, Universal Grant, Universal Income Tax Credit. (Sheahen, 2012: 178)

'Basic Income', on the other hand, always means the same thing: 'Basic Income gives every citizen a check for the full basic income every month, and taxes his or her earned income ...' (USBIG Network). This is a genuine Basic Income as defined in the previous section of the chapter. So 'Basic Income' is an unconditional income, but 'Basic Income Guarantee' is a guaranteed income level that can be met in a variety of different ways. Basic Income Guarantee and Basic Income are clearly very different concepts, but unfortunately the presence of the words 'Basic Income' in both of them means that they can easily be confused. The Basic Income Canada Network causes even more problems by defining both Basic Income and Basic Income Guarantee as income level guarantees, which implies that means-tested benefits will be paid (Basic Income Canada Network, 2021). We have already encountered the unfortunate use of 'Basic Income' to describe an experiment with an income-tested benefit in Ontario (Ontario, no date). Equally unfortunate is the assumption that the results of historic experiments with Minimum Income Guarantees in the United States can be interpreted without qualification as predicting the effects of Basic Income schemes, which of course they cannot.

The problem emerges in academic literature as well. Bent Greve suggests that increasing automation requires a 'guaranteed minimum income', but is not clear as to whether he wishes to see guaranteed a Basic Income—an unconditional income for every individual of the same age—or a minimum net household income (Greve, 2017: 95, 127) (Greve is equally confused about the meanings of Citizen's Income and Basic Income: Greve, 2017: 96). And perhaps even more problematic, Thomas Piketty employs the term 'basic income' to mean a 'minimum guaranteed income' that would 'decline as other income increased', and so a means-tested benefit: and he continues to use 'basic income' terminology while explicitly rejecting the idea of an unconditional income, on the basis that it would risk weakening the link between income and work and could be

instrumentalized to favor hyper-flexibilization and the fragmentation of labor. This could lead to an artificial inflation of the tax level, with the danger of decreasing resources available for the social state: (Piketty, 2020: 1002–3) none of which would occur with a carefully designed Basic Income scheme (Torry, 2020a: 77–9; 2020b).

If debate is to be rational, then clear communication between participants is essential, which in turn requires that all of the parties to a discussion should mean the same thing by the same words. Clarity matters. There is so much difference between a guaranteed minimum income and a Basic Income that it would be helpful if the term 'Basic Income Guarantee' were to be abandoned, along with all use of 'guarantee' terminology (Torry, 2020a: 22–3).

'Unconditional'

'Unconditional' is found in such combinations as 'unconditional cash transfers' and 'unconditional benefits': but what does it mean? The *Oxford English Dictionary* defines 'unconditional' as

Not limited by or subject to conditions or stipulations; absolute, unlimited, complete;

it defines 'condition' as:

… Something demanded or required as a prerequisite to the granting or performance of something else; a provision, a stipulation;

and the entry on 'stipulation' includes

The action of specifying as one of the terms of a contract or agreement; a formulated term or condition of a contract or agreement.

The dictionary gives as an example of the use of 'unconditional', 'The Kuwait authorities insisted that the [hijackers'] surrender was "unconditional"'; and as a use of 'condition' it offers a quotation from John Wesley: 'The word *condition* means neither more nor less than something sine quâ non, without which something else is not done.'

If usage is the key to a word's meaning, and we are seeking the meaning of 'unconditional' as it might be used in debate on the reform of benefits systems, then it is in such a context that we must study its use. Take these examples of uses of the words 'conditional', 'condition' and 'unconditional' drawn from an International Labour Organization publication:

Improvements in schooling are not restricted to conditional cash transfer programmes. Positive effects on schooling can also be observed for unconditional transfers or workfare programmes. … Brazil's *Bolsa Familia* provides income transfers to poor households, on condition that they regularly send their children to school and that household members attend health clinics. … In Chile, *Programa de Pensiones Asistenciales*, a non-contributory and unconditional social pension programme, is found to have reduced poverty amongst people in old age by about 9.2 per cent. (International Labour Organization, 2010: viii, 2, 11)

In relation to the first use of 'unconditional', we find the word employed in direct contrast to 'conditional', where the conditionality is clearly 'something demanded or required as a prerequisite': that is, that parents send their children to school. In relation to the second use of 'unconditional', the author adds 'non-contributory', suggesting that 'unconditional' does not preclude the income transfers being conditional on contributions having been paid. The 'unconditional' nature of the pension is clearly not compromised by its payment being conditional on the recipient's age.

We might categorize conditionalities as follows: 1. Conditions that we cannot affect (such as our age); 2. Conditions that we have affected and that relate to events in the past (such as the payment of social insurance contributions); and 3. Conditions that we can affect and that relate to future or current events (such as paid employment). The first use of 'unconditional' in the passage quoted above suggests that none of these kinds of conditions applies. The second use permits age being a condition, which is the first type of conditionality; and the fact that the pension is stated to be non-contributory suggests that here 'unconditional' does not exclude the condition that contributions have to have been paid, which is the second type of conditionality.

We find a similar variety of meanings in the modern Basic Income debate. In relation to the Citizen's Basic Income Trust's definition of Basic Income, 'unconditional' means that the Basic Income 'would vary with age, but there would be no other conditions: so everyone of the same age would receive the same [Basic Income], whatever their gender, employment status, family structure, contribution to society, housing costs, or anything else' (Citizen's Basic Income Trust, 2018a: 3). However, when Charlie Young uses the word 'unconditional' in a report for the Royal Society of Arts, sometimes it can mean 'is not dependent on other earned or unearned income, is not means-tested and is not withdrawn as earnings rise', and at other times it can mean that although the income is not subject to a work test, it can be withdrawn as earned income rises (Young, 2018: 9, 22).

Because 'unconditional' can imply a variety of meanings, even within a single document, it might be important to state a working definition for the purposes of this history. In relation to this history, unless stated otherwise, 'unconditional' should be taken to mean 'not limited by or subject to any conditions or stipulations, except the age of the recipient' (Torry, 2017a; 2020a: 10–11).

'Universal'

The word 'universal' can be found in such phrases as 'universal benefits' and 'Universal Basic Income', and the *Oxford English Dictionary* defines 'universal' as follows:

> Extending over or including the whole of something specified or implied, esp. the whole of a particular group or the whole world; comprehensive, complete; widely occurring or existing, prevalent over all. … Affecting or involving the whole of something specified or implied. … Of a service or facility: extended to, provided for, or accessible to all members of a community, regardless of wealth, social status, etc. …

The last part of the entry is particularly relevant. The most recent example of usage given is from the *South China Morning Post*: 'By last year, 94 per cent of the mainland's populated areas had provided nine years of universal compulsory education.' The definition makes it clear that any use of the word 'universal' requires the specification of the community to which the 'service or facility' is extended, for which it is provided, or to which it is accessible.

We shall seek examples of the use of 'universal' in the same International Labour Organization publication that we quoted above:

> But despite the progress made in the materialization of the universal right to social security, very important gaps remain. … Non-contributory schemes include a broad range of schemes including universal schemes for all residents, some categorical schemes or means-tested schemes. … Categorical schemes could also be grouped as universal, if they cover all residents belonging to a certain category, or include resource conditions (social assistance schemes). They may include other types of conditions such as performing or accomplishing certain tasks. (International Labour Organization, 2010: 1, 39)

The community envisaged by the first use of 'universal' is the whole of the human race; but the community envisaged by the second and third uses is constituted by the residents of places served by particular non-contributory schemes. However, the second and third uses are different. The second instance of 'universal' implies a benefits scheme that is neither means-tested nor restricted to a particular category of residents, because those kinds of benefits are listed separately. This means that the same amount will be paid to everyone of the same age, and that here 'universal' implies unconditionality. The third use flatly contradicts the second use, because it implies that universal schemes *can* be categorical or means-tested. So while 'universal' always means 'extending over or including the whole of something specified or implied', great care will always have to be taken when interpreting uses of the word 'universal'. It might mean that the same amount of money would be paid to every resident of a given community; or it might mean that it would be paid to every *eligible* resident, with eligibility being determined by whether someone belonged to a particular category (for instance, whether they were unemployed or disabled), or by whether their existing income fell below a specified level. The UK's 'Universal Credit' is a means-tested and work-tested benefit (and ought to be called 'Unified Benefit'), whereas 'Universal Basic Income' is another name for Basic Income: an unconditional income paid at the same rate to everyone of the same age.

As with 'unconditional', 'universal' has been used with diverse meanings, so the reader will always need to study the context in order to discover the meaning that an author is giving to the word. In this history, 'universal' will always apply to a particular community, whether national, regional or global: so 'Universal Basic Income' will mean a Basic Income paid to everyone within a specified community. Strictly speaking, the 'universal' is redundant here, because 'Basic Income' implies unconditionality, which in turn implies universality: so the purpose of adding 'universal' to 'Basic Income' is presumably to emphasize the fact that everyone in a particular community would receive the income, regardless of any circumstances other than their age. Similarly, this history will take 'universal benefit' to mean an unconditional income for a particular age group: so, for instance, the UK's Child Benefit is a universal benefit because it is paid for every child. If quotations employ 'universal' to mean something different—for instance, that an income will be paid to everyone in a community who happens to be somehow eligible to receive it—then that will be discussed.

'Unconditional' will always imply 'universal', and if 'universal' means unconditional within a community then 'universal' will imply 'unconditional'. However, if 'universal' means 'every eligible individual within a community', then 'universal' does not imply 'unconditional'. This means that we cannot automatically replace 'unconditional' with 'universal' (Torry, 2017a; 2020a: 11–13).

WHAT SHOULD BE INCLUDED IN THIS HISTORY?

Clarity of definition will be a primary concern and aim of this history. This is for two reasons. Firstly, in relation to the history itself: any history-writing requires a clear boundary to define what the history is about; and clear boundaries require clear definitions of terms. Secondly, in relation to any use to which this history might be put in connection with the global debate on Basic Income: only if definitions are clear and understood can that debate be rational. A concern for clarity of definition draws our attention to aspects of the Basic Income debate where clarity is lacking, and raises an important question as to what should be included in this history and what should not.

Take for instance the significant recent upsurge in popular futurist literature in which Basic Income proposals are found. Two examples that argue from technological and employment market change to Basic Income are *Utopia for Realists* by the journalist Rutger Bregman (2017), and *The Second Machine Age* by Erik Brynjolfsson and Andrew McAfee (2014). Bregman tells us that he is an enthusiast for Basic Income, but many of his examples have conditionalities attached to them, and there is no initial definition against which he evaluates the different mechanisms that he discusses. Similarly, *The Second Machine Age* does not distinguish between Basic Income schemes and Minimum Income Guarantees that imply means-tested benefits (Brynjolfsson and McAfee, 2014: 232–3). So should these two books appear in a history of Basic Income? The fact that they are ambiguous in relation to the subject-matter might suggest that they should not: but the fact that they and books like them have been significant elements in the modern debate about Basic Income suggests that they should. The policy of this history will be that texts, discussions, experiments and anything else that has been relevant to the Basic Income debate, will be included. This means that texts, discussions, experiments and anything else about Basic Income, and also texts, discussions, experiments and other activities that are either ambiguous in relation to the central subject matter of Basic Income, or that do not relate to it at all, will be included if, and only if, such material has been directly relevant to the Basic Income debate. So yes, *Utopia for Realists* and *The Second Machine Age* are ambiguous in relation to Basic Income, but they have played a part in the modern Basic Income debate, so they are relevant to that debate's history.

Similarly, the Ontario experiment with an income-tested benefit that they called a 'Basic Income' (Ontario, no date) was not about Basic Income at all, but it had a variety of effects on the global Basic Income debate and therefore belongs in the history. And a lot further back, Thomas Paine, often credited with initiating the modern Basic Income debate, did not in fact write about a Basic Income (Paine, 1797), whereas Thomas Spence did write about one at around the same time (Spence, 1797). However, what Paine wrote was a significant contribution to the Basic Income debate, so his name and what he wrote must appear.

A particularly important question relates to whether such reform proposals as Minimum Income Guarantee, Negative Income Tax, Tax Credits (of various kinds) and Participation Income, belong in this history. The following section therefore describes those ideas, raises the important question of their administration, and asks to what extent they belong in this history.

Minimum Income Guarantee, Negative Income Tax, Tax Credits, Basic Income and Participation Income

There are a number of ways in which a Government can provide incomes to individuals and households: by guaranteeing that a household will not fall below a specified minimum income; by implementing a Negative Income Tax, which pays out below an earned income threshold; by allocating a Tax Credit that is withdrawn as earned income rises; by providing a Basic Income: an unconditional income at the same level for everyone of the same age; or by providing a payment that would be a Basic Income if there were no behavioural conditionalities attached to it. Relationships between these different mechanisms are quite complex, which raises the question as to which of these belong in a history of Basic Income.

Minimum Income Guarantee

A Minimum Income Guarantee (MIG) is a level of income below which a household is not allowed to fall, with different levels applying to different types of household. A means-tested or income-tested benefit is then provided to fill the gap between the set level and existing earned and savings income (an income-tested benefit takes income into account when a benefit level

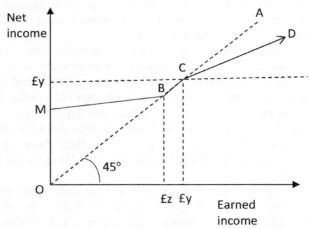

Note: A means-tested benefit enables a household's disposable income to reach the Minimum Income Guarantee level M. By the time earned income reaches £z the benefit has been completely withdrawn. Tax is paid from earnings level £y. Net income is given by the line MBCD.

Source: Author's own.

Figure 1.1   Minimum Income Guarantee

is calculated, whereas a means-tested benefit might take other factors into account, such as wealth) (see Figure 1.1). If the rate at which the means-tested benefit is withdrawn is the same as the rate at which income tax is paid, and if the means-tested benefit is totally withdrawn when the earned income tax threshold is reached, then the relationship between disposable income and earned income can be represented by a straight line on the graph with earned income on the horizontal axis and disposable income on the vertical axis, as in Figure 1.2.

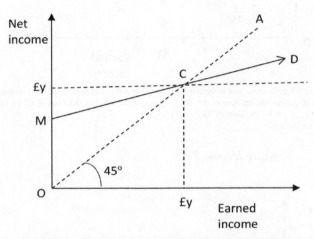

Note: M is the Minimum Income Guarantee. If the means-tested benefit is withdrawn at the same rate as income tax is collected, and the benefit is withdrawn completely at the tax threshold £y, then the relationship between disposable income and earned income is represented by the straight line MD.
Source: Author's own.

Figure 1.2   Minimum Income Guarantee

Negative Income Tax
A Negative Income Tax works in the same way but is administered through the tax system. If the employer is responsible for deducting income tax and passing it to the Government, then above a tax threshold the employer will deduct tax, and below it will pay out a Negative Income Tax proportional to the amount by which earned income falls below the threshold (see Figure 1.3). If the rates of deduction and the rate of payment are the same on either side of the threshold, then the relationship between earned income and disposable

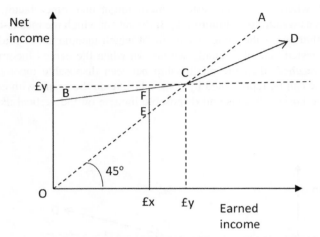

Note: A Negative Income Tax is paid below an earned income threshold, and income tax is
deducted above it. At earned income of £x, the Negative Income Tax paid out is given by the line
EF. Net income is given by the line BCD.
Source: Author's own.

Figure 1.3   *Negative Income Tax*

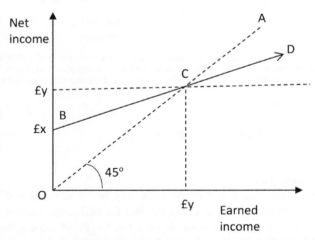

Note: Where the rate of deduction above the earned income threshold £y and the rate of
payment below the threshold are the same, the relationship between disposable income and
earned income is represented by the straight line BD.
Source: Author's own.

Figure 1.4   *Negative Income Tax*

income will be represented by a straight line on a graph with earned income on the horizontal axis and disposable income on the vertical axis, as in Figure 1.4. If with a Minimum Income Guarantee the means-tested benefit happens to be zero at the tax threshold (that is, when income tax begins to be paid), then the Minimum Income Guarantee works in the same way as a Negative Income Tax, except in relation to its administration, on which see below.

Tax Credit

'Tax Credit' can have a variety of meanings.

a. As used by the UK's Heath Government during the early 1970s, it meant a fixed sum allocated each week to each individual by the Government. If there was no other income, then the sum would have been paid in full. As earned income rose, the Tax Credit would have been withdrawn at a specified rate until it was exhausted at an earnings threshold. Above the threshold income tax would have been charged. To specify a Tax Credit amount fulfils the same function as specifying the rate at which a Negative Income Tax would be paid below the earnings threshold (see Figure 1.5). If the Tax Credit is withdrawn at the same rate as income tax is paid, then the relationship between earned income and disposable income can be

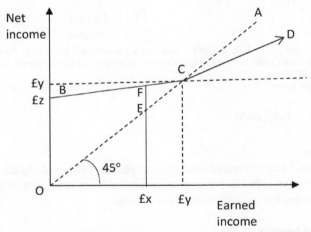

Note: A Tax Credit of £z is allocated. If there is no other earned income, the Tax Credit is received in full. As earned income rises, the Tax Credit is withdrawn until at earned income of £y it is exhausted. At earned income of £x the Tax Credit is represented by the line EF. Net income is given by the line BCD.
Source: Author's own.

Figure 1.5   Tax Credit

represented by a straight line on a graph with earned income on the horizontal axis and disposable income on the vertical axis (see Figure 1.6).

b. The United States Earned Income Tax Credit (EITC) is paid annually to families in employment following the submission of an annual tax return. A formula determines the amount of EITC to be paid.

c. The 1997 New Labour Government in the UK called means-tested benefits for families in employment 'Tax Credits'.

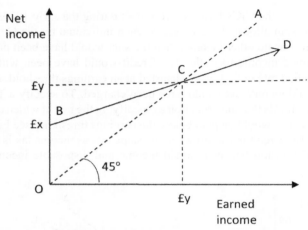

Note: Where the rate of deduction of tax above the tax threshold is the same as the rate of withdrawal of the Tax Credit, the relationship between net income and earned income is given by the straight line BD.
Source: Author's own.

Figure 1.6   Tax Credit

Basic Income
A Basic Income is an unconditional income paid to every individual. Figure 1.7 represents a Basic Income scheme in which the Basic Income is paid for by collecting income tax on all or most other income.

Participation Income
During the early 1990s, Professor Tony Atkinson proposed a 'Participation Income' (see Chapter 7): a Basic Income in all respects other than the conditionality that there would have to be evidence of some kind of 'participation' in society, or evidence that participation ought not to be expected. He thought that a Participation Income would be more acceptable politically than a Basic

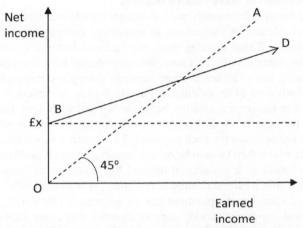

Note: The Basic Income of £x provides a secure financial platform. Tax is then collected on all or most other income. Net income is given by the straight line BD.
Source: Author's own.

Figure 1.7   Basic Income

Income. Those who were ill, disabled, retired or looking for work, would receive a Participation Income without having to prove participation in society, but otherwise at least one participation condition would have to be met: employment, self-employment, education, training, voluntary work, or caring for the young, older people or disabled dependents (Atkinson, 1993; 1996; Fitzpatrick, 1999: 101, 111–22; White, 2003: 170–75). (No graph has been offered in relation to a Participation Income, because this would be the graph for a Basic Income: but that graph's caption would have to make it clear that only those who satisfied one of the 'participation' conditions would actually receive the Participation Income.)

Comparisons between Minimum Income Guarantee, Negative Income Tax, Tax Credit, Basic Income and Participation Income

As we can see from the graphs, it is possible to choose parameters for means-tested benefits, Negative Income Tax and Tax Credit (definition (a)) that would enable them to exhibit the same relationship between earned income and disposable income as for a Basic Income. This can lead to an assumption that they are the same as Basic Income (Sommer, 2016). They are not. Significant differences between them, particularly in relation to their administration, mean that they are very far from being the same, and very far indeed from having the same effects.

The administration of means-tested benefits
Means-tested benefits are usually paid in arrears by a Government agency on the basis of a calculation that relates to household composition and earned and other income. Either housing costs are factored into the calculation of a single means-tested benefit, or a separate means-tested benefit might be paid to cover housing costs. Either average earnings during a previous period of several months is used in the calculation, in which case the benefit is awarded at the same rate for several months before it is recalculated, or the income earned since the benefit was last paid is used in the calculation, in which case the benefit is recalculated for each payment. The former method can result in overpayments which then have to be repaid, causing financial problems for the household, whereas with the second method the Government agency has to know the household's earned income in real time (as with the UK's Universal Credit) so that each benefit payment can be accurately calculated. Multiple jobs, occasional earnings, varying earned incomes and other factors, make accurate administration difficult to achieve, resulting in wildly gyrating benefit levels, periods without benefits and calculation errors (Unite Research, 2019).

The administration of Negative Income Tax
Income tax deducts money from earnings above an earnings threshold, and a Negative Income Tax pays money to the employee below the threshold. The Negative Income Tax can be administered by the Government or by the employer. If the Government administers the Negative Income Tax, then it becomes a means-tested benefit calculated by the second of the two methods described in the previous section. The employer must provide regular and accurate earnings information to the Government (as with the UK's Universal Credit). If the employer administers the Negative Income Tax, then if someone moves between employers their Negative Income Tax administration has to be transferred between employers; and if they have a period of unemployment then administration has to be handed to the Government and then on to the new employer. If someone has two employments then the employers have to decide which of them will administer the Negative Income Tax; and if someone has occasional other earnings then their employer will need to be informed so that the employee can be paid the correct amount of Negative Income Tax, if any.

If every working age adult is treated in the same way for Negative Income Tax purposes, then neither their employer nor the Government needs to know any personal details. If people in different circumstances are treated differently (for instance, in relation to household structure), then their employer and the Government will need to know individuals' circumstances in order to calculate the correct income tax or Negative Income Tax.

Many income tax systems are cumulative. An annual amount of income is not taxed: so each week, or each month, the employer has to calculate how much tax to deduct so that by the end of the tax year the correct amount of tax has been deducted. With Negative Income Tax, the tax system would be non-cumulative. Each week, or each month, the correct amount of the Negative Income Tax would have to be paid in addition to earnings, or no Negative Income Tax would be paid and earnings would be taxed. A non-cumulative system requires a single tax rate, so anyone paying higher rate tax would have to pay additional income tax at the end of the tax year.

The administration of Tax Credits
A Tax Credit scheme of variety (a) would be administered in the same way as Negative Income Tax. The only difference would be in the specification. For a Tax Credit scheme, the amount to be paid out if there are no earnings is speci-fied, along with a withdrawal rate as earnings rise. For a Negative Income Tax, the threshold is specified along with tax rates above and below the threshold. Administration of Tax Credits (of definition (a)) and Negative Income Tax would be identical.

The administration of Basic Income
A Basic Income is an unconditional income paid to every individual by a Government agency, and it is not withdrawn as earnings rise. Income tax is paid on all or most earned income, and this would continue to be administered in the normal way. Administration of the Basic Income would be extremely simple. As the only conditionality permitted would be someone's age, the Basic Income could be turned on at each person's birth, or at whatever age had been agreed, and could be turned off at their death. Very rarely would any active administration be required in between.

The administration of Participation Income
First of all, a test would have to be applied to find out if someone was exempt from meeting the participation conditions, and, if they were not, evidence would have to be provided that they were meeting at least one of the con-ditions. The test and the evidence-seeking would have to be undertaken at regular intervals.

Comparing the schemes
Administration matters. Take, for example, a Participation Income. At face value the argument that it would more politically feasible than a Basic Income might appear to be persuasive, but once we take account of the administra-tive realities things look rather more complicated. 'Street-level bureaucrats' (Lipsky, 1980) would find themselves with considerable discretion as they decided whether someone was exempt from meeting a participation condition, and, if they were not, whether they could meet at least one of the partici-

pation conditions. The kind of demeaning enquiry that has always plagued means-tested benefits would have to be applied to millions of people in relation to what would otherwise be an unconditional income. Each condition would have to be minutely specified; 'creative compliance' would become a wasteful industry (De Wispelaere and Stirton, 2008; De Wispelaere and Noguera, 2012: 25–6); and, taking England and Wales as an example, this huge and stigmatizing administrative effort would exclude a maximum of 1 per cent of the population from the Participation Income (Torry, 2016a: 134–8). Public attitudes would quickly sour. Once the administrative realities are factored in, the supposed political feasibility of Participation Income begins to look rather less convincing.

Negative Income Tax and genuine Tax Credit (definition (a)) schemes would be simple to administer for any individual with a single long-term permanent employment and no other income. As we can see from the descriptions above, administering them for anyone else would present a serious challenge. And we already know how complex, stigmatizing and error-prone is the administration of the means-tested or income-tested benefit required by a Minimum Income Guarantee.

But might we have to take factors other than administration into account? Survey data from Japan suggests that a Negative Income Tax could be a more popular option than Basic Income (Takamatsu and Tachibanaki, 2014: 205), so even if the administration might be onerous, Negative Income Tax might still be preferred to Basic Income. However, the Japanese public opinion survey took no account of the difficulty of administering a Negative Income Tax, and if information on the administrative complexities had been conveyed before the survey questions had been asked then the outcome might have been different. An additional problem with the survey is that questions about Negative Income Tax were only put to people in employment (Takamatsu and Tachibanaki, 2014: 201), whereas questions about Basic Income were put to members of the public regardless of their employment status. It is difficult to see how a legitimate comparison can be made between the two sets of figures.

Here a general point must be made: few people are able to understand the complexities of the tax and benefits system of a developed country, so it is difficult to see how most people would be able to deliver a well-informed opinion about alternative income maintenance mechanisms to a public opinion researcher. A further difficulty is that, as we have recognized, the different mechanisms can look very similar if drawn on a graph. This misleads economists and other academics into thinking that they are basically the same, when they are in fact very different from each other. Both a Negative Income Tax and a Tax Credits (type (a)) scheme would be either impossible or very difficult to administer, whereas a Basic Income could not be easier. The UK's recent experience with 'Universal Credit' (a combined means-tested benefit) is a classic example of consultants proposing a system without taking sufficient account of the administrative challenges that the proposal would face (Centre for Social Justice, 2009), and of a Government and civil service not sufficiently aware of how benefits systems are administered in practice. A Participation Income was proposed by an eminent academic who was either unable or unwilling to factor in the complex, wasteful and demeaning administration that would be required. The only reform option that we have discussed that could be administered easily is Basic Income, and it is also the only one for which the transition from the current system would be easy to manage (Torry, 2015a).

Do these reform proposals belong in this history?

Some authors begin their discussions of the history of Basic Income with histories of means-tested and contributory benefits (Van Parijs and Vanderborght, 2017: 51–69), as the evolutions of these very different benefits have 'deeply shaped the context in which interest for basic income has developed and into which it will need to be fitted in due course' (Van Parijs and Vanderborght, 2017: 51). There is some logic to this. However, that will not be the approach of this history. This is a history of Basic Income, so an unconditional income for every individual must remain its focus. However, readers will discover references to the histories of means-tested and contributory benefits, and to the various mechanisms just discussed, where these are relevant to the main theme. For instance, Basic Income will often be found being advocated as a replacement for, or complement to, means-tested benefits, and Minimum Income Guarantee experiments have often been employed as evidence for the likely effects of Basic Income, which of course they cannot be in any direct sense. A Negative Income Tax has sometimes been argued for as a form of Basic Income (which it is not), and a Participation Income became an important element in the debate during the early 1990s, and was still being proposed by Tony Atkinson as an alternative to Basic Income not long before he died in 2015 (Atkinson, 2015: 297). This is not a history of a variety of reform proposals: it is an account of the history of Basic Income, and important elements of that history have been the ways in which other proposals have been compared with Basic Income, have drawn attention towards themselves and away from Basic Income, have been either properly or erroneously employed to provide evidence for or against Basic Income, and so on. Timothée Duverger suggests that any 'minimum income' should be regarded 'as a prefiguration or a reduced form of Basic Income' (Duverger, 2018: 6–7), and includes a variety of income-tested and otherwise conditional benefits in his history. We shall do the same where those other mechanisms are relevant to the history of Basic Income, but not otherwise: and we shall always distinguish clearly between Basic Income and other kinds of income provision.

Any author who writes a history inevitably encounters multiple interesting aspects of the subject about which the history is being written. It is therefore tempting to detour through discussions of those aspects. While readers will find a number of such detours in this book, an attempt has been made to keep them to a minimum, and in particular to keep them to discussions that might illuminate the history of Basic Income: which is, after all, what this book is meant to be about.

The Selection and Ordering of Material

There is of course a sense in which this book is not a history of Basic Income. No country has ever implemented one, so perhaps there is no history to be written. However, as Kovce and Priddat point out, if ever a Basic Income is implemented, it will not be without a history (Kovce and Priddat, 2019: 26). However, to recognize that if ever a Basic Income is implemented it will have a history, and that here we intend to record that history from early mentions of Basic Income to the present day, does not tell us precisely what to include, nor how to order the material.

For instance: should this be a history of ideas, and of the ways in which they have emerged, evolved, and often disappeared? Should it be about texts? Should it record discussions that have taken place, among activists, academics, policymakers, and so on? Should it be a history of events: for instance, of pilot projects and experiments of various kinds, and of the implementation of unconditional incomes of various kinds? It would be impossible to separate these different aspects of the global Basic Income debate, so this history must be about all of those. Ideas and texts have driven pilot projects and experiments, and those in turn have generated ideas and texts. Discussions and texts have resulted in implementations, and implementations have resulted in ideas, texts and discussions. Although there will be a clear subject-matter boundary in the sense that the focus for this history will be Basic Income, no other restriction will be imposed on the kinds of material to be included.

However, saying that does not tell us how to choose or order the material. A study of existing histories of Basic Income reveals that several of the authors have chosen a 'waves of enthusiasm' pattern, as they have noticed that periods of substantial activity have always been followed by troughs during which the debate has subsided and has sometimes disappeared from view. The fact that authors differ in relation to how many waves there have been rather suggests that the material itself does not suggest a single waves and troughs pattern, and that the wave patterns have to some extent been imposed on the material. A study of the histories finds that in order to populate some of the waves, material that might not strictly belong in a history of Basic Income has some-times been given rather too much attention. This applies particularly to waves that are better described as waves of activity in relation to Minimum Income Guarantee schemes rather than waves of activity about Basic Income schemes (Torry, 2020a: 28–47). The policy of this book will be to avoid overarching patterns, and instead to seek out material on the Basic Income debate and then to order it both geographically and chronologically. Once that has been done, patterns might be discovered.

But having described what might look like a carefully structured method backed by apparently normative processes for choosing and ordering material, it is of course essential to recognize that many different histories of Basic Income have been written, could have been written, and will be written: and as one of those who commented on an early draft has quite rightly pointed out, it would be possible to write a book about each of the many aspects of the history only briefly mentioned in this volume. This means, of course, that a vast amount of potential material has been omitted, which inevitably reduces the objectivity of the resulting history. A further related problem is that the limits imposed by the requirement to write a single-volume history has meant that much that others might have wished to see either explained or contextualized has not been. It is entirely true that what the reader will find here is a highly subjective selection and ordering of material, and I look forward to one day reading the equally subjective histories that will be written by scholars more experienced at history-writing than I am.

THE STRUCTURE OF THE BOOK

Following this introductory chapter, Chapter 2 will ask who first thought of the idea of Basic Income, and from then on a broadly chronological structure will be followed. Chapter 3 will record relevant individuals and movements during the nineteenth century; and Chapters 4 and 5 will explore the debate in the United Kingdom during the first half of the twentieth century. Chapter 6 will discuss the quite distinctive debates in Canada and the United States of America; Chapter 7 will ask about the character of recent debate in the UK; and Chapter 8 will explore the multiple approaches of the debate in continental Europe. Chapter 9 finds that during the twenty-first century debate about Basic Income has occurred all over the world; and Chapter 10 discusses what is now a single global debate. Chapter 11 draws conclusions.

CONVENTIONS

A normal convention in social policy is employed throughout the book: taxes and benefits in general are not capitalized, whereas the particular specified taxes and benefits of particular countries are, so 'income tax' means any tax on income, whereas in the context of a discussion of the UK's tax and benefits system 'Income Tax' will be the UK's Income Tax along with all of its regulations. Clearly defined mechanisms, such as Negative Income Tax, Tax Credit and Basic Income, will also be capitalized.

A HISTORY OF BASIC INCOME

To reiterate, this is a history of Basic Income: an individual, unconditional and nonwithdrawable regular income, of the same amount for every individual of the same age, without work test and without means test. Peter Sloman suggests that 'any attempt to understand the intellectual history of basic income must start by recognizing the fluidity of the idea and the ambiguity of many real-world proposals' (Sloman, 2019: 4–5). This history takes a different approach. As far as *Basic Income: A History* is concerned, the definition of Basic Income is clear and definite, and it is not fluid. The difference in the two approaches might be due to the fact that Sloman is a historian, and that for historians everything is in process, including ideas; whereas this author's first job after leaving university was the administration of means-tested benefits, and he has spent much of the last 35 years researching social policy, a field in which clear definitions are essential.

Sloman suggests that 'we can only understand the history of basic income … in relation to a wider nexus of cash transfer schemes' (Sloman, 2019: 10), and that the history of an idea such as Basic Income requires us to understand the diverse and changing economic, social and social policy contexts within which the idea has been discussed or trialled (Sloman, 2019: 12). This no doubt correct insight underlies a number of collections of texts relating to the Basic Income debate (Cunliffe and Erreygers, 2004; Kovce and Priddat, 2019; Widerquist et al., 2013) in which texts about a 'guaranteed income' will often be found alongside texts about Basic Income. The intention in the writing of this history will be distinctive. It is a history of Basic Income: an unconditional and nonwithdrawable income for every individual: so the most significant context for any particular instance of discussion or experience of Basic Income will be discussion and practice of the same idea at different times and in different places. This book is a history of Basic Income, and other cash transfer schemes will only be discussed to the extent that they are relevant to that history.

2.   Who thought of Basic Income first?

INTRODUCTION

Early human communities that survived by hunting animals and gathering naturally growing fruit, fungi, and other edible plants, have sometimes been regarded as early exemplars of Basic Income, as has the thirteenth-century English Charter of the Forest that was written and signed at the same time as Magna Carta (Floyd, 2020; Standing, 2017a: 1–11; 2019b: 1–25). Neither of these were about cash payments to individuals, so however interesting and important they might be, they will not be discussed here. Neither shall we regard as a Basic Income the silver mined at the Laurion mines near to Athens during the sixth and fifth centuries BCE and paid to Athenian citizens (Widerquist, 2015). First of all, silver coins appear to have been distributed only to citizens, and so not to women or slaves; secondly, the payment appears to have been a single grant rather than a regular income; and thirdly, it appears that the coins were not for citizens' own use, but to contribute towards the money that they were obliged to find to build a fleet of triremes (Aperghis, 2013: 13).

So who was the first person to think of paying an unconditional income to every individual? We cannot know, of course: but we can at least attempt to discover the earliest example, whether in relation to a record of a Basic Income having been provided, or in relation to the earliest extant description of it. We shall first of all ask whether Thomas More or John Locke might have proposed a Basic Income; and we shall then turn to two writers at the end of the eighteenth century, Thomas Paine and Thomas Spence.

AN EARLY START?

Thomas More

Thomas More (1478–1535) was a lawyer, statesman, and author, and his *Utopia*—which can mean 'no place', 'good place' or both—describes a fictional island and its society. There is 'one rule of justice, equality and community solidarity' (More, [1516] 1995: 253), and the community is characterized by 'communal living and [a] moneyless economy' (More, [1516] 1995: 247).

The narrator believes that 'unless private property is entirely abolished, there can be no fair or just distribution of goods' (More, [1516] 1995: 102), and describes the so far non-existent community as one in which

> everything belongs to everybody, [and] no one need fear that, so long as the public warehouses are filled, anyone will ever lack for anything for his own use. For the distribution of goods is not niggardly; no one is poor there, there are no beggars, and though no one owns anything, everyone is rich ... At the very moment when money disappeared, so would fear, anxiety, worry, toil, and sleepless nights. Even poverty, the one condition which has always seemed to need money, would immediately decline if money were entirely abolished. (More, [1516] 1995: 241, 247)

This all looks rather like a perfect monastery, and one can understand why some might have found in More's *Utopia* a foreshadowing of the Basic Income debate: but in the absence of a money economy it is difficult to credit the book with a role in the history of Basic Income.

John Locke

In 1690, John Locke argued in his *Second Treatise of Government* that in the state of nature the

> estate all men are naturally in ... [is] a state of perfect freedom to order their actions, and dispose of their possessions and persons as they think fit, within the bounds of the law of Nature ... A state also of equality. (Locke, [1690] 1884: 192)

Whilst 'God has ... given [the world] to mankind in common' (Locke, [1690] 1884: 203), we have 'property' in our 'persons' and in our 'labour' (Locke, [1690] 1884: 204), so if we mix our labour with some part of the common wealth, then we gain private property rights over that part.

> Whatsoever, then, he removes out of the state that Nature hath provided and left it in, he hath mixed his labour with it, and joined to it something that is his own, and thereby makes it his property ... Nor was this appropriation of any parcel of land, by improving it, any prejudice to any other man, since there was still enough and as good left, and more than the yet unprovided could use, so that, in effect, there was never the less for others because of his enclosure for himself. (Locke, [1690] 1884: 204, 207)

Locke recognizes that a money economy and automated industry have resulted in 'disproportionate and unequal possession of the earth' (Locke, [1690] 1884: 215), and as we are now far from the 'state of nature', it is generally not true that if some individual or corporation takes for themselves some part of the common wealth then there will be 'enough and as good' left over for others: so if we wish to justify the private appropriation of the common wealth then we shall have to ensure that there will again be 'enough and as good' for everyone. Widerquist finds that Locke's arguments relating to private appropriation have been and can be variously interpreted, and that in particular the proviso and its consequences have been and can be variously interpreted (Widerquist, 2010b). Fleischer and Lehto argue that the 'Lockean Proviso'—that 'enough and as good' will be available for everyone—provides the basis for an argument for Basic Income once it is recognized that a Basic Income might be the most efficient way to ensure that 'enough and as good' actually becomes available to everyone (Fleischer and Lehto, 2019: 442, 444–5). Layman, on the other hand, interprets 'enough and as good' as applying to the resources that should be available to everyone so that when they mix their labour with those resources they end up with sufficient to live on (Layman, 2011: 8–9). Layman concludes that

[e]very household has a right to whatever support is necessary in order to reach a point at which its adult members are in a position to support themselves and their dependents at whatever level is necessary for human lives to go reasonably well. If all or some of the adults in a household are able to work, then that household is entitled to whatever degree of state support will, in conjunction with full-time work, raise it to the sufficiency level. If, for whatever reason (including a sluggish labor market, recognized educational commitments, maternity or paternity, etc.), no one in a household is in a position to work, that household is entitled to the full amount necessary to bring it to the sufficiency level. (Layman, 2011: 9)

Layman recognizes that a Basic Income might be the most efficient method to ensure that these requirements will be met (Layman, 2011: 10): but that only proves the point that Locke does not provide an argument for Basic Income. We have also seen that although Fleischer and Lehto find in the Lockean Proviso the basis for an argument for Basic Income, they have to provide an additional argument from the efficiency of Basic Income before they can construct a Lockean libertarian argument for Basic Income as the best method for providing 'enough and as good' for everyone. We have to conclude that although Basic Income is perfectly compatible with Locke's libertarian political economy, Locke does not himself provide a sufficient argument for Basic Income, and nor does he argue for one: and indeed, in 1697 he wrote 'An Essay on the Poor Law' (Locke, [1697] 1997) in which the proposals could not be further from an unconditional income. We therefore have to turn to the eighteenth century for our first explicit modern discussion of Basic Income.

THE EIGHTEENTH CENTURY

In order to discover the first mention of a genuine Basic Income we must first of all distinguish between Basic Income and Basic Capital. The former is a regular unconditional income for every individual, whereas the latter is one-off grants to individuals when they reach a particular age. It is the first author who wrote about a Basic Income that we are seeking. However, this does not mean that we shall not be interested in texts that are not about Basic Income, because we shall be interested in authors whose works have contributed to the Basic Income debate. For instance, however different they might be in some of their effects, the similarities between Basic Capital and Basic Income mean that the arguments that authors offer for Basic Capital will often be those that we shall find to be significant in relation to debate about Basic Income, and in that sense texts about Basic Capital will be relevant to our history (Pateman, 2003).

To take one particular example: from the eighteenth century onwards we shall find a theme in both Basic Capital and Basic Income literature that we shall discover throughout the modern debate on Basic Income: the desire to tackle both the inequality and the poverty that eighteenth-century industrialization and the growing cities and towns had made all too visible. We shall find that during the eighteenth and nineteenth centuries discussion of increasing poverty and inequality was often vigorous, and sometimes revolutionary in character; and we shall also find a consensus that the cause of both inequality and poverty was the ownership of land and other property by a few, to the detriment of the rest (Sloman, 2019: 32–3). To quote a selection of the authors whom we shall encounter in this chapter and the next:

> On one side the spectator is dazzled by splendid appearances; on the other, he is shocked by extremes of wretchedness. (Paine, 1797: 10)

> Hear me! Ye oppressors! Ye who live sumptuously every day! Ye, for whom the sun seems to shine, and the seasons change, ye for whom alone all human and brute creatures toil, sighing, but in vain, for the crumbs which fall from your overcharged tables. (Spence, 1797: 7)

> Though the oppressions of the poor and sighings of the needy arise from a multiplicity of circumstances, yet the following, among other causes, demand particular attention … 1st, Interests. 2d, Rents. 3d, Duties. 4th, Inheritances … (Blatchly, 1817: 195)

> The property rights of the landed goods, which among men are unjustly held by a small number to the detriment of the great mass of people, are the cause of the disorder of society in which all kinds of misery and distress press upon mankind. (De Keyser, [1854] 2004: 57)

When the land is individually appropriated ... genuine society is not constituted by the whole population, but only by the group of the rich. The rest are treated as mere objects: they are the political slaves or proletarians. (De Potter, 1874: I/308; [1874] 2004: 74)

If one considers the abundance of all kinds of products in the shops, side by side with this mass of men, women and children in rags, does it need more than a little bit of common sense to understand that the cause of industrial anarchy does not reside in the exuberance of the population, but in the poverty of the masses who on average are merely able to meet 1/5 of their needs? (Charlier, 1848: 33–4; [1848] 2004: 109)

In this and the subsequent chapter we shall find not only that increasing poverty and inequality motivated attempts to understand their causes: we shall also discover a certain amount of consensus in relation to the cause, and suggested solutions that have clear family resemblances to each other.

THE END OF THE EIGHTEENTH CENTURY: BASIC CAPITAL AND BASIC INCOME

Before we discuss the writings of Thomas Paine and Thomas Spence it will be important to discuss an eighteenth-century wage subsidy scheme. It is essential to do this because the Speenhamland scheme is sometimes regarded as an early example of a Basic Income. It is not, and it is important to know that.

Speenhamland

It has been claimed that the Speenhamland reforms of 1795 were 'an experiment in a kind of basic income' (Pitts et al., 2017: 150; cf. Block and Somers, 2005: 14). They were not. They were an example of the extension of poor relief to the working poor permitted by an Act of Parliament passed in 1782, and they constituted a Minimum Income Guarantee. The difference is crucial. A Minimum Income Guarantee is a minimum income level below which a household's income is not allowed to fall, and the minimum income is achieved by paying a means-tested benefit. The modern equivalents in the UK are Working Tax Credits and Universal Credit. The Speenhamland wage supplements were designed to fill the gap between the worker's earned income and a specified minimum income that was related to the size of the family and also to the price of bread. This could not have been further from the idea of a Basic Income.

The Speenhamland payments fell if earnings rose, and rose if earnings fell. A Basic Income remains the same whatever the individual's earnings. This means that the effects are very different. The Speenhamland supplements functioned as a dynamic subsidy. They rose if wages fell, so employers who cut wages knew that the supplements would make up for the wage cut. A Basic Income would be a static subsidy, which means that it would not rise if wages fell, so both employers and employees would know that if wages fell then employees' families would be worse off. Both collective bargaining and national minimum wages would be even more important than they are in the context of today's in-work means-tested benefits, and the effort to maintain them would intensify. As well as being a dynamic wage subsidy, the Speenhamland scheme also functioned as a dynamic price subsidy. If the price of bread increased, then the supplement would rise, and part of the additional cost would be paid by the community as a whole, and not by the individual in receipt of the supplement. It is therefore possible that the scheme contributed to price inflation. We would expect a Basic Income to be uprated annually, but uprating would not automatically track price inflation, and Basic Incomes would constitute only a proportion of average income, so there is no reason to think that a Basic Income would have any more of an effect on inflation than today's income tax allowances.

Another difference between Speenhamland and Basic Income relates to employment incentive. Within the communities that were paying the Speenhamland supplement, for a large family with a single low-wage breadwinner there was no financial advantage to seeking increased wages, a better-paying job or additional skills. Increased wages would mean a lower supplement. This and the other effects of the Speenhamland payments were well understood at the time (Van Parijs and Vanderborght, 2017: 58, 61). Because a Basic Income would never change, anyone currently on means-tested benefits whose Basic Income enabled them to come off them would immediately experience increased incentives to seek higher wages, or to seek additional skills in order to obtain a better-paying job. No longer would an increase in wages result in a loss of benefits, so an increase in earned income would result in a far greater increase in net income.

It is quite true that means-tested in-work benefits such as the Speenhamland supplements, Working Tax Credits and Universal Credit, 'keep the cost of labour competitive with machines so that employers keep workers hanging on for longer than otherwise would be the case' and restrict 'the freedom of workers to sell their capacity to labour to employers as equal parties to a contract' (Pitts et al., 2017: 149–50). A Basic Income, on the other hand, would never compromise 'the bargaining power of labour', and so would not contribute to 'falling or stagnating wages and deteriorating employment prospects' (Pitts et al., 2017: 151). By providing a secure financial platform on which individuals and households could build, a Basic Income would increase workers' ability to turn down badly paid jobs, to argue for wage increases or to start their own businesses.

Yet another difference between the Speenhamland provision and Basic Income is that Basic Income would be an unconditional income at the same level for every individual in a country, province or region, whereas there was considerable local variation in relation to the administration of relief for the working poor in England in the eighteenth century. There is evidence that few parishes made use of the 1782 permission to extend Poor Law relief to working families; that even fewer of them did so for any length of time; that the ways in which the Act of Parliament was interpreted varied; and that the ways in which local officers administered relief for the working poor were quite diverse (Block and Somers, 2005; Fraser, 1984: 36): but the main problem at the time was that some of the inevitable dynamic subsidy effects had caused reputational damage to in-work benefits, and progressively, and definitively in 1834, out-relief for able-bodied workers was replaced by workhouses (Sloman, 2019: 33–6; Torry, 2018b).

Thomas Paine

Thomas Paine was writing in the wake of the French Revolution, and in the context of debate about the constitution of the United States of America, in both of which he and his writings were involved. Both the French Revolution and the US constitution were informed by democracy, individual rights, the inviolability of private property, and a conviction that vulnerable members of society needed to be cared for by society as a whole (Duverger, 2018: 12–13). In his *The Rights of Man*, Paine wrote that all citizens are 'born, and always continue, free and equal in respect of their Rights' (Paine, [1792] 2006: 62), so he wanted to see the State

> pay ... to every poor family out of surplus taxes ... four pounds a year for every child under fourteen years of age ... To pay to every ... person of the age of fifty years, and until he shall arrive at the age of sixty, the sum of six pounds per annum out of the surplus taxes, and ten pounds per annum during life after the age of sixty, (Paine, [1792] 2006: 146, 148)

but only for the 'aged poor' (Paine, [1792] 2006: 146; cf. Claeys, 1989: 25; Quilley, 1994). These were all means-tested benefits.

Paine's ideas then moved in a less means-tested direction. In 1797 he published *Agrarian Justice*, written, according to the preface, 'in the winter of 1795 and 96' (Paine, 1797). At the heart of the argument is a distinction between property gained by work, which belongs to the worker, and property that belongs to no one, and therefore to everyone (Duverger, 2018: 14). Because land had been given by God to be owned in common by everyone (a religious argument), and because all other property had been created as much by society as a whole as by individual effort (a secular argument) (Claeys, 1989: 197), Paine believed that anyone who now owned land or other property should pay compensation into a common fund, out of which unconditional grants could be made: the method for collection of the compensation being an inheritance tax at 10 per cent of the value of someone's wealth at their death (Cunliffe and Erreygers, 2004: xiv; Paine, 1797: 17–28).

> The earth, in its natural, uncultivated state was, and ever would have continued to be, the COMMON PROPERTY OF THE HUMAN RACE, ... every proprietor ... of cultivated lands owes to the community a GROUND-RENT ... for the land which he holds; and it is from this ground-rent that the fund proposed in this plan is to issue.
>
> ... *out of which there shall be paid to every person, when arrived at the age of twenty-one years, the sum of* Fifteen Pounds sterling, *as a compensation in part for the loss of his or her natural inheritance, by the introduction of the system of landed property.*
>
> AND ALSO,
>
> *the sum of* Ten Pounds per annum, *during life, to every person now living, of the age of fifty years, and to all others as they shall arrive at that age*
>
> ... to every person, rich or poor, to prevent invidious distinctions. It is also right it should be so, because it is in lieu of the natural inheritance, which, as a right, belongs to every man, over and above the property he may have created, or inherited from those who did. ...
>
> Land ... is the free gift of the Creator in common to the human race. Personal property is the EFFECT OF SOCIETY; and it is impossible for an individual to acquire personal property without the aid of Society, as it is for him to make land originally. ... All accumulation, therefore, of personal property, beyond what a man's own hands produce, is derived to him by living in society; and he owes on every principle of justice, of gratitude, and of civilization, a part of that accumulation back again to society from whence the whole came. (Paine, 1797: 12–17, 29–30)

The aim was not only to ameliorate poverty, but to prevent it from occurring in the first place by providing sufficient capital for every young adult to start a business, and by ensuring a decent standard of living for elderly people and people with disabilities (Paine, 1797: 25–8). The remarkable title of Paine's book summarizes the plan:

> Agrarian Justice opposed to Agrarian Law and to Agrarian Monopoly, being a plan for meliorating the condition of man by creating in every Nation a National Fund ... to pay to every Person, when arrived at the age of Twenty-one years, the Sum of Fifteen Pounds Sterling, to enable him or her to begin the World; and also Ten Pounds Sterling per Annum during life to every Person now living of the Age of Fifty Years, and to all others when they shall arrive at that Age, to enable them to live in Old Age without wretchedness, and go decently out of the World. (Paine, 1797)

The proposal that every individual, 'her' as well as 'him', should receive a capital sum at the age of twenty-one, is clearly a proposal for Basic Capital; and the annual grants for people blind and lame would have been early disability benefits, with the individuals receiving them tested in some way for disability: but what should we call the provision of an annual income for everyone aged over fifty years of age? A pension, yes: but would it have been what we might now call a Citizen's Pension: that is, a Basic Income for individuals over fifty?

As we recognized in Chapter 1, an unconditional income paid to every individual of the same age constitutes a Basic Income; and because Paine envisaged that the payment to everyone over the age of fifty would be of the same amount every year, the annual payments would have conformed to the normal assumption that the amounts of a Basic Income would not vary. However, we also recognized in Chapter 1 that a further normal assumption is that a Basic Income would be paid regularly, say once a week or once a month. An annual payment to every adult aged over fifty years of age would not conform to this assumption. We would therefore expect it to have some effects similar to those that we might expect from a Basic Income, and some that would be different. Today's closest parallel would be the Alaska Permanent Fund Dividend: a varying annual dividend paid equally to every Alaskan citizen who has lived in the state for more than a year. The dividend has reduced inflation, reduced poverty and inequality, and created employment: effects that we might expect of a Basic Income (Goldsmith, 2012: 53; Sommeiller et al., 2016; Widerquist, 2010a; Zelleke, 2012: 150). However, the pattern of expenditure has been different. A Basic Income would provide the basis for a normal domestic budget, and would be spent on such basics as food, clothing, electricity, rent and so on. The Alaska Permanent Fund Dividend is sometimes used to stockpile food and fuel for the winter, but it tends to be spent on larger items bought infrequently (such as televisions), on clearing debts, on the costs of Christmas celebrations, and on travel (Feloni, 2019). It is no surprise that Thomas Paine is credited with being an early advocate of a Basic Income (Piketty, 2020: 984), but the difference between the effects of an annual payment and a weekly or monthly payment, along with the difference in the frequency of the payment, probably means that we ought not to count his proposal as a proposal for a Basic Income.

Paine was careful to employ government data and some reasonably acceptable assumptions to prove that the levels at which the grants would have been paid would have been feasible. The figures for national wealth and population were clearly approximate, but at least the attempt was made to prove financial feasibility. And in other ways, too, Paine's proposals reflect aspects of the modern Basic Income debate: for instance, the appeal to justice, and the attempt to prevent rather than ameliorate poverty (Torry, 2018a: 81–4; 2020a: 60–64).

Whilst Thomas Paine's proposals were not strictly for Basic Incomes, their unconditionality, the grounds on which they were advocated, and the attempt to prove financial feasibility, have meant that references to them have been numerous throughout recent Basic Income debate; and it is neither surprising nor inappropriate that Paine should frequently be credited with starting the modern debate about Basic Income (Torry, 2013: 32; 2018a: 22; Widerquist, 2019a: 33).

Thomas Spence

In 1796, the same year that Thomas Paine wrote his *Agrarian Justice*, Thomas Spence published *The Meridian Sun of Liberty: or, the whole rights of man displayed and most accurately defined* (Spence, 1796), which claims to be the text of a lecture given to the Philosophical Society in Newcastle-upon-Tyne on 8 November 1775, for the printing of which Spence was expelled from the Society (Rudkin, 1927: 42).

> That property in land and liberty among men, in a state of nature, ought to be equal, few, one would fain hope, would be foolish enough to deny. (Spence, 1796: 5)

Denying the members of a community the right to live off the commons amounts to 'denying them a right to live' (Spence, 1796: 5): but that is what has happened, because 'the land ... has been claimed by a few' (Spence, 1796: 5). Spence then outlines his plan for righting this wrong:

> Let it be supposed then, that the whole people in some country, after much reasoning and deliberation, should conclude that every man has an equal property in the land in the neighbourhood where he resides. They therefore resolve ... that every one may reap all the benefits from their natural rights and privileges possible. (Spence, 1796: 8)

In each parish a corporation would be formed, of which every resident would be a member.

> The land with all that appertains to it, is in every parish made the property of the corporation or parish; (Spence, 1796: 8)

the land would be let, and the rents then used 1. to contribute to the costs of central government; 2. 'in maintaining and relieving [the parish's] poor, and people out of work' (Spence, 1796: 9); 3. on salaries for parish officers; 4. for repairing bridges and other infrastructure; 5. in maintaining the streets; 6. 'in making and maintaining canals'; 7. in maintaining waste ground; 8. to buy arms and ammunition; and 9. in paying premiums to encourage local agriculture. And then each quarter day, the people of the community would meet to settle the accounts, and

> then the residue of the public money or rents after all public demands are thus sat-isfied, which is always two-thirds, more or less, of the whole sum collected, comes lastly to be disposed of, which is the most pleasant part of the business to every one. The number of parishioners, and the sum thus left to be divided among them being announced, each, without respect of person, is sent home with an equal share.
> So if by sickness or mischance
> To poverty some wane,
> Their dividend of rents will come
> To set them up again. (Spence, 1796: 12)

After his celebratory poem, Spence goes on:

> Though I have only spoke of parishioners receiving dividends which may be under-stood as if men only were meant to share the residue of the rents, yet I would have no objection, if the people thought proper, to divide it among the whole number of souls, male and female, married and single in a parish, from the infant of a day old to the second infantage of hoary hairs. (Spence, 1796: 12)

Spence then reiterates the argument that everyone had the right to live 'on the public common' (Spence, 1796: 12), which is why the rents due on the land should be 'equally enjoyed by every human being' (Spence, 1796: 12); and because the corporations and the financial arrangements would prove to be stable, 'the whole earth shall at last be happy and live like brethren' (Spence, 1796: 12).

Spence published what purported to be the text of the 1775 lecture several times: in 1775, 1779, 1792, 1793 and 1796 (twice), although there is some doubt about some of these datings as not all of the printings were dated, and some of them are now lost. Chase thought that none of the 1775 printing had survived (Chase, 1988: 21), but it now appears that one copy has (Bonnett, 2014; Thomas Spence Society, 2020).

Fortunately, original printings or reprintings of a sufficient number of the different pamphlets are available (Spence, [1775] 2014; [1775] 1882; [1793] 1893–95; 1796) to enable us to draw some tentative conclusions as to how Spence's ideas evolved. In the earlier printings, there is no mention of a residue being distributed to every resident of the parish, which means that the only payment made to residents is a means-tested benefit for people who are 'poor, and people out of work'. It is in the 1796 printing, titled *The Meridian Sun of Liberty*, that we find the addition of the passage quoted above in which 'each, without respect of person, is sent home with an equal share' of the residue of the rents, along with the four-line poem, and the discussion of whether women as well as men might receive an equal share of the rents (Spence, 1796: 12).

Additional evidence as to the evolution of Spence's ideas is found in *Pigs' Meat*, a collection of many of Spence's numerous pamphlets. In an undated pamphlet we find this:

> The people in every district or parish should appoint collectors to receive the rents, and divide them equally among themselves, or apply them to what public uses they may think proper. (Spence, [undated] 1893–95)

This could mean either that the collectors should receive the equal payments, or that all of the residents should do so. Let us assume that it means the latter: but then we also have to recognize that such an equal payment to every resident is one option among others, and is not necessarily a settled element of a plan. As the pamphlet is undated, and the pamphlets reprinted in *Pigs' Meat* are not necessarily in the order in which they were published, we cannot be sure of the date on which Spence wrote this paragraph: but the somewhat ambiguous wording suggests a date between the earlier printings of the 1775 lecture and the 1796 publication of *The Meridian Sun of Liberty*.

Further evidence for the evolution is found in a song published in 1783:

> … The rents throughout that happy state,
> Each parish deals so fair,
> That every householder therein
> Does get an EQUAL SHARE. … (Spence, [1783] 1893–95)

We might conclude that a possible chain of events went like this: the 1775 lecture proposed a number of uses for the rents to be collected by the parish corporations, among which was a means-tested benefit, but not an equal distribution to every resident of the parish. At some point Spence was won- dering whether a proportion of the rents might be paid to every member of the community, and so mentioned this as a possibility in a pamphlet, and the ambiguous wording might be a symptom of his initial hesitancy about the idea. By 1783 he was confident enough about the proposal to suggest in a song that 'every householder' should receive an equal share of the rents; and then, by 1796, in *The Meridian Sun of Liberty*, an equal distribution of the residue of the rents to every resident of the community has become a definite part of the plan, and perhaps the most important part, and he was also willing to discuss the possibility of every man, woman and child receiving an equal share. By 1797, when Spence published *The Rights of Infants* (Spence, 1797)—discussed below—the plan for an equal payment to every member of the community had taken centre stage, and rather than one third of the rents being paid out as equal quarterly payments to all of the residents, as envisaged in *The Meridian Sun of Liberty*, two thirds were now to be paid out as equal incomes.

As the undated *Pigs' Meat* pamphlet is found between pamphlets published in 1792 and 1793, it is not impossible that 1792 was the year during which Spence began to formulate the plan for an equal distribution of a proportion of the rents to every individual in the community. This was the year during which Spence left his wife in Newcastle, abandoned schoolteaching, and moved himself and his son to London, where he became a printer and bookseller and participated in a variety of radical campaigns and organizations (Rudkin, 1927: 54). In Newcastle, Spence might have felt as if he was rather a lone voice crying in the wilderness, but in London there were plenty of radicals with whom to discuss ideas, and it might be that it was such discussions in a new context that facilitated Spence's innovation: because an innovation it was.

Spence's *The Rights of Infants* had been written in 1796, but when Thomas Paine published his *Agrarian Justice*, Spence added a preface and appendix excoriating Paine for the timidity of his proposal to charge inheritance tax at only 10 per cent, because in his view the whole of a deceased individual's estate belonged to the local community (Spence, 1797: 3): that is, land owner-ship should be socialized rather than being left in private hands and the value of the land taxed in compensation (Duverger, 2018: 17–18). The extended *The Rights of Infants* was published in 1797. The importance that Spence gave to his disagreements with Paine might be gleaned from the full title of *The Rights of Infants*:

> The Rights of Infants, or the Imprescriptable Right of Mothers to such a Share of the Elements as is sufficient to enable them to suckle and bring up their Young. In a DIALOGUE between the ARISTOCRACY and a MOTHER OF CHILDREN, to which are added BY WAY OF PREFACE AND APPENDIX STRICTURES ON PAINE'S AGRARIAN JUSTICE. (Spence, 1797)

Paine had proposed a 10 per cent inheritance tax on the basis that it was unimproved land that properly belonged to the whole community, and that the proceeds of any improvements that had been made to it belonged to the indi-vidual who had made the improvements. Spence's point was that the owner of the land was not necessarily the person who had made the improvements:

> Did the proprietors alone work and toil at this improvement? And did we labourers and our forefathers stand … idle spectators of so much public-spirited industry? I suppose not. Nay, on the contrary, it is evident to the most superficial enquirer that the labouring classes ought principally to be thanked for every improvement. (Spence, 1797: 15)

As Spence put it in a dialogue:

Young man:	I hear there is another Rights of Man by Spence, that goes farther than Paine's.
Old man:	Yet it goes no farther than it ought.
Y.M.:	I understand it suffers no private Property in Land, but gives it all to Parishes.
O.M.:	In so doing it does right, the earth was not made for individuals. (Spence, n.d.: 3)

Having taken possession of estates, the local authority would then lease them out for cultivation, and use the rent to pay for public services and quarterly unconditional incomes that would be distributed

> fairly and equally among all the living souls in the parish, whether male or female; married or single; legitimate or illegitimate; from a day old to the extremest age; making no distinction between the families of rich farmers and merchants ... and the families of poor labourers and mechanics. ... This surplus [after public services have been funded], which is to be dealt out again among the living souls in a parish every quarter-day, may be reasonably supposed to amount to full two-thirds of the whole sum of rents collected. But whatever it may amount to, such share of the surplus rents is the imprescriptible right of every human being in civilized society, as an equivalent for the natural materials of their common estate, which by letting to rent, for the sake of cultivation and improvement, they are deprived of. (Spence, 1797: 8–9)

Spence not only describes the quarterly income for every individual and its funding method: he also discusses the many advantages that he foresaw accruing to society. Following the preface and dialogue that constitute most of *The Rights of Infants*, Spence added four pages of text in two columns, with the likely effects of Paine's scheme—'Agrarian Justice'—on the left, and the

likely of effects of his own scheme—'The End of Oppression'—on the right.
To quote from the right-hand column:

> The people will receive, without deduction, the whole produce of their common
> inheritance.
> The people will be vigilant and watchful over the public expenditure, knowing that
> the more there is saved their dividends will be the larger.
> The people will be all intent upon the improvement of their respective parishes,
> for the sake of the increased shares of the increased revenues, which on that account
> they will receive.
> Universal suffrage will be inseparably attached to the people both in parochial and
> national affairs, because the revenues, both parochial and national, will be derived
> immediately from their common landed property.
> The government must of necessity be democratic. ...
> There will exist only the robust spirit of independence mellowed and tempered by
> the preference and checks of equally independent fellow citizens. ...
> There can be no taxes nor expences of collecting them, because the government
> would be supported by a poundage from the rents which each parish would send
> quarterly to the national treasury, free of all expence, thus leaving the price of
> commodities unencumbered with any addition but the price of labour. ... . (Spence,
> 1797: 11–12)

The quarterly dividends would have meant that after experiencing financial
difficulties anyone would be able to 'start again' in the economy; 'as both
young and old share equally alike of the parish revenues, children and aged
relatives will ... be accounted as blessings'; the dividends would provide the
means to enable people to be educated (Spence 1797: 13); and

> What with the annihilation of taxes and the dividends of the parochial rents ... the
> people will rarely be driven to the dire necessity of using a substitute for bread. ...
> The people's oppressors must either submit to become undistinguishable in the
> general mass of citizens or fly the country.
> Domestic trade would be at an amazing pitch because there would be no poor.
> The quarterly dividends, together with the abolition of taxes, would destroy
> the necessity of public charities; but if any should be thought necessary, whether to
> promote learning, or for any other purpose, the parochial and national funds would
> be found at all times more than sufficient. (Spence, 1797: 13–14)

The predictions are flawless. As we shall see, when genuine Basic Income
pilot projects were carried out in Namibia and India, pilot communities
developed democratic structures to control aspects of the local economy;
money was pooled to enable such infrastructure as toilets and a post office
to be built; women, people with disabilities and elderly people experienced
emancipation and respect; economic activity increased, especially among
individuals with low earnings; new businesses were established; children
were better cared for; greater social cohesion was experienced; crime was

reduced; no unwanted economic effects occurred; school attendance and results improved; people's health improved; nutrition improved; and staff members of development charities were left wondering whether they would still have jobs if Basic Incomes were to become the means for promoting social and economic development (Basic Income Grant Coalition, 2009; Davala, 2019; Davala et al., 2015; Haarmann and Haarmann, 2007; 2012; Haarmann et al., 2019; Torry, 2013: 69–73; 2018a: 134–5). While the social and economic conditions prevalent in the communities in which the recent pilot projects took place might not have been very different from conditions in rural parishes in eighteenth-century England, there was a significant difference between the pilot projects and Spence's proposals: the former were externally funded, and so injected additional money into local economies, whereas Spence's incomes and endowments were to be funded by reallocating existing land rents. It must therefore be open to doubt as to whether Spence's predictions would have been as substantially realized in his own context as they were during the modern pilot projects. A genuine parallel would require new pilot projects in which the Basic Incomes would be funded entirely from within the resources of the community. But having said that, it is not insignificant that Spence's predictions were so closely mirrored in modern Basic Income pilot projects.

Leaving aside for the time being the objections levelled against Spence's plan: for instance, that it took no notice of landlord claims that might have been legitimate, that parishes would not necessarily be effective managers of property, and that the scheme was simply not practicable (Ley, 1888: 4–5), the important issue here is that the payments envisaged by Spence from at least 1796 onwards, probably in outline from 1792, and possibly from as early as 1783, would have constituted an unconditional income for every individual. The only questions relate to the frequency of the payments and to the stability of the amounts that would have been paid. The payments would have been made quarterly, and they would have varied in amount in relation to the rents being paid on the estates leased out by the community. This locates the payments somewhere between a varying annual dividend and a weekly or monthly income paid permanently at the same rate. The number of estates being let out by the community would grow as their former owners died, so Spence would have been able to envisage rents of an increasing rather than a decreasing value: but once all of the land was in the ownership of the community, and all of it was leased, the quarterly payments would have varied as the rental market fluctuated.

What we can say is that Spence's plan is very close to being one for a Basic Income, and that because he envisaged the regular payments being made to every member of the community, and not only to individuals over the age of fifty, he has a better claim than Paine to be thought the first person to think of the idea of a Basic Income. He was certainly the first to predict in a specific and probably accurate manner the effects that we might expect to occur if a Basic Income were to be established.

CONCLUSIONS

We have discovered that Thomas More and John Locke might properly be viewed as contributing ideas that have remained important elements of the Basic Income debate, and that Thomas Paine might properly be regarded as the first author to propose Basic Capital. However, it is Thomas Spence who should be regarded as the first author to propose a recognizable Basic Income. While we might justifiably quibble that quarterly payments are not frequent enough to be regarded as a regular income, we would have to recognize that shorter intervals might not have been feasible or expected, and that quarterly intervals might actually have been appropriate in relation to quarterly rental and other payments; and while we might quibble that varying amounts cannot constitute a Basic Income, again we might have to recognize that the funding method envisaged would not have permitted any other option. Spence's proposal was probably as near as anyone was going to get to a Basic Income at the end of the eighteenth century.

While Thomas Paine's *Agrarian Justice* has been frequently referenced during recent debate about Basic Income (Torry, 2013: 32; 2018a: 22; Widerquist, 2019a: 33), it would appear that it had little or no influence on the proponents of Basic Capital or Basic Capital during the intervening years (Van Parijs, 2020). This would not be true of Thomas Spence, whose proposals for unconditional regular incomes were actively taken up and developed during the following century, as we shall see.

3. Basic Income during the nineteenth century

INTRODUCTION

In the previous chapter we have described proposals by both Thomas Paine and Thomas Spence. Paine's proposal for a one-off endowment for every young adult might be termed 'Basic Capital', and Spence's proposal for quarterly incomes 'Basic Income'. In this chapter we shall find nineteenth-century authors discussing both Basic Capital and Basic Income—that is, unconditional lump sums and unconditional regular incomes, respectively—so we shall divide the chapter accordingly; and we shall find arguments for both Basic Capital and Basic Income that are still in circulation today.

BASIC CAPITAL

Rather like Thomas Paine, three nineteenth-century authors in the United States recommended Basic Capital funded by an inheritance tax. Whether they had read *Agrarian Justice* is not clear, and it would appear that they had not read each other's proposals (Cunliffe and Erreygers, 2004: xv). They belong in this history because the arguments that they employed were similar to those later employed by advocates of Basic Income. Three Belgian authors belong in the history for the same reason.

The United States

Cornelius Blatchly
In 1817, Cornelius Blatchly rehearsed arguments similar to Paine's for the redistribution of property:

> Rents of houses and lands, and interest of money, are probably the effects of ancient usurpation, tyranny, and conquest. ... If property is considered in respect to its origin, it is social and individual: being the result and fruits of social protection, policy, and assistance, or of individual care, wisdom and industry. (Blatchly, 1817: 198, 205)

Blatchly's title is

SOME CAUSES OF POPULAR POVERTY ARISING FROM THE ENRICHING NATURE OF INTER-
EST, RENTS, DUTIES, INHERITANCES, AND CHURCH ESTABLISHMENTS, investigated in
their principles and consequences, AND AGREEMENT WITH SCRIPTURE: (Blatchly,
1817)

so as well as wanting to extract wealth from ecclesiastical establishments, he
offers a lengthy argument based on the biblical creation stories:

Man, created a little lower than the angels, had *dominion* given to him (not in his
individual, but in his *aggregate* capacity) … If individuals usurp what is the divine
right only of the aggregate, they deprive *man* (a term including all men and women)
of his rights and privileges granted to him in the beginning by *God*, his creator,
and the *sole* proprietor of angels, men, beasts, birds, fishes, serpents, insects, vegetables, minerals, lands, seas, air, and heavens … All men should therefore esteem
themselves as deriving their titles from him, for general use and benefit, and not for
individual aggrandizement and oppression of the multitude. (Blatchly, 1817: 199)

Blatchly asks, 'How can a man who is dead, be said to will?' (Blatchly, 1817:
205) and concludes that when someone dies, their property should

revert … to its most immediate source, to the society, the community, the nation
whence his property was derived. … the property does, of right, belong to the whole
community, and to every man and woman an equal portion … children … have also
a right to their averaged share, which is due from the society. (Blatchly, 1817: 206)

Cornelius Blatchly's proposal would have constituted an inheritance tax of 100
per cent of the value of the property of the person who had died: ten times the
tax rate recommended by Thomas Paine.

Thomas Skidmore
In 1829, Thomas Skidmore wanted to go even further in order to achieve
a division of property that would recognize that originally land and natural
resources belonged to everybody, and that all wealth is a product of social
functions, such as education and the law, as well as of individual effort
(Skidmore, 1829: 244–5). He proposed not only that the whole of the property
of everyone who died should be divided equally among the population (except
that if one member of a couple died, half of the property should be transferred
to the surviving member, and half to the State), but also that at the beginning of
the process there should be 'an equal division of all … property among the citizens, of and over the age of maturity … a patrimony, and that an equal one too,
to every individual on arriving at the age of maturity' (Skidmore, 1829: 137–8,
229). The State's subsequent role was then to ensure an 'equal transmission

to every individual of every succeeding generation' (Skidmore, 1829: 211). In relation to the initial redistribution: '… the owner should be answerable for the forth-coming of so much as may be left in his possession, at the peril of imprisonment for fourteen years …' (Skidmore, 1829: 140); and in relation to the subsequent distribution of someone's property at their death, 'punishment by imprisonment, for a term of fourteen years, should be visited upon him, who, during his life time, gives away his property to another. …' (Skidmore, 1829: 143–4). Not only a 100 per cent inheritance tax rate, but also a 100 per cent wealth tax, based on Skidmore's rather optimistic assumption that

> the universal sentiment of mankind is opposed to inequality, as well in property as in other things. Never, since man has existed, has there been found a human being, who has thought that an equal share with his fellow-beings, was likely to be, or by any possibility could be, an injury to him. (Skidmore, 1829: 214)

To what extent might we call this a scheme for 'Basic Capital' (Cunliffe and Erreygers, 2004: xiv–xvii)? Once we begin to look at the detail, it looks rather less like one. The plan was for an inventory to be taken of all 'real property', mainly land, along with all personal property and State property that could be sold. 'Let there be, next, a dividend made of this amount, among all such citizens, who shall be of and over the age of eighteen … male and female'. The sale would then take place, and anyone would be able to bid for the property. 'Delivery may be made of the whole, if it be real property and the receiver may stand charged with the overplus. If it be personal property—delivery to be made, only to the amount of the dividend …'. Once the sale was complete, a new dividend would be made that in total came to the exact amount of the sale revenue, and the difference from the original dividend calculated. Then, 'by comparing the amount of each person's purchases with this patrimony, it will be seen whether he is creditor or debtor to the State, and how much; and he will be entitled to receive the same, or required to pay it to, the State accordingly' (Skidmore, 1829: 138–9). This means that if during the sale someone had bid for property of a value greater than the final dividend, then they would have had to pay the difference; and if someone had bid for property of a lower value than the final dividend then they would have received the difference. Each individual would have received the same value, but in varying amounts of money and property. This means that while any subsequent division of property of people who had died might be ambiguously regarded as an example of 'Basic Capital', the original distribution of wealth could only be regarded as 'Basic Capital' if the value of property bid for at the sale were to be counted along with any money paid to individuals. A further complication is that Skidmore proposed that when a dividend was assigned to every male adult, 'it shall be at their option, after the dividend is made, to receive it in cash, or to use the credit of it, in the future purchase of other property' (Skidmore, 1829: 141–2): meaning that the value of such credit would have to be counted along with cash paid and property bid for if the scheme were to be regarded as granting Basic Capital, which by definition is of the same value for every individual of the same age.

Both Blatchly and Skidmore based their proposals on the fact that land was a gift to humanity as a whole, and that wealth is as much a product of society as of the individuals who happen to own it. Although their plans were for financial mechanisms very different from Basic Income, their justifications for the division of wealth after death, and in Skidmore's case immediately, were the same as those employed by early advocates of Basic Income from Thomas Spence onwards (Spence, 1797).

Orestes Brownson

A third United States advocate of providing one-off capital grants to young adults was Orestes Brownson, a Christian minister who belonged in turn to the Presbyterian, Universalist, Unitarian and Roman Catholic churches (Lapati, 1965: 44–52). Social reform was a constant theme of his journalism:

> The cause of the crime and misery now prevalent is chiefly owing to the inequality which exists among us and which almost every institution tends to perpetuate and increase ... it were thinking meanly of man, meanly of his social powers, to say he is susceptible of no better state of society than the present ... Equality must be introduced ... Secure to every man the products of his own labor and the evil will disappear. (Brownson, [1829] 2007: 85, 88)

By 1840, following a recession, inequality and class divisions were serious issues (Ryan, 1976: 164–5), and Brownson's view was that wage labour had become even more oppressive than slavery (Brownson, 1840: 10), and that only a more equal distribution of capital would enable labourers to escape from wage slavery and own their own businesses. 'There must be no class of our fellow men doomed to toil through life as mere workmen at wages' (Brownson, 1840: 13). The solution proposed was first of all the replacement of what Brownson saw as the corrupt Christianity of the churches and the revival of 'the Christianity of Christ' (Brownson, 1840: 22; Butler, 1992: 60), and then the abolition of the power of the banks, the abolition of hereditary property, the passing of everyone's property to the State at their deaths, and the payment of one-off grants to every adult on reaching maturity (Brownson, 1840: 4, 22–4; [1840] 1978: 54, 59, 61–2, 70).

> In giving, in this way, an equal share to all of what we have shown belongs in equal portions to all, society treats all her members alike. But, after having done this, which depended on her, she leaves them to fare according to their works. Society

is not required to keep them equal, or to labor to make them equal. She is simply obliged to treat them as equals, so far as she is concerned. She must, in that which it belongs to her to do, treat them all alike, and give no advantage to one over another. But, if one can honestly, by his own exertions, become richer than another, that is his own affair, with which she has nothing to do. It is no part of our plan that the idle and profligate should fare alike with the industrious and thrifty. What we ask is, that society shall, in the distribution of that, which none of the generation it concerns have had any hand in producing or accumulating, should treat all alike, for thus far the claims of all are equal. (Brownson, [1840] 1978: 78)

Brownson thought that his proposal would assist the Democratic Party during an election campaign. He was wrong. Brownson's scheme was widely publicized by the opposition because they believed that changing inheritance laws in the way envisaged would be unpopular. It was: and even though the Democratic Party tried to distance itself from the proposals, the party's presidential candidate lost the election partly because of it (Lapati, 1965: 58–9; Ryan, 1976: 173).

Belgium

Paul Voituron

During the late 1840s, a group of students of the philosopher François Huet, along with some other philosophers, formed the Societé Huet (the Huet Society). Among the topics discussed was that of a 'dotation': a one-off capital grant to every young adult to enable them to purchase some means of production. This idea first made its appearance in 1848, both in the proceedings of the Society, and in a previously unpublished manuscript by the secretary, Paul Voituron (Cunliffe and Erreygers, 2004: 48). An important objective of paying for the Basic Capital by socializing proportions of everyone's wealth at their death via an increasing inheritance tax rate (Cunliffe and Erreygers, 2004: xviii; Voituron, [1848] 2004: 54), and using the revenue obtained to pay a one-off grant to every young adult, was to construct a compromise between full property rights and the complete absence of property rights in communism (Voituron, [1848] 2004: 53–4): but the main aim was to give effect to the conviction that

> three indissolubly linked rights derive from the fact of man's existence on earth. These three rights are: the right to live, the right to work, and the right to instruments of labour. They form each other's condition. The first cannot be exercised legitimately without the other two. That is why they form one single right that we shall call: the right to live by one's labour. The right to property is intimately linked with this right. (Voituron, [1848] 2004: 49)

The plan to provide capital to every young adult is later described in terms of an 'economic emancipation' that requires work to be disconnected from 'the tyranny of both need and salary' via a 'generalization of individual property' (Voituron, 1876: 165, 173).

We shall find reappearing later in this history the arguments that unconditional payments would enhance the ability to earn a living, and at the same time would emancipate the individual, along with evidence that this is in fact what happens (Basic Income Grant Coalition, 2009: 13–17; Davala et al., 2015: 73, 76, 92–6, 113, 134, 153–5; Haarmann and Haarmann, 2007; Standing, 2017a: 232, 236; Rhys Williams, 1943: 147; Torry, 2018a: 41–8, 151–9).

Napoleon De Keyser

In Napoleon De Keyser's publication of 1854, we find a rather complex proposal that involves a distribution of land by lottery, rents payable on the land occupied, a one-off grant for every young adult,

> [a]nd to each and everyone without exception: nature's support. In every state, everyone should receive an equal share of the general rental revenues of the land and of the revenues derived from everything which is held in common: mines, forests, pasture, rivers, trees along streets, etc. (De Keyser, [1854] 2004: 70)

'Nature's support' would be paid quarterly (Cunliffe and Erreygers, 2004: xix), and it is not clear to what extent the rate at which it would be paid would vary over time, which locates it somewhere between a varying annual dividend and a Basic Income paid at the same rate weekly or monthly: so whether De Keyser should be credited with discussing a Basic Income is an interesting question. Of equally clear interest is one of the motives for the plan. Each individual's disposable income would be made up of the proceeds of cultivating their own land, receiving 'nature's support', and earning an income in other ways: and because by these means earning a sufficient income would take relatively little time,

> [a] quiet and necessary state of mind will prevail to keep everyone mentally busy with the extension and improvement of the powers of reason. By allocating to everyone his precious portion of the inheritance of all, everybody can therefore get his share of the moral or immaterial treasures: erudition, wisdom and sciences. To this end institutions of education will be founded, so that every human being can without costs reach the highest degree of knowledge, this knowledge being the great and unfinished mission in life.
>
> When natural rights, the generosities of Creation, are enjoyed like that, they will raise every single individual to his human dignity, and they will for all people together bring about a society at the level of man's elevation and of the insights in Creation! (De Keyser, [1854] 2004: 60)

De Keyser belongs in this history not because his 'nature's support' might or might not have been a Basic Income, but because of his understanding that providing every individual with an income, and with a means of acquiring income without spending too much time on doing so, would provide time for other pursuits. One of the reasons still given for pursuing a Basic Income is that it would provide people with the time and resources to undertake a wide variety of work, with 'work' broadly defined to encompass cultural, community, political and caring work (Torry, 2018a: 47–8).

Agathon De Potter

Our third Belgian writer, Agathon De Potter, studied the ways in which land was divided and owned (De Potter, 1874: II/88), and concluded that justice required that the 'social economy' should serve the people's 'wellbeing', and that this required that they should have sufficient resources (De Potter, 1874: II/143). If workers recognized that needs were not being met, then they experienced 'mal-être', poor-being, rather than 'bien-être', wellbeing (De Potter, 1874: II/153): hence the need for society to provide resources (De Potter, 1874: II/230–31).

However, when De Potter turned to the practicalities of this provision, we discover ambiguity: and an important reason for including his writings in this chapter is that at this point they illustrate an important issue of which we shall need to be aware throughout this history:

> To whom does [society] advance capital? Especially to the labourers who do not yet have any, or to those who have lost it through bad luck. To the first, who are minors upon their entering the society of majors, it advances a social dowry [une dot sociale]; to the latter it lends some capital. As to the unfortunates who are unable to work or the mentally disadvantaged who are incapable of normal conduct: it lends them nothing. To those society owes the means to live, and gives it to them. (De Potter, 1874: I/312; [1874] 2004: 76)

Does he mean that capital will be given to everyone as they reach adulthood, or just to those 'who do not yet have any'? It is not clear. Later on, De Potter thought that 'land and rent should constitute collective property' (De Potter, 1886: 47), and then later still that 'the land must be equally available to all, and there must be no further division and distribution' (De Potter, 1897: 81): and that if the condition of the poor did not improve then eventually there would be 'violent death' and 'war between poor and rich' (De Potter, 1886: 13, 59). But whether any of this implied a distribution of either capital or income is not clear; and there is certainly no Basic Income in view, as the only people who would receive a regular income of any kind would be those who had passed some kind of disability test.

Throughout this history, clarity as to the definition of Basic Income will be essential, and equally essential will be clarity as to what any particular author is proposing. Where clarity is lacking in the latter respect it will be important to point that out.

BASIC INCOME

As for Basic Income, debate on Thomas Spence's plan continued in England, and a rather different tradition emerged in France. Between them, they represent themes still highly visible in the contemporary Basic Income debate. However, before we study authors who discussed the possibility of providing unconditional incomes to every individual, we must ask to what extent the British philosopher John Stuart Mill might have believed that providing an unconditional income would balance the requirements of justice and maximum aggregate utility.

Great Britain

John Stuart Mill
John Stuart Mill's work as an administrator in the London office of the East India Company gave him an understanding of practical politics; and both this and his study of political economy convinced him that 'political philosophy' was a system 'much more complex and many-sided than [he] previously had any idea of, and its office was to supply, not a set of model institutions, but principles from which the institutions suitable to any given circumstances might be deduced' (Mill, [1873] 1924: 57, 113). Two of those principles were equality and individual private property, which he constantly tried to reconcile by advocating self-help accompanied by equality of opportunity rather than equality of outcome (Kurer, 1998: 339). So, for instance, if someone makes improvements to the farmland that he occupies, he

> must have a sufficient period before him in which to profit by them: and he is in no way so sure of having always a sufficient period as when his tenure is perpetual [and] ... the rents or profits ... are at his disposal. (Mill, [1848] 1965: 227, 232)

However, the State remains 'at liberty to discard' landowners if it compensates them (Mill, [1848] 1965: 230), and 'the balance in all cases of doubt should incline against the proprietor' (Mill, [1848] 1965: 232).

Mill entered Parliament, where he became concerned about the increasing gap between rich and poor, and particularly that between the idle rich and the industrious poor. His studies in economics had led him to believe that competition was essential to a healthy economy, so he was sceptical of revolutionary and centralized socialism and of government interference with wage levels (Kurer, 1998: 339, 351), and concerned that co-operatively owned enterprises did not provide sufficient incentive for productivity and innovation: but he was attracted to the kind of socialism represented by Charles Fourier, whose call for a 'decent minimum', as we shall see, was somewhat vague as to whether what was intended was a Basic Income or a minimum to be assured by a means-tested benefit. Mill's reading of Fourier was that 'in the distribution, a certain minimum is first assigned for the subsistence of every member of the community, whether capable or not of labour' (Mill, [1848] 1965: 211–12). It appears that Mill interpreted Fourier's call for a 'decent minimum' as an appeal for a Basic Income, which might not have been what Fourier had intended, but might have been what Mill quite early in his literary and political career had come to understand as a way of righting the wrongs consequent upon private land holding, and as the best way to provide for the poor at the same time as ensuring no reduction in employment incentive. This understanding of Mill's reading of Fourier is encouraged by later passages expressing a desire for a communist utopia (Ten, 1998: 389–92, 395). In Parliament, Mill argued for limitations and prohibitions on large land holdings, the heavy taxation of income from land, and changes to the laws on inheritance (Halliday, 1976: 100–101; Stafford, 1998: 126–9), and in particular the taxation of inherited wealth rather than the taxation of estates: a change designed to encourage greater dispersion of someone's wealth at their death (Mill, [1848] 1965: 224–5; Cappelen and Pedersen, 2018: 320).

Mill correctly understood that the income-tested Speenhamland scheme, discussed in Chapter 2, had contributed to the depression of wage levels and to employment disincentives (Torry, 2018b), but instead of seeing Speenhamland's means-testing as the problem, he located the problem in workers' unwillingness to work and therefore approved of the stringent conditions imposed on Poor Law recipients from 1834 onwards (Hollander, 1985: 742–7). However, once in Parliament, Mill

> looked forward to a time when … the division of the produce of labour, instead of depending, as in so great a degree it now does, on the accident of birth, will be made by concert on an acknowledged principle of justice … The social problem of the future we considered to be, how to unite the greatest individual liberty of action, with a common ownership in the raw material of the globe, and an equal participation of all in the benefits of combined labour. We had not the presumption to suppose that we could already foresee, by what precise form of institutions these objects could most effectually be attained, or at how near or how distant a period they would become practicable … . (Mill, [1873] 1924: 162)

In his *Utilitarianism*, published in 1863, Mill argued that if someone had 'a sufficient claim … to have something guaranteed to him by society, we say that he has a right to it': and that two essentials to which every individual had a right were therefore 'physical nutrient' and 'security' (Mill, [1861] 2001: 53, 54). Skorupski calls these 'primary utilities', and suggests that

if a person has a right to such and such primary utilities, then providing them for him and protecting him in the possession of them is a requirement ... which has priority over the direct pursuit of general utility, or the private pursuit of personal ends. (Skorupski, 1989: 328)

Satisfying the requirements of justice in this way does not appear to either Mill or Skorupski to compromise the maximization of aggregate utility which is at the heart of Mill's political economy, presumably because autonomy as well as happiness counts towards utility: so ensuring that basic necessities are provided for ought to be compatible with maximizing general utility. However, as Ryan suggests,

justice is a principle independent of, and in some ways opposed to, that of maximising general happiness. To desire an equal, or a fair, distribution of goods is not the same thing as desiring to maximise goods; (Ryan, 1987: 229)

and, as Skorupski points out, the logic of rights suggests that providing the essentials should have priority over the maximization of aggregate utility, because if it does not then human beings become 'expendable resources' (Skorupski, 1989: 334). With this adaptation to Mill's utilitarianism, 'an equal participation of all in the benefits of combined labour' (Mill, [1873] 1924: 162) might have become an argument for a Basic Income: an argument that Mill might have made if he had correctly understood why the Speenhamland scheme had had the unfortunate consequences that it did; and an argument that he might also have made in 1879 when he described a Fourier-inspired community in which the first call on resources was an equal division among the members of the community (Mill, [1879] 1965: 747).

Whether or not Mill was entirely clear about the difference between a Basic Income and a Minimum Income Guarantee, it appears that at least in connection with Fourier's writings he was happy to countenance a Basic Income for every member of the population (Van Parijs and Vanderborght, 2017: 76–7).

Allen Davenport, Richard Carlile
In one sense there is nothing new in Allen Davenport's description of a scheme for the community taking possession of land, leasing it out, and using the rents to pay unconditional incomes to every member of the community, which he published in the journal *The Republican* in 1824. Davenport did more than anyone to revive interest in Thomas Spence's writings, whose poetry he had read on arrival in London in 1804 (Duverger, 2018: 19); and he was explicit

that his scheme was that of Spence (Chase, 2004; Davenport, n.d.). 'Let every individual have an equal interest, or profit in that land which gave him birth, and from which is extracted the sustenance of every thing that has life' (Davenport, 1824: 391–2). Later on, Davenport extended this principle by asking for a 'community of property' that included the common ownership of machinery (Davenport, 1826: 356):

> The working man ... would not only enjoy the whole fruits of his industry, untaxed, but an equal share, in every respect, of the elements and spontaneous productions of nature also ... (Davenport, n.d.: v, 12)

The justification for the community owning land and leasing it out for cultivation might be Spence's, but the justification for paying regular incomes to every individual is somewhat different. Davenport argues that members of the royal family receive regular allowances from the State, so

> Why should not every child that is born in the country be entitled, at its birth, to a revenue from the state, from the common farm, from the productions of the earth, as well as the child of a king? (Davenport, 1824: 396)

Also new is a discussion of objections to Spence's plan. In his article in *The Republican* Davenport responded to objections to Spence's plan previously raised by the journal's editor, Richard Carlile, himself an author heavily influenced by Spence (Chase, 2016: 3); and Carlile then exercised an editor's privilege by responding in footnotes. Carlile's objections still function as objections in the modern debate, which is why both Davenport and Carlile can be regarded as significant authors in the history of Basic Income.

Carlile's first objection was that an equality of property was 'impracticable'. Davenport responded:

> Why, Sir, many things seem impracticable, and impossible too, until they are attempted. ... The discovery of the origin of matter and motion seems to me quite impossible; and yet, what time is not spent, and what volumes are not written on that mysterious subject? I contend that an equality of property in land is practicable. (Davenport, 1824: 394)

Carlile responded in a footnote: 'All a people can fairly desire is, to be an untaxed people; and if those ... who hold the land pay a tax for its use to those who do not hold, "*agrarian equality*" is fully accomplished' (Davenport, 1824: 394).

Few of those who engage in the modern debate on Basic Income would advocate the appropriation of every piece of land by the State on the death of its owner, and most might well regard Spence's plan as 'impracticable'.

The objection of impracticability, or infeasibility, is still frequently heard in relation to the whole idea of a Basic Income. By 'infeasible' or 'impracticable' the objector will often mean 'financially infeasible'; and what they often mean by that is that they have chosen a level of Basic Income, a funding method, and a variety of ways in which current taxes and benefits would be changed; they have pronounced the scheme infeasible; and they have therefore declared Basic Income to be infeasible (Rothstein, 2018; Torry, 2018d). This is a failure of logic, and ought to be called that, although we might be a little more circumspect in our expression of that verdict than Davenport was:

> It is the want of reflection, and entertaining that readiness of doubt of every thing that does not spring from our own brain, that keeps us continually in the dark, and makes us cherish the very system that destroys us. (Davenport, 1824: 398)

We are probably more aware than either Davenport or Carlile that feasibility is a complex idea, and that it might be better to ask about feasibilities in the plural. First of all, for Basic Income to be financially feasible we need just one particular Basic Income scheme to be affordable, and also for it not to impose net disposable income losses on low-income households. What is then required is for the scheme to be administratively feasible, psychologically feasible (that is, is the idea understood, and is it understood to be beneficial?), behaviourally feasible (that is, does the Basic Income do what it says it will do?—a feasibility only testable after implementation), politically feasible, and policy process feasible (that is, can it navigate the policy process from idea to implementation?) (Torry, 2016a; 2019a). If there is a single Basic Income that can pass those tests in a particular country, then Basic Income is entirely feasible.

Davenport describes and responds to a further objection:

> Others object to [Spence's] plan, and say, that if such a plan was to be acted upon, many of the working people, knowing that they would have something whether they were industrious or idle, would cease to labour, and the consequence would be, that the land would run to waste, and not produce enough of the necessaries of life for the general support of the population; which would produce discontent, anarchy, and every species of petty warfare ... (Davenport, 1824: 398)

Davenport offers a response:

> Those who are afraid that the people would become idle, the land cease to be cultivated, and every thing thrown into confusion, have only to look around them; let them look at the East India Company, the Banking Company, or any other Joint Stock Company, and see if they can discover any idleness, any inactivity, or any confusion among them; or whether they are not the most prosperous, the most wealthy, and the most powerful people, according to their number, of any people on the earth. (Davenport, 1824: 398–9)

We might not attempt precisely the same argument today, but similar arguments are still offered: that there are examples that we can indicate that show that providing someone with an unconditional income does not make them idle. Today the examples chosen would be a handful of natural experiments that show that to reduce the rate at which earned income is withdrawn by the tax and benefits system as earned income rises incentivizes rather than disincentivizes employment; and also a variety of Basic Income pilot projects, and other experiments with similarities to Basic Income pilots, that show that Basic Incomes have in fact increased rather than reduced economic activity (Torry, 2018a: 151–9).

Carlile refused to publish anything further about the scheme described by Davenport, whether from Davenport or from anyone else, because although 'no one disputes [the scheme's] worth ... it is so far from being practicable' (Carlile, 1825: 57).

Both Davenport and Carlile belong in this history, not because the reform proposals that they were discussing were new, which they were not, but because the same objections to Basic Income are still heard, and the rebuttals are still heard as well, at least in relation to their general structure. The two authors also belong in this history because Carlile's plan for a tax on land (rather than Davenport's plan to appropriate the land on the death of the owner) has remained an important element in the debate.

The United States

Henry George
In 1888, the American Henry George suggested that private land ownership was 'a robbery in the present', not just in the past; that purchasing land in good faith gave no right of possession; and that 'rent, the creation of the whole community, necessarily belongs to the whole community'. As he put it in one of his many pamphlets:

> Since ... all the Scottish people have the same equal right to live, it follows that they must all have the same equal right to the land of Scotland. ... they must all have the same equal rights to the elements which Nature has provided for the sustaining of life—to air, to water, and to land. For to deny the equal right to the elements necessary to the maintaining of life is to deny the equal right to life. (George, 1888: 3–4)

George rejected John Locke's view that land was property to the extent that human labour had improved and cultivated it. There was no property in land, and the only property was in the fruits of human labour (George, [1898] 1932: 365–6). Everyone 'has a right ... to his own labour and the fruits of his labour' (George, 1884a: 130): but because every worker now 'finds every foot of land enclosed against him' (George, 1884a: 132), and so must work for the owners of land, increasing inequality has become 'the main source' of social problems (George, 1884a: 255). The obvious solution to inequality and poverty was 'the common ownership of land', but in practice it would not be necessary to confiscate land, and we find George shifting from Davenport's proposal to Carlile's:

> You cannot divide land and secure equality: … in our complex civilization that cannot be done. It is not necessary to divide the land, when you can divide the income drawn from the land. (George, 1884b: 14)

That income could be divided

> by concentrating all taxation into a tax upon the value of land, and making that heavy enough to take as near as may be the whole ground rent for common purposes. (George, 1884a: 276; cf. [1879] 1907: 280, 326, 363–4, 403, 404)

There would be 'a single tax' (George, [1891] 1947: 94), everyone would be released from other taxes, no land would be left idle, and a fund would be provided for 'public use' (George, [1879] 1907: 403).

> Here is a fund belonging to society as a whole from which without the degradation of alms, private or public, provision can be made for the weak, the helpless, the aged; from which provision can be made for the common wants of all as a matter of common right to each. (George, 1884a: 287)

George was aware that it was often private interests that determined what was taxed and what was not (Borcherding et al., 1998: 175–8; George, [1898] 1932: 132), and he must have been well aware that certain private interests would be particularly concerned to avoid any significant taxation of land rents: but he still thought it worth proposing a land value tax, and the use of the revenue for public purposes, because that combination would

> raise wages, increase the earnings of capital, extirpate pauperism, abolish poverty, give remunerative employment to whoever wishes it, afford free scope to human powers, lessen crime, elevate morals, and taste, and intelligence, purify government and carry civilization to yet nobler heights. (George, [1879] 1907: 404)

George's somewhat prolix style leaves us in some doubt as to precisely how 'common wants' (George, 1884a: 287) were to be met, what the 'public uses' (George, [1879] 1907: 403) of the new taxation revenue would be, and in particular whether a Basic Income was intended. Because his single land tax proposal could have provided funding for a Basic Income, it is no surprise that George has been regarded as 'the forgotten forbearer of UBI' (Stern, 2020);

and we can sometimes find brief suggestions that unconditional incomes for every individual might have been a possibility that he considered—the revenue would be 'distributed in public benefits to all [of the community's] members' (George, [1879] 1907: 438–9)—but no details are offered, so it is impossible to decide the matter. Contemporary discussions of Land Value Tax can be rather more explicit about the employment of land value tax revenue to pay for a Basic Income (Farley, 2017).

France and Belgium

Charles Fourier
Charles Fourier's *Lettre au Grand Juge* (*Letter to the High Judge*), is important not only because it might or might not discuss a Basic Income, but also because it represents an early example of the unclear terminology, and therefore ambiguity, that has afflicted the Basic Income debate from that day to this.

Fourier was writing during a period of social and economic change following the French Revolution: a period during which older forms of solidarity were disappearing and new ones were emerging. During this period, increasing industrialization, alongside social and economic turbulence, was generating the poverty that so much concerned Fourier (Duverger, 2018: 23–5; Spencer, 1981: 55–6):

> It is easy to prove that all social crimes out of ambition proceed from the poverty of the people, from their efforts to escape poverty, from the anxiety which is instilled in society by the presence of poverty, from the fear of falling into it, and from disgust for the odious habits which it encourages. (Fourier, [1803] 1874: 19; [1803] 2004: 100)

As for the solution: 'When the people enjoy constant comfort and a decent minimum, all the sources of discord will be dried up or reduced to very little', and this will be achieved by a system that will 'assigner en salaire ou en vétérance un minimum décent au-dessous duquel il ne puisse pas tomber', which Beecher and Bienvenu translate as 'guarantee a salary or in old age a decent minimum below which they cannot fall' (Fourier, [1803] 1874: 20; [1803] 2004: 100). This passage contains two ambiguities.

The fifth edition of the *Dictionnaire de l'Académie Française*, published in 1798, among other definitions defines 'assigner' as 'placer', which in turn is defined as 'situer, mettre dans un lieu'; and it defines 'salaire' as 'récompense, paiement pour travail, ou pour service' (Académie Française). The passage should probably be translated: 'provide by wage or in old age a decent minimum below which they cannot fall'. This looks like a Minimum Income Guarantee, provided for working age adults by a statutory minimum wage high enough to ensure that a specified minimum is attained, or by a pension, which could be either means-tested or not. Cunliffe and Erreygers conclude from a study of several of Fourier's texts that he intended a distribution in kind and not in money; and that the distribution was intended for the poor, and not for everybody. Although the intention was not to work-test the income, what he was describing was far from being a Basic Income (Cunliffe and Erreygers, 2001: 462).

Fourier moved on to more wide-ranging and often rather fantastical descriptions of an ideal society, and it was these, as well as his detailed prescriptions, that influenced authors who read his works (Spencer, 1981: 153–5): for instance, Victor Considérant, who, during the middle of the nineteenth century, following Thomas Paine's logic, argued that the privatization of land required compensation in the form of a right to work rather than in the form of unconditional grants and incomes (Duverger, 2018: 28–34). As for Fourier himself, in 1829 he was still writing about 'un minimum copieux, d'une garantie de nourriture et d'entretien décent ...' ('a generous minimum, a guarantee of food and of decent maintenance ...').

Le remboursement du minimum avancé sera garanti par l'attraction industrielle ou passion du peuple pour des travaux très agréables et très lucratifs. (Fourier, 1829: 24)
[The reimbursement of the advanced minimum will be guaranteed by the attraction of industry or people's passion for very pleasant and very lucrative work.]

Does he mean that a Basic Income would be paid, which would then be reimbursed to the State by people doing the work that needed doing: work that would now be attractive; or does he mean that people would be reimbursed for their work, and that that reimbursement would provide the 'generous minimum'? The description of the minimum as 'avancé' ('advanced'), might suggest the former: except that Fourier goes on to explain that the minimum would be constituted as 'dividends', one of which would be related to 'work', one to capital, and one to the level of someone's skills:

à chaque individu, homme, femme ou enfant, trois dividendes affectés à ses trois facultés industrielles, Capital, Travail et Talent, et pleinement satisfaisants pour lui. (Fourier, 1829: 24)
[to each individual, man, woman or child, three dividends allocated to their three industrial faculties, Capital, Work and Talent, and fully satisfactory for him.]

We remain in doubt as to what Fourier intended.

Joseph Charlier

One of the authors influenced by Fourier's writings was the Belgian Joseph
Charlier. The foundation of his argument is one that we have met before, but
here it is particularly clearly expressed:

> L'homme en naissant apporte avec lui le droit de vivre; de ce droit ... découle
> comme conséquence obligé le droit de demander au sol, patrimoine commun des
> hommes, sa part dans les fruits nécessaires à son existence ... D'où il suit que la
> nue-propriété du sol est inaliénable de sa nature: elle est indivisé et appartient non
> aux individus en particuliers, mais à la collection, à l'ensemble des êtres créés.
> (Charlier, 1848: 20)
> [When he is born, man brings with him the right to live; from this right ... follows
> as a necessary consequence, the right to demand from the land, the common patri-
> mony of men, his share of the fruits that he needs for his existence. ... from which
> it follows that full property to the land is unalienable by nature: it is joint property
> and does not belong to private individuals but to the collectivity, to all creatures as
> a whole.] (Charlier, [1848] 2004: 103–104)

Private ownership of land is 'usurpation', and it 'has wrecked and will wreck
every attempt to improve the condition of the masses' (Charlier, 1848:
21; [1848] 2004: 104). However, Charlier recognizes the rights of current
landowners, so although the land should be taken by the State, the present
occupiers should be left in place and permitted to benefit from what they legitimately thought they owned by receiving compensation: substantial annual
compensation for the first generation, progressively less for the second, third
and fourth generations, and none for the fifth. Such compensation would be
paid out of tenants' rents, and, after paying compensation to former owners,
the proceeds would fund 'un minimum garanti' ('a guaranteed minimum'),
the level of which would slowly grow as the amounts paid out in compensation declined (Charlier, 1848: 44–7, 33; [1848] 2004: 114–15, 110). This
'guaranteed minimum' would eventually satisfy everyone's 'absolute or
vital needs' (Charlier, 1848: 24; [1848] 2004: 106): but is the 'guaranteed
minimum' a Basic Income? Because this somewhat ambiguous phrase, 'guaranteed minimum', is subsequently substituted by 'la garantie d'un minimum
obligatoire pour chacun tout en laissant le travail facultatif' ('the guarantee of
an obligatory minimum for all, leaving labour optional') (Charlier, 1848: 33;
[1848] 2004: 111), we can conclude that Charlier intended the quarterly payments not to be work-tested: but did he mean by 'guaranteed minimum' a net
income below which nobody would be allowed to fall, which would imply
a means-tested benefit to bring everyone up to that minimum; or did he mean
a Basic Income: an equal unconditional income payable to every individual
without being means-tested?

Although we can find no statement in the *Solution du Problème Social*
(*Solution of the Social Problem*) that removes all possibility of ambiguity,

the evidence suggests that Charlier intended a non-means-tested income by 'guaranteed minimum'. The logic of the argument that each person's right to live gives to each individual 'the right to demand from the land ... his share of the fruits that he needs for his existence' (Charlier, 1848: 20, 23; [1848] 2004: 103–4, 106), suggests an equal division of land rents. The argument that anyone can find themselves impoverished, and that 'the rich themselves have an interest in the success of this system, which in offering a guaranteed minimum to all, provides everyone with a perfect security ... it can guarantee that in future not one single human being can die of hunger' (Charlier, 1848: 43; [1848] 2004: 116–17), suggests the 'perfect security' of a Basic Income. Charlier discusses whether women should receive amounts different from men, and whether children should receive less than adults, and in both cases decides for equality, and that 'an equal minimum *for all* has to be acknowledged as the invariable rule based on the equal, uniform, indivisible rights of everyone' (Charlier, 1848: 46; [1848] 2004: 118). All of this suggests non-means-tested payments. However, there are occasional suggestions that the 'guaranteed minimum' might be provided by a variety of means. There are passages that suggest that some individuals already have their needs met, which might lead us to think that because they already had a 'guaranteed minimum' they would not need to have one provided:

> Domestic staff, employees, people with small private means ... all of them people whose vital needs have been safeguarded. ... a man whose first needs are secured, whose material life is supported, is generally speaking more steady, more active and more industrious. ... Arrived at well-being [bien-être] he will want to rise to prosperity ... . (Charlier, 1848: 36; [1848] 2004: 111)

However, it becomes clear that the lesson he wishes to draw is that to provide everyone with an unconditional income would encourage rather than discourage productive work, because anyone who

> enjoys a guaranteed minimum ... will be energetically incited by the direct and personal advantages it provides, because from the moment his labour has to satisfy only his acquired needs, it becomes attractive in that it enlarges the sphere of well-being and spreads the benefits of capital, adopting its characteristics and realizing its enjoyments. (Charlier, 1848: 36; [1848] 2004: 112)

While recognizing that Charlier's terminology can be ambiguous, taking the passages as a whole we can legitimately decide that Charlier's argument was that every individual, whatever their age or gender, whatever their employment status, and whatever their other income, should regularly receive the same proportion of the surplus of land rents once compensation had been paid to the former owners.

Charlier's *Solution du Problème Sociale* is not only of interest because he was probably an early advocate of a Basic Income. It is also of interest in that it responds to objections that are still heard today (Duverger, 2018: 36–7).

As we have seen, Charlier tackles an objection already answered by Thomas Spence and Allen Davenport: that providing a Basic Income would make people idle. Charlier has already distinguished between 'absolute or vital needs' and 'relative or acquired needs' (Charlier, 1848: 24; [1848] 2004: 106), and on that basis suggests that

> since man will no longer need to take care of his vital needs he will prefer ... to develop his acquired needs, which he can only satisfy through labour. (Charlier, 1848: 36; [1848] 2004: 111)

Charlier then tackles a further objection: in today's terminology, who will do the lousy jobs? And the response is the same as the one generally offered today:

> No doubt the establishment of a guaranteed minimum, by raising and bettering the material conditions of the popular masses, will render them more fastidious in their choice of a profession; but since this choice is, generally speaking, determined by the wages of labour, the industries concerned have to offer their employees, because they are absolutely necessary, sufficiently high wages for them to accept as a fair compensation for the inconvenience they incur. (Charlier, 1848: 37; [1848] 2004: 112)

But it is not only objections about which Charlier writes. He is also aware of the advantages that providing a Basic Income would offer to society, particularly in relation to both 'the mutual independence of individuals with respect to each other' and at the same time what we would call an increase in social cohesion.

> Once the right to conservation is guaranteed for all by means of a minimum, man will no longer be forced to demean himself to often shameful acts in order to snatch his existence from the urgent needs inherent to his nature. As a result the mistrust, which today keeps them more or less at a distance, will no longer have a reason to exist and will disappear in the light of the general conviction that from now on friendship will no longer be a burden, but will be profitable for all. (Charlier, 1848: 38; [1848] 2004: 113)

Charlier's proposal looks similar to that made by Thomas Spence. The payments would be quarterly (Charlier, 1848: 51; [1848] 2004: 120), for the first four generations they would tend to rise, and thereafter they would fluctuate with the rent revenues. The proposal lies somewhere between an annual dividend and a Basic Income.

Cunliffe and Erreygers suggest that Charlier had offered 'a fully developed basic income scheme' (Cunliffe and Erreygers, 2001: 477), and Duverger that Charlier was 'the first to formulate so distinctly … the proposition of a Basic Income for all, without conditions, in monetary form' (Duverger, 2018: 37). They are probably correct: but whether they are or not, we can legitimately see Charlier's *Solution du Problème Sociale* as an argument for providing a Basic Income. He sets out the need to tackle poverty, a proposal for tackling it by paying an unconditional income to every individual, and a funding method; he responds to objections; and he explains some of the advantages for individuals, for the economy, and for society. Here is the closest we have come so far to a modern treatment of Basic Income.

CONCLUSIONS

Many of the proposals that we have discussed in the previous chapter and in this one fulfil the definition of Basic Income as an unconditional income for every individual, with the clearest examples being those of Spence and Charlier. As we recognized at the end of the previous chapter in relation to Thomas Spence's pamphlets, what the proposals do not fulfil are the assumptions often made of how a Basic Income would function: that is, payments would have been quarterly rather than weekly or monthly, and they would have varied in amount; but we should probably recognize that in relation to the nineteenth century, as in the eighteenth, quarterly varying payments might have been the only practicable proposal that could have been made. We can conclude that, given what our authors wanted their unconditional incomes to achieve, if they had been able to propose a weekly or monthly payment of a stable amount then they would have done so. On that basis, and given the context, we probably ought to conclude that in terms of the eighteenth and nineteenth centuries we ought to accept that a quarterly and somewhat variable unconditional income should probably count as a Basic Income. Thomas Spence's pamphlets should therefore be counted as the earliest extant texts in which we find the idea of a Basic Income evolving, and Joseph Charlier should be credited with being the first to develop what looks remarkably like a modern discussion of Basic Income and its likely effects.

A reading of the dates of the literature cited in this chapter somewhat disproves Henderson and Quiggin's suggestion that 'there is a big gap in the Basic Income literature between the 1850s and the 1920s' (Henderson and Quiggin, 2019: 494), but it might be accurate to suggest that the literature of that period was more derivative than the literature of the previous sixty years and of the period after the First World War. The Basic Income debate did not take new directions between 1850 and 1918, and Henderson and Quiggin are of course correct to point out that the period

> coincides with the rapid growth of the labour movement, labour parties, and socialist parties. Perhaps the idea of a world of propertied independence seemed increasingly out of step with the emerging world of industrial capitalism, and the more ambitious goals of socialists in relation to the collective ownership of the means of production. (Henderson and Quiggin, 2019: 494)

They go on to chart a subsequent century of disinterest in Basic Income among trades unions (Henderson and Quiggin, 2019: 495–500): but that did not prevent the debate from taking interesting new directions after the First World War; and nor did it prevent it from becoming the diverse global debate that it is today.

4. Basic Income in the United Kingdom during the early twentieth century

INTRODUCTION

Following the First World War, a number of writers in the United Kingdom (UK) explored the possibility of paying an unconditional income to every individual: a phenomenon no doubt partly generated by the way in which during the war it had become normal for people to expect the Government to manage the economy in ways that might not have been expected before (Duverger, 2018: 39–40). These writers set out from a wide variety of perspectives, they offered a variety of methods for funding their Basic Incomes, and between them they represented a powerful case for Basic Income. We shall be left wondering whether their different individual research and educational activities might have had more effect on the policymaking process if there had been better institutional connections between them, and perhaps if they had used similar names to describe their proposals.

BERTRAND RUSSELL'S 'VAGABOND'S WAGE'

Bertrand Russell was a mathematician, philosopher and campaigning pacifist, who wrote substantial mathematical and philosophical academic texts. He also wrote for a more general market a number of books that he regarded as being philosophical in a broad sense of the word. These were intended to make a difference to the world (Pigden, 2003: 481–2, 493). Russell wanted to see a society characterized by both anarchism and socialism, which in practical terms meant a socialist state in which the individual's freedom would be maximized (Sloman, 2019: 68–9).

In 1917, Russell wrote *Political Ideals*:

> I am not prepared to maintain that economic justice requires an exactly equal income for everybody. Some kinds of work require a larger income for efficiency than others do; but there is economic injustice as soon as a man has more than his share, unless it is because his efficiency in his work requires it, or as a reward for some definite service. ... except in cases of unusual laziness or eccentric ambition, most men would elect to do a full day's work for a full day's pay. ... ordinary work

should, as far as possible, afford interest and independence and scope for initiative. These things are more important than income, as soon as a certain minimum has been reached. (Russell, [1917] 2012: 18, 21)

By the following year, when he wrote *Roads to Freedom*, Russell's ideas about the 'certain minimum' had become more specific:

A certain small income, sufficient for necessaries, should be secured to all, whether they work or not, and ... a larger income—as much larger as might be warranted by the total amount of commodities produced—should be given to those who are willing to engage in some work which the community recognizes as useful. (Russell, [1918] 2006: 93)

The income that Russell envisaged was to be 'secured' to all, and Russell might have meant by this a Basic Income, and his proposed income has been understood as that (Sloman, 2019: 69), even when he calls it a 'vagabond's wage'.

The necessaries of life should be free, as Anarchists desire, to all equally, regardless of whether they work or not. Under this plan, every man could live without work: there would be what might be called a 'vagabond's wage', sufficient for existence but not for luxury. (Russell, [1918] 2006: 133)

The 'certain small income' should presumably be interpreted in the light of the socialist and anarchist framework within which the book as a whole is framed. Russell envisages 'the community' rather than the market determining the monetary value of work: and so it is 'the community' that pays both the 'certain small income, sufficient for necessaries', and the 'larger income ... given to those who are willing to engage in some work which the community recognizes as useful' (Russell, [1918] 2006: 93). So what in fact is being recommended here is the abolition of the 'wage system' (Russell, [1917] 2012: 54) and the implementation of a State-provided work-tested income for every individual: an income that could not be means-tested simply because there would be no other sources of income. The way in which the income would be increased by the community's valuation of the individual's work means that it would not have been a Basic Income according to the definition: although of course that part of it that would have been paid to everyone—the 'vagabond's wage'—could have been regarded as one, and in Russell's view it is that part that would have promoted artistic activity, scientific innovation (Russell, [1918] 2006: 131–4), and the economic independence of women:

Women in domestic work, whether married or unmarried, will receive pay as they would if they were in industry. This will secure the complete economic independence of wives, which is difficult to achieve in any other way, since mothers of young children ought not to be expected to work outside the home. (Russell, [1918] 2006: 145)

This passage should presumably be read in the light of the 'certain small income' that would be 'sufficient for necessaries' and 'secured to all' (Russell, [1918] 2006: 93) and could be seen as an early 'wages for housework' campaign.

Russell believed that 'if men had to be tempted to work instead of driven to it, the obvious interest of the community would be to make work pleasant' (Russell, [1918] 2006: 87): but he was content with the idea that his proposals might result in 'idleness', about which he later wrote an essay, 'In Praise of Idleness':

> In a world where no one is compelled to work more than four hours a day, every person possessed of scientific curiosity will be able to indulge it, and every painter will be able to paint without starving, ... medical men will have time to learn about the progress of medicine ... above all, there will be happiness and joy of life, instead of frayed nerves, weariness, and dyspepsia. ... Modern methods of production have given us the possibility of ease and security for all; we have chosen, instead, to have overwork for some and starvation for others. (Russell, [1935] 1996: 14–15)

Russell had read both Charles Fourier and John Stuart Mill. In Fourier he would have found a 'guaranteed minimum', and in Mill's *Chapters on Socialism* he would have read about Fourier communities in which 'a certain minimum [was] first ... set apart for the subsistence of every member of the community, whether capable or not of labour' (Mill, [1879] 1965: 747). These might have been the sources for Russell's own 'certain small income ... secured to all' (Russell, [1918] 2006: 93; see also Duverger, 2018: 42).

A STATE BONUS

E. Mabel and Dennis Milner

Bertrand Russell was not a Quaker—far from it—but he was a conscientious objector during the First World War, and Dennis and E. Mabel Milner, both Quakers, would have been aware of that, and were aware of his writings (Van Trier, 2020). (This will not be the last time that we shall notice Quaker engagement with the Basic Income debate.) Following service in an Ambulance Unit during the First World War, Dennis Milner worked as an engineer in the Quaker-founded Rowntree chocolate factory in York, and while there he developed his idea for a State Bonus. He soon left the factory to work full-time on the idea, publishing booklets (sometimes alone, sometimes with his wife

E. Mabel Milner, and sometimes with others) and running the State Bonus
League (Cunliffe and Erreygers, 2004: 121; Van Trier, 1995: 31–142).
   The plan for a State Bonus was that

(a)   Every individual, all the time, should receive from a central fund some small
      allowance in money which would be just sufficient to maintain life and liberty
      if all else failed.
(b)   That as everyone is to get a share from this central fund, so everyone who has
      any income at all should contribute a share each in proportion to his capacity.
      …
Every man, every woman, and every child must have it in their own right; it must
be theirs irrespective of the faults and errors of the past, making it possible for the
fallen to start out on life again with a new hope: it must be clear of all taxes and
legal obligations. It must be ours like the air and the sunshine. (Milner and Milner,
1918: 7)

As today, the employment market after the First World War was characterized
by casualization and seasonal employment, so all of a household's income was
permanently at risk.

The need for a subsistence income is a continuous need, and much injury to health
and steadiness of habits has resulted from it being met discontinuously. (Milner,
1920: 29)

A national minimum wage was no answer to this, and it was also

economically quite unsound because it attempts to assess an economic unit of work
in terms of humanitarian need. (Milner, 1920: 29; cf. Price, 1920: 10)

And there was no reason to think that a wage should permanently pay for the
subsistence costs of a family with children when there would be periods of
life without them; neither was there any reason for seasonal employers to pay
workers for the whole year (Milner, 1920b: 44–7, 77). A Basic Income was
clearly required, and the fact that the amount to be paid to every individual
was given, and calculations of the net cost of the scheme was based on every
individual receiving the same amount (five shillings, or £0.25), makes it clear
that the income that the Milners intended was individual, nonwithdrawable and
without means test or work test (Milner and Milner, 1918: 7), and that it was
therefore a genuine Basic Income. When in 1920 the terms 'Minimum Income'
and 'guarantee' were used to describe a scheme—'The Minimum Income is
a permanent guaranteed income backed by the whole Community' (Milner
and Milner, 1920: 3)—it is clear from the context that the Milners were still
discussing a Basic Income.

As with many of the authors whom we studied in Chapter 2, the main motive was to find a solution to poverty (Milner and Milner, 1918: 1):

> The Scheme for a State Bonus is an attempt to outline a method of dealing with the problem in a simple, direct, and yet comprehensive way: suitable for immediate legislation, yet making a fundamental change in our social relationships. It appeals to the family unit by making for a juster proportioning of money payment to the needs of the family, and by so doing will re-establish confidence, not only in the State organization, but between all classes. (Milner and Milner, 1918: 4)

Such arguments from a Basic Income's ability to improve social cohesion would be heard again, as would arguments from fairness: Unemployment Benefit was 'a reward for unemployment' (Milner, 1920: 29), 'the Community should help all alike, not only those who have failed to help themselves' (Milner and Milner, 1918: 6), and 'any attempt to confine the allowance to those who are unemployed penalizes those who are employed' (Milner, 1920: 28). Also to be heard again would be the argument that the Basic Income would improve both employment conditions and the health of workers:

> No one should be driven by the threat of destitution into accepting work which is underpaid, unhealthy, or even dangerous. Therefore destitution must not exist. (Milner and Milner, 1918: 6)

> The Minimum Income [State Bonus] is … an attempt to secure capability for work by abolishing destitution … and an attempt to encourage willingness to work in an atmosphere devoid of Industrial Compulsion. (Milner, 1920: 19)

The State Bonus would keep people

> fit for the next work and, because no deductions are made from this maintenance on account of employment, each job brings a return comparable with their effort, adds to their self-respect, and this in turn makes them more capable of doing useful work. (Milner, 1920: 78)

A more general argument from the need for efficient workers was offered in a booklet for which Dennis Milner wrote a foreword:

> Every man, woman and child should have the legal right to an income from the State of a sufficient sum to maintain a national minimum standard of physical efficiency … the removal of all cause for worry on account of the actual necessities of life would make enormously for increased efficiency in all directions. (Price, 1920: 8, 9)

Similar arguments based on a Basic Income's likely effect on mental health are still heard today (Psychologists for Social Change, 2017).

The Milners were aware that if the level of the State Bonus were to be set too high then employment incentives would fall and the funds available to pay for the Bonus would also fall: but they were also clear that at the level of five shillings (£0.25) per week at pre-war prices (Milner and Milner, 1918: 7), which equated to £27.25 per week in 2018 (Morley, 2020), there would have been no disincentive effect: and in any case, 'of the wisdom of maintaining people in health by proper nourishment, before attempting to induce them to work, there can be no question' (Milner and Milner, 1918: 13). Arnold Price went further: with a State Bonus in payment,

> work will come to be regarded more as a moral duty ... and as a means to create individual and collective wealth. (Price, 1920: 10)

As well as having to deal in this way with the objection that the State Bonus would result in 'slacking' (Milner and Milner, 1918: 14), the Milners also had to face other objections, and in particular one offered more frequently now than in the past, perhaps because Basic Income is now looking both more desirable and more feasible than it used to. This is the objection that discussion of Basic Income distracts us from studying other reform options regarded by some as both more feasible and more useful, and that to implement a Basic Income scheme would mean less money for solving social problems by reforming the existing welfare state (Gough, 2017: 185; Lawrence and Lawson, 2017: 72; Piachaud, 2016: 19): but as the Milners pointed out, their scheme was 'not antagonistic to other methods of reform' (Milner and Milner, 1918: 6), and it was 'not an alternative, but [was] an additional method of tackling a small part of all these problems' (Milner and Milner, 1920: 11). The same can be said of many illustrative Basic Income schemes today (Torry, 2018a: 173). As for the objection that the State Bonus would not be affordable, Dennis Milner argued that the additional income tax required would be 'a 20 per cent deduction at source on all incomes' (Milner, 1920: 21): a fixed proportion so that both the pool available for distribution, and therefore the State Bonus itself, would vary with national income (Milner, 1920: 21).

Not every argument that the Milners offered for the State Bonus was as robust as this. By 1920 the argument was being offered that because any increase in productivity would be shared by all, workers would no longer reduce their productivity in order to maintain the level of employment, and so industrial productivity would increase. The reason for the greater prominence of this argument was that the level of productivity was becoming a national concern (Duverger, 2018: 47–8; Milner, 1920b: 49–50, 52): but the argument fails because there was no reason to believe that a share in the proceeds of an increasing aggregate national productivity would prevent an increase in an individual firm's workers' productivity from resulting in posts being declared redundant and a consequent loss of net disposable income for the workers.

The Milners proposed that contributions towards the fund from which the Bonus would be paid should be paid by 'everyone with any income at all' (Milner and Milner, 1918: 8) at a flat rate. This was to ensure that 'the Bonus would not come as a sudden net addition to wages', and that

> the transfer of money from rich to poor would be reduced to a minimum. It cannot be too clearly stated that the object of the Bonus is to introduce this feeling of security, not to make an arbitrary addition to wages. It is, in short, a very comprehensive insurance scheme. Therefore, as with other insurance schemes, the contribution must be from all, while the benefit would be most felt by those in need. (Milner and Milner, 1918: 8)

This is the kind of wise adaptation to public opinion from which the modern debate might still have lessons to learn: a further example of which was the Milners' description of their scheme as an example of 'moderate Communism' as opposed to 'suggestions which are being made for complete socialistic schemes, to be arrived at by revolutionary methods' (Milner and Milner, 1918: 10). The Milners were writing in the shadow of the Russian Revolution. And in order to show that no major redistribution of income was in view, the Milners offered what would now be called a 'typical household' calculation that showed that a family of five earning £500 per annum would be better off by just £10 per annum. Only the top decile—the tenth of families at the top of the earnings range—would have experienced a net loss of income, and they would have been 'chiefly people who can appreciate the other advantages of the Scheme' (Milner and Milner, 1918: 11).

By 1920 the Milners were writing that

> single women or men would find it hard to manage on the sum proposed, but if they seem to be taxed by the scheme it should be remembered that it helped their parents and it will help themselves later when they are married or old, (Milner and Milner, 1920: 3)

presumably because objectors had pointed out that the 1918 scheme would redistribute from single people to couples.

In their 1918 *Scheme for a State Bonus* the Milners suggested that employers would gain from 'the general satisfaction of all the workers, and the consequent reduction in strikes' (Milner and Milner, 1918: 12), from healthier workers, from an increase in demand, and from the fact that a wage would no longer have had to provide for the entire cost of a large family: a factor used to argue for Family Allowances during the Second World War (Harris, 1981: 249). The Milners also argued that the Bonus would mean children staying longer in school, that women would be less dependent on men and so 'freer to make proper choice about marriage', and that 'many of the higher and nobler aspirations' would be released (Milner and Milner, 1918: 13). The penultimate argument adduced in the book was the one most common during previous centuries:

> On a point of justice most people are agreed that everyone ought to have access to the land, but it is clear that in our existing civilization this right is denied, so that it would seem only reasonable for Civilisation to give in exchange the cash equivalent of what a man could grow with very little effort. Obviously giving the equivalent in cash is a great deal simpler than reorganizing our whole land system! (Milner and Milner, 1918: 14)

The final argument was that the Bonus would 'help to maintain the unity of purpose which has been developed by the War, because it perpetuates the idea of "each for all and all for each"' (Milner and Milner, 1918: 15).

The conclusion of the Milners' *Scheme for a State Bonus* says this:

> ... this scheme has not been worked out for the benefit of one class more than another, and it is hoped that enough has been said to indicate its value to all.
>
> To the economic failure it offers life and liberty. This means that for every man with a moderate income there will always be in the back of his mind a sense of security, which will make for greater stability throughout the whole of industry; and for the fallen there will be fresh hope.
>
> It removes from all the fear that Peace will bring dislocation accompanied by strikes and further restrictions on personal liberty, and ensures that no mistakes in demobilizing will lead to the destitution of anyone.
>
> For the children it means more equal opportunities for development; to their parents, less anxiety and less difficulty in meeting the growing expenses.
>
> It removes, for all of us, the reproach of the existence in our midst of extreme and dire poverty.
>
> In short, it makes men and women, rather than materials, the basis of Reconstruction. (Milner and Milner, 1918: 16)

This is a Basic Income scheme of a 'modern' variety: it was argued for on the basis of its predicted social and economic effects rather than on the basis of the common ownership of land on which Paine and Spence had relied (Duverger, 2018: 45); and it was fully specified in its details. In these respects, the Milners' proposal was a new departure. But where did it come from? Van Trier suggests that reading Edward Bellamy's novel *Looking Backward* might have inspired ideas that led to the invention of the State Bonus (Van Trier, 1995: 129–38): but perhaps more significant is the fact that Dennis Milner was an engineer (Sloman, 2019: 66). An engineer looks at a problem and seeks a practical solution; and, most importantly, seeks the simplest possible solution. I suspect that this is where the Milners' proposal came from. They could see the poverty of many people in the UK; they knew that the Poor Law was not the answer; so they sought the simplest possible solution to the problem: an unconditional income for every individual, paid for by an income tax.

If further reasons were to be required for describing the Milners' proposal as 'modern', then it would be these: their scheme was feasible then, and an appropriately updated version would be feasible today; they expressed many of the arguments for the scheme that would be offered today; and they recognized many of the objections that might be heard today, and offered appropriate responses. It might not be inappropriate to regard the Milners' plan for a State Bonus as the first modern fully specified and feasible illustrative Basic Income scheme.

The booklet in which a State Bonus ('Minimum Income') scheme was published in 1920 described a set of proposals that the Labour Party might have decided to implement if it had found itself in government: 'Old Age Pension at 60 ... Widows' Pensions ... Women's Endowment' (Milner and Milner, 1920: 9); and it then pointed out that a Basic Income would have cost the same, would have provided the same income security as other methods, would have been 'in line with the public utterances of the Labour Party', and would have been attractive to voters because of its simplicity and the fact that it could be implemented straight away 'without great disorganization' (Milner and Milner, 1920a: 12). In 1921, the Labour Party's Executive Committee asked the party's Advisory Committee on Trade Policy and Finance to prepare a memorandum on the State Bonus Scheme. The memorandum was then discussed and approved by the Executive Committee.

(a)   The State Bonus Scheme is attempting to do the right thing in the wrong way. All that it raises would be better achieved by the bringing into force of the Labour Party's existing programme.

(b)   It takes no account of the peculiar problem of the Labour Party which has to fit its programme to three periods: (a) The present capitalist period; (b) The transitional period; (c) The ultimate period.

(c)   Substantially it proposes to raise money without any regard to ability to pay and to distribute it without any regard to need. (Labour Party, 1921: 60)

The 'existing programme' is summarized as 'nationalisation, workers' control, the raising of all wages, the raising of unemployment insurance ...' (Labour Party, 1921: 60), and the memorandum suggests that the problems of carrying out the programme would already be significant without adding an 'industrial disorganisation such as would follow on the State Bonus Scheme' (Labour Party, 1921: 60). A list of detailed objections is offered: the high tax rates required, the flat rate of tax, the low level of the payments, administrative difficulties, and so on. A summary follows:

> In so far as the scheme is designed to meet poverty, unemployment, and other ills, the Labour Party's programme is already designed to cope with them. The Party is already committed to high wages, good housing, increased education, nationalisation, high unemployment insurance, widows' pensions, high and earlier old age pensions, sickness pensions, mothers' pensions, full and adequate provision for orphans. All this can be done in the transitional period without upsetting the machinery of production on which we subsist. It is quite conceivable that by the time many of the measures to which the Labour Party is committed have been brought into operation, the need for the State Bonus Scheme will have disappeared. The change will have been gradual, the disturbance will have been reduced; the growth of the communised state will have been cautious and therefore sound. A large measure of industrial amelioration will have been achieved instead of being sacrificed to the odium of possible failure. (Labour Party, 1921: 62)

As Van Trier points out, what is particularly interesting is that no mention is made of the 'something for nothing' argument (Van Trier, 1995: 127). Might members of the Advisory Committee on Trade Policy and Finance have disagreed over the legitimacy of unconditional incomes? Might there have been some who understood unconditional incomes as entirely coherent with a socialist society, and others who wanted to see labour properly valued by adequate wages and conditions and who saw the State Bonus Scheme as a distraction?

No further discussion of the State Bonus appears to have taken place, and by 1922 the State Bonus League appears to have ceased to exist (Macnicol, 1980: 9; Van Trier, 1995: 128).

Bertram Pickard

Another Quaker and founder member of the State Bonus League, and another who knew of Bertrand Russell's writings, was Bertram Pickard, and a year after the Milners published their *Scheme for a State Bonus* Pickard published *A Reasonable Revolution* (Pickard, 1919). The State Bonus described is the same as that discussed by the Milners (Pickard, 1919: 19), but the reasons for it are given different weights and are differently expressed. For Pickard, the State Bonus

> must be deemed the monetary equivalent of the right to land, of the right to life and liberty, and must carry with it no taint of pauperism. That is why it must be paid to all alike, the rich, the poor, the deserving, the undeserving. (Pickard, 1919: 21)

The State Bonus would 'increase the bargaining power of the "worker"', enhance the status of women, enable the children of all classes to benefit from 'higher education', 'foster the spirit of co-operation', make it possible for the low paid worker 'to demand fair value in return for his services', enable people to start their own businesses, and cause wages for undesirable jobs to rise (Pickard, 1919: 33–6, 40, 61). The Bonus would incentivize employment, because anyone currently on 'public or private charity' would seek a job,

> for they would receive a full return in added comfort for the money earned, whereas to-day they are rewarded by charity in proportion to their indigence. ... Thus the Scheme, whilst based upon the belief that Man is normally industrious, takes human frailty into account and is essentially a sane admixture of idealism and common sense. (Pickard, 1919: 37)

An important difference between Pickard's and the Milners' arguments for a State Bonus is that the Milners argued that the scheme would redistribute only mildly from rich to poor (Milner and Milner, 1918: 11), whereas Pickard regarded it as an instrument for obtaining a 'more equitable distribution of wealth', with the aim of creating a 'new Social Order' and avoiding a 'bitter and protracted' class conflict. The State Bonus would found the social order 'upon a basis of income rather than of capital, and thus interfere for the present as little as possible with the machine of Production, so that industrial stability may be maintained' (Pickard, 1919: 37–8). Pickard does not remark on the difference in emphasis between his and the Milners' preferences in relation to the amount of redistribution that would be achieved by the State Bonus, but the difference is there nevertheless. That difference is yet another similarity to today's debate, in which there is a substantial amount of discussion and disagreement over the level at which a Basic Income should be paid (Torry, 2017b), and much related discussion over Basic Income's relationship to redistribution, and in particular over whether what matters is the redistribution of income or the redistribution of the ability to increase net income through additional earned income (Bryan, 2005: 39; Harrop, 2012: 9; Parker and Sutherland, 1994; Torry, 2018a: 86–90).

SOCIAL CREDIT

The Basic Income debate is replete with engineers. Dennis Milner was one; and an early contributor to the UK's 1980s Basic Income debate was the engineer Keith Roberts:

> Economic Engineering is the discipline that is concerned with the design of model economic systems to meet specified requirements, and with the prediction and evaluation of the performance of such systems. ... Here we think of the economic

system as a machine that is amenable to human design and control, and examine a particular model based on the National Dividend scheme that appears to provide a positive answer. (Roberts, 1983: 14)

It was as an engineer that Clifford Douglas—Major Douglas—approached the problem of the mismatch between increasing production and stagnant purchasing power during the early 1920s.

> In considering the design, either of a mechanism or of an undertaking, it is first of all necessary to have a specific and well-defined objective, and, after that, a knowledge not only of the methods by which that objective can be obtained, but also of the nature and treatment of the forces which will be involved, the materials available, and their reaction to those forces. (Douglas, 1933: 168)

This was the problem: if A is total wages, dividends and other incomes, and B is other costs of production, then $(A + B) = P$, where P is equal to the total price of all goods and services. This meant that total income would be less than the total price of goods, creating poverty in a context of overproduction, and handing control of purchasing power to banks 'which have acquired the monopoly of money-making' (Douglas, 1951: 49). Douglas's solution to the problem was that the Government should both control prices and add money to the economy in the form of an unconditional 'national dividend' (Douglas, 1951: 35–6; Duverger, 2018: 50–51; Sloman, 2019: 70–71). The argument is often overly complex, and there are secondary infeasible aspects to Douglas's plan that need not detain us; but the main elements of the plan are clear: the State and not the banks should issue credit for investment and other purposes, and the purchasing power that that debt represents could then be distributed to households (Douglas, 1920: 115–17). In practical terms, the State would be purchasing production capital and allocating the fruits of production to the population in order to fill the gap between prices and earned and other incomes. There is something of a logical gap in the sense that until a loan is repaid the value cannot be allocated and spent, but the principle still makes sense, and we shall come across this argument again.

Douglas offered a detailed description of a social credit scheme for Scotland, perhaps presciently including a 'Scottish Treasury empowered by the Scottish people' and a 'Scottish Government' (Douglas, 1933: 206–7). The proposal was for a national dividend of an amount equal to 1 per cent of the total capital value of assets in Scotland, 'the dividend to be paid monthly by a draft on the Scottish Government credit, through the Post Office and not through the banks' (Douglas, 1933: 207). No national dividend would have been received by someone whose 'net income ... is more than four times that receivable in respect of the national dividend' (Douglas, 1933: 207–8), and anyone who turned down the offer of appropriate employment would have suffered 'suspension of benefit in respect of the national dividend' (Douglas, 1933: 211). This means that the dividend would not have been a Basic Income, but it would have been an interesting experiment if Scotland had been independent and had decided to implement the plan.

The social credit idea faded in the UK during the 1930s, partly due no doubt to the diversity of the descriptions and explanations of social credit that we find in Douglas's writings, and the frequently confused nature of the text. A precise engineer he might have been, but a precise author he was not: and Van Trier's research suggests that it was the edited (or rather, rewritten) versions of Douglas's ideas that Alfred Orage published in his journal *The New Age* that ensured that Douglas's ideas received an audience (Van Trier, 2005). Interest took a long time to decline. There was sufficient interest in social credit for a third edition of Douglas's 1931 *The Monopoly of Credit* to be published in 1951, and there were still enthusiasts attending Basic Income Research Group seminars during the mid-1980s. In Canada, where farmers were experiencing poverty because grain prices had fallen during the 1929 recession, a Social Credit Party was formed, won power in Alberta in 1935, and then failed to implement a provincial dividend (Duverger, 2018: 54; Sloman, 2019: 71; Van Parijs and Vanderborght, 2017: 80). Interest in the idea that governments should provide incomes to fill the gap between purchasing power and the value of production can still be found today (Crocker, 2015; 2019; 2020).

Charles Marshall Hattersley

The same year that the Labour Party's National Executive Committee rejected the idea of a State Bonus, C. Marshall Hattersley published *The Community's Credit*, which based its argument for a 'National Dividend' on another argument frequently rehearsed today (Bregman, 2017; Daugareilh et al., 2019: 29; Hughes, 2018: 41; OECD, 2019: 117): that increasing automation means that wage income can no longer be the only source of the income that people need to enable them to consume essential goods and services.

> The object of the application of Science to Industry is the production and distribution of goods and services for the use and enjoyment of mankind with the minimum expenditure of human energy; and as the years pass, and scientific invention and discovery succeed still further in replacing human energy by the power of machines, increasing unemployment will render an already inadequate system more and more so. So much the more necessary does it therefore become with every advance made in this direction to devise some means of distributing purchasing-power to those for whom Industry has no longer any need. (Hattersley, 1922: 102)

Everyone needs greater purchasing power because 'every year the power to supply man's needs and material desires is increasing with bewildering rapidity' (Hattersley, 1931: 3). Not only is Hattersley's automation argument for a National Dividend one that we hear today, but the main objection that he tackles, that the National Dividend would be 'something for nothing', is also one that we still hear (Piachaud, 2016: 4–10). Hattersley made the point that if only people who were not employed were to receive benefits from the State, then they would always have an incentive to remain unemployed (Hattersley, 1922: 144). Further arguments followed: all of us have very similar subsistence needs (Hattersley published minimum needs scales in his *Wealth, Want and War* (1937: 29, 33–4)); there is no reason why employment income should be 'practically the sole mechanism for providing people with the power to claim the goods and services they need'; the fact that this is so is 'an instrument of Government, deliberately limiting the leisure and energy available for creative efforts of mind or muscle outside the regimented and disciplined activity of industrial production' (Hattersley, 1937: 187) (an interesting argument that might be made more often); and 'economically, leisure only presents a problem when unaccompanied by the means of livelihood' (Hattersley, 1937: 190). Putting these arguments together: 'a person's power to claim goods and services must in future be less and less dependent on his or her direct contribution to production' (Hattersley, 1937: 195). Further advantages of 'dividends for all' (Hattersley, 1937: 211) would be that women would become financially independent; the poor would have secure incomes; begging would not be necessary (Hattersley, 1931: 35); and everyone would be better able to resist 'tyranny' (Hattersley, 1922: 108).

As for where the money might come from, Hattersley follows Major Douglas in suggesting that the National Dividends should be paid for by 'Industry', and not by '*adding to the load borne by the taxpayer*' (Hattersley, 1922: 109: italics in the original). This is somewhat disingenuous, as raising costs to industry causes the prices of its products to rise: but the logic is correct, because 'Industry' benefits financially from increasing automation, and as it is increasing automation that is the cause of the reduction in purchasing power, it is from 'Industry' that the funds to pay for Basic Incomes should come. If this funding method were to be employed, then another advantage of paying a National Dividend would become clear: because at the moment industrial workers do not directly benefit from increasing automation, they have every reason to resist it, but if increased automation were to increase the National Dividend, then workers would benefit, and might not resist to the same extent (Hattersley, 1922: 109–10).

An additional funding method was also proposed by Hattersley and by the Social Credit Movement more generally: 'new money' (Hattersley, 1931: 32–4), paid out until demand met potential industrial supply. We have already encountered this argument when we discussed Major Douglas, and we hear similar 'new money to pay for Basic Incomes' arguments today: that because the proceeds of production are going increasingly to capital, and the wage share of the proceeds of production is falling, the Government should distribute new money as unconditional incomes in order to fill the gap and enable the whole of Gross Domestic Product to be purchased (Crocker, 2015; 2019; 2020). First of all, the claim that the wage share of the proceeds of production is falling is contested (Whittaker, 2019); and secondly, whilst it is true that Quantitative Easing since the financial crisis (that is, central banks creating new money to buy government bonds) appears not to have increased inflation, what is not clear is whether new money constantly paid as unconditional incomes would not do so, particularly if a proportion of that money were to be spent on imports rather than on domestic production. It is probably true, though, as Hattersley claimed, that a National Dividend would enable 'Science' to be 'no longer hampered in its work of lessening human toil by fear of creating want and despair' (Hattersley, 1931: 35): but care would have to be taken if money creation were to be used to fund the National Dividend. Taxation of industry would be the safer of Hattersley's two funding methods.

SOCIALIST INTEREST

G.D.H. Cole

The Labour Party's rejection of the State Bonus idea in 1920 was not the end of socialist interest. In 1929, George (G.D.H.) Cole, a socialist academic, discussed the way in which 'distribution according to need' (by which he meant that every individual had equal basic needs that could be met by equal and unconditional incomes) was beginning to replace 'payment for economic value received' (Cole, 1929: 198). He cited the examples of publicly funded education and the contemporary debate over family allowances. But when he discussed the proposal for a State Bonus, he could not believe that the idea would be acceptable to the general public. He suggested that an 'ordinary worker in industry' would

> agree to a minimum distribution according to need as a basis for the protection of childhood and for other special purposes; but he still wants to reward each according to his works – according, that is, to his own revised estimate of what each man is worth. ... He believes in a wage-system shorn of class-exploitation, and not in a society based on communistic principles. (Cole, 1929: 200)

Cole therefore proposed that family allowances and free education should be encouraged, because

> though these things can be regarded as steps towards complete economic equal-
> ity, they can be regarded no less reasonably as steps towards an accommodation

between the rival principles of remuneration for work and income as a social right based on need. The practical political maxim for the present is not full economic equality, but the recognition of an all-round minimum of human needs below which no human being must on any account be allowed to fall. (Cole, 1929: 200)

This is an important early example of a discussion of what today we might call the question of 'psychological feasibility' (Torry, 2016a: 87–117). However much Cole might have understood and valued the idea of an unconditional income for every individual, he simply could not believe that it would be acceptable without an accompanying requirement to accept paid employment (Sloman, 2019: 73). Hattersley had already offered what amounted to a response, which, although logical, would have satisfied neither Cole's 'ordinary worker' nor Cole himself at that stage:

> Production by Industry to-day is the result of the combined effort of three distinct factors. ... Capital, ... Labour, ... the Common Cultural Inheritance of the Community. [This] comprises ordered government, industrial, social and political organization, education, religion, and the hundred and one amenities of civilization. ... The heirs to this splendid heritage are the members of the Community. ... The members of the Community ... , as well as Capital and Labour, are justly entitled to a share in the produce of Industry. ... And so we look forward to the time when every member of the Community as an individual shall, apart from and in addition to his or her remuneration as a producer, receive, as a matter of course and of right, his or her Communal Dividend – his or her proper share in the increase in the Real Credit of the Community as a whole. *National Dividends as such should be distributed irrespective of whether the recipient is employed or not, or of his or her financial status.* (Hattersley, 1922: 104–6, italics in the original; cf. 1931: 36)

If we put the Milners', Pickard's and Hattersley's proposals and arguments together, then we discover that by the 1920s many of the details of some useful and potentially feasible Basic Income schemes had already been described; that many of the arguments for establishing a Basic Income had already been explained; that many of the objections that we still hear today had already received an answer; and that questions about psychological feasibility were already being asked. A further connection between the first half of the twentieth century and the second decade of the twenty-first is that just as academics today change their minds about Basic Income (Lister, 2017), so academics then could do so. Influenced by his reading of the Milners' State Bonus Scheme, this is G.D.H. Cole writing in 1935, and therefore in the context of the recession of the early 1930s, the austerity measures that the UK Government had implemented, and particularly the onerous and degrading means test (Duverger, 2018: 58, 62–3):

> Incomes will be distributed partly as rewards for work, and partly as direct payments from the State to every citizen as 'social dividends'—a recognition of each citizen's

claim as a consumer to share in the common heritage of productive power. ... The aim should be, as speedily as possible, to make the dividend large enough to cover the whole of the minimum needs of every citizen. Being paid as a civic right, it will be of equal amount for all, or rather for all adults, with appropriate allowances for children. ... Work will have its sufficient reward; but the main part of the national income will no longer be distributed as a by-product of industry. (Cole, 1935: 235)

The reason that Cole decided that he wanted to see adults receiving unconditional and equal incomes was that it would make it easier to predict demand for goods and services. The reason that Ruth Lister is now more favourable towards the idea of a Basic Income than she once was is that a Basic Income would be a 'means of ensuring everyone a modicum of basic security in an increasingly insecure world' (Lister, 2017). The world changes, and people change their minds.

There would appear to be little that is new in today's Basic Income debate.

CONCLUSION

During the early twentieth century all of the initiatives that we can properly identify as elements of the history of Basic Income occurred in the UK. There was of course discussion of minimum income schemes of various kinds in France and elsewhere (Duverger, 2018: 68–71; Van Parijs and Vanderborght, 2017: 82), but discussion of an unconditional income for every individual was a UK prerogative. As we shall see in the next chapter, this characteristic of the Basic Income debate will still be evident beyond the middle of the century.

5. Basic Income during the mid-twentieth century in the United Kingdom

INTRODUCTION

This chapter continues the UK-focused theme of the previous one: not only because more happened in the UK in relation to the debate on unconditional incomes than in most other countries, but also because some of the things that did happen find echoes in later activity elsewhere.

ELEANOR RATHBONE AND FAMILY ALLOWANCE

Following the First World War, during which soldiers' families had received an addition to their income for each child, Eleanor Rathbone established both the Family Endowment Society and the Children's Minimum Council, and published a pamphlet that argued that because a worker's wage would never be sufficient to support a large family, the State should contribute towards the costs of bringing up children (Macnicol, 1980: 5–10, 20–23; Thane, 1996: 63–4, 202). Then, in 1924, she wrote *The Disinherited Family* (Rathbone, [1924] 1986: 139, 167, 353), an argument for unconditional incomes to contribute towards the costs of bringing up children. William Beveridge experienced 'instant and total conversion' (Beveridge, 1949: 270) and in 1925 suggested that mine owners should pay child allowances as a way of keeping costs down at the same time as paying a wage that would provide subsistence incomes for families of all sizes. The General Strike prevented that from happening, but Beveridge was able to try the idea at the London School of Economics, where he was the Director, and when he was asked to chair a committee set up to reform social insurance, he wrote unconditional child allowances into the preface as one of the report's presuppositions. An important reason for paying child allowances to all families was that child allowances were already being paid with Unemployment Benefit, which meant that when unemployed men with large families found employment, they could find that the wage was less than the Unemployment Benefit; and a further argument for the unconditionality of the payments was that 'little money can be saved by any reasonable income test' (Beveridge, 1942: 154, 157, 163, 177). For some, including Beveridge, increased employment market incentive was an important argument; for others, including John Maynard Keynes, child allowances meant that wage inflation would not be driven by men having to pay the whole cost of bringing up large families; for others, the equality represented by the unconditional nature of the allowances was what mattered; yet others hoped that the plan would reduce pressure for a national minimum wage; and trades unions had more women members than before, and they wanted child allowances. A short paperback summary of the arguments for child allowances published in 1940 contributed to public understanding (Rathbone, 1940); and when Beveridge's report came to be debated in Parliament, Members of Parliament were aware of public understanding and approval. Because members on both sides of the House of Commons had their own reasons for wanting to see happen what were by then being called Family Allowances, and because they knew that their reasons might not be shared by others, the debate was subdued. The Family Allowance Act was passed in 1945, and the first Family Allowances were paid in 1946 (Harris, 1977: 449; 1981: 249; Land, 1975: 169, 173–9, 195–6, 205, 221; Macnicol, 1980: 93, 172, 176, 191–3, 202; Thane, 1996: 63–4, 226).

Beveridge did not get it all his own way. He wanted the allowances to be paid for every child, and he wanted them called 'Child Allowance'; but the Treasury excluded the first child in each family, and insisted on 'Family Allowance'. If the same amount had been paid for every child, then the Family Allowance would have been a true Basic Income according to the definition. As it was, it was close; and during the late 1970s it got closer still when regressive Child Tax Allowances were abolished and Family Allowance became Child Benefit for every child as a response to significant poverty among families with children. Child Benefit survives as an unconditional income for children. It is unfortunate that high earners in households receiving Child Benefit now have to pay additional Income Tax, and that women have been withdrawing their Child Benefit claims in order to avoid the tax being paid: but still, Child Benefit itself remains an unconditional income for children (Spicker, 2011: 120; Torry, 2013: 22–7).

JULIET RHYS WILLIAMS

As well as Family Allowances, the preface of Beveridge's 1942 report, *Social Insurance and Allied Services*, proposed a National Health Service, and the body of the report contained a great deal of detail on proposals for National Insurance (State Pensions, work-tested Unemployment Benefit, and Sickness Benefit, paid on the basis of contribution records) and for means-tested, work-tested and household-tested National Assistance benefits for any family with an income that did not reach a stated minimum (Beveridge, 1942). The report was a success: the public liked it, and most of it was legislated, at least in principle, after the end of the Second World War.

However, not everyone agreed with the report. Lady Juliet Rhys Williams, Secretary of the Women's Liberal Federation (Harris, 1981: 258), issued a minority report, which was then published as *Something to Look Forward To* (Rhys Williams, 1943). She had experienced the way in which the withdrawal of means-tested unemployment assistance as earned income increased was preventing workers in South Wales from accepting temporary or part-time employment (Sloman, 2019: 77), so she objected to the time-limited nature of Beveridge's proposed National Insurance benefits because it would mean too many families finding themselves on disincentivizing means-tested National Assistance benefits. Coercion would therefore be required in the employment market, which to a Liberal was simply not acceptable.

> Once the power of the State is made use of as a means of making a man work against his will, there is no certainty that ... ancient methods of coercion will not sooner or later be resorted to ... The hope of gain is infinitely preferable to the fear of punishment and the fear of want as a motive for human labour ... *The real objection to the Beveridge scheme does not lie in its shortcomings in respect of the abolition of want, which could be made good, but in its serious attack upon the will to work.* ... the rewards of idleness will approximate very nearly to the wages of the regular worker, particularly after the various contributions, taxes, subscriptions and other impositions required from him, but not required from the unemployed man, have been deducted from his pay. (Rhys Williams, 1943: 13, 45, 141, 142: italics in the original)

Under Beveridge's plan, a man, wife and child could earn £3 per week and be better off by only five shillings (25p, which would have equated to £11.87 per week in 2019). Under Rhys Williams' proposal for flat-rate and nonwith-drawable payments for every individual, conditional only on working-age men and single women either being in employment or seeking employment, a man, wife and child would have been better off by £1/16/– (one pound and sixteen shillings: £1.80, which equates to £85.45 per week in 2019) (Booker, 1946: 232; Meade, 1948: 44–5; Morley, 2020; Sloman, 2019: 78). A further problem with Beveridge's scheme was that whereas Family Allowances would not be paid for the first child in the family, child allowances were to be added to Unemployed Benefit, again benefiting the unemployed individual and not the employed. Rhys Williams' point was that every worker should receive '*the whole benefit of wages (less taxation)*' (Rhys Williams, 1943: 147: italics in the original), which was clearly what was not going to happen.

But as well as this practical concern, there was also a principle involved that we have already found expressed in Chapter 3 by the American Orestes Brownson in 1840:

> *The State owes precisely the same benefits to all of its citizens, and should in no circumstances pay more to one than to another of the same sex and age, except in return for services rendered* ... the State owes precisely the same advantages to every citizen, *and should consequently pay the same benefits to the employed and healthy as to the idle and sick. ... The prevention of want must be regarded as being the duty of the State to all its citizens, and not merely to a favoured few.* (Rhys Williams, 1943: 139, 144, 145: italics in the original)

Rhys Williams' plan would have granted to every individual an income that would not have been means-tested, but it was not entirely unconditional because it would have required workers (apart from married women) to sign a 'social contract' that committed them either to be employed or to attend the Labour Exchange and accept any employment offered. The condition meant that the proposal was not for a Basic Income, but was instead close to Tony Atkinson's proposal for a Participation Income (see Chapter 7). Rhys Williams clearly hoped that because the non-means-tested income would not be withdrawn as earned incomes rose, there would be very few workers who would not willingly add employment income to the universal but work-tested 'Social Contract allowances' (Rhys Williams, 1943: 145, 146).

To cope with different housing costs in different areas, Rhys Williams suggested that the income should be paid at different levels in different regions; and although every woman would have received an income in her own right, it would have been 19 shillings per week (95p, which would have been £45.10 in 2019) rather than the 21 shillings (£1.05, which would have been £49.84 in 2019) that would have been paid to men (Morley, 2020; Rhys Williams, 1943: 145, 163–4). We therefore have three reasons for not calling Rhys Williams' suggestion a Basic Income: it was work-tested; women and men would have received different amounts; and the payment would have varied by region: although arguably if this third consideration had been the only one then we might have been able to say that within each region a Basic Income would have been paid.

But whether strictly a Basic Income or not, as Rhys Williams wrote ten years later, her scheme would have resulted in greater administrative simplicity than Beveridge's, along with the abolition of poverty, increased employment incentives, more stable prices, the abolition of means-testing, full employment, the encouragement of part-time and occasional employment if no full-time employment was available, increased social cohesion and an enhanced status for women (Rhys Williams, 1953: 138).

> The Social Contract proposals represent a genuine means of escape from the economic dilemma which bids us choose between a continuance of want, on the one hand, and the destruction of the desire for gain as the motive for labour on the other, with its implied reversion to compulsion as the only means available to provide the labour required to sustain our civilization. (Rhys Williams, 1943: 148)

By the time Rhys Williams published *Something to Look Forward To* in 1943, the Beveridge Report (1942) had experienced substantial public, trade union, political and parliamentary approval, and although the male-breadwinner assumption that had informed Beveridge's report had its critics, the criticism was motivating attempts to influence the way in which the Beveridge proposals were implemented rather than inspiring a campaign for Rhys Williams' proposals. Those proposals were treated sympathetically by a number of economists, in Liberal circles during the mid-1940s, and in some Conservative circles later in the decade: but the high rates of taxation that would have been required to fund the allowances were clearly a problem, and although unemployed individuals would have experienced lower marginal deduction rates with Rhys Williams' scheme than with Beveridge's National Assistance, and therefore a higher employment incentive, individuals who would have been earning less than the Income Tax Personal Allowance might have found themselves paying Income Tax and therefore suffering higher Marginal Deduction Rates and a lower employment incentive.

Rhys Williams' final opportunity to showcase the benefits of her scheme came in the form of a Royal Commission on Taxation of Profits and Income during the first half of the 1950s. The Commission rejected radical reform, and for fifteen years there was little discussion of reform of the structure of the benefits system (Duverger, 2018: 76–7; Sloman, 2019: 79–82, 86–7; 2020). Whilst Rhys Williams' proposals had struck a chord with a number of policymakers, Henderson and Quiggin's verdict is that the failure to see her ideas implemented

> highlights the limitations of being an individual policy entrepreneur, the strong support within the bureaucracy and the political class for Beveridge's model of social insurance and targeted welfare, and Rhys Williams' personal hostility towards socialism, which prevented even the possibility of an alliance with the labour movement. (Henderson and Quiggin, 2019: 495)

Juliet Rhys Williams' scheme clearly has an importance of its own within the history of Basic Income, because although her own plan was not for a Basic Income scheme, it was not far off, and it showed that Beveridge could have proposed a Basic Income scheme if he had extended to working-age adults the unconditional principle that he was happy to apply to child allowances and to the National Health Service, which he also wrote into the preface of his report as a prerequisite for his proposals. Like the Milners' scheme, Rhys Williams' proposal was framed as an adjustment of the tax and benefits system, rather than as an expression of social justice. She thus contributed to the UK's Basic Income debate being firmly located in a growing and distinctively British social administration tradition (Sloman, 2019: 92–3). But Rhys Williams is significant to this history in another way as well. She was the mother of Brandon Rhys Williams, the Conservative Member of Parliament who in 1982 proposed a genuine Basic Income scheme to a parliamentary committee: a scheme that in many respects mirrored his mother's, as it would have been funded by general taxation, and aimed to replace the majority of other social security provision (Sloman, 2019: 65).

JAMES MEADE

James Meade was one of the circle of young economists surrounding John Maynard Keynes during the 1930s. In 1937, he became editor of the World Economic Survey of the League of Nations; during the Second World War he joined the Economic Section of the Cabinet Office and became its Director at the age of thirty-nine; he was responsible for the 1944 White Paper on Employment Policy; and in 1947 he returned to academic life, first at the London School of Economics, and then as Professor of Political Economy at the University of Cambridge from 1957 to 1967. In retirement, he chaired the Meade Committee on the structure of direct taxation, and he continued to write about economics into his ninth decade, which is why this section seriously transgresses the stated chronological boundary of this chapter.

For sixty years, from the early 1930s to his death in 1995, James Meade studied production, distribution, money, taxation, the welfare state and the economy's international dimensions; his interests spanned economics, history, social policy and politics; and although his thought developed in line with a changing political consensus, he consistently pursued themes established early on in his career: the need to stimulate demand in the economy in order to reduce unemployment; administrative and economic efficiency; the market as the efficient way to produce and distribute goods and services (Sloman, 2019: 48); the reduction of economic inequality; and (particularly latterly) the importance of individual freedom. Whether our interest is the development of his thought or the substantial consistencies across sixty years, we shall find the 'social dividend' idea occurring over and over again, and in relation to every one of Meade's major interests.

In 1935, Meade wrote a paper for the Labour Party, *Outline of Economic Policy for a Labour Government*, in which he recommended an 'increase [in] the equality of distribution of the national income' (Meade, [1935] 2016: 33), in particular 'by paying a smaller or larger part of [the profits of State-owned industry] as a social dividend to the members of the community'. This would enable the Government to

> control the amount of the national income spent on consumption and the amount allocated to capital development. When even at very low interest rates very little development is profitable, a large proportion can be paid out as a social dividend; whereas if new and profitable fields of development appear a much larger part can be apportioned to the capital budget for this capital development. (Meade, [1935] 2016: 53)

This was a true 'social dividend', in the sense that it was a proportion of the profits made by industry. Although he was influenced by Major Douglas's Social Credit ideas, as well as by G.D.H. Cole and Abba Lerner, Meade did not accept the detail of Douglas's argument, as he initially thought the equation $MV = PT$ (M is the money supply, V the velocity of circulation, P the price level, and T the volume of transactions, or the national output) to be a better guide to the workings of the economy than Douglas's $A + B$ = the total price of goods and services (where A is labour incomes, and B is the non-labour costs of production) (Duverger, 2018: 63). Meade did not believe that a social dividend could be funded by a government creating new money, but instead argued for its funding from within the existing economy. He would have preferred the social dividend to be funded by the profits of nationalized industries, but he also recognized that funding it by increasing Income Tax or by taxing inheritances might also be possibilities (Duverger, 2018: 65; Meade, [1936] 1938: 212, 267, 246).

One of Meade's abiding concerns was economic efficiency, and the economic efficiency of an equal social dividend for every citizen made the concept particularly attractive. In 1944, Abba Lerner published a book that he had been writing since 1932, *The Economics of Control*, in which he justified the payment of a Social Dividend first of all on the basis that it would fill the gap between the total of incomes and the total of prices due to the non-labour costs of production, and also because it would increase total utility (Duverger, 2018: 61; Lerner, 1944). Meade reviewed the book:

> Mr. Lerner argues ... that the total satisfaction achieved from any given income will be maximised if that income is so divided among individuals that its marginal utility is the same for everyone; but he adds an interesting and elegant proof of the proposition that (on the assumption that the marginal utility of income declines in the case of each individual) the maximisation of probable total satisfaction is attained by an

equal division of income, even though we cannot directly compare the satisfactions of different individuals. (Meade, 1945: 48)

But however important such efficiency might have been, the maintenance of demand in the cause of reducing unemployment was for Meade a social dividend's major attraction (Meade, 1945: 48; Sloman, 2019: 74).

By 1948, we find Meade's concerns for a free society, a free market, administrative efficiency, the maintenance of demand, the reduction of unemployment, and a more equal division of income and property, all in a single book, *Planning and the Price Mechanism*, the thesis of which is

> that a large measure of state foresight and intervention is required to guide the economy from war to peace, to prevent inflationary and deflationary pressures, to ensure a tolerably equitable distribution of income and property, and to prevent or to control the anti-social rigging of the market by private interests, but that these objectives can be achieved in an efficient and a free society only if an extensive use is made of the mechanisms of competition, free enterprise and free market determination of prices and output. (Meade, 1948: v–vi)

It is surely no accident that, in the context of this combination of all of Meade's interests, we find a sustained discussion of a social dividend: in this case in the form of Rhys Williams' scheme (Rhys Williams, 1943). Meade wrote of it:

> It is suggested that a straightforward monetary payment or allowance or 'social dividend' should be paid to every man, woman and child in the country—although the rate of payment might, of course, be lower for children than for adults. This would take the place of all social security benefits, such as unemployment benefit, old-age pensions, health benefits, children's allowances. Every man, woman and child would thus have his or her basic minimum whether in sickness or in health, in work or out of work, young or old. There need be no means test and no tests whether a man was seeking work or whether a man was genuinely ill. Doctors could stop writing out health certificates and get on with their job of curing their patients. Employment exchanges would stop fussing about unemployment insurance and get on with their job of introducing employers with vacancies to workers without jobs. The Ministry of National Insurance could be closed down.
>
> These universal personal allowances would also take the place of the whole apparatus of allowances under the income tax. All income (other than the 'personal allowances' [the social dividends] which would be tax-free) would be taxed at a standard rate of tax. The whole apparatus of Pay-as-You-Earn would disappear; and the only task of the Inland Revenue in this field would be to ensure that all income was taxed at the standard rate of tax. All personal assessments would cease for income tax purposes. (Meade, 1948: 43)

Meade appears not to have noticed that Rhys Williams' scheme envisaged differing rates for women and men, a work test, and different levels of payment for different regions of the country. What he saw in the scheme was administrative simplicity, greater personal freedom, and more equal incomes, and that it would 'afford a perfect instrument for the most effective and prompt control over total national expenditure in the interests of avoiding inflation and deflation' (Meade, 1948: 44).

Meade was, of course, aware of a social dividend's problems, and in particular that an unconditional payment might reduce the incentive to work (Meade, 1948: 45): but in spite of the possible difficulties, Meade's conclusion was that a Rhys Williams social dividend scheme

> has the greatest attraction from the point of view of social security, equity, personal freedom, administrative simplicity and the provision of a means of exercising a prompt and effective control over purchasing power as a measure against inflation and deflation ... Could the scheme with modifications be made workable? Certainly it deserves the most careful and serious examination. (Meade, 1948: 46)

Meade's later works offer little new on the social dividend except by way of emphasis (Meade, 1964). *The Controlled Economy*, published in 1971, returned to a social dividend's demand-generating function, and added that 'there would be no insuperable administrative difficulty in reducing the payments in times of unexpected inflationary pressures and increasing them in times of unexpected deflationary pressures' (Meade, 1971: 239). In 1975, Meade returned to the problem of funding a social dividend. Without telling us where the figure came from, he suggested that a 50 per cent income tax rate would be needed for a social dividend at Supplementary Benefit (now Universal Credit) levels, and, believing that this would be a disincentive if imposed across a broad wages spectrum, suggested a 75 per cent rate on the first slice of earned income, which would have allowed a rate below 50 per cent on the rest (Meade, 1975: 91). Again, the administrative simplicity of a social dividend is stressed (and particularly the simplifying effect of an individual-based rather than a household-based system); and again we find a social dividend proposed because it would enable market-mechanisms to work more freely (Meade, 1975: 101).

Meade was more aware of administrative realities than were some other economists, and it was the administrative complexity of a Negative Income Tax that led him to reject it, even though it would have had many of the same effects on the poverty and unemployment traps as a social dividend (Meade, 1972; Parker, 1989: 149). A social dividend would not need to adjust to changes in someone's other income or in their labour market status, whereas a Negative Income Tax would.

Meade's somewhat Keynesian programme had some influence on post-war economic policy in the UK: but he rightly recognized that by the late 1970s a great deal had changed. No longer did investment mean more jobs (indeed, it could mean fewer jobs); no longer could Government fix prices and wages (except in utilities over which they had some control); and no longer would increasing spending power automatically translate into demand for goods or services produced in a particular country. Meade recognized that now 'much more attention must be paid to measures other than price and wage setting in order to achieve a fair and acceptable distribution of income and property' (Meade, 1984: 130). Again, a social dividend was his instrument of choice.

Meade's *Agathotopia*, published in 1989, is, according to Walter Van Trier, an 'intellectual testimony' which

> presents the results of a long intellectual career dedicated to the search for an institutional framework congenial to his view of a good economic life—a view resting on a deeply rooted life-long moral conviction based on the equal importance of liberty, equality and efficiency. (Van Trier, 1995: 346)

In *Agathotopia*, Meade foresees a time when each of us will receive income from a variety of sources: labour shares (issued to workers, and producing dividends reflecting the firm's profits); capital shares; wages; and a social dividend—the social dividend being particularly important as a stable element making it less of a problem when the other income elements fluctuate (Meade, 1989: 27, 30; cf. Van Trier, 1995: 365). The aim of the social dividend is 'the promotion of equality, the alleviation of risk-bearing, the improvement of incentives for low earners, and the simplification of the welfare state' (Meade, 1989: 34). Meade offers a detailed description of how a transition to a social dividend might be possible (Meade, 1989: 36), and again suggests a 'surcharge' on the first slice of earned income in order to make the scheme affordable (Meade, 1989: 38). His conclusion is that

> the higher the social dividend and the higher the general rate of tax imposed to finance it, the greater will be the beneficial effects on the equalisation of adjusted incomes and on the mitigation of risk-bearing. But both the rise in the social dividend (which enables people to enjoy a given income without earning so much) and the higher marginal rate of tax (which reduces the net return on any additional earnings) will tend to reduce economic incentives for work and enterprise. In the choice of policies these results must be weighed against each other. (Meade, 1989: 67)

But however much Meade grapples with the problems posed by the attempt to fund a social dividend out of tax revenue, he has not given up hope of a social dividend being what it says it is: a distribution of profits produced by national assets (which he hopes might one day replace the national debt), assets made up of shares owned by the State, and possibly whole companies owned by the State but not managed by it.

> If the merits of a competitive system are to be preserved, and at the same time excessive inequalities are to be avoided, we need to consider radical ways in which part of the high returns on capital can be used to supplement the earned incomes of the representative worker ... A familiar suggestion is to institute a progressive structure of taxation which falls on the rich, the revenue from which can be used to finance adequate social benefits for the relief of poverty and for the raising of standards at the lower end of the income scale. This raises a serious danger of introducing disincentives into the productive system. If the social benefits are confined strictly to the support of those in poverty, the system will inevitably lead to serious disincentives in the form of the well-known poverty trap, since any additional earnings will be offset by withdrawal of social benefits as the recipients work themselves out of poverty.
>
> On the other hand, if the benefits are not confined to citizens who are in need, but are paid on an adequate scale in the form of a Basic Income or Social Dividend to every citizen, the marginal rates of tax on private incomes needed for their finance would become intolerably high—perhaps implying a rise from 25% to 80% in the basic rate of income tax. The disincentive effects at the upper end of the scale become intolerable.
>
> There is one possible radical change in our present economic system which would resolve this dilemma: a structural reform which we should, in my opinion, be considering very seriously.
>
> Imagine the following happy state of affairs. The state, instead of being burdened with a large national debt, has not only repaid the whole of that debt but has in addition accumulated an amount of public savings which enables it to own a substantial National Asset ... This would provide a very solid base for the introduction of a true Social Dividend. [This scenario] presents a vision of a future society in which private competitive enterprise is the ruling mode of production, but in which the state receives a substantial share of the yield on the nation's real capital resources, thus enabling it to fulfil its proper social role without the immoderately high rates of taxation which would destroy private enterprise and initiatives. (Meade, 1990)

As we shall discover in Chapter 7, Meade was over-pessimistic about the increase in the rate of Income Tax that would be required to fund a useful Basic Income. He was perhaps over-optimistic about the possibility of paying off the national debt and amassing a social wealth fund.

There is nothing new on the social dividend in Meade's final publication, *Full Employment Regained?*. However, the final paragraph makes an important point:

> A main objective of a Citizen's Income is to provide a reliable income from some source other than earned income (thus making the rate of pay less important relative to other sources of income) and to do so in a way which makes the personal distribution of the total national income more egalitarian. (Meade, 1995: 57)

This publication comes full circle, listing the social dividend as one of twenty-one control variables by which the economy might be managed (Meade, 1995: 85). All the old themes return: full employment; demand management; greater income equality; and a social dividend (now called a Citizen's Income). But there are also some new emphases. Since his earliest publications, Meade was interested in 'external relations': the effects of one nation's economy on another's. In his 1991 book *The Building of a New Europe* he looked particularly at the new European context of our national economy, and solved the problems that would be posed by a Basic Income in only one European country by proposing a Europe-wide Basic Income.

[T]he central Community authority should allow free national experimentation in these policies but should itself introduce and administer a positive form of egalitarian intervention of its own. For example, it might itself raise a general community levy or tax of some form and use the proceeds to pay a modest Basic Income to all the citizens of the member countries. The national governments could be left to top this up with their different national schemes. Movements of people and capital would ... put a brake on the most extreme egalitarian experiments; but the existence of the modest Community scheme would mean that the outcome of the competition between the national experiments would be less markedly inegalitarian than would otherwise have been the case. This solution would permit more national experimentation and would involve a less complicated central bureaucratic apparatus than ... solution through centrally administered full national harmonisation. (Meade, 1991: 24–9)

So in this instance, too, there is continuity and development, the development being a response to changing times, the continuity being a reflection of Meade's continuing pursuit of both the free market and a more equal society in an international context.

Meade was a child of his time, and for most of his career he believed that the abolition of unemployment was the route to the abolition of both idleness and poverty, of both Idleness and Want (Beveridge, 1942: 6): but by 1981 he had recognized that the technological revolution had created a new situation in which either wages and unemployment would rise together, or wages would decline and inequality grow (Meade, 1984)—both of which have happened in different sectors of the economy; so the unconditional incomes that he had proposed early in his career appeared increasingly relevant as time went on (Torry, 2005).

James Meade's work foreshadowed a variety of aspects of today's Basic Income debate: the concept of a social dividend; the idea of a social wealth fund, the dividends of which might constitute a Basic Income (Lansley et al., 2018); and the proposal for a Eurodividend (McKnight et al., 2016: 67–8, 80; Van Parijs and Vanderborght, 2017: 230–41). Where did he get these ideas? Van Trier finds that even though Meade knew Bertram Pickard, that is not where the idea for a social dividend came from. Instead, it was G.D.H. Cole's discussion of a 'social dividend' that might have been the source of Meade's enthusiasm for the idea, and it was Juliet Rhys Williams' proposal in *Something To Look Forward To* that gave the idea the institutional framework required (Van Trier, 2002; 2018b: 464–5).

GOVERNMENT PROVISION OF INCOME

While the provision of public services, represented by the National Health Service, free secondary as well as primary education, and large local authority housing projects, were important elements of the UK's welfare state after the Second World War, during the first half of the twentieth century poverty came to be understood largely in terms of a lack of income, and this somewhat one-dimensional conceptualization persisted after the war. Sloman suggests that the understanding of poverty as insufficient income was to a large extent a result of a research tradition that had the calculation of subsistence incomes, and surveys of the extent to which households' incomes fell below those levels, at its heart: perhaps simply because such aspects of poverty can be measured, whereas others—such as the squalor of housing—cannot; and yet others—such as health—can only be measured with difficulty (Sloman, 2019: 37–42). It might be argued that the centrality of social security benefits to the Government's response to inadequate incomes lasted until the first National Minimum Wage was legislated at the very end of the twentieth century: a provision that both managements and trades unions had initially resisted, the former because they believed that a National Minimum Wage might compromise their ability to negotiate over their members' wage levels, and the latter because they were concerned about increasing costs; and which they both eventually recommended, trades unions because it would protect low paid workers, and businesses because it would set a floor to the market and reduce unfair competition from low-paying firms (Torry, 2016a: 209–12). But that was by no means the end of the centrality of social security benefits to government income maintenance policy. Means-tested in-work benefits were at the heart of the 1997 Labour Government's attempt to abolish child poverty, and Housing Benefit rather than the required increase in residential property remained the strategy for ensuring that housing remained something like affordable.

For the entire twentieth century, government attempts to ensure that everyone had enough money was at the heart of its social policy: but as Juliet Rhys Williams rightly understood, if this was to be achieved by increasing the coverage of means-tested benefits, then first of all an injustice would be done—for why *should* a government give more to some members of the population than to others?—and secondly, poverty and unemployment traps would be the inevitable outcome of benefits being withdrawn as earned incomes increased. In the context of the continuing centrality of means-tested benefits, the National Minimum Wage implemented in 1999 could never have been the solution to poverty that it was meant to be, simply because it will always be of less value to anyone on in-work means-tested benefits than to someone not on them because the benefit recipient's net income will always rise by less than the net income of someone not on benefits whose pay has risen by the same amount. The answer had to be the Government providing incomes to everyone: an argument that was not going to go away all the time the Government relied on means-testing to provide sufficient incomes for the country's population. Because the UK's Government is still doing that, the argument for Basic Income has not gone away.

CONCLUSION

During this period, all of the initiatives that we can properly identify as elements of the history of Basic Income occurred in the UK. There was of course discussion of minimum income schemes of various kinds in France and elsewhere (Duverger, 2018: 68–71; Van Parijs and Vanderborght, 2017: 82), but little if anything related to Basic Income. As we shall see in subsequent chapters, this would soon change.

James Meade's work has taken us well into the 1980s, and represents an important stage in a fairly continuous if sometimes low profile exploration of unconditional incomes from the First World War to the present day in the UK. One of the quieter periods was the 1960s. Just occasionally we find discussions of genuine Basic Incomes emerging during this period: for instance, in a booklet published in 1963 in which Gilbert Rae describes a genuine Basic Income funded by an additional income tax (Rae, 1963: 11–13):

> The government could make an equal payment to all regularly, weekly if required … The payment would give the right to everyone to choose between leisure and work, for whatever reason concerned them. … The payment could appropriately be called a National Dividend. (Rae, 1963: 11–12)

But such instances are rare. For interesting action during this period on the reform of benefits and tax systems in less conditional directions we have to turn to the United States and Canada, so in the next chapter that is where we shall study the history of Basic Income, and particularly some important experiments during the 1970s in mechanisms with some characteristics similar to those of a Basic Income.

6.   Basic Income and diversity in Canada and the USA

INTRODUCTION

Both Canada and the United States of America fulfil a somewhat different role in the history of Basic Income from the countries that we have discussed so far and that we shall go on to discuss in subsequent chapters. This difference relates both to practical experiments and to terminology. In Canada and the US, 'Basic Income Guarantee' can mean anything from a Minimum Income Guarantee, through a Negative Income Tax, to a Basic Income. There is a history to this terminology. Among early members of what became the USBIG (United States Basic Income Guarantee) Network, founded in 1999, were supporters of both Basic Income and Negative Income Tax, because the Negative Income Tax option for reform had been more discussed in the United States than it had been elsewhere. Because the new organization wanted to be a forum for all of these early supporters, it looked for terminology that would recognize both the similarities and differences between Basic Income and Negative Income Tax. 'Universal Basic Income' was chosen for Basic Income, 'Negative Income Tax' was already well-understood terminology, and 'Basic Income Guarantee' was used to represent the set containing Universal Basic Income, Negative Income Tax and similar reform options. There was a hope that this threefold terminology might catch on elsewhere, but that did not happen. As Karl Widerquist suggests, 'It's unfortunate the movement has not settled on a standard word for UBI, a standard word for NIT, and a standard word for the set. BIG might not be the best word for that set, but sadly we have no standard word at all for that set' (Widerquist, 2021). This author can only agree with that sentiment.

So in relation to this chapter, 'Basic Income Guarantee' can mean any one of a set of reform options from means-tested benefits through Negative Income Tax to Basic Income; 'Negative Income Tax' means a Negative Income Tax; and 'Basic Income' normally means a genuine Basic Income: but it might not. Martin Luther King's advocacy for a Minimum Income Guarantee delivered by an income-tested but not work-tested benefit has correctly been interpreted as advocacy for a 'Basic Income Guarantee' (Lewis, 2020: 120) and not for a Basic Income (Lewis, 2020: 121), but a Minimum Income Guarantee has also been called a 'Basic Income' (Frankel, 2020: 150). This can be somewhat confusing.

In Canada, 'Basic Income' is even more likely to mean an income-tested benefit than it is in the United States. The Ontario experiment discussed later in this chapter was for an income-tested and household-based benefit, but the Ontario Government called it a 'Basic Income' experiment; and on the website of the Basic Income Canada Network (2021) the terms 'Basic Income' and 'Basic Income Guarantee' are used interchangeably, and they always mean a 'Minimum Income Guarantee' except where the income is stated to be unconditional and is called a 'demogrant'. Experiments during the 1970s were with Minimum Income Guarantees rather than with Basic Incomes, and yet in Canada they could be called 'Basic Income' experiments (Frankel, 2020: 150); and even when they are understood not to have been Basic Income experiments, the assumption has often been made that research results relating to Minimum Income Guarantee experiments are directly relevant to the Basic Income debate, which of course they are not. More recent experiments have been about a wide variety of different mechanisms, including sometimes a Basic Income, and the experiments have sometimes been discussed together as if they are about the same thing.

A further problem is the frequent assumption that a Minimum Income Guarantee and a Negative Income Tax are the same thing, whereas they are only the same if the means-tested benefit used to raise household incomes to the Minimum Income Guarantee ceases to be paid at the same point on the earnings range as income tax begins to be extracted, and this is the case for every household; and even then Minimum Income Guarantee and Negative Income Tax should only be regarded as the same if they are administered in the same way, which normally they would not be: a Minimum Income Guarantee would normally be administered by a Government, and a Negative Income Tax through employers.

Given this diversity, and the significant disconnection from mainstream terminology in North America, and in particular in Canada, why are we giving so much space to Canada and the US in this history? The reason is that academics, policymakers and historians have often regarded Minimum Income Guarantee and Negative Income Tax proposals, and practical experiments with Minimum Income Guarantees, as important elements in the Basic Income debate (Van Parijs and Vanderborght, 2017: 82–4; Widerquist, 2019a).

In Chapter 1, we have explained the differences between a number of income maintenance mechanisms, and particularly Minimum Income Guarantee, Negative Income Tax and Basic Income. As we shall see throughout this chapter, those debating how to reform tax and benefits systems in the USA and Canada have frequently regarded a Negative Income Tax (NIT) as an administratively feasible reform option, and have often seen it as equivalent to a Basic Income. This makes it important to describe the similarities and differences between the two at the beginning of this chapter.

A NIT is what it says it is: a negative income tax. Above an earnings threshold, the employee pays tax, which is generally collected by the employer before being transferred to the Government. Below the threshold, an addition to wages is paid, the amount of the addition being proportional to the difference between the threshold and earned income (see Figures 1.3 and 1.4 in Chapter 1). The NIT can be administered by the Government or by the employer. If the Government administers the NIT, then the employer must provide regular and accurate earnings information to the Government, as with the UK's current Universal Credit. If the employer administers the NIT, then if someone moves between employers, their NIT administration has to be transferred between employers. If they have a period of unemployment, then administration of the NIT has to be handed to the Government and then on to the new employer. If someone has two employments, then the two employers have to decide between them which one will administer the NIT; and if someone has occasional other earnings, then their employer has to be informed so that the NIT can be withdrawn accordingly.

If every working-age adult were to experience the same NIT rate and earnings threshold then neither their employer nor the Government would need to know any personal details. However, if people in different circumstances were to receive different levels of NIT (for instance, in relation to marital status, wealth or any other conditionality), then their employer and the Government would need to know individuals' circumstances in order to allocate the correct amount of NIT.

Many income tax systems are cumulative. An annual amount of income is not taxed. Each week, or each month, the employer has to calculate how much tax to deduct so that, by the end of the fiscal year, the correct amount of tax has been deducted. With NIT, the tax system would have to be non-cumulative, because if NIT is due to the employee then the correct amount has to be paid out every week or every month in relation to current earnings, and not in relation to annual earnings and annual allowances. This means that each week, or each month, the employer would have to pay the correct amount of NIT in addition to earnings, or no NIT would be paid and earnings above the threshold would be taxed. A non-cumulative system requires a single tax rate, so anyone paying higher rate tax would have to pay additional income tax at the end of the tax year. One of the reasons for this not being felt to be a problem in the United States and Canada is that end of year tax bills and refunds are already a common experience, particularly in relation to the Earned Income Tax Credit in the US: an end of year payment to low income families with at least one adult in employment (Sloman, 2019: 112, 120; 2020; Torry, 2016a: 126–8).

Given the complexity of the administration of a Negative Income Tax, and the potential for so much Government and employer interference in the lives of individuals and households, it is always something of a surprise when academics and policymakers towards the libertarian and therefore 'small Government' end of the political spectrum prefer a Negative Income Tax to the entirely interference-free Basic Income. The only conclusion that I can draw is that they have neither experience nor understanding of how different taxes and benefits are administered.

Whilst Canada is the location for a certain amount of terminological confusion, it is in the USA that we find the most extreme conflation of Minimum Income Guarantee, Negative Income Tax and Basic Income. Peter Sloman has suggested that the reason for this is the extremely fragmented nature of income maintenance provision in the United States (Sloman, 2020). 'Social security' means federally funded pensions and disability and survivor benefits, with other income maintenance being 'welfare': a state responsibility, and therefore quite diverse in structure and levels, with the Federal Government exercising a certain amount of control through conditions attached to federal funding arrangements. Income Tax, on the other hand, is a federal responsibility, which means that the important Earned Income Tax Credit is administered at the federal and not the state level. It is not entirely surprising that compared with this fragmented diversity, federal-level Minimum Income Guarantee, Negative Income Tax and Basic Income might all feel rather similar.

HUEY LONG AND ROBERT THEOBALD: MINIMUM INCOME GUARANTEE PROPOSALS

In 1888, Edward Bellamy published a novel in which he envisaged an income conditional on participating in an 'industrial army'. This was one of the inspirations for a radio broadcast in 1934 in which Senator Huey Long proposed 'a guaranty of a family wealth of around $5,000', 'a fair share of the income of this land', and an 'old-age pension of £30 a month for everyone that is sixty years old' (Long, 1934). However, the pension was not in fact for 'everyone': 'we do not give this pension to a man making $1,000 a year, and we do not give it to him if he has $10,000 in property, but outside that we do' (Long, 1934). In a 'Statement of the Share Our Wealth movement' in 1935, more detail is given of the regular income for families: 'The yearly income of every family shall be not less than one-third of the average family income, which means that … no family's annual income would be less than from $2,000 to $2,500' (Long, 1935). The regular annual income is therefore an income-tested benefit designed to bring each family's income up to a specified level, and the pension is both wealth-tested and income-tested, so we can make the reasonable assumption that the 'guaranty of a family wealth of around $5,000' implies a grant to each family to bring their wealth up to the specified level. We are here in the world of a Minimum Income Guarantee and a Minimum Wealth Guarantee, and not of a Basic Income.

As we discovered in Chapter 4, a year after Huey Long's broadcast a Social Credit Party won power in Alberta and then failed to implement a provincial social dividend (Duverger, 2018: 54; Sloman, 2019: 71; Van Parijs and Vanderborght, 2017: 80). Both the US and Canada then had to wait until the 1960s for any significant public debate to occur about the future of tax and benefits policy. In 1963, Robert Theobald suggested that in a context of 'cybernation', and of the inevitable destruction of jobs, the existence of 'abundance' meant that the 'job-income link' could be broken, and every individual could be given a 'due-income', a 'Basic Economic Security', that would create 'an economic floor under each individual' (Theobald, 1963: 145–7). A constitutional right

> would guarantee to every citizen of the United States, and to every person who has resided within the United States for a period of five consecutive years, the right to an income from the federal Government sufficient to enable him to live with dignity. (Theobald, 1963: 184)

The level of Basic Economic Security would be

> based on the individual's total income record of the year … any family (or individual) with some private [earned or investment] income of their own would not only receive payments to make up the difference between their private income and their regular entitlement under BES [Basic Economic Security], but also a premium of 10 per cent of the value of their private income. (Theobald, 1963: 196)

This is a Minimum Income Guarantee that would have paid the full amount of a means-tested benefit to anyone with no earned income and that would have been withdrawn at a rate of 90 per cent of any earned or investment income (Theobald, 1963: 196). It is not a Basic Income. Theobald sometimes employs the term 'basic income', but he means by it a means-tested benefit:

> Basic economic security can be provided most easily through the guaranteed income. This proposal for making a basic income available as a matter of right is rapidly moving toward the center of the political stage. (Theobald, 1968: 18)

What was moving towards 'the center of the political stage' was discussion of a Minimum Income Guarantee.

MILTON FRIEDMAN AND NEGATIVE INCOME TAX

An important trajectory of the United States debate on taxation and benefits reform began in Paris, where in 1938 a group of libertarian intellectuals coined the term 'neoliberalism':

> Neoliberals started to recognize the growing need 'to organize individualism' in order to counter what was perceived as an unfortunate but irreversible politicization of economics and science ... To achieve their goal of the 'Good Society', neoliberal agents agreed on the need to develop long-term strategies projected over a horizon of several decades, possibly to involve several generations of neoliberal intellectuals. (Mirowski and Plehwe, 2015: 15)

By 'politicization of economics and science' they meant such politically active economists as John Maynard Keynes, whose *General Theory of Employment, Interest, and Money* had concluded that it was the role of Government to establish 'certain central controls in matters which are now left in the main to individual initiative' (Keynes, 1936: 377–8).

In 1947, Friedrich (von) Hayek, then working at the London School of Economics, Milton Friedman, then at the University of Chicago, and other like-minded economists, met in the Swiss village of Mont Pelerin. The outcome was the Mont Pelerin Society, which from then until now has argued for a free market economy, private rather than public ownership, and the freedom and responsibility of the individual: that is, neoliberalism. Whether or not the establishment of neoliberal think tanks around the world was a strategy is debated, but what happened is clear: think tanks that argued for the neoliberal paradigm circulated staff into and out of Governments and academia, resulting in a critical mass of influential individuals advocating the paradigm, so that as soon as the Keynesian paradigm hit a variety of crises during the 1970s the new one was ready for action. Public assets and services were privatized, trades unions were weakened, exchange rates and capital movements were set free, and individuals were tasked with looking after their own economic destinies (Berry, 2018: 5–6, 8; Fevre, 2016; Russell and Milburn, 2018: 45, 47–8).

As Sloman points out, attitudes towards Government provision of incomes varied among the members of the Mont Pelerin Society. Some did not wish to see any Government distribution at all, but Hayek recognized that Governments might have a responsibility to provide 'security against severe physical privation, the certainty of a given minimum of sustenance for all ... there can be no doubt that some minimum of food, shelter, and clothing, sufficient to preserve health and the capacity to work, can be assured to everybody' (Hayek, [1944] 2008: 147–8). Hayek did not specify the mechanism by which the 'given minimum' should be achieved (Van Parijs and Vanderborght, 2017: 86–7), but recently Burczak has shown that the provision of a sufficient minimum along-side a Hayekian wish to reduce coercion in the employment relationship can between them form a coherent Hayekian argument for Basic Income (Burczak, 2013). Most significantly for the future debate on Basic Income, at the first meeting of the Mont Pelerin Society Milton Friedman advocated a Negative Income Tax (NIT) (Sloman, 2019: 47–8), an idea that he had developed five years previously while working for the US Treasury (Duverger, 2018: 78–9). As Friedman saw it, a NIT, which paid to an employee an additional income proportional to the amount that their earned income fell below a threshold, recommended itself 'on purely mechanical grounds' (Friedman, [1962] 2002: 191–2) and because it would be 'a single program designed to give assistance to persons with low incomes, regardless of the reason why their incomes are low', and would enable the abolition of a variety of existing means-tested programmes that in his view encumbered the economy (Cohen and Friedman, 1972: 45; Duverger, 2018: 82). The Negative Income Tax would be

> directed specifically at the problem of poverty. It gives help in the form most useful to the individual, namely, cash. It is general and could be substituted for the host of special measures now in effect. It makes explicit the cost borne by society. It operates outside the market. Like any other measures to alleviate poverty, it reduces the incentives of those helped to help themselves, but it does not eliminate that incentive entirely, as a system of supplementing incomes up to some fixed minimum would. An extra dollar earned always means more money available for expenditure. (Friedman, [1962] 2002: 192)

In 1971, John Rawls recommended a NIT (Rawls, 1971: 275) on the basis that 'the market is not suited to answer the claims of need' and so cash transfers is the 'way of dealing with the claims of need [that] would appear to be more effective than trying to regulate income by minimum wage standards, and the like' (Rawls, 1971: 277). Anything beyond the meeting of needs and provid-ing sufficient for 'an appropriate standard of life' should be provided by the market in labour (Rawls, 1971: 277). The following year, during a debate on the relative virtues of NIT, means-tested benefits and social insurance (which he did not think should be called insurance) (Cohen and Friedman, 1972: 23–8, 37), Friedman suggested that a NIT would

> do efficiently and humanely what our present welfare and social security system does inefficiently and inhumanely—namely, provide an assured minimum to all persons in need regardless of the reason for their need without destroying their char-acter, their independence, or their incentive to better their own conditions. (Cohen and Friedman, 1972: 23)

The NIT's chief virtue was that it avoided Governments having to intervene in society or contravene individual freedom by providing public services and means-tested benefits (Sloman, 2019: 95–6). A further advantage was that it would function as a macroeconomic regulator by providing an anti-cyclical increase to household incomes during recessions; and yet another that it made available to the poor the efficiency of the price mechanism, which the provision of public services by Governments could never achieve (Sloman, 2019: 47–8).

NIT has always been more popular than Basic Income in libertarian/neo-liberal circles (Story, 2015; Fleischer and Lehto, 2019), even though a Basic Income delivers the same relationship between gross and net income as NIT. NIT's greater popularity might be because Basic Income's universality and unconditionality can be viewed as socialist. But as pointed out at the beginning of this chapter, there is an irony here. While Friedman understood that there might be 'problems of administration' (Cohen and Friedman, 1972: 45; Friedman, [1962] 2002: 192), he did not recognize that administratively a NIT behaves in much the same way as means-tested benefits, and that to do the same job with a Basic Income would have avoided both the Government intervention in society, and the contravention of individual liberty, that are inevitably associated with NIT. Basic Income would have served Friedman's libertarian ideology far more effectively than a NIT could ever do.

The importance of the longstanding interest in Negative Income Tax for the Basic Income debate among libertarian thinkers, and therefore for this history, is that because a NIT can deliver the same relationship between gross and net income as a Basic Income, the two have often been conflated, particularly in relation to Friedman's espousing of NIT, as we find Preiss doing here:

> A substantial basic income furthers effective economic freedom (on Friedman's own understanding), redeems his central claim that markets enable cooperation without coercion, and enables him to address his lifelong interlocutors by mitigating concerns for the ways in which economic dependence and inequality undermine both freedom and democratic legitimacy. (Preiss, 2015: 169)

A substantial Basic Income would do all of that, and a smaller one would go a long way towards it: and either of them would be a great deal easier to administer than a Negative Income Tax.

This raises the question as to why economists and politicians to the right of the political spectrum prefer Negative Income Tax to Basic Income. One possibility is that a Negative Income Tax can apply different rates above and below the earnings threshold, enabling a low income tax rate to accompany an even lower NIT rate: that is, a lower rate at which the NIT is paid in relation to the amount by which earned income falls below the threshold. This enables recipients to be clearly distinguished from taxpayers and to be disadvantaged in relation to them. A Basic Income would pay the same amount to everyone, and income taxes would generally be progressive: a combination that would not distinguish between net recipients and net payers, and that would privilege individuals with low earned incomes or no earned incomes at all.

A further and related reason for preferring Negative Income Tax to Basic Income might be because the latter might allocate either no income tax allowance or only a small one, meaning that income tax would be paid on all or most earned income, whereas the former requires a higher earnings threshold below which the NIT is paid out and above which income tax is collected. Treating tax allowances differently from income maintenance payments is a mechanism for distinguishing between taxpayers and benefits recipients, and they are also a way of minimizing public expenditure figures in the national accounts. If a country's tax allowance were to be replaced with a Basic Income of the same value, then the Government's financial position would not alter and neither would that of any individual: but because the Basic Incomes might be counted as public expenditure, and revenue foregone in the form of tax allowances might not be, it would look as if the Basic Income was far more expensive than the tax allowance, which it would not be. The only solution to this problem would be for revenue foregone in the form of tax allowances to be counted as public expenditure: a change that Governments are understandably hesitant to make (Sloman, 2020).

JAMES TOBIN'S BASIC INCOME

James Tobin's proposal for a Negative Income Tax is quite rightly discussed alongside other Negative Income Tax proposals: but in the context of the US debate of this period it is an outlier in the sense that one of the options considered for administering the NIT would have turned it into something very close to a Basic Income.

In a paper published by Tobin, Pechman and Miezkowski in 1967, the authors propose that a 'NIT allowance' should be established, and they offer two payment methods. One of them administers the Negative Income Tax as if it were a means-tested benefit: that is, families would have to apply for it if they believed that their annual incomes would fall below specified levels. Regular payments would then be made, with their calculation taking into account the basic allowance, an offsetting tax and predicted net earned income. With the other method,

> the full basic allowance would be mailed out at the beginning of each period—week, or half-month—to all families. The checks would be received by families who may ultimately have incomes in excess of the break-even point, as well as those who will be eligible for net benefits. Likewise, all families would be subject to withholding at the rate of the offsetting tax on the first X dollars of their earnings, and would be required to pay the offsetting tax on other income by quarterly declaration. Final

adjustment would be made by the tax return for the year filed the next April 15th. (Tobin et al., 1967: 21)

Families with higher incomes who wished to avoid the additional tax would be able to decline to receive the basic allowance. The paper includes detailed costings, and a discussion of which existing benefits might be adjusted on the implementation of the 'Negative Income Tax'.

The one characteristic of the plan that means that strictly speaking the payments of the basic allowance would not be payment of a Basic Income is that the basic allowance would have been calculated on the basis of the family structure and would have been paid as a single sum to each family. To be a genuine Basic Income, it would have had to be the same amount for each individual, and paid to the individual. But apart from that, the proposal was for a Basic Income. Just as we must take care to study the detail of mechanisms called 'Basic Income' to ensure that they are what they say they are, so we should study the detail of proposals for a 'Negative Income Tax': they might not be what they say they are, and they might be proposals for a Basic Income.

J.K. GALBRAITH'S CHANGE OF MIND

Just as in the UK G.D.H. Cole changed his mind, so in the United States John Kenneth Galbraith came to see the value of a guaranteed income. As Van Parijs and Vanderborght point out, in the first edition of his *The Affluent Society*, published in 1958, Galbraith suggested that education and slum clearance, rather than the provision of incomes, could be the most useful way to tackle poverty: but by the time of the second edition, first published in 1969, he had changed his mind, and a new paragraph appeared (Van Parijs and Vanderborght, 2017: 87–8):

> Within the last ten years, the provision of a regular source of income to the poor, as a matter of broad social policy, has come to seem increasingly practical. The notion that income is a remedy for indigency has a certain forthright appeal. As elsewhere argued, it would also ease the problems of economic management by reducing the reliance on production as a source of income. The provision of such a basic source of income must henceforth be the first and the strategic step in the attack on poverty. (Galbraith, 1970: 264)

A footnote is added: 'In the first edition the provision of a guaranteed income was discussed but dismissed as "beyond reasonable hope"' (Galbraith, 1970: 264).

But the question is this: what does Galbraith mean by 'the provision of a regular source of income to the poor' (Galbraith, 1970: 264)? The addition of 'to the poor' suggests a means-tested benefit, and this interpretation is confirmed by an earlier discussion about

> various proposals for guaranteed income or a negative income tax. The principle common to these proposals is provision of a basic income as a matter of general right and related in amount to family size but not otherwise to need. If the individual cannot find (or does not seek) employment, he has this income on which to survive. With income from employment, part of the payment is withdrawn and above a certain level is converted into a payment *to* the state. (Hence the term negative income tax.) To work is always to have more income. (Galbraith, 1970: 243)

What is envisaged here is a family-based and income-tested benefit. The difference between Galbraith's proposal and the welfare regime of the United States at the time is that as earnings rose the income provided by the Government would have been withdrawn slowly rather than dollar for dollar as could happen with the existing system (Van Parijs and Vanderborght, 2017: 88). Galbraith's change of mind belongs to the history of a Negative Income Tax, and for that reason it is relevant to the history of Basic Income: but its direct relevance is minimal.

PRESIDENT NIXON'S FAMILY ASSISTANCE PLAN

Just as in the UK the 1960s saw a rediscovery of poverty, so in the United States a greater understanding of the extent of poverty led to a variety of calls for a 'guaranteed annual income', by which was usually meant an income-tested benefit (for 'the poor'), although the benefit was generally not intended to be asset-tested or dependent on behavioural conditions being met (Fox Piven and Cloward, 1966). Occasional calls for the implementation of a Negative Income Tax continued to be heard, and it was a plan for a Negative Income Tax for families with children that was proposed to President Richard Nixon in 1969. The rate at which the NIT would have been paid was 50 per cent of the amount by which earned income fell below a threshold: a substantial improvement on the 100 per cent withdrawal rate for the Aid to Families with Dependent Children (AFDC) that the new scheme was designed to replace. Originally intended not to be dependent on behavioural conditions, the scheme finally announced as the Family Assistance Plan (FAP) was subject to a work test, and it suffered criticism both from those who believed that the scheme would have resulted in employment disincentives, and from those who thought that the behavioural conditions would stigmatize the poor and would in practice be racist (Duverger, 2018: 85–7; Van Parijs and Vanderborght, 2017: 90–91). The statement of the withdrawal rate also came in for criticism because it did not state the total deduction rate. As Milton Friedman commented:

> The President's Family Assistance Plan is in principle a far-reaching proposal for restructuring public assistance. Its aims are, first, to establish a national minimum welfare standard, thereby reducing the incentive for poor people to move in order to qualify for higher welfare; second, to give persons on relief a strong incentive to work themselves off relief by enabling them to improve their lot substantially by additional earnings; and third, to substitute an objective income standard for the present means test and thereby provide more equal treatment.
>
> These objectives are admirable, and the general principle embodied in the proposal—a negative income tax—is well suited to achieve them. But unfortunately, the specific embodiment of these principles is so defective that the bill, at least in the form in which it was submitted to the Senate Finance Committee last year, would make matters worse rather than better. ... After the first $720 of earnings a year, the President proposes that the welfare payment be reduced by 50 cents for every dollar of additional earnings, supposedly leaving the worker 50 cents for himself. However, [because of other taxes and changes to existing benefits], the actual marginal tax rate reaches 80 percent and more. (Cohen and Friedman, 1972: 42–4)

A lower withdrawal rate would have solved the problem; and to have matched the withdrawal rate to the rate of income tax charged on earned income above $720 a year would have replicated the relationship between earned income and net income that would be delivered by a Basic Income.

The Family Assistance Plan was eventually blocked by the Senate Finance Committee, with both conservative Republicans and progressive Democrats voting against it, the former because they thought that the plan went too far, and the latter because they thought that it did not go far enough (Henderson and Quiggin, 2019: 495; Sloman, 2019: 96). With hindsight, it was probably a good thing that the plan was abandoned, as the 'problems of administration' (Cohen and Friedman, 1972: 45; Friedman, [1962] 2002: 192) associated with a Negative Income Tax really are significant. The plan's failure left the path open for the establishment of more stringent regulation of the existing welfare structure and for the Earned Income Tax Credit (on which, see below) (Steensland, 2008: 157–81).

The period from the mid-1960s to the early 1970s was a window of opportunity for tax and benefits reform in the United States. Poverty was recognized as a problem; existing rather chaotic welfare provision was also recognized as a problem; and there was a willingness across the political spectrum to study and discuss reform options. Steensland suggests that Nixon's Family Assistance Plan and previous reform proposals failed to be implemented because the cultural currents against the plans' partial dissolution of the deserving/undeserving and work-requirement/unconditional distinctions were simply too strong for the proposal, and the reasons that lawmakers on both the left and the right of the political spectrum had found for liking the idea of a guaranteed annual income were not sufficient of a counter-current.

> Because [Guaranteed Annual Income] plans so directly challenged the tacit cultural perceptions on which the existing welfare system was based, the structuring role these perceptions play in policy development was more visible than usual. ... [I]n the same way that historical institutionalists have argued that aspects of the American policymaking process bias the trajectory of reform in particular directions, so too do cultural structures like the enduring distinction between the deserving and undeserving poor. For instance, given the expense of the program, a number of commentators have expressed surprise at the [Earned Income Tax Credit]'s ease of passage in the mid-1970s and its subsequent growth in the following years. Yet the creation and growth of this program is far less puzzling when one recognizes that it not only conforms to categories of worth but reinforces them. (Steensland, 2008: 245)

The Family Assistance Plan was not the only option on the table. Another emerged during the 1972 presidential election that pitted Richard Nixon against the Democrat George McGovern.

GEORGE MCGOVERN'S MINIMUM INCOME GRANT

In 1972, presidential candidate Senator George McGovern proposed a 'Minimum Income Grant', sometimes called a 'demogrant' or a 'national income grant'. The aim was to tackle the problems associated with the current welfare system:

> The poor find that, as soon as they go to work, they are subject to extremely high rates of income taxation because of their sudden sharp reduction of public aid when they earn their first dollar. The net result is mounting frustration for those in the middle and a future of poverty for those who are heavily penalized when they seek to work their way out of welfare dependence.
> There are other weaknesses of the public assistance or welfare program. Many people in need are not covered; family groups are penalized; benefits are insufficient; migration from one state to another is encouraged; extensive controls are applied; and it is possible for taxpayers to be worse off than those receiving public assistance. ...
> I propose that every man, woman, and child receive from the federal Government an annual payment. This payment would not vary in accordance with the wealth of the recipient. For those on public assistance, this income grant would replace the welfare system. It has also been suggested that the national income grant could replace certain social security benefits. ... the payments are made on an individual basis. Thus, there would be no incentive for a family to break up in order to receive higher total benefits. (McGovern, 1972)

Different methods and levels of payment were discussed, including James Tobin's proposal, discussed above; and the administrative detail was left for later discussion and decision. Anyone who stopped reading McGovern's article in the *New York Review of Books* at the end of the section titled 'The Minimum Income Grant' and did not read the section on 'Financing the Minimum Income Grant' would have been left with the impression that a Basic Income might have been intended. Anyone who continued to read would soon have realized that this was not necessarily the case.

> It is expected that those below the poverty line would keep all of the grant, while those between the poverty line and the break-even point would keep a gradually decreasing amount as their incomes rose. The loss of grant benefits would thus be sufficiently gradual as not to discourage those on welfare from seeking a job (in fact, it would encourage them to seek work) and would provide a significant income supplement to the millions of Americans in the medium-income range. Thus, for example, a family of four with its own income of $8,000 would be able to retain an additional $2,000 of the Minimum Income Grant. (McGovern, 1972)

When the different parts of the article are read together, what is not clear is whether the grant itself would be withdrawn, or whether its value would be withdrawn by charging additional income tax. If the former option was intended then McGovern intended an income-tested benefit; if the latter, then a Basic Income or a household-based variant of it. Three conclusions are possible: that McGovern had not thought sufficiently about the difference between on the one hand income-tested benefits and on the other unconditional incomes the value of which would be withdrawn through the tax system; that he did understand the difference but had not made up his mind which might be the best method and so wanted to leave his options open (Van Parijs, 2020); and that the ambiguity was purposefully designed to enable voters with different preferences to find what they were looking for.

McGovern won the Democratic Party nomination with his plan, but then came under sustained attack from the Nixon administration in relation to the cost of the demogrant. The plan was reshaped as a benefit only for the poor: but the incumbent president still won the election, and one consequence was the final abandonment of the Family Assistance Plan and the implementation of the Earned Income Tax Credit (EITC), paid annually to poorer working families with children on the basis of a complex formula following the submission of an annual tax return. The EITC is the polar opposite of a Basic Income: it is means-tested, work-tested, family-based, paid annually—and popular, because it assists poor children and is paid to workers. The credit has since then been extended to some workers without children, but the structure is still much the same as it has been since the programme was implemented during the mid-1970s. Various proposals have been made that would shift the

EITC in the direction of a Basic Income: for instance, that payments could be more frequent than once a year; but the problem with that is that a worker's pay might rise during the year, meaning that money would have to be paid back. As means-tested and work-tested benefits go, the EITC might be optimal. This suggests that the way forwards for the Basic Income debate in the US might be to frame Basic Income as a foundational layer of income alongside such existing programmes as the Earned Income Tax Credit (Duverger, 2018: 89; Leff, 2019; Van Parijs and Vanderborght, 2017: 91–2).

The USA was fortunate to avoid having to manage the administration of a Negative Income Tax, and the high marginal deduction rates of a Minimum Income Guarantee. Instead, it got the Earned Income Tax Credit, which is preferable. A combination of the EITC and a Basic Income would be even better. But soon after the 1972 election the window of opportunity for doing anything significant about income maintenance closed. The popularity of the EITC, rapid inflation caused by the oil price increase during the mid-1970s, and public opinion turning against taxation, all contributed to the birth of an era of tax cuts and public expenditure cuts.

PRACTICAL EXPERIMENTS IN THE UNITED STATES

While President Nixon's Family Assistance Plan (FAP) was defeated in the Senate, and while there was still sufficient interest in doing something about the US's chaotic income maintenance system, one element of the planning for the FAP's implementation experienced a significant afterlife. In order to provide evidence on which to base detailed planning for Nixon's plan, four experiments were initiated in which households were randomly allocated either to a group subject to a Minimum Income Guarantee (that is, their household incomes were topped up to specified levels based on their household structures) or to a control group that continued to experience the existing system, with each experiment applying a variety of guaranteed income levels and a variety of rates of withdrawal as earned incomes rose. The largest and longest experiment was held in Seattle and Denver (the 'SIME/DIME' experiment), and smaller ones in New Jersey, in Iowa and North Carolina, and in Gary, Indiana. The aim was to evaluate the Minimum Income Guarantee's effects on such indicators as weight at birth, school performance, divorce rate, and particularly employment market behaviour. Widerquist has aggregated results across the four US experiments and the Canadian Mincome experiment in Dauphin and Winnipeg discussed below, and has found that

> relative work reduction varied substantially across the five experiments from 0.5% to 9.0% for husbands, which means that the experimental group worked less than

the control group by about ½ hour to 4 hours per week or 1 to 4 fulltime weeks per year. …

    The response of wives and single mothers was somewhat larger in terms of hours, and substantially larger in percentage terms because they tended to work fewer hours to begin with. Wives reduced their work effort by 0% to 27% and single mothers reduced their work effort by 15% to 30%. These percentages correspond to reductions of about 0 to 5 fulltime weeks per year. The labor market response of wives had a much larger range than the other two groups, but this was usually attributed to the peculiarities of the labor markets in Gary and Winnipeg where particularly small responses were found. (Widerquist, 2019b: 308)

As Widerquist points out, these results should not be taken to represent what would happen if a population-wide Minimum Income Guarantee were to be implemented. Only the Canadian experiment involved a saturation site. The four US experiments selected already poor sections of the population from which to randomly select experiment participants, so for all of the participants the guaranteed annual income would have been sizeable in relation to existing earned incomes. The saturation site experiment in Dauphin exhibited far lower reductions in employment hours, which suggests that with a community-wide Minimum Income Guarantee labour supply would fall, wages would rise and labour supply would then bounce back. This effect would not be expected among a randomly selected sample.

    A serious problem occurred when the results of the experiments were published. Politicians and journalists assumed that the average reductions reported meant that every worker had worked less, whereas what was actually happening was that workers were taking longer to find new jobs, which is arguably a good thing, as it probably meant that workers were finding appropriate jobs rather than just any job (Widerquist, 2019b: 308–10). And perhaps new mothers were re-entering the employment market less quickly than before so that they could spend more time with their young children; and maybe parents generally were choosing to spend more time with their children: again good outcomes (Forget, 2011: 286).

    The 'quality of life' results of the experiments were also in the right direction. School attendance and test scores rose; young people were remaining in education for longer; more adults participated in continuing education; there were fewer low birth weights; the nutritional quality of diets improved; and there was less domestic abuse and mental illness. However, one result of the SIME/DIME experiment caused some rather too significant controversy. Initial analysis suggested that in that experiment the divorce rate rose, suggesting that the guarantee of an income was enabling women to leave their husbands. If this had been the case then there would have been two ways to interpret the finding: that a Minimum Income Guarantee would have disastrous social effects, or that if all that is holding a relationship together is financial dependence, then perhaps the relationship should end. But this was not the case. The initial reporting of high separation rates had been a mistake. When Cain and Wissoker re-examined the data of the SIME/DIME experiment they found that

> [t]he plans (specifically, the negative income tax plans in the experiment) had no effect on the rate of marital dissolutions among the 'treatment' couples relative to the control couples. (Cain and Wissoker, 1990: 1235)

The saturation site Dauphin Mincome experiment reported below found that the dissolution rate actually dropped (Widerquist, 2019b: 312).

Taking an overall view of the US experiments, a positive interpretation of the overall results would be that a Minimum Income Guarantee can reduce poverty and many of its effects, and that the changes in employment market behaviour would be both useful and sustainable. A less positive interpretation would be that the experiment had shown that a Minimum Income Guarantee would reduce employment and would have some disastrous social effects at considerable financial cost.

Only interim results of the four US experiments were available when the US Congress was discussing President Nixon's Family Assistance Plan (Forget, 2011: 286; Widerquist, 2019b: 313). A further complication is that it might not have been clear to Congress that the experiments were about Minimum Income Guarantees, whereas the Family Assistance Plan was closer to being a Negative Income Tax. By the time discussions were reaching a conclusion in Congress, Jimmy Carter was President and the plan was not so clearly a Negative Income Tax: but both the press and therefore the politicians were drawing extreme conclusions from the research results, and particularly those that indicated reduced employment hours and a higher divorce rate. As Widerquist concludes, 'an environment with a low understanding of complexity is highly vulnerable to spin with simplistic or nearly vacuous interpretation' (Widerquist, 2019b: 315). (Author's note: I am writing this while the UK is in the process of leaving the European Union: the result of a referendum undertaken in an environment with 'a low understanding of complexity' and 'highly vulnerable to spin with simplistic or nearly vacuous interpretation'.)

Widerquist continues:

> Whether the low information content of the discussion in the media resulted more from spin, sensationalism, or honest misunderstanding, is hard to determine. But whatever the reasons, the low-information discussion of the experimental results put NIT [and Minimum Income Guarantee] (and, with hindsight, Basic Income by proxy) in an extremely unfavourable light, when the scientific results were actually mixed-to-favourable. (Widerquist, 2019b: 315)

Even those who should have understood the complexity, and ought to have worked harder to understand and communicate the research results, failed to do so. As the *New York Times* reported:

Senator Daniel Patrick Moynihan, long a leading proponent of a 'negative income tax' as a substitute for the welfare system, today declared that he now had serious doubts the concept would work. ...

The Senator, a Democrat from New York who heads the Senate Subcommittee on Fiscal Assistance, is widely considered an academic authority on welfare problems. He attributed his doubts to recent research indicating that such programs, the equivalent of a guaranteed annual income for the poor, tend to reduce work efforts and increase marital instability.

'We must now be prepared to entertain the possibility that we were wrong', Senator Moynihan said in a statement issued as he began three days of hearings on the recent research.

In so doing, he also opened a good-natured but pointed argument with the Carter Administration, whose proposals for welfare reform rely in large part on a cash-assistance plan similar to the negative income tax. The proposals were rejected in the last session of Congress. (*New York Times*, 1978)

The outcome was a virtual end to political consideration of a Negative Income Tax and of Minimum Income Guarantee schemes generally, and, by association, of Basic Income (Van Parijs and Vanderborght, 2017: 92–3).

THE MINCOME EXPERIMENT IN CANADA

A number of reports published in Canada during the late 1960s and early 1970s floated a variety of reform options, including a Minimum Income Guarantee (known as a Guaranteed Annual Income in this context) (Forget, 2011: 287; Van Parijs and Vanderborght, 2017: 93, 277); and between 1974 and 1979 two Minimum Income Guarantee experiments took place in Manitoba: a saturation site experiment in the town of Dauphin, population 10,000, with control communities elsewhere in the state, and an experiment among households randomly selected across Winnipeg, with matched control households.

The 'Mincome' experiment specified an annual income level below which a household would not be permitted to fall, with the level depending on the structure of the household. Households with no other income received payments equal in value to the whole of the guaranteed income, and households with earned income had the payments reduced by 50 cents for every C$1 of earned income. This meant that wealthy households received no payments. The difference between the Mincome payments and normal means-tested benefits was that the Mincome payments were not work-tested: that is, there was no conditionality related to employment status, and there were no job search or occupational training requirements. This meant that the character of the payments lay somewhere between normal means-tested benefits and Basic Income.

Rapid oil price rises and consequent inflation during the mid-1970s precipitated both changes of Governments at both state and national levels and spiralling Mincome costs, and the new Governments brought the experiment to an end. The only evaluation that took place was of the randomly selected households across Winnipeg. On average, husbands reduced their employment hours by just 1 per cent, wives by 3 per cent, and lone parents by 17 per cent (Forget, 2011: 288–9; Widerquist, 2019b: 310).

Data collection ceased after two years, little analysis was undertaken, and all data records were stored. Thirty years later, rather than pursue the original agenda of the experiment, which was to study the employment market effects of a Minimum Income Guarantee, Professor Evelyn Forget studied Dauphin's health and education service records, on the basis of hypotheses that the reduction in income risk experienced in Dauphin (including among families who did not receive any payments, but would have done so if their earned incomes had declined) might have improved the population's wellbeing, and that the temporary Minimum Income Guarantee might have made it more likely that young people would remain in full-time education for longer than usual. Forget found that

> [o]verall hospitalizations, and specifically hospitalizations for accidents and injuries and mental health diagnoses, declined for MINCOME subjects relative to the comparison group. Physician claims for mental health diagnoses fell for subjects relative to comparators. ... Overall, the measured impact was larger than one might have expected when only about a third of families qualified for support at any one time and many of the supplements would have been quite small. This we attribute to social interaction. Because Dauphin was a saturation site, the involvement of friends and neighbours in the scheme may have led to changes in social attitudes and behaviours that influenced individual behaviour even among families that did not receive the supplement. (Forget, 2011: 299–300)

Forget found no change in the birth rate due to the experiment, no change in the family dissolution rate, and young people remaining longer in full-time education: and we have already discussed the potentially useful changes in employment market activity (Forget, 2011: 291–2, 299–300).

Another scholar who has revisited the research data of the Dauphin experiment is David Calnitsky, who has found that

> the design and framing of Mincome led participants to view payments through a pragmatic lens, rather than the moralistic lens through which welfare is viewed. ... Mincome participation did not produce social stigma. ... The social meaning of Mincome was sufficiently powerful that even participants with particularly negative attitudes toward Government assistance felt able to collect Mincome payments

without a sense of contradiction. By obscuring the distinctions between the 'deserving' and 'undeserving' poor, universalistic income maintenance programs may weaken social stigmatization and strengthen program sustainability. (Calnitsky, 2016: 27)

Forget's work, and that of other scholars who have sought out the results of the 1970s experiments, interpreted them and communicated them, has contributed important scientific content to the Basic Income debate. The process is circular. In the absence of a sufficient number of genuine Basic Income pilot projects, the Basic Income debate has looked for the results of experiments with similar mechanisms, and interpreted them as results relevant to the Basic Income debate, sometimes without making allowance for the differences between Minimum Income Guarantee, Negative Income Tax and Basic Income; and the use that Basic Income researchers and campaigners are making of the results drives the search for the results of the experiments and also the interpretative effort. The process has been largely positive, with journalists understanding that it might be useful for workers to have the ability to seek an appropriate new job, for young people to stay longer in full-time education, and for parents to spend more time with their children, and particularly useful for health, mental health and other social indicators to improve, all at relatively modest cost, or perhaps at no cost at all if reduced healthcare costs were to outweigh the cost of a Minimum Income Guarantee, a Negative Income Tax or a Basic Income (Widerquist, 2019b: 316).

The question for this history is the extent to which the results of the US and Canadian experiments can be counted as predictors of what would happen if a Basic Income were to be implemented. A Basic Income would be paid to everyone, rather than to only one third of a population at any one time; the payments would be utterly predictable, rather than varying as earned income changed; and the payments would be made to the individual rather than to the household. The hypothesized reason for the beneficial effects of Dauphin's Minimum Income Guarantee was the sense of economic security that it generated. That sense would arguably be greater with a Basic Income, provided existing means-tested benefits were left in place in order to ensure that no low-income household would suffer a net disposable income loss at the point of implementation. We can therefore hypothesize that any population that experienced a genuine Basic Income in the context of continuing means-tested benefits would experience the kinds of enhanced health, mental health and educational outcomes experienced in Dauphin; and we can also hypothesize that they would experience even less stigma than the Mincome participants: but it still has to be said that none of the US and Canadian experiments were testing Basic Incomes, so there will always be some doubt as to the extent to which the results obtained during the experiments might predict what would happen if a Basic Income were to be implemented (Van Parijs and Vanderborght, 2017: 141–2).

Perhaps one of the reasons that most of the debate in the United States and Canada during this period was about a Minimum Income Guarantee and not a Basic Income was simply that it is far more difficult to run a Basic Income pilot project than it is to run a Minimum Income Guarantee pilot project. A Minimum Income Guarantee pilot project can leave in place the existing tax and benefits structure and pay to each household, either at the end of the tax year or more frequently, a sum of money to bring the household's total income up to a specified level based on the household structure. A genuine Basic Income pilot project would need to change the existing tax and benefits system for the pilot communities, simply because that is what would have to happen if an affordable Basic Income were to be implemented for an entire population. This would require a substantial amount of work on the part of Government departments, and probably employers as well, and would therefore require the kind of sustained political commitment that can never be guaranteed. There are good reasons for there never having been a saturation site Basic Income pilot project in a country with a more developed economy.

While there are reasons for claiming that the means-testing required for a Minimum Income Guarantee can 'simulate the effect of taxes on beneficiaries' (Widerquist, 2019b: 304), and can 'mimic the post-tax-and-transfer profile entailed by some conceivable household-based scheme for the bottom part of the income distribution' (Van Parijs and Vanderborght, 2017: 141), there are also significant differences between an unconditional income given to every individual and a means-tested benefit that cannot avoid the complexity, bureaucratic intrusion and stigma inevitably associated with means-testing. It also has to be said, as Van Parijs and Vanderborght correctly point out (2017: 142–3), that even if a genuine Basic Income were to be tested on a whole community, and if the changes to the tax and benefits system were to be made that would have to be made if a permanent scheme were to be introduced, then the limited duration of any pilot project would mean that every individual's decisions would be made in the light of the fact that the project would end, and, because of the small size of any sample relative to the population of the country, the employment market would not change as it would over time in the context of a permanent Basic Income, meaning that the results of the experiment would still not accurately predict what would happen if a permanent Basic Income were to be implemented.

As we shall see, genuine Basic Income pilot projects have taken place in Namibia and India: these were possible to undertake because there were no complex tax and benefits systems that had to be altered to make the projects possible. We are therefore left with some significantly positive results from Minimum Income Guarantee experiments undertaken in the context of more developed economies, and Basic Income pilot projects in the context of less developed economies. In the absence of a genuine Basic Income pilot project in the context of a more developed economy we shall have to predict the likely effects of a Basic Income in that context on the basis of experiments with something different in the same context and of Basic Income pilot projects in a different context. That might be sufficient for the time being.

Ontario

In 2017, the Canadian province of Ontario began what it called a Basic Income experiment. It was not one: it was very similar to MINCOME. The incomes paid were based on the household rather than the individual (that is, a couple received less than two individuals living alone would have received in total), and the payments were income-tested: that is, they were withdrawn as earned income rose. The characteristic that brought the incomes closer to a Basic Income than the existing social assistance benefits was that the incomes were not work-tested. The income was a 'revenu de base sous condition de ressources', a 'resource-conditional basic income': so not a Basic Income (Duverger, 2018: 129).

The project began in several communities, but was then abruptly cancelled when a new provincial Government took office in 2018 (Ontario, no date; 2018; 2019). The Ontario Government did not evaluate the project, although an independent effort was made to do so. Following the last payments in March 2019, an online highly detailed questionnaire was circulated by McMaster and Ryerson Universities and was completed by 217 former recipients; and forty in-depth interviews were carried out (Ferdosi et al., 2020; Taekema, 2020). Here are the report's findings:

- Many recipients reported improvements in their physical and mental health, labour market participation, food security, housing stability, financial status and social relationships.
- Basic income also had a noticeable impact on the use of health services, with many of the survey respondents indicating less frequent visits to health practitioners and hospital emergency rooms.
- For a significant number of participants, basic income purportedly proved to be transformational, fundamentally reshaping their living standards as well as their sense of self-worth and hope for a better future.
- The majority of those employed before the pilot reported working while they were receiving basic income. Many reported moving to higher paying and more secure jobs.
- Those working before the pilot reported even greater improvements on some measures of well-being than those who were not working before. (Ferdosi et al., 2020: 4)

Not surprisingly, these results look similar to those obtained during the Mincome experiment nearly half a century earlier. As with those results, it must be a matter of debate how different the Ontario results would have been if a genuine Basic Income had been paid for the three years originally intended.

THE ALASKA PERMANENT FUND DIVIDEND

A sovereign wealth fund is a fund owned by a nation state's Government. The revenue for the fund is often composed of royalties paid by companies in exchange for licences to extract natural resources, and the proceeds of the fund are either left in place in order to increase the capital, or they are used for public or other projects at the Government's discretion (Lansley, 2016: 41–54).

In 1966, oil drilling began at Prudhoe Bay in Alaska. Early royalties paid by the oil companies for permission to extract oil were widely regarded as having been wasted by the Alaskan Government: so in 1974 a new Governor, Jay Hammond, suggested founding a permanent fund, both to prevent the royalties from being spent on public projects driven by interest groups, and to provide continuing benefit for Alaskan citizens once the oil ran out. The fund was established in 1976 and began to receive royalties in 1977, with the State Constitution requiring that at least one quarter of State oil revenues should be added to the fund's capital (Alaska Permanent Fund Corporation, 2021). In order to protect the fund from future political interference, Hammond's next move was to establish the Alaska Permanent Fund Dividend: the payment to every Alaskan permanent citizen of a proportion of the proceeds of the fund (Hammond, 1994). Unlike the Fund, which found favour across the political spectrum, the dividend proved more difficult to establish, and is not protected by a constitutional amendment (Rose and Wohlforth, 2008): its only protection is that it is received by every resident who has lived in Alaska for more than a year and intends to stay there. Initially the plan was that each citizen's annual dividend would be proportional to the length of time for which they had lived in Alaska, but a legal challenge resulted in equal annual payments for every eligible citizen (O'Brien and Olson, 1991). The dividend has been paid since 1982. In view of the pandemic, the 2020 dividend of $992 was paid in July rather than in the usual October, and at the end of the year the fund had a value of $72.3bn (Brehmer, 2020; Mathews, 2020).

As for the dividend's effects, research has shown that employment has increased slightly in non-tradable sectors (that is, in sectors in which inter-national trade does not occur), presumably because the universal grants have enabled people to increase their consumption of local goods and services. In tradable sectors (that is, in sectors subject to international trade) there has been a reduction in employment, and an increase in the proportion of part-time employment, presumably because the dividends have enabled some workers to reduce their employment hours. Overall there has been no effect on employment, presumably because the two trends have balanced each other out (Jones and Marinescu, 2018). The dividend has had an anti-inflationary effect (Goldsmith, 2012); and whereas in 1980 Alaska exhibited the highest inequality in the United States, by 2018 it was the state with both the lowest inequality and the lowest inequality growth (CNBC, 2018; Goldsmith, 2012: 53; Sommeiller et al., 2016).

Could the Alaska Permanent Fund model be transferable? That is, could other countries build sovereign wealth funds and pay dividends to their populations out of the profits? Yes, of course, given the political will (Lansley, 2016). Every country possesses resources from which the State could extract value in order to build a fund; and once the fund was large enough, the profits could fund an annual dividend, or even a small Basic Income (Widerquist, 2010a; Widerquist and Howard, 2012), although in years in which investment profits were low, additional funds would be required to maintain the value of a Basic Income. In Alaska, pressure on the public finances has sometimes meant the value of the dividend being reduced so that public services could be paid for: but the lesson that we can draw from Alaskan experience is that once a permanent fund and an annual distributed dividend have been implemented, public approval can be guaranteed. The Alaskan Permanent Fund and its dividend survived Sarah Palin as Governor of Alaska.

Is the Permanent Fund Dividend a Basic Income? It is paid on an individual basis, is not work-tested, and is not means-tested, and it is paid unconditionally to every Alaskan citizen who has lived in Alaska for more than a year and intends to stay there. However, it is an annual payment and not a regular weekly or monthly income, and the amount fluctuates from year to year, sometimes substantially (Alaska Department of Revenue, 2020). During occasional years in the future the dividend might not be paid at all (Kitchenman, 2019). So while the payments might satisfy normally stated summary definitions of Basic Income, they do not conform to at least two assumptions about a Basic Income: that the payment should be regular, either weekly or monthly; and that the payments should be of the same amount every week or every month (Zelleke, 2012: 150). But having said that, the Alaska Permanent Fund and its annual dividend are remarkable achievements. For forty years, the citizens of Alaska have been receiving an unconditional annual dividend, the effects of which have been entirely positive. There are now over fifty countries with sovereign wealth funds, but only Alaska's pays a dividend to citizens (Van Parijs and Vanderborght, 2017: 95). The others could clearly learn from Alaska's experience; and countries without sovereign wealth funds could learn both from Alaska's Permanent Fund and from the effects of its dividend.

CONCLUSION

During the 1960s and 1970s, the United States saw plenty of debate about Negative Income Tax and Minimum Income Guarantee, and occasionally about Basic Income: but perhaps that was the problem. Those who knew the difference between a Negative Income Tax and a Minimum Income Guarantee would have known what they were discussing, but there would have been many who would have been hazy about the difference, few would have understood that they only function in the same way if the means-tested benefit that operationalizes the Minimum Income Guarantee were to cease to be paid for all household types at the same time as income tax comes into payment, and perhaps even fewer would have understood the differences between Basic Income and both a Minimum Income Guarantee and a Negative Income Tax. And, as we have seen, there were plenty of experiments, and they eventually generated significantly positive results: but only eventually; and there were several examples of experiments decided upon and begun by one administration, and either cancelled or not evaluated by the next. The short-term concerns of politicians rarely fit well with the long time period required to plan and carry out experiments and pilot projects (Duverger, 2018: 130).

In 2017, a group of psychologists reviewed a variety of what they called 'Basic Income-oriented experiments', and concluded that

> Evidence from previous Basic Income-oriented experiments indicates the potential for UBI [Universal Basic Income] to increase all five psychological indicators of a healthy society: agency, security, connection, meaning and trust. The security and flexibility of a UBI is likely to give citizens a stronger sense of agency, greater personal mastery and more control over their lives, which evidence shows would lead to an increase in life satisfaction. The population could have more time to spend with friends, family and in their communities and would experience higher levels of social support as a result, which is incredibly important for well-being. People might gain a renewed sense of purpose and meaning through activities outside of currently constructed 'paid' employment, leading to a weakening of the current over-importance placed on paid work as part of the 'good life'. UBI is likely to lead to a general increase in social trust and a lessening of the shame, humiliation and devaluation that comes with relying on means-tested welfare benefits or being occupied in unpaid caring. In the light of all these positive social impacts of UBI, its introduction has the potential to be a hugely significant and beneficial public health intervention. (Psychologists for Social Change, 2017)

It is a pity that the results of Canada's Mincome experiments were not fully evaluated at the time; that the results of experiments in the USA were so misunderstood and misinterpreted by journalists and politicians; and that no other states, either in the US or Canada, followed Alaska's lead. As it was, by the end of the 1970s there was little debate about a Minimum Income Guarantee, a Basic Income or a Negative Income Tax, either in the USA or in Canada. Occasional publications emerged (Sheahen, 1983) to keep a modicum of debate going; and in Canada a commission tasked with studying the possibility of free trade with the United States and a more flexible economy suggested that the reforms should be accompanied by a 'Universal Income Security Program'. The commission studied both an income-tested benefit and 'a universal demogrant-based delivery system', with the income taxed back from wealthier families through the tax system, and it recommended the latter. A 'family unit' approach would have been taken to implementation, but apart from that the recommendation would have been for a Basic Income (Minister of Supply and Services, 1985: 794–5, 800). The Federal Government focused on the free trade recommendations of the report and ignored the Universal Income Security Programme proposal (Pasma and Mulvale, 2014: 8). The MacDonald Commission's report was a rare expression of interest in anything like Basic Income; and by the late 1980s the Basic Income debate had migrated back to Europe (Duverger, 2018: 90).

In 2000, the Canadian Prime Minister, Jean Chrétien, floated the idea of a Guaranteed Income, but soon dropped it when it came in for criticism (Pasma and Mulvale, 2014: 8). More recently, both Canada and the US have participated in the global interest in Basic Income. As we have seen, the brief Ontario experiment was not a Basic Income pilot project: but in the United States Andrew Yang, a candidate for the Democratic Party's presidential nomination, ran on an agenda dominated by a genuine Basic Income that he called a 'Freedom Dividend' (Stevens and Grullón Paz, 2020). As we shall see in Chapter 9, the USA is back in the Basic Income debate. Canada is still mainly talking about a Minimum Income Guarantee.

7. Basic Income, research and feasibility in Great Britain and Ireland

INTRODUCTION

As we have discovered in Chapters 2, 4 and 5, the United Kingdom was where the first and then the most significant subsequent steps were taken in the modern Basic Income debate. In Chapter 3 we have discussed activity in more diverse locations, and in Chapter 6 a somewhat different debate in Canada and the US. In this chapter we return to the UK, because for the final thirty years or so of the twentieth century this was again where many of the developments in the Basic Income debate occurred, and where issues and events occurred that were in various ways representative of the debate in other countries as well. By the end of the chapter we shall be straying into the new millennium. Because of the distinctive character of the Basic Income debate in Scotland, we shall be treating some of its aspects separately; and because of some similarities to the debate in the UK we shall also be discussing the Basic Income debate in the Republic of Ireland.

THE UK FROM BEVERIDGE TO THE 1980S

The Context

In order to understand some of the possible reasons for a brief upsurge of interest in Basic Income in the UK during the early 1980s, and continuing interest since then, a discussion of elements of the social and economic context is required, and also an understanding of some of the attempts that were made to solve problems that were afflicting the benefits system.

The period from the end of the Second World War to the early 1970s was one of fairly full employment in a variety of industries. The weekly wage or monthly salary provided a reasonable standard of living for most families, and the nationwide contributory National Insurance benefits and the means-tested National Assistance benefits established by legislation based on the Beveridge Report (Beveridge, 1942) were filling most income gaps, albeit in a highly labourist and male-oriented way (Sloman, 2019: 65). At the same time, free healthcare and education had reduced considerably the poverty that had existed before the Second World War. However, by the 1960s, National Insurance benefits were not keeping up with inflation, and increasing housing costs, which were paid with National Assistance benefits but not with National Insurance benefits, meant that increasing numbers of both elderly and working-age adults were receiving means-tested benefits. National Assistance was no longer the residual safety net that Beveridge had intended, and the UK found itself with a means-tested benefits system supplemented by short-term social insurance benefits rather than with a social insurance system supplemented by means-tested benefits. Instead of fostering social cohesion, as Beveridge had intended, the benefits system had become a source of division, stigma and poverty (Atkinson, 1969: 24; Bradshaw and Bennett, 2011; Sloman, 2019: 97–100, 103; Thane, 2011: 218).

The deindustrialization of the 1970s, due largely to global competition, began to look like Government policy by the 1980s as the Conservative Government declared war on the trades unions. No longer was the average single breadwinner wage sufficient to ensure that families did not fall into poverty: hence the implementation of rent rebates and in-work means-tested benefits during the 1970s. As Sloman concludes,

> The Conservative Governments of 1979–97 … presided over a significant shift away from the Beveridgean vision of contributory National Insurance towards a system of means-tested income support which complemented the neoliberal restructuring of the labour and housing markets. (Sloman, 2019: 174)

Even though a National Minimum Wage (now erroneously called a 'National Living Wage') was implemented in 1999 (Torry, 2016a: 209–14), the expansion of in-work means-tested benefits (first Family Income Supplement in 1971, renamed as Family Credit, then Tax Credits, and now Universal Credit) has enabled wages to fall in real terms without an eruption of public anger, has embedded a presupposition that income distribution is better regulated by cash transfers than by wage regulation (Sloman, 2019: 55), and has helped to 'stabilize, reproduce, and legitimize neoliberal capitalism' in both the UK and elsewhere (Sloman, 2019: 19, 56–7). The resulting 'redistributive market liberalism' (Sloman, 2019: 29) has turned the UK from a 'tax state' to a 'transfer state', and a consequence of this is that increasing numbers of people have found themselves both paying Income Tax and National Insurance Contributions and receiving in-work means-tested benefits, putting in question the previous clear division between taxpayers and benefits recipients (Sloman, 2019: 19–26, 149). This, along with turbulence in the employment market due to globalization and increasing automation, and the increasing conditionality and stigmatization of means-tested benefits, is the context that has given birth to attempts to simplify the UK's complex tax and benefits systems, and to solve its problems.

From the late 1950s onwards, occasional calls for a Negative Income Tax (NIT) were heard, in tune with similar proposals in the United States (see Chapter 6), although these became more muted once the administrative difficulties were recognized, and after a thorough examination of the proposal at the end of the 1960s the Government concluded that NIT was unworkable. The same conclusion was reached following a further thorough examination of the administration of NIT in 1970 (Sloman, 2019: 147–8); and when the Labour Government that took power in 1997 suggested that its new 'Tax Credits'—in fact a means-tested benefit for households in employment—should be paid via employers, employers' organizations' protests about the administrative burden that that would imply resulted in the plan being dropped (Sloman, 2019: 189–90). In spite of these attempts to distance the Government from means-testing, spirited attempts to control spending on means-tested benefits, and frequent problems with administration, particularly when benefits regulations changed (Sloman, 2019: 198), the chief tendency of the previous four hundred years—means-testing by Government—did not go away. Another continuing trend was the constant renaming of benefits, as National Assistance became Supplementary Benefit, Family Credit became Working Families Tax Credits, Working Families Tax Credits became Working Tax Credits and Child Tax Credits, and lots of means-tested benefits were then bundled together into Universal Credit, which is neither universal nor a credit (Sloman, 2019: 100–109, 114–17, 121, 124, 130, 152, 177–80; Torry, 2013: 17–21). Van Parijs and Vanderborght (2017: 163) call Universal Credit a 'household-based negative-income-tax scheme, restricted to those working or willing to work' (Van Parijs and Vanderborght, 2017: 163). There is a sense in which it is that, but the household-based nature of it, and the monthly payments based on real-time submissions from employers, have made the benefit's administration extremely complicated, and the means-tested and household-based nature of it make it stigmatizing and unreliable. It ought to be called the means-tested benefit that it is, and neither a Tax Credit nor a Negative Income Tax.

Proposals for Tax Credits

A proposal examined by a parliamentary committee in 1972
The problem with the term 'tax credit' is that it has been used to describe a variety of different mechanisms. In the United States, the Earned Income Tax Credit (EITC) is a payment made at the end of the tax year for anyone in employment, with the amount of the payment depending on the level of earned income, the level of a spouse's earned income, and the number of dependent children. Only those with dependent children would normally benefit finan-

cially from the EITC (Leff, 2019). In the United Kingdom, the last Labour Government implemented 'Working Tax Credits' and 'Child Tax Credits' for individuals in employment. The payments could be weekly or four-weekly, and, like the EITC, the amounts paid depended on household structure and household earned income. What is interesting about these uses of the term 'tax credit' is that the payments bear no direct relationship to the amounts of tax paid or to the system for collecting taxes (although the EITC is paid on the basis of an end of year tax return).

During the early 1970s, the UK Government seriously considered a scheme for genuine tax credits proposed by Sir Arthur Cockfield, a former Inland Revenue official who twenty years previously had prepared the Inland Revenue's critique of Juliet Rhys Williams' proposals: which is somewhat ironic as his plan for tax credits would in many ways have been similar to Rhys Williams', although it would have been administered rather differently (Sloman, 2019: 132). Instead of an Income Tax Personal Allowance (an amount of earned income on which tax is not paid), each individual in the Tax Credit scheme would have received a specified Tax Credit. This would have been paid in full if they had no other income, and would have been withdrawn at a specified rate as earned income rose. As earned income continued to rise, the Tax Credits would have been exhausted, and beyond that point Income Tax would have been collected.

> The tax credit system is a reform which embodies the socially valuable device of paying tax credits, to the extent that they are not used against tax due, positively as a benefit ... [so as to] bring together what people pay and what they receive ... Fewer people will be means-tested and others means-tested less often, and for the community there will be a large saving in administrative staff. (Her Majesty's Government, 1972: iii)

A Tax Credit is a simple concept, but the scheme proposed was rather complicated. The self-employed, anyone earning less than £8 per week, and married women, would have been excluded from receiving Tax Credits; and a married man would have received a larger Tax Credit than a single man. Anyone receiving a Tax Credit would have lost their Income Tax Personal Allowance, whereas anyone who did not receive a Tax Credit, including married women, would have retained theirs. A parliamentary committee insisted that married women should also receive Tax Credits, on the basis that if their earned incomes were below the Income Tax Personal Allowance then they would not have benefited from the full value of the Income Tax Personal Allowance, whereas they would have benefited from the full value of the Tax Credit. The parliamentary committee also recommended that the Child Tax Credits should be paid to the mother as cash payments at the Post Office, whereas the original proposal was for Child Tax Credits to be added to the father's Tax Credit. The effect of this latter recommendation was to increase the Family Allowance rather than to contribute to the Tax Credit scheme. This recommendation was an interesting recognition of the efficiency and effectiveness of unconditional incomes for children, and therefore of unconditional incomes more generally (Dilnot et al., 1984: 82–4; Her Majesty's Government, 1972: 5, 18; House of Commons Select Committee on Tax-Credit, 1973: 20–24; Sloman, 2019: 132–43).

A significant administrative difference between the Tax Credits scheme and the existing Income Tax system was that the latter had to be managed on a cumulative basis, because by the end of the tax year an employee had to have paid the correct amount of Income Tax in relation to their Income Tax Personal Allowance and the relevant Income Tax rates, whereas the Tax Credit scheme would have been managed on a weekly basis, with each week the Tax Credit added to wages, or Income Tax deducted from them, purely in relation to the single 30 per cent rate. Partly because it would have been essential for an employer to calculate accurately every week the amount of Tax Credit that would have been paid to each worker earning below the threshold, administration was clearly going to be complicated. Additional complications were that someone already earning below £8 per week would not have received a Tax Credit, whereas someone in the scheme whose income then fell below £8 per week would have remained in it (the aim being that eventually everyone would have been in the scheme); and if someone lost their job, then a Government department would have taken over payment of their Tax Credit, with administration then passing to the new employer when they found another job.

The chief difference between Basic Income and genuine Tax Credits is administrative, and that difference is significant: but because individuals in the Tax Credit scheme would have experienced the same relationship between earned income and disposable income as that delivered by a Basic Income, genuine Tax Credits are sometimes confused with Basic Income. In Chapter 6, we have discussed Negative Income Tax (NIT) proposals emanating from the United States, and the 'problems of administration' (Cohen and Friedman, 1972: 45; Friedman, [1962] 2002: 192) inevitably associated with any Negative Income Tax (Sloman, 2019: 130). We can now see that the Tax Credits proposal was simply a NIT differently described. A Negative Income Tax scheme specifies the rate at which the NIT is paid as earned income falls below a threshold, whereas a Tax Credit scheme specifies the amount of the Negative Income Tax that would be received when earned income was zero. With the Tax Credit amount, the threshold, and the rate of payment of the NIT all carefully chosen, a Tax Credit scheme and a Negative Income Tax can create precisely the same relationship between earned income and disposable income. Just as a Negative Income Tax would be fairer than an increasing Income Tax Personal Allowance because a rising allowance does not benefit anyone earning an income less than the allowance, whereas a rising NIT threshold benefits everyone, so a Tax Credit scheme is fairer than a rising Income Tax Personal Allowance because the rising allowance benefits only those with earned incomes greater than the allowance, whereas a rising Tax Credit benefits everyone (House of Commons Select Committee on Tax Credit, 1973: 3, 28). However, much can still depend on personal circumstances. When Tony Atkinson evaluated the UK's 1970s Tax Credit proposal, he discovered that the impact for an individual would depend 'critically on individual circumstances'—on such factors as whether they were receiving means-tested benefits, how high their working expenses were, and the ages of their children—whereas extending Family Allowance to the first child in every family would have made every family with children better off (Atkinson, 1973: 54–5). Whether Atkinson's rather wholesale criticism of the scheme might have been partly a result of Labour Party committee members' suspicion of it is an interesting question (Sloman, 2020).

The parliamentary committee split along party lines, with Labour Party members objecting that the tax credits could subsidize low wages, and that the scheme's requirement for a single tax rate would make progressive income taxation impossible (Sloman, 2019: 138), and the Conservative majority ensuring that the committee recommended acceptance of the scheme, largely because it would have improved employment incentives. Tax Credits would have been withdrawn at 30 per cent as earned income rose, and the same rate would have been used to deduct Income Tax once the Tax Credit had been exhausted. This would have achieved a linear relationship between earned income and disposable income, and would therefore have provided more employment incentive than the more steeply withdrawn means-tested Family Income Supplement that the Tax Credit scheme would have replaced. As the committee's report put it, the scheme seemed

> to offer the possibility of improving the amount of income retained from increased earnings … The effect of the scheme [was] to give the same treatment to the very large majority of the population, with scope for differential treatment by giving selective help to those in greatest need and levying differential taxation on the highest paid. (House of Commons Select Committee on Tax-Credit, 1973: 7)

The General Elections of 1974 delivered a Labour administration, which decided that the Tax Credits scheme was unaffordable, and preferred the means-tested Family Income Supplement to Tax Credits, but was happy to retain the proposal for unconditional incomes for every child payable to the mother. The new Labour Government was particularly pleased to have been able to retain the existing Income Tax system, because it allowed for differential tax rates across the earnings range, whereas the Tax Credits scheme would have required the same rate to apply to the majority of employees (Sloman, 2019: 140). A difference between NIT and Basic Income rather too little noticed is that for a Negative Income Tax scheme to be anything like administrable the NIT has to be paid out, and tax collected, on a weekly or monthly basis. Multiple tax rates become almost impossible to administer, which means that income tax related to higher tax rates has to be collected at the end of the tax year on the basis of a tax return; which in turn means that higher rates can only be applied to a limited number of households. A genuinely progressive income tax system therefore becomes impossible. A Basic Income would not pose the same problem, because unconditional incomes and the tax system would remain entirely separate, making a Basic Income and a progressive tax system entirely compatible.

It might be thought that it is a pity that the scheme did not happen. The Tax Credit scheme was designed to reduce poverty among working families, to offer greater incentives to seek additional earned income, and to be more efficient to administer than means-tested benefits. If the Conservative Party had won the General Election in 1974 then the UK might by now have found itself with some real Tax Credits. Additional lessons would have been learnt: for instance, that Government revenue foregone in the form of income tax personal allowances (that is, levels of income not taxed) ought to be counted in the national accounts in the same way as benefits paid out, because they can both have the same effect on individuals' and households' disposable incomes as well as on Government revenues (Torry, 2013: 29–31). However, the 'problems of administration' would have been significant, not only because any NIT scheme faces administrative challenges greater than those faced by the UK's 'Universal Credit', and both employers and the Government would have been involved in their administration, but also because the Tax Credits scheme envisaged was itself complicated both by exclusions and by different rates for people in different household circumstances. For the scheme not to have been implemented might have been a lucky escape.

A Liberal Party proposal

In 1979, Philip Vince developed for the Liberal Party a scheme of 'tax-free credits, some of them universal and some withdrawn as other income rises' (Vince, 1986: 5; see also Parker, 1989: 168–89); and in 1983, Richard Wainwright, a Liberal Party Member of Parliament, presented an uprated version of the scheme to a parliamentary committee (Creedy and Disney, 1985: 38–46, 198; Parker, 1989: 168–89; Vince, 1983; 2011). In 1988, the Liberal Party merged with the fairly new Social Democratic Party to become the Liberal Democratic Party, and for a while Basic Income was party policy (Vince, 1990), but then ceased to be in 1994 (Goodhart and Parker, 1994; Goodwin, 1994).

When Atkinson and Sutherland evaluated the 1983 proposal, they found that many families with children would have seen increases in their disposable incomes, and that many households would have experienced less of a poverty trap (that is, less of any additional earned income would have been withdrawn than was the case with existing means-tested benefits, so they would have been able to climb out of poverty more easily) (Atkinson and Sutherland, 1984: 11, 13); but they also discovered a problem: that the scheme would have imposed substantial losses on too many low-income households. As they put it, redistribution would have occurred among the working population (Atkinson and Sutherland, 1984: 10, 17). We shall find the same problem occurring with some Basic Income schemes, and particularly those schemes funded from within the current tax and benefits system and that abolish existing means-tested benefits. Such schemes inevitably impose significant losses on large numbers of low-income households (Torry, 2013: 31–2).

From Family Allowance to Child Benefit

Just for once, a name change was not just that. Child Benefit really was an improvement on Family Allowance. By the mid-1960s, the real value of Family Allowance, an unconditional income for the second and subsequent children in every family, had been allowed to fall; Child Tax Allowances were benefiting those with earned incomes above the Income Tax Personal Allowance, and particularly individuals paying higher rate Income Tax; research had shown that poverty remained a serious problem, particularly among families with children; and in 1966 the film *Cathy Come Home* had shown how easy it was for a family with children to slip into destitution (Abel-Smith and Townsend, 1966; Atkinson, 1969: 24; Banting, 1979: 66, 95; Barr and Coulter, 1991: 279–80; Titmuss, 1962; Townsend, 1979: 151). The new Child Poverty Action Group (CPAG) had begun by arguing for a Negative Income Tax, but was soon asking that Family Allowance should be paid for every child, that its value should be increased, and that the cost of these changes should be paid for by abolishing the Child Tax Allowance; and when the Labour Party returned to Government in 1974, legislation was passed to turn Family Allowance into Child Benefit for every child (Atkinson, 1969: 141; 2011: 83; Hill, 1990: 41; Sloman, 2019: 111–12). However, by 1976 there was no sign of Child Benefit being implemented, and in May of that year the Government's decision to postpone implementation by three years was reported to Parliament. Frank Field, Director of CPAG, published an article based on leaked cabinet minutes that revealed the Prime Minister's and Chancellor's anxiety that to pay Child Benefit and abolish the Child Tax Allowance would reduce male disposable incomes and lead to wage inflation, and that it would look as if public expenditure had increased even though the Government's fiscal position would not have changed. The leaked minutes also revealed the way in which the Prime Minister and Chancellor had manoeuvred the cabinet into agreeing with them (Field, 1982). The fact that to pay a Basic Income, even if it were to be paid for by reducing the Income Tax Personal Allowance, would make it look as if public expenditure had risen when it had not, remains a problem for the Basic Income debate in the UK and in other countries in which turning tax allowances into cash payments would be the obvious method for funding a Basic Income. This is a problem that will only be solved when revenue foregone through tax allowances is treated in the same way as expenditure on benefits in the national accounts (Spicker, 2011: 118; Torry, 2013: 24–5; Walley, 1986). The important connection between Child Benefit and Basic Income, though, is the fact that Child Benefit was and remains an unconditional income for every child: not at the same amount for every child, because more is paid for the first child in a family than for subsequent children, but apart from that minor difference, the income is unconditional. In 2010, the new Conservative Government said that it wished to withdraw Child Benefit from households containing higher-rate taxpayers. Having discovered that it could not do that because there was no database that connects Child Benefit recipients with higher rate taxpayers, an additional tax charge was imposed on higher rate taxpayers living in households in receipt of Child Benefit, which has had the unfortunate effect of mothers in high-earning households withdrawing their Child Benefit claims in order to avoid themselves or their partners having to pay the tax charge. The UK is now in the rather strange position of paying an unconditional income for children and at the same time collecting a tax on children (Torry, 2018a: 19–20).

Campaigns During the 1970s

During the 1960s and 1970s, an important element of the Basic Income debate in the UK was provided by the claimants' unions that emerged to assert their rights to benefits payments and to campaign for improvements to the system: and as Bill Jordan points out, the claimants' movement was very different from the still fairly new Child Poverty Action Group (CPAG). CPAG was a predominantly middle class and highly structured exercise, and the emerging claimants' unions were working class in origin and participative in character, with no regular roles or permanent officers at either local or national level. Although the terminology was often that of 'Guaranteed Minimum Incomes', this was generally interpreted to mean Basic Incomes, and the charter adopted by the National Federation of Claimants Unions in 1970 demanded 'the right to adequate income without means test for all' (Jordan, 1988: 259). Jordan suggests that the reason for claimants' unions taking off in the UK, in ways that they did not in other European countries, is that in the UK social insurance benefits were of lower value and of shorter duration than in many other countries, so more workers found themselves on means-tested and therefore stigmatizing benefits than was the case elsewhere. A further reason for the growth of the movement in the UK was that the social assistance system is a national one rather than being locally administered, as it is in many other European countries, so a national federation of claimants' unions made sense, as did a demand for a change in the system. Jordan offers evidence of a highly active claimants' union membership involved in advocacy, advice, campaigning and a wide variety of work of various kinds, thus supporting his contention that people without paid employment could be 'busy, active and purposeful, and more cheerfully creative than many workers who were tied to routine jobs' (Jordan, 1988: 263). Already automation was reducing the number of secure and well-paid jobs and giving rise to more temporary and part-time employment; and it is this trend, as well as the intrusive and degrading character of means-tested benefits, that gave rise to claimants' unions' demands for a Basic Income (Jordan, 1988).

A factor related to the feminist aspects of the subsequent Basic Income debate in the UK was the 'wages for housework' campaign. Feminists disagreed over 'wages for housework', some believing that the idea gave in to a gendered division of labour; and feminists were equally split over Basic Income, with some arguing for it, and others objecting to it on the grounds that it might detract from the fight for equal rights and pay in the workplace, and particularly in the professions (Miller et al., 2019: 138–42).

From the 1970s onwards, forerunners of the Green Party, and then the Green Party itself, have argued for a Basic Income on the basis that it would maintain incomes during a transition to a more sustainable economy (Lord, 1993); and academics and others concerned about the prospect of higher unemployment have argued for Basic Income on the basis that it would stimulate new jobs because employers would no longer have to pay the whole of subsistence incomes (which of course they were not doing anyway as individuals on low pay were already receiving in-work means-tested benefits). Loud voices were already being heard objecting to Basic Income on the basis that it would compromise the work ethic (Sloman, 2019: 154–9).

Brandon Rhys Williams' Basic Income Proposal

In Chapter 5, we discussed Juliet Rhys Williams' proposal for something very close to a Basic Income. Her son, Sir Brandon Rhys Williams, was a member of the Conservative Party rather than a Liberal, but he shared his mother's enthusiasm for reforming the tax and benefits system. In 1967, he wrote a booklet proposing a 'universal flat-rate allowance' that would provide a 'minimum income for everybody', but with additions for 'the disabled, pensioners, widows and other people in any number of special categories' (Rhys Williams, 1967: 7); he was elected to Parliament to represent South Kensington in a by-election in 1968; and from then on he attempted to interest his parliamentary colleagues in his mother's scheme (Sloman, 2019: 117). In 1972, he had printed a lecture that he had given on the same subject in 1971; in March 1973, he was a witness during the select committee hearings on the 1972 Tax Credit proposal (House of Commons Select Committee on Tax-Credit, 1973: 65); and in 1982, he recommended a 'Basic Income Guarantee' to another select committee. In this context, 'Basic Income Guarantee' meant that every individual would be guaranteed to receive an unconditional income, and so meant 'Basic Income', as did the term 'minimum income guarantee' in the 1967 publication. This was before 'guarantee' was usually employed to mean a guaranteed income level that would be attained by implementing a means-tested benefit, so its use was not ambiguous. As Brandon Rhys Williams put it: 'Every British Citizen should be awarded a personal allowance of a value related to personal status, not to resources'; and as Hermione Parker's synopsis of the scheme explained: 'Every citizen would be entitled to a personal basic income or PBI. These guaranteed basic incomes would replace virtually all existing benefits and allowances' (House of Commons Treasury and Civil Service Committee Sub-Committee, 1982: 423, 425; see also Parker, 1982; 1989: 224–53; 1995). This is how the committee's final discussion with Brandon Rhys Williams concluded:

Chairman
942. There seem to me to be many benefits of this system.
   There are.

943. Clearly you are expressing them very eloquently. Clearly they would go a long way toward easing the unemployment and poverty traps.
   There would not be any unemployment under these schemes. You would not need to register as unemployed. There would be people who were not in full-time work but they would not need to have themselves labelled as unemployed. If they got an opportunity of work or casual work they could take it and nobody would have to know.

944. Are you saying that the unemployment benefit trap would be virtually eradicated by this?
   Certainly.

945. Also it would be administratively much simpler.
   Yes, it would.

946. I wonder what degree of redistribution of resources there would be or is that one of the matters that could be flexible within the system?
   This is optional. This is why I have not put figures in my paper because you could make the scheme do what you liked. If you want to help people on low wages or low

incomes you can tilt the tax and benefit structure in such a way that it is redistributive in certain directions.

Chairman: May I say that you will observe that owing to pressure of other engagements we have lost our third member and are now therefore non quorate. Thank you very much. (House of Commons Treasury and Civil Service Committee Sub-Committee, 1982: 459)

While the committee did not come to any agreement as to the best way forwards for the tax and benefits system, it recommended that Basic Income should be regarded as a serious option for reform, that more work should be done, and that 'the Government should put such work in hand. ... Meanwhile, it is desirable that changes to the present system should be compatible with an eventual move to an integrated structure of tax and social security' (House of Commons Treasury and Civil Service Committee, 1983). A General Election ensued and nothing was done about the sub-committee's recommendation: but the exercise had given rise to a certain amount of research and discussion related to Basic Income, and there was now a sufficiently large group of people engaged with the issue to enable some more long-term and co-ordinated activity to begin (Sloman, 2019: 165; Torry, 2013: 32–6).

The Basic Income Research Group

Inspired by Brandon Rhys Williams' submission of a proposal for a Basic Income to a parliamentary committee in 1982, and the announcement of a Government review of social security benefits (which eventually gave birth to a report that left the UK's benefits structure unchanged), in 1984 a group of individuals met at the offices of the UK's National Council for Voluntary Organisations (NCVO) in Bedford Square in London to form the Basic Income Research Group (BIRG). This was the first organization with a sole focus on Basic Income since the State Bonus League more than sixty years earlier. A further significant aspect of the event was the name chosen. An unconditional income for every individual was called a 'State Bonus' during the early years of the twentieth century, and then until the early 1980s a 'social dividend', particularly in the writings of James Meade. It would appear to have been Brandon Rhys Williams and Hermione Parker who first employed the name 'Basic Income Guarantee', Parker who then dropped the 'Guarantee', and the Basic Income Research Group that institutionalized the term 'Basic Income'. The 'Basic Income' terminology was then firmly embedded in the movement by the Europe-wide organization established at a conference in Louvain-la-Neuve in Belgium in 1986 calling itself the Basic Income European Network (BIEN). 'Basisinkomen' was already in circulation in the Netherlands, 'Grundeinkommen' in Germany and 'revenu de base'

in France, so to follow the Basic Income Research Group's employment of
'Basic Income' terminology might have seemed the obvious choice both for
the name of an unconditional income and for the name of the Europe-wide
organization, an additional factor no doubt being the nice acronym that 'Basic
Income European Network' would generate (Hall, 1988: 309–10; Van Trier,
2002: 3–5).

The NCVO had received a grant to enable it to establish a research project
on Basic Income, and this enabled the group to publish the *BIRG Bulletin*: initially two cheaply printed single-page editions, and then a third well-designed
and expensively printed edition in the spring of 1985. What began as a loose
association of individuals with ideological commitments right across the
political spectrum, and as an organization initially intended to last only two
years in order to prepare a report for a report-back conference (Hall, 1988:
309), slowly developed a structure, with Hermione Parker (the *Bulletin*'s
editor) and Bill Jordan (a Reader in Social Studies at Exeter University) as
'joint chairmen', and Peter Ashby, an NCVO staff member who had already
written a booklet for the NCVO about Basic Income (Ashby, 1984), providing
administrative support. The NCVO's financial support ended in 1987; Tony
Walter was elected Chair; in 1988 the administrative base migrated to the
home of the then secretary (this author), who became the Trust's Director in
a voluntary capacity; and from 1988 to 1992 BIRG relied on small charitable
grants and individual subscriptions and donations to enable it to employ
part-time administrative staff, to continue to publish the *BIRG Bulletin* and
other publications, and to hold occasional conferences. Most of these were
one-day events, usually at Toynbee Hall in London: an appropriate venue as
William Beveridge had been sub-warden there from 1903 to 1905 (Briggs and
Macartney, 1984: 61–70; Harris, 1977: 39–63). BIRG occasionally persuaded
high-profile speakers to speak at its conferences: in 1991, Paddy Ashdown
MP, Leader of the Liberal Party, who in 1989 had recommended a Basic
Income in his book *Citizen's Britain* (Ashdown, 1989); and Michael Meacher
MP, a member of the Shadow Cabinet. In 1992, a 24-hour event was held at
St George's House, Windsor, attended by both Government and opposition
ministers and by trade union leaders. Working groups were held on particular
issues, both short-term ones—for instance, on how Basic Incomes would be
paid to individuals—and longer-term enquiries, such as the working group
on Basic Income and employment, to which Ken Mayhew of the National
Economic Development Office contributed, and that published a substantial
report (Parker, 1991). Seminars were held, mainly at the London School of
Economics. Mimi Parker, along with Holly Sutherland, then a research assistant working with Professor Tony Atkinson, continued to research illustrative
Basic Income schemes, which Parker published in the *BIRG Bulletin* (Basic
Income Research Group minutes and reports; Sloman, 2019: 232); in 1988,

Atkinson and Sutherland published an analysis of a Basic Income scheme that turned the Income Tax Personal Allowance into a Basic Income and retained and recalculated all other benefits (Atkinson, 1995; Atkinson and Sutherland, 1988); and the same year Parker explained a similar scheme at the second BIEN conference in Antwerp (Parker, 1990). As research progressed during this period, it became even clearer that only this kind of scheme was ever going to be financially feasible in the short to medium term: that is, that it would not be feasible to establish a Basic Income scheme for the UK that would at the same time enable means-tested benefits to be abolished, tax rates to rise by a feasible amount and poor households not to be made poorer (Torry, 2014a; 2019a). Early editions of the *Bulletin* described a Basic Income as an unconditional income 'sufficient to meet basic living costs'. By 1988, the question of political as well as financial feasibility was taking a central role in the debate (Purdy, 1990), and 'sufficient to meet basic living costs' was dropped.

In 1989, BIRG registered as a charity, and in 1992, Geoffrey Hubbard, a trustee of the Joseph Rowntree Charitable Trust, persuaded his fellow trustees to make grants of £50,000 per annum for a period of three years on condition that an unconditional income would be called a 'Citizen's Income' rather than a 'Basic Income'. BIRG's trustees agreed; this author resigned from the voluntary post of Director so that a new paid Director could be appointed; and the Trust, which became the Citizen's Income Trust (CIT), moved its administrative base to a hired office at the London School of Economics. Richard Clements, who had been editor of the left-wing journal *Tribune*, and had been advisor and office manager to Michael Foot and Neil Kinnock while they were leaders of the Labour Party, was looking for a new job because the Labour Party had lost the 1992 General Election and Neil Kinnock had resigned as Labour Party leader. CIT's trustees were pleased to be able to appoint Clements as Director of the Trust in April 1993, and he did useful work during the following three years, using his networks to persuade journalists and policymakers to begin to take the idea of unconditional incomes seriously. Sadly, his wife became ill, and then he did, so he retired in 1996, which was earlier than expected. The Joseph Rowntree Charitable Trust's grant was extended twice, enabling two further paid Directors to be appointed; and an additional grant was agreed for a research project on the dynamics of tax and benefit reform and on opportunities for Basic Income (Jordan et al., 2000): but in 2000 the grants came to an end, the Director resigned, and the trustees asked this author to return as Director in a voluntary capacity. He agreed to do so. The Chair, Evelyn McEwen, was dying of cancer, and so resigned, and Anne Miller was elected in her place (Basic Income Research Group, 1986a; 1986–93; Citizen's Income Trust, 1993–2001; Sloman, 2019: 148, 227–8; Torry, 2020c: 187).

The late 1980s and early 1990s were a period of increasing interest in Basic Income among policymakers and academics, an interesting stimulus to the debate during the late 1980s being the Archbishop of Canterbury's Commission on Urban Priority Areas' positive assessment of Basic Income in 1985 (Archbishop of Canterbury's Commission on Urban Priority Areas, 1985: 224; Hall, 1988: 310); but by the mid-1990s this interest had dissipated. Sloman suggests that anxieties about the cost, and a concern that a Basic Income would compromise the work ethic, were major reasons (Esam and Berthoud, 1991: 60, 68; Sloman, 2019: 234): hence an increasing interest in the idea of Participation Income (on which, see below), which might itself have been an additional reason for the mid-1990s dissipation of interest in Basic Income. And then economic growth and 'welfare to work' achieved increasing employment levels during the later 1990s and early 2000s, and although an increasing number of jobs were less secure than before, the reduction in the unemployment rate largely removed unemployment levels as an argument for Basic Income (Sloman, 2019: 235).

Since 2001, the Citizen's Income Trust (renamed the Citizen's Basic Income Trust in 2017) has published a website (which was completely rede-signed during 2015), maintained a library, published numerous articles both on its website and in the quarterly *Citizen's Income Newsletter*, published a monthly email update, convened small expert study groups to prepare reports on particular issues related to Basic Income (for instance, on implications for housing costs, on who should receive a Basic Income, and to prepare draft legislation), and organized occasional larger events. The largest recent events were a day conference organized with the British Library in 2014, and a day conference in 2018 organized in collaboration with a variety of London School of Economics (LSE) departments and other organizations during which, for the first time as far as we could tell, representatives of all of the major recent, current and planned Basic Income pilot projects and similar experiments were together in the same room. The day culminated with a sold-out debate between Philippe Van Parijs and the Oxford academic John Kay, an opponent of Basic Income (Torry, 2020c: 189–95). In many ways this event was the culmination of a relationship between the LSE and the Basic Income debate that had been significantly assisted during the 1990s by Professor Tony Atkinson and Holly Sutherland, and more recently by Hartley Dean, Professor of Social Policy.

Whenever possible, evidence has been submitted to parliamentary enquir-ies. In 2007 the Citizen's Income Trust submitted to a parliamentary commit-tee's enquiry into benefits simplification a fully costed Basic Income scheme that would have been funded from within the current tax and benefits system (House of Commons Work and Pensions Committee, 2007: Ev. 84–90). Unfortunately, the committee called no witnesses from the Trust. Donald Hirsch, representing the Joseph Rowntree Foundation, was called as a witness, and informed the committee that the Trust's scheme would have increased the basic rate of Income Tax to 46 per cent (House of Commons Work and Pensions Committee, 2007: Ev. 14). The Trust's written evidence had stated that a total income tax rate of 33 per cent would be required (22 per cent Income Tax and 11 per cent National Insurance Contribution). Members of the committee appear not to have read the Trust's evidence, as none of them questioned Hirsch's statement. As we shall see, there has been something of a history of selective employment of evidence during parliamentary discussion of Basic Income.

At the time of writing, this author has recently retired as Director after being first the Trust's secretary and then its Director for a total of twenty-five years, and the trustees are considering how the Trust might best serve the UK's Basic Income debate in a context in which an increasing number of organizations are now working on Basic Income, and in which the debate is becoming livelier by the day.

Schemes with Some Similarities to Basic Income

Participation Income
In 1992, Professor Tony Atkinson assisted the Citizen's Income Trust to move into offices at the London School of Economics, and invited the Director to attend a lecture titled 'Towards a European social safety net' that he was to give at the Annual General Meeting of the Institute for Fiscal Studies. The context was the Maastricht Treaty that established the European Community's Common Internal Market, and the decision of the UK Government not to sign up to the Social Charter attached to the treaty. During the lecture, Atkinson suggested that 'in considering the form of social protection, we should perhaps look wider than at income-tested social assistance. Although it is the latter which is apparently envisaged in the Social Charter, it is not obvious that the Elizabethan Poor Law provides the best model for Europe of the next century' (Atkinson, 1992: 52); and during the discussion following the lecture he suggested that while Basic Income would fulfil the requirements for a European social safety net, he did not believe that it would be politically acceptable (Atkinson, 1993; 1996: 67). He suggested instead a 'Participation Income' that would require every individual to be 'participating' in society in some way, unless prevented from doing so, before they could receive the otherwise unconditional income. Anyone who was employed, self-employed, retired, caring for children, caring for the elderly, caring for disabled dependents, absent from work because of sickness or injury, unable to work because of disability, unemployed but available for work, studying or training on approved courses, or undertaking approved voluntary work, would have received the Participation Income (Atkinson, 1993: 10; 1996: 69).

During the intervening thirty years the Participation Income proposal has been recognized as a useful way to satisfy a social reciprocity norm, because it requires the individual to contribute to society's resources before they receive from them, rather than the receipt of resources inviting reciprocation, as with a Basic Income (White, 2003: 170–75). Atkinson's view was that a Participation Income could be a useful step towards a Basic Income (Fitzpatrick, 1999: 101, 111–22); and in 1994, the Labour Party's Commission on Social Justice report *Social Justice: Strategies for National Renewal* suggested that it

> would be unwise ... to rule out a move towards Citizen's Income [Basic Income] in future: if it turns out to be the case that earnings simply cannot provide a stable income for a growing proportion of people, then the notion of some guaranteed income, outside the labour market, could become increasingly attractive. (Commission on Social Justice, 1994: 264)

The report proposed that a Participation Income should be considered, and concluded that National Insurance should remain at the heart of benefits policy and that the difficulties of moving from unemployment into employment resulting from the rigidities of the benefits system should be addressed (Clinton et al., 1994: 42; Sloman, 2019: 184–5).

However politically feasible a Participation Income might at first appear, scholars with some understanding of administrative realities have recognized the near impossibility of administering it, the bureaucratic intrusion that would be required in order to test for adherence to the participation conditions, and the 'creative compliance' that would be generated to enable individuals to meet the 'approved voluntary work' condition (De Wispelaere and Stirton, 2008: 4, 6). Research undertaken by this author (Torry, 1996), and subsequently updated (Torry, 2016a: 134–9), has shown that approximately 1 per cent of the adult population of the UK would not fulfil the participation conditions, raising the obvious question as to whether it would ever be feasible for a Government to commit to such a large, expensive, and intrusive administrative burden in order to prevent such a small number of individuals from receiving an otherwise unconditional income. If a Participation Income were ever to be implemented, then either the participation conditions would soon be dropped, or the administrative process would be so unpopular that Basic Income and anything like it would be off the agenda for a very long time. Rather proving the first possibility, in 1988 France implemented a 'Revenu Minimum d'Insertion' (RMI): an income-tested income conditional on the signing of an individualized 'insertion' contract that committed the individual to activities that would enable them to be 'inserted' into mainstream society, with an aim of insertion into paid employment. A subsequent history of failure to monitor insertion contracts damaged the project's credibility (Euzéby, 1994; Whitton, 1993: 13–14) and led to its replacement in 2009 by the 'Revenu de Solidarité Active': similar, but without the individualized insertion contracts.

In 1994, Hermione Parker suggested that provisions intended as steps along the way to a Basic Income, such as a Participation Income, might be less than helpful because 'a major public education exercise is necessary before voters are likely to adjust their value systems to the problems of post-industrial societies. Fudging the issues could delay this process' (Parker, 1994: 9): but Atkinson continued to promote his Participation Income, and in his last book, *Inequality*, he was still arguing for the proposal. The chapter section on the subject contained what purported to be a graphical representation of the results of a simulation of the effects of a Participation Income scheme on disposable incomes (Atkinson, 2015: 297; Citizen's Income Trust, 2015). However, the EUROMOD microsimulation programme employed to obtain the results cannot simulate Atkinson's participation conditions, so what was in fact published were the results of a simulation of a Basic Income scheme. The fact that it would not be possible to represent the participation conditions in the computer programme is of course an indication that administration of the conditions would be labour intensive and intrusive.

The Single-Tier State Pension
A Citizen's Pension is a pension paid unconditionally to every resident of a country. No contributions have to be paid during a working life in order to receive it, and it is not means-tested. If it is high enough then it can take elderly households off means-tested benefits. New Zealand has had such a pension for eighty years (O'Connell, 2004).

In 2011, the UK's Department for Work and Pensions published a consultation paper about the future of state provision of pensions. One of the options on offer was a Single-Tier State Pension, designed to replace the previous mixture of state provision that comprised a Basic State Pension based on the number of National Insurance Contributions made; an earnings-related element; and a means-tested element if the household does not have enough to live on (Department for Work and Pensions, 2011). The Single-Tier State Pension—named the 'New State Pension' when it was implemented in 2016—is not a Citizen's Pension, but it would have been one if it had replaced the National Insurance Contributions condition with a residency condition.

The scheme's architect was Steven Webb, a Liberal Democrat Member of Parliament and Pensions Minister in the coalition Government that governed the UK from 2010 to 2015, and it is not insignificant that in 1990 Webb had co-authored a book on a social security reform option that would have been a Basic Income if it had been individual-based rather than household-based (Brittan and Webb, 1990), and that the Liberal Party, which had merged with the Social Democrats in 1988 to form the Liberal Democrats, had a history of advocating unconditional or near-unconditional benefits, from Juliet Rhys Williams' scheme, through Beveridge's unconditional Family Allowance, to party leader Paddy Ashdown's advocacy for Basic Income in 1989 (Ashdown, 1989: 80–84).

The reason given for implementing the Singe-Tier State Pension was that a report had shown that a large and increasing number of elderly households were eligible for the means-tested pension; that for those households saving for a pension was of less value than for other households; and that the means-tested pension therefore imposed a disincentive to save for retirement, and left people uncertain as to how much they would have to live on after retirement age (Salter, 1997; Salter et al., 2009). The Single-Tier State Pension is designed to be of greater value to someone with a full contribution record than was the combination of the old Basic State Pension and the means-tested Pension Credit: so for households on the new pension, the New State Pension makes means-testing redundant, apart from the means-testing of the Housing Benefit that many pensioners still need (Salter, 1997). As the Institute of Actuaries pointed out, to turn the New State Pension into a Citizen's Pension would have cost just one third of the tax relief granted to those paying contributions towards private pensions (Salter et al., 2009: 178); would have given to individuals a degree of certainty as to how much money they would have to live on during retirement; would have taken no account of savings, and so would not have penalized saving; and would have created a pensions system that would have gone a long way towards equalizing women's and men's pension incomes (Basic Income Research Group, 1986b; Creedy, 1998; Ginn, 1996; Salter, 1997).

Steven Webb would have connected receipt of the Single-Tier State Pension to everyone's National Insurance Contributions records to ensure the acceptability of the plan to the majority of voters who see reciprocity as the State demanding some kind of service before the payments could be released (Torry, 2013: 38–42).

Steps along the way? Universal Credit

While still in opposition, Iain Duncan Smith, Shadow Work and Pensions Secretary and a former Leader of the Conservative Party, established a Centre for Social Justice. Duncan Smith had recognized the difficulty caused by different means-tested benefits, with different regulations, being available for individuals employed for less than sixteen hours per week and for more than sixteen hours per week. The transitions between the benefits caused by changes in employment hours meant administrative complexity for both claimants and Government departments: the Department for Work and Pensions (which administered Job Seeker's Allowance: available to households in which nobody was employed for more than sixteen hours per week), and Her Majesty's Revenue and Customs (which administered so-called 'Tax Credits' for households with someone employed for more than sixteen hours per week), and could result in a significant disincentive to seek additional paid employment. The Centre for Social Justice published a report, *Dynamic Benefits* (Centre for Social Justice, 2009), that recommended that several different means-tested benefits should become one single means-tested benefit, and when in 2010 a Conservative and Liberal Democratic coalition formed a new Government, legislation was passed to implement 'Universal Credit'. Although the aim was benefit simplification, roll-out has been slow; the taper rate was raised from 55 per cent to 63 per cent, and work allowances reduced, thus reducing employment incentives; and some of the aspects of the new benefit have caused substantial problems, such as the often severe sanctions relating to employment market conditionalities, a long waiting period between claiming the benefit and receiving the first payment, no payments for third and subsequent children in a family making a new claim, and benefit restrictions if a household in rented accommodation is deemed to have too many bedrooms. At each stage of the evolution of Universal Credit the Citizen's Basic Income Trust has contributed evidence to enquiries, always arguing for the advantages of a Basic Income, and always recognizing that, in principle, Universal Credit might be regarded as a useful step towards an income maintenance system based on Basic Income. Increasing difficulties with Universal Credit have caused that view to have become rather more muted over time (Citizen's Income Trust, 2010; Citizen's Basic Income Trust, 2020; Sloman, 2019: 213–16).

How should we regard aspects of current benefits systems that bear similarities to Basic Income, or that look as if they might be steps along the way towards one? We can conclude from the evidence offered here that a case by case approach should be taken. If an aspect of the current system, or a policy proposal, could in some definable way be seen as a step towards a social security system based on Basic Income, then that should be stated, unless the current aspect or the policy proposal either causes difficulties, or could cause difficulties, that would mean reputational damage for Basic Income.

Research and Education

Research on the financial feasibility of Basic Income, and a research-based educational approach, had been significant aspects of the debate in the UK since Dennis and Mabel Milner offered detailed calculations on the net cost of their State Bonus scheme, and also 'typical household' calculations: that is, calculations of the effects of the scheme on particular household types (Milner and Milner, 1918: 7, 11; Van Trier, 2018a: 1–5, 10). The Basic Income scheme presented to a parliamentary committee by Brandon Rhys Williams was accompanied by similar calculations by his research assistant, Hermione (Mimi) Parker (House of Commons Treasury and Civil Service Committee Sub-Committee, 1982: 459; House of Commons Treasury and Civil Service Committee, 1983; Parker, 1989: 100; Torry, 2020c: 188). Throughout the period, the Basic Income Research Group's publications were in a firmly educational rather than campaigning mode, as were a number of books and other publications (Brittan and Webb, 1990; Fitzpatrick, 1999; Parker, 1989; 1995; Parker and Sutherland, no date; Walter, 1985; 1989). Net cost and typical household calculations were often included both in books (Brittan and Webb, 1990; Parker, 1989; Parker and Sutherland, no date) and in articles (Parker 1988; 1994; Parker and Dilnot, 1988; Parker and Sutherland, 1988); and by the time Parker wrote *Instead of the Dole* (1989: 166–7, 398–400), an early microsimulation programme, TAXMOD (see Chapter 10), was available, so the extent of household disposable income gains and losses could be calculated for the whole of the UK's population: a method and results increasingly important as the debate turned decisively towards questions of feasibility during the twenty-first century.

THE UK DURING THE TWENTY-FIRST CENTURY

During the first few years of the twenty-first century, the Basic Income debate in the UK remained of much the same character as during the previous century: occasional interest from parliamentary committees (House of Commons Work and Pensions Committee, 2007; Work and Pensions Committee, 2017), but little academic, media or public debate. The Basic Income Research Group (which in 1992 had become the Citizen's Income Trust, and then in 2017 the Citizen's Basic Income Trust) continued to maintain a website, and to publish the *Citizen's Income Newsletter* three or four times a year, along with occasional booklets and pamphlets.

And then in 2014 things began to change. Attributing causality is always difficult, but the pilot projects in Namibia and India might have been factors, and publicity around both the Swiss referendum and the Finland experiment certainly was. (See below on the influence exerted by the Finland experiment on the UK debate.) One specifically UK factor was the first article explicitly about Basic Income in the mainstream press. In 2013, the Policy Press had published this author's *Money for Everyone* (Torry, 2013): the first general introduction to Basic Income to have appeared in English since Hermione Parker's *Instead of the Dole* and Tony Walter's *Basic Income* in 1989 (Parker, 1989; Walter, 1989). A trustee of the Citizen's Income Trust knew the journalist Larry Elliott, and arranged a meeting with him. Elliott read the book, and in August 2014 wrote an article about Basic Income in *The Guardian* (Elliott, 2014).

Think tanks began to take an interest: first of all the Royal Society of Arts (Painter and Thoung, 2015); then the more libertarian Adam Smith Institute with a report mainly about Negative Income Tax (Story, 2015); and then the more left-wing Compass (Reed and Lansley, 2016; Lansley and Reed, 2019).

Throughout this period, the Citizen's Basic Income Trust maintained its research-based educational approach, a stance assisted by the birth of the more campaigning Basic Income UK, originally established in 2013 to collect UK signatures for the European Citizens' Initiative (European Commission, 2014; see also Chapter 8). The two organizations have worked well together, a process assisted by the Chair of Basic Income UK being also a trustee of the Citizen's Basic Income Trust. A more recent ingredient is the expanding network of 'UBI labs' in which partnerships between local authorities, university departments and other organizations have proposed Basic Income schemes and pilot projects and encouraged local authorities to pass resolutions accordingly. At the time of writing, fourteen such resolutions had been passed. The movement started in Sheffield and has now formalized itself as the 'UBI Lab Network' (UBI Lab Network, 2020), and, like much else in the Basic Income debate, it has begun to globalize. There are now UBI Labs in Jakarta and Bucharest. A complex network of organizations is emerging: the UBI Labs Network is affiliated to Basic Income UK; Basic Income UK is affiliated to UBI Europe; and UBI Europe is affiliated to BIEN: the Basic Income Earth Network. In the UK, Basic Income UK fulfils something of a co-ordinating role by bringing together the different groups to ensure co-operation over strategy and action (Jacobson, 2021).

The most recent organizational initiative in the UK occurred in 2019 when, with the assistance of the Citizen's Basic Income Trust, the left-leaning think tank Compass established the Basic Income Conversation. Sufficient money was raised to appoint two paid staff members with a brief to employ community organizing methods to encourage discussion of Basic Income among policymakers and the general public (Basic Income Conversation, 2021). The Basic Income debate was beginning to receive the resources that it deserved.

RESEARCH METHODS

Throughout the period under review, the UK Basic Income debate continued to be characterized by financial feasibility research, the extent and quality of which remained unique in the global debate. In order to understand some significant incidents in the UK Basic Income debate, the different financial feasibility research methods that have been used during the period must first be explained.

Initially, only two methods were available for researching the financial feasibility of proposed Basic Income schemes: a method that uses the national accounts and census data to work out the net cost of an illustrative scheme, and a 'typical household' method. The 'national accounts' method can work out how much a Basic Income would cost by multiplying the proposed amounts for different age groups by the numbers of individuals in those groups given by census data; and it can work out from the national accounts how much money could be made available by abolishing other benefits, reducing tax allowances and increasing tax rates. For a revenue neutral scheme, the cost of the Basic Incomes must balance the amount of money made available. The problems with the method are that it cannot discover whether the combination of tax changes, the abolition of means-tested benefits, and the payment of Basic Incomes, would result in net disposable income losses for low-income households; and it can only discover the net costs of Basic Income schemes that entirely abolish existing means-tested benefits rather than adapting or recalculating them (because if existing benefits are adapted, or are recalculated on the basis that households are now receiving Basic Incomes, then the method cannot determine how much money would be saved). The 'typical household' method takes a particular household, with a specified number of adults, a specified number of children of various ages, and specified earned incomes and housing costs, and works out the change in disposable income that a proposed Basic Income scheme would generate. This method can of course handle Basic Income schemes that leave current means-tested benefits in place and either adapt or recalculate them, but it can only deliver calculations for the particular household structures and circumstances chosen. It cannot calculate the net cost of a scheme, or discover whether other kinds of households with low incomes would suffer net disposable income losses. Because initially the 'national accounts' and 'typical household' methods were the only ones available (House of Commons Work and Pensions Committee, 2007), questions about net household disposable income losses could not be answered. In a context in which the Basic Income debate was far from widespread, and in which more general questions about the desirability of paying everyone some money were at the top of the agenda, this was not too much of a problem. The difficulty occurred when the debate became more widespread, and questions about feasibility and implementation were beginning to be asked, because in that new context researchers who used the national accounts and typical household research methods could not answer questions being put to them (Miller, 1983; 2017; Painter and Thoung, 2015).

The main reason that financial feasibility research has been such a distinctive feature of the Basic Income debate in the UK is that the UK has been in the forefront of developing research methods for evaluating the financial effects of proposed changes to the tax and benefits system. When computers were large mainframe machines that took up vast amounts of space, the Cambridge academic Tony Atkinson constructed a computer model of the British Income

Tax system. He and his research assistant Holly Sutherland continued to work in this field, first in Cambridge, and then at the London School of Economics, where Sutherland assisted Hermione Parker with *Instead of the Dole* (Parker, 1989). Sutherland then moved the project back to Cambridge, and finally moved what had by then become a European Union funded project to the Institute for Social and Economic Research at the University of Essex. TAXMOD had become POLIMOD, and then POLIMOD had become EUROMOD (Immervoll et al., 1999): a computer programme into which are coded the regulations of the benefits and income tax systems of every European Union country, and through which can be passed financial data on a statistically significant sample of every EU country's population. For each country, the programme's own statistics function can deliver poverty, inequality and other statistics, and the output files can be used to discover multiple other results, such as the numbers of households on particular means-tested benefits. Researchers can then write new benefits into the programme, and can change existing taxes and benefits, in order to model proposed changes to the tax and benefits system. The programme is then run again, and a new set of statistics obtained, which can be compared with the results for the current system in order to discover the real-world effects of the proposed policy change. It is this powerful research tool that has enabled the increasing number of financial feasibility questions to be answered because it enables illustrative Basic Income schemes to be tested for net household disposable income losses among low-income households, for changes in poverty and inequality indices, and so on (Sloman, 2019: 160; Sutherland, 2016; Torry, 2014b; 2015b; 2016d; 2016e; 2017c; 2018c; 2020c: 188).

Different researchers employ different strategies when they evaluate illustrative Basic Income schemes using microsimulation. Reed and Martinelli both select a number of illustrative Basic Income schemes and test them for effects on poverty, inequality, household disposable income losses and so on (Lansley and Reed, 2019; Martinelli, 2017a; 2017b; 2017c; Reed and Lansley, 2016). This author starts by setting feasibility criteria: the annual net cost of the scheme has to be within £2bn of zero; poverty and inequality indices must fall; no low-income households should suffer significant losses at the point of implementation; no households should suffer unmanageable losses; Income Tax rates should normally rise by no more than three percentage points; and a significant number of households should be removed from means-tested benefits, and even more households should be brought within striking distance of coming off them. Once the criteria have been set, a trial and error method is used to test a wide variety of illustrative Basic Income schemes until one is found that fits the criteria (Torry, 2019a; 2020b; 2020c: 188–9).

While microsimulation functions as a highly reliable predictor of the immediate financial effects of Basic Income schemes, and therefore as a selector of feasible schemes, what it cannot do is predict dynamic effects—that is, how the economy would evolve over time in the context of a Basic Income—and it cannot predict employment market effects. Theoretical models of the employment market, informed by evidence on how employment market behaviour is affected by changes in tax rates, might be able to tell us something about how employment market behaviour might change (Colombino et al., 2010), but those models' construction is theory-driven and often makes substantial assumptions: for instance, that a progressive tax system would be exponential; that is, with disposable income equal to earned income to the power of $1 - t$, where t is the tax rate. No tax system would ever be of that character. This means that the extent to which the models' predictions would be reflected in the real world must always be open to a level of doubt that is difficult to quantify. An equally significant problem with such attempts to model employment market change is that the statistics employed to set the parameters of the model will be drawn from particular employment markets at particular times and places and would therefore depend on multiple factors such as the availability of childcare, the occupations available, and so on, whereas those might not be the context of any other employment market. A further problem is that what cannot be modelled is the ability that a Basic Income would give to workers to say yes to lower paid employment if they wished, and no to jobs with poor pay and conditions (Van Parijs and Vanderborght, 2017: 145–7). That it would be difficult to simulate the effects of a Basic Income and its attendant funding method on employment market behaviour is a problem that was recognized quite early in the modern Basic Income debate (Boulanger, 1988).

Microsimulation itself employs real-world tax and benefits regulations and real-world data, and employs no exogenous theory, and so can be regarded as delivering reliable results. While attaching an employment market model (de Jager et al., 1994) might look as if it would improve the quality of predictions because it would tell us something about the employment market changes that might result from implementation of a Basic Income scheme, enabling us to microsimulate on the basis of changing employment market behaviour, the increasing effects of the models' assumptions as the number of iterations rises means that results would become less and less reliable. Long-term large-scale saturation site pilot projects will therefore be the only way to deliver anything like reliable predictions about how financially feasible Basic Income schemes would affect employment market behaviour.

As well as providing the Basic Income debate with a robust research method for evaluating the financial effects of illustrative Basic Income schemes, a further benefit of the UK's social science research expertise is the availability of regularly recalculated Minimum Income Standards. An earlier method for calculating the amount of money that households needed to live on involved researchers asking about the amounts and kinds of food required for physical survival, along with the costs of the most rudimentary housing, clothing and so on, and then calculating the costs: but by the 1970s the inadequacy of that approach was clear (Townsend, 1979), and the 'Breadline Britain' approach was developed in which a representative sample of the population is interviewed to discover the goods that they regard as essential for participation in society as well as for mere survival. Using this method, the Joseph Rowntree Foundation publishes annually a set of Minimum Income Standards for a variety of household types (Davis et al., 2018; Hirsch, 2019; Lansley and Mack, 1983; 2015; Torry, 2020d: 322). Microsimulation research has consistently shown that individuals' Basic Incomes set at levels that would add up to the appropriate Minimum Income Standard for each household type would be financially infeasible, but that Basic Income schemes with lower Basic Income levels and that retained means-tested benefits could bring household disposable incomes closer to Minimum Income Standards (Sloman, 2019: 160–61; Torry, 2020d: 322–7).

An increasingly important aspect of social science has been opinion polls. A European survey and then a UK survey sponsored by the University of Bath and the Royal Society of Arts have both shown that public support for Basic Income now reaches 50 per cent, although this falls when it is pointed out that taxes would have to rise to pay for the Basic Incomes (Fitzgerald, 2017; Ipsos MORI, 2017; Van Parijs and Vanderborght, 2017: 172–4; Young, 2018: 3). Similar opinion surveys have been held in other countries; and the Swiss referendum about Basic Income in 2016 might be regarded as the largest ever opinion survey (see Chapter 8). Given that policymakers watch how public opinion is shifting before they will consider change that looks anything like radical, it might be that opinion surveys will prove to be the most important research politically, with financial feasibility research an essential accompaniment.

POLITICS, FAKE NEWS, MISREPRESENTATION AND THE EXCLUSION OF EVIDENCE

Four events related to the Basic Income debate in the UK offer some important lessons.

A Green Party Manifesto

The Green Party manifesto published for the UK's General Election in 2015 said this:

> The idea in a nutshell is this. Scrap most of the existing benefits apart from disability benefits and Housing Benefit. Abolish the income tax personal allowance.

> Then pay every woman, man and child legally resident in the UK a guaranteed, non-means-tested income, sufficient to cover basic needs—a Basic Income. For those who earn, the Basic Income compensates for the loss of the personal allowance. (Green Party, 2015: 54)

Natalie Bennett, the leader of the Green Party, then said in a television interview that they envisaged a Basic Income of £72 per week for working-age adults. A *Guardian* journalist had read the Citizen's Income Trust's website and had found research results that showed that a Basic Income of that level, in the absence of retained means-tested benefits, would impose significant disposable income losses on lots of low-income households, and published an article saying that. The Trust's Director did not say everything in the article attributed to him, but the journalist's conclusion was correct: that the scheme was not feasible (Wintour, 2015). What the article did not say, which it might have done, is that the same research project had shown that a £72 per week Basic Income would be perfectly feasible if means-tested benefits were left in place and recalculated (Torry, 2014b; 2015b).

Why had a newspaper that had previously published Larry Elliott's article on how useful a Basic Income might be have taken such a negative attitude to the subject? The only reason that some of us could think of was that *Guardian* journalists wanted to see a Labour Party victory at the forthcoming General Election, were concerned that the Green Party might attract votes that would prevent Labour from winning, and had therefore decided to criticize Green Party policies. Fortunately, the article, and the many articles that followed it, contributed to a significant rise in interest in Basic Income, prompted new research on the financial feasibility of Basic Income schemes, and did nothing to dent the Green Party's enthusiasm for Basic Income (Torry, 2020c: 195–6).

Fake News About Finland

One of the reasons for the recent significant increase in interest in Basic Income globally was the experiment that took place in Finland between January 2017 and December 2018 (Chapter 8; see also Kangas 2016; Kansaneläkelaitos Kela 2016). This experiment randomly selected 2,000 unemployed individuals from across the country and made their means-tested and work-tested unemployment benefits unconditional for a period of two years. But that was not what news media were saying: they were saying that Finland was planning to implement a Basic Income for all of its citizens. This author's research suggests that ambiguous phrasing in an article in the *New Statesman* (Penny, 2016) might have been the source of the misunderstanding: but there might not have been a single source of the fake news. Wherever it came from, it could not be stopped, however much the Citizen's Income Trust and others put out accurate information. Some outcomes of the fake news were positive for the Basic Income debate: one of the Citizen's Income Trust's trustees appearing on BBC 2's *Newsnight* programme, a BBC radio *Money Box Live* programme dedicated to Basic Income, and other requests for radio and press interviews (Torry, 2020c: 190).

Misrepresentation During a Parliamentary Debate

Debates in Westminster Hall, adjacent to the UK Parliament's two main debating chambers, allow Members of Parliament to debate matters of interest not currently being considered for legislative action but that might one day require legislation. The resolution is always in the form 'This house has considered ...'. In 2016, Ronnie Cowan MP, a Scottish National Party Member of Parliament, introduced a debate on Basic Income. Following his introduction to the topic, during which a working paper by the Director of the Citizen's Income Trust was quoted, Julian Knight, a Conservative Member of Parliament, asked whether Mr Cowan

saw the part of the report in which it is stated that, in order to support a universal basic income, the basic rate of income tax would have to rise to 48 pence in the pound. Can he say how on earth that is supportable in a modern economy? (Hansard, 2016)

Not having the Working Paper in front of him, Mr Cowan was unable to respond that the paper had stated that a Basic Income scheme that would require that level of Income Tax would be infeasible, but that the same paper also contained research results on an entirely feasible scheme that would require only a three percentage points increase in the basic rate of Income Tax.

Later in the debate, Damian Hind MP, the Minister for Employment, said that

UBI would create too many losers among the poorest families and dramatically increase the number of children living in poverty—a point confirmed through modelling even by the Citizen's Income Trust. (Hansard, 2016)

These statistics again related to a Basic Income scheme that the working paper had declared to be infeasible, and the minister had not mentioned that other schemes avoided such losses and reduced child poverty (Torry, 2020e).

Following the debate, the Citizen's Income Trust's trustees decided that the Trust would no longer publish research results on financially infeasible schemes.

Exclusion of Evidence During a Committee Hearing

Much of the UK Parliament's business is done by Members of Parliament forming committees to submit reports on their respective policy areas and to question relevant ministers, civil servants and other interested parties. In 2016, the House of Commons Work and Pensions Committee was to hold a hearing on Basic Income, and issued the usual request for interested individuals to apply for invitations to give evidence. Three microsimulation researchers applied for invitations, but none were invited. Instead, a researcher who still used a national accounts method was invited, even though she had not requested an invitation. When committee members asked what had by 2016 become normal financial feasibility questions, such as whether it was possible to avoid disposable income losses for low-income households, and what Income Tax rises would be required, the first question could not be answered, and only schemes that would require large increases in Income Tax rates were described. There was nobody present who could show that a meaningful Basic Income scheme could be constructed that would require only a three percentage point rise in Income Tax rates and that would not impose losses on low-income households (Hansard, 2017; Torry, 2020e). The committee's chair was able to publish a report that said that

> A universal Citizen's Income would either require unthinkable tax rises or fail to deliver its objectives of simplification and a guaranteed standard of living. There are problems in the welfare system, but CI is not the solution to them. Rather it is a distraction from finding workable solutions. (Work and Pensions Committee, 2017)

A further Work and Pensions Committee hearing in 2020, with a different Chair, received and heard evidence on a feasible Basic Income scheme based on microsimulation research results.

Lessons From the Four Incidents

It is unfortunate that journalists have allowed what appear to be political motives to determine what they write about Basic Income, and that from similar motives Members of Parliament have misrepresented research results and excluded them from consideration. It is equally unfortunate that fake news about experiments has been difficult to correct. Lessons were learnt. It is particularly unfortunate that a decision had to be taken not to publish negative research results, but perhaps more significant was the increasing effort expended on researching feasible Basic Income schemes. The general lesson to be drawn is that financial feasibility research using the best available methods is now essential, and that equally essential is the wide and diverse dissemination of the positive results of such research (Torry, 2020c: 200).

Among the lines projected on the wall at a conference to celebrate the history of microsimulation research in Europe was the sentence 'EUROMOD is the reason that the Basic Income debate in the UK has been so intelligent'. But it is not just microsimulation research that is the reason for that: it is the long tradition of high-quality social science research that has informed the debate, and the educational approach that continues to characterize discussion of Basic Income in the UK. Whatever the setbacks, the research and education must go on. Reliable research results might one day be heard.

AN INCREASINGLY LIVELY DEBATE

Since 2013, the UK has seen an increasingly lively debate about Basic Income, matched by similar increases in the extent of the debate in the United States and worldwide. A graph showing the number of Google searches for 'Basic Income' exhibits a general increase with some interesting peaks, one of which clearly relates to news about the Finland experiment (Sloman, 2019: 236).

No doubt the increasing number of books and articles on the subject has been a significant reason for the increasing extent and depth of the debate about Basic Income in the UK. Factors that could only be causal are increasing anxiety about the effects of automation, computerization, artificial intelligence, and globalization on the security of both employment and earned incomes; and most recently the way in which the coronavirus pandemic has revealed the extent of income insecurity. We cannot know what the future employment market will look like, but we can confidently predict that it will be characterized by increasing turbulence as jobs disappear, new jobs appear, jobs change and the security of employment changes (Breemersch et al., 2017; Standing, 2011a; Torry, 2020c: 194–5). We are increasingly clear that existing benefits systems will not be able to provide the income security required as turbulence increases; and increasing numbers of people are now aware that a Basic Income would make a significant contribution to making incomes more secure.

As Peter Sloman has pointed out, whereas previous periods of interest in Basic Income have coincided with increases in unemployment, the current increase in awareness and debate of Basic Income occurred while employment was high: so an important driver of the debate is not unemployment, but more precarious employment, and anxiety about the future of employment (Sloman, 2019: 224–5, 238). Shocks to the employment market and the economy during the coronavirus pandemic during 2020 have revealed just how fragile they are, resulting in even greater interest in Basic Income. A further significant change is that both the Labour Party and trades unions are now showing more interest in Basic Income, having recognized that for many households wages on their own can no longer prevent poverty; and in 2018 John McDonnell, the Shadow Chancellor, commissioned Guy Standing to write a report on how Basic Income pilot projects might be organized in the UK (Sloman, 2019: 238; Standing, 2019a).

As Sloman also points out,

> where British activists once set the pace in basic income research, the latest wave of interest has been powerfully shaped by developments in the global south, including pilot schemes in Namibia and India and the wider enthusiasm for tackling poverty through cash transfers. (Sloman, 2019: 225)

In this globalized world, news about pilot projects in Namibia and India (Sloman, 2019: 237), news about a referendum on Basic Income in Switzerland, and fake news about an experiment in Finland, all became British news. Growing interest in Basic Income in one part of the world now means growing interest in another; but the corollary might also be true: that waning interest in one part of the world might mean waning interest in another. There are pressures within the UK debate that might facilitate such a decline in interest, and particularly the difficulty of implementing a Basic Income scheme that would not require significant tax rises, would not impose losses on low income households, would take a significant number of households off means-tested benefits, and would reduce both poverty and inequality. Such schemes exist (Torry, 2019a; 2020b): but plenty of schemes are published that do not fulfil these criteria, which rather unfairly damages the concept of Basic Income and not just the undesirable schemes. One strategy that attempts to bypass the problem is the proposal that a social wealth fund should be built, the proceeds of which would fund a Basic Income (Lansley, 2016; Lansley et al., 2018). This was James Meade's proposal, and the experience of the Alaska Permanent Fund Dividend has provided some useful modern backing for it (Sloman, 2019: 244). However, this strategy could only be a long-term one, so if a Basic Income is to be implemented in the short to medium term then only a scheme that funds the Basic Incomes by altering the current tax and benefits systems could possibly be feasible.

As Sloman suggests, conditional cash transfers have become the default method for maintaining the incomes of poor families, and in this globalized world it would be difficult for the UK or any other country to buck that trend. It ought to be no surprise that the UK is trying to roll multiple means-tested benefits into one means-tested benefit. Framing Basic Income in ways relevant to a country's needs will be essential if pressures to curtail the debate are not to overwhelm those encouraging it. In the UK, with its increasingly fractured employment market and increasingly insecure incomes, framing Basic Income as a secure layer of income that would protect household disposable incomes at the same time as making the employment market more efficient could be the most effective stimulus to increasing interest (Sloman, 2019: 243, 250, 253). Even if pilot projects really are what they say they are—that is, local Basic Income schemes that it would be feasible to roll out nationwide—the results can be spun in a variety of directions: so whether or not pilot projects take place, only public understanding and approval of the advantages of an unconditional and therefore secure layer of income would enable the Basic Income debate to continue to increase in both extent and depth (Sloman, 2019: 245). The public understanding that is required is that a system based almost entirely on means-testing is not fit for purpose in a context of deep and rapid employment market, economic and social change, whereas even a relatively small Basic Income would provide the layer of income security that everyone will need (Sloman, 2019: 255):

> If Governments want to help citizens navigate a rapidly shifting labour market, they should prioritize forms of social security which provide a stable and predictable income floor that individuals can build on through work and saving. (Sloman, 2019: 254)

SCOTLAND

As has often been the case, the history of the Scottish Basic Income debate was considerably shaped by some significant individuals. In Edinburgh in 1983, Anne Miller was writing about regular incomes for individuals that would have been unconditional if the addition for people with disabilities had been treated as a separate benefit (Miller, 1983). She was a founder member of the Basic Income Research Group (now the Citizen's Basic Income Trust), becoming its Chair in 2001, and she attended the first meeting of the Basic Income European Network in 1986. Ailsa McKay, until her untimely death in 2014 while Professor of Economics at Glasgow Caledonian University, was both a prominent feminist and a prominent advocate for Basic Income, both in the academic world (Campbell and Gillespie, 2016: 3–12; McKay, 2005) and from 2013 as a member of the Scottish Government's Expert Working Group on Welfare. The group gave serious consideration to the possibility of a Basic Income scheme being implemented in an independent Scotland, and concluded that 'introducing a full CI [Citizen's Income] scheme would be such a significant reform that it may be best considered after the early years of independence have passed and the Scottish economy is maturing. For these reasons we would not recommend the introduction of a CI at this time. However, it is an option that could be revisited in the future' (Expert Working Group on Welfare, 2014: 59).

When the referendum on independence took place in 2014, the majority voted to remain in the United Kingdom, so the existing Scottish Government continues to exercise a number of powers devolved from the UK Government in Westminster, but still has almost no control over the tax and benefits systems. This means that implementation of a Basic Income scheme for Scotland cannot now be regarded as an immediate or even medium-term option. But that has not stopped a lively debate from continuing. In 2015, the Fairer Fife Commission, chaired by Martyn Evans, who is Chief Executive of the Fife-based Carnegie UK Trust, and who had already chaired the Expert Working Group on Welfare, suggested that Fife Council should select a town in which to hold a Basic Income pilot project (Fairer Fife Commission, 2015: 24–5). (It is perhaps unfortunate that the model recommended in the Commission's report was that of the experiment in Utrecht in the Netherlands, which was not in fact a Basic Income pilot project.) In 2016, the charity Reform Scotland published a detailed report on Basic Income (Mackenzie et al., 2016), and in the same year the Scottish National Party agreed a motion proposed by Ronnie Cowan MP—another significant figure in the Scottish debate—that Scotland should introduce a Basic Income when it was able to do so. The Scottish Green Party included the idea in its 2015 General Election manifesto, as had the Green Party of England and Wales.

For more than thirty years, the Basic Income debate in Scotland was facilitated by the UK's Citizen's Basic Income Trust (CBIT: formerly the Basic Income Research Group), but by the time of the independence referendum the debate in Scotland had already diverged from the debate in the rest of the UK, mainly because the prospect of independence would have meant a Scottish Government deciding whether to implement a Basic Income scheme, which many saw as a more likely prospect than the UK Government deciding to do so. And so, in 2015, the Citizen's Basic Income Network Scotland (CBINS) was formed; in 2016 it constituted itself and registered as a Scottish Charitable Incorporated Organisation; and in November 2016 it held a launch event, at which Guy Standing gave a presentation, and also at which a Glasgow Councillor, Matt Kerr, announced that Glasgow would like to host a Basic Income pilot project (McFarland, 2016). In 2017, the Scottish Social Security Committee heard oral evidence for and against Basic Income, and recognized that without additional powers it would be difficult for the Scottish Government to implement a Basic Income scheme (Scottish Parliament, 2017); both North Ayrshire and Edinburgh City Councils joined the ongoing discussions about the possibility of pilot projects in Scotland; the Scottish Government committed £250,000 for the planning stage of Scottish pilot projects; a meeting heard from Jurgen De Wispelaere, who had been involved in the planning for the Finnish experiment; and by the end of 2017 a steering group had been established to study the feasibility of a Basic Income pilot project in Scotland (Miller, 2019). The steering group reported its findings in June 2020:

- Pilot model recommendations:
  - It is recommended that a pilot should be a randomized controlled study, with two study areas where the whole community receives a CBI [Citizen's Basic Income] (one receiving the high payment, the other receiving the low payment).
  - The preferred model for piloting a CBI pilot in Scotland is based on 5 key principles: universal (paid to all); unconditional (no requirement to search for work); individual (not paid to households, like Universal Credit); periodic (paid at regular intervals); and made as a cash payment.
  - The model proposes two levels of CBI payments—one 'high level' based on the Minimum Income Standard and one 'low level' more closely aligned with current benefit levels. For both levels of payment, suspension of a range of existing income-related benefits is proposed, while others, primarily related to disability, housing, childcare and limited capability for work would continue.
- Care should be taken that participants who are vulnerable and/or with low incomes should not experience detriment (financial or otherwise) compared to individuals not involved in the study.
- Direct intervention costs of a pilot based on the proposed model (net of savings on benefits and pensions and excluding administration and evaluation costs) are approximately £186m over three years for a study including both low and high levels of CBI.
- There is significant interest and value in exploring the potential benefits of CBI via piloting, however there are substantial challenges associated with institutional arrangements for a pilot. This research has determined it is not currently feasible for any one level of Government alone to deliver a pilot model of a CBI as described by the Steering Group. There would be substantive and complex legislative, technical and delivery changes required to ensure that a CBI interacts with the existing social security system in a way that avoids detriment to those on benefits and lowest incomes.
- The majority of social security benefits a CBI would need to interact with are reserved to the UK Government, particularly those in relation to housing, child-care support and other top-up payments. Within current welfare and tax governance arrangements, political will and support across all levels of Government (local, Scottish and UK) including the Department for Work and Pensions (DWP) and HM Revenue and Customs (HMRC) would be required to overcome these challenges. Without such support, the feasibility of a pilot, that minimizes detriment, would require legislative changes to be made. (Citizens' Basic Income Feasibility Study Steering Group, 2020: 7–8)

The Labour Party had promised Basic Income pilot projects if it won the 2017 UK General Election, which could have meant the 'legislative, technical and delivery changes' required for pilot projects in Scotland being implemented. The Labour Party lost the election.

IRELAND

The ethos of the Basic Income debate in Ireland has been similar to that of the UK debate, and the assumptions underlying Ireland's benefits system are the same as those for the UK: full employment; permanent employment; and only short-term unemployment—hence the inclusion of Ireland in this chapter rather than in Chapter 8 on the rest of Europe. The effects of the current benefits system are also the same as the effects of the UK's system: 'a complex and inadequate system which is now failing to meet the needs of the people trapped within it' (Healy and Reynolds, 2000: 238) in a context of rapid technological, social and employment market change. For forty years, the Conference of Religious of Ireland's (CORI) Justice Commission, and in particular two members of religious orders, Seán Healy and Brigid Reynolds, have energized the Basic Income debate in Ireland, and have had considerable success in putting the idea on the political agenda and keeping it there.

In 1977, Ireland's National Economic and Social Council, a Government-sponsored organization bringing together employers, trades unions, and farming, community, voluntary and environmental organizations, studied Basic Income as one of three options for reform of social security; and then in both 1982 and 1986 Government commissions rejected Basic Income as an option, claiming that it would be too expensive and that it would distract attention from the need to raise the levels of existing benefits (Healy and Reynolds, 2012: 151–2). Ireland was already struggling to pay for its not very generous social security benefits because of the country's high dependency ratio—a relatively small number of employed individuals supporting large numbers of unemployed, elderly and young people (Callender, 1988), and CORI's Justice Commission agreed with those who were saying that too high an Income Tax rate would be required to fund a high Basic Income: and it then found that the double message—advocacy for its own Basic Income scheme, alongside rejection of a scheme with higher Basic Incomes—was difficult for the public to absorb (Healy and Reynolds, 2000: 241). This is a problem that has intensified. Simple messages are easy for both the media and the public to absorb and amplify, whereas more complex ideas—'Some Basic Income schemes are feasible, and some are not'—can be more difficult to process and so fail to be heard and understood. (A recent obvious example of this process occurred in the UK during the Brexit referendum campaign: 'Take Back Control'—that is, take back legislative control from the European Union institutions—was a simple message that was easy for the media and the public to understand. The more complex message—that countries have to pool their sovereignty if they are to keep control of their markets, economies and legislation, rather than have them controlled by more powerful countries and by transnational corporations—is a lot more difficult to understand and amplify.)

In spite of the difficulties, support for Basic Income did not disappear. By the mid-1980s, a section of the more right-wing Fine Gael party was supportive of Basic Income; members of the Green Party were advocating a Basic Income; and the small Workers' Party had published a detailed proposal for a Basic Income scheme (Callender, 1988: 291–2). CORI's Justice Commission responded to the 'complex message' dilemma by creating more accessible explanations of its own proposal, including a video, with the result that the message that there are different Basic Income schemes, with different levels of feasibility, began to be understood. From 1994 onwards, CORI publications, and associated briefings and discussions, proliferated; and further research in 1997 found that a larger Basic Income could be envisaged if implemented gradually over a period of three years (Healy and Reynolds, 2000: 241–2). A contribution to the intelligence of the debate in Ireland, as in the UK, was microsimulation research that offered high-quality predictions of the financial effects of illustrative Basic Income schemes: and one particularly interesting exercise of this kind was a comparative study of the microsimulation programmes available in the UK and Ireland and of illustrative Basic Income schemes for the two countries (Callan et al., 1999).

In 1996, the Irish Government's national planning process added an additional pillar to the existing pillars of employers, trades unions and farmers' organizations, with the result that CORI was able to join the new 'voluntary and community' pillar and persuade the other social partners in the process to include a section promising a study of Basic Income in the 1997 to 1999 'Partnership 2000' programme. A steering group was established to prepare a Green Paper: a discussion document to inform future debate. In parallel with this project, CORI's Justice Commission engaged with the parties contesting the 1997 General Election in Ireland, with the result that the coalition Government formed after the election promised a Green Paper on Basic Income by June 1999. The debate then turned towards a proposal to make existing tax credits (Ireland's version of an income tax allowance) refundable: that is, that they should function as a Negative Income Tax, and so deliver the same relationship between gross and net income as a Basic Income. CORI's Justice Commission encouraged this debate on the basis that once refundable tax credits had been implemented, to move to a Basic Income would simplify the administration (Healy and Reynolds, 2012: 159–63). An important contribution to the debate was research that showed that a number of pathways to the implementation of a Basic Income would be available (Clark and Healy, 1997).

The CORI Justice Commission was not purely focused on the Basic Income debate, so it did not fulfil the requirements for affiliation to BIEN, the Basic

Income Earth Network. In 1995, an organization specifically tasked with promoting debate on Basic Income was formed and was subsequently affiliated to BIEN: but it was Seán Healy and others related to the CORI Justice Commission, assisted by John Baker of BIEN Ireland, who organized the BIEN annual congress in Dublin in 2008. Quite righty, CORI's work is diverse, as it represents the interests of Roman Catholic religious communities across Ireland; and when its social justice activity was hived off into an independent stand-alone organization named 'Social Justice Ireland' in 2009, still directed by Healy and Reynolds, the activity continued to be driven by a diverse social justice agenda that included Basic Income as a regular theme (Healy, 2021). In 2011, BIEN Ireland (now 'Basic Income Ireland') was reactivated, with Social Justice Ireland's involvement, and since then it has fulfilled educational, research and campaigning roles (Ryan and Baker, 2012). As in the UK, it can be useful to the debate if different organizations with different functions can work well together.

The Green Paper promised by the Irish Government in 1997 was published in 2002 by Social Justice Ireland on behalf of the steering group and for many years featured on the Prime Minister's Department website (Social Justice Ireland, 2002; Healy, 2021), and during the same year Charles Clark, a professor of economics in New York, published a wide-ranging analysis of a detailed Basic Income scheme for Ireland (Clark, 2002: 41–125): but Government disinterest meant that the process went no further (Healy and Reynolds, 2012: 164). More recently, engagement with political parties has continued, and the parties that have formed the current coalition Government—Fine Gael, Fianna Fáil and the Green Party—have committed themselves to hold a Basic Income pilot project during the lifetime of the Government (Basic Income Ireland, 2020).

Although it has not yet seen a Basic Income implemented, Ireland has seen an unusual degree of Government interest in Basic Income, no doubt to a large extent as a result of the consistent research and educational activity undertaken by Social Justice Ireland, now accompanied by Basic Income Ireland. Seán Healy has suggested that one reason for significant Government interest is that Ireland is a small country in population terms, so the barriers that exist between Government ministers and civil society organizations and their personnel in countries with larger populations do not exist to the same extent in Ireland. As he has said, you might meet the Taoiseach (Prime Minister) in the lift. Communication of ideas can therefore be rapid and well informed. Whether the current commitment to hold a pilot project will result in a genuine pilot project is an interesting question: but the country's Government's commitment to doing so is a good way to start—an advantage not available to the UK.

CONCLUSIONS

Neither in the UK nor elsewhere are the social and economic problems revealed and exacerbated by the pandemic going away in a hurry. Inequalities of various kinds look likely to increase, and employment and earned incomes will continue to be insecure (Sowels, 2018). Increasing recognition of these social and economic facts, and the advantages that a Basic Income would have over means-tested benefits, mean that the research and the educational approach that have typified the UK approach to the Basic Income debate must continue, and must increasingly be the experience in other countries as well.

The UK has always played a prominent part in the Basic Income debate, and it will continue to do so, as will the Republic of Ireland, and as would an independent Scotland if independence were to occur: but by the 1980s the debate was becoming increasingly European: and it is to the rest of Europe that we now turn.

8. Multiple approaches to Basic Income in continental Europe

INTRODUCTION

As we have discovered in Chapters 2, 4 and 5, the United Kingdom was where the first and then subsequent steps were taken in the modern Basic Income debate. In Chapter 3 we have found that following the earliest period of the debate there was a broader geographical spread of engagement with the possibility of unconditional incomes, and in Chapter 6 we have discovered that the USA and Canada have hosted some important experiments in mechanisms that bear some similarities to Basic Income: but that makes it even clearer that until 1980 the UK was the main location for debate specifically about an unconditional and regular income for every individual. As we shall now see, that began to change during the 1980s, and by the end of the century the Basic Income debate was a pan-European phenomenon.

It is at this point in the book that selection of material begins to become difficult. Quite a lot of European countries have experienced debates with similar characteristics during the past thirty-five years or so, and in order to keep the chapter somewhere close to a manageable length a selection has had to be made. A comprehensive treatment of the recent European debate would be simply impossible within the confines of a single chapter. What the reader will find here are discussions of those events that have been particularly formative for Europe's Basic Income debate, and also explorations of national debates that represent important characteristics of the European debate as a whole. An attempt has been made to choose countries that represent several characteristics of the debate so that the maximum number of characteristics can be included while at the same time restricting the number of countries discussed. Even though that has been a consistent aim, the selection of countries to be discussed, and the selection of material for each of those countries, inevitably remains something of a personal choice. A future book-length history of the recent Basic Income debate in Europe might be able to offer a more comprehensive picture.

THE EUROPEANIZATION OF THE BASIC INCOME DEBATE

The rediscovery of poverty during the 1960s that was an important driver of the Basic Income debate in both the UK and the USA was a largely anglophone phenomenon: but the poverty and high unemployment that emerged during the late 1970s and the 1980s affected the whole of Europe as increasing automation, competition from rapidly industrializing countries elsewhere in the world, and higher fuel prices, caused significant and rapid change in all European economies and employment markets (Duverger, 2018: 91–2). Existing benefits systems were ceasing to cope with the demands imposed on them, and reform options were being discussed. This is the context in which multiple new aspects of the Basic Income debate emerged during the 1980s. Not that debate on Basic Income was entirely lacking on the continent of Europe before 1982: but it was during the 1980s that occasional discussions of an unconditional income among academics and a few others around Europe transformed into a more co-ordinated network of activity as people in different countries got to know each other. As always, not everyone was careful about terminology and definitions, so it is sometimes difficult to tell whether an event or a national debate was about Basic Income or about a Minimum Income Guarantee: but there are enough texts and events unambiguously about Basic Income for us to draw the conclusion that the 1980s saw the Europeanization of the Basic Income debate, particularly if the UK is included in Europe, as of course it must be. During this period Basic Income failed to wrest discussion about the reform of benefits systems away from the embedded social insurance and means-testing presuppositions firmly entrenched across Europe, but the foundations had been laid for a diverse and widespread debate about Basic Income that for once looked as if it was not going to go away.

BELGIUM

In 1983, a group within 'Links', the Flemish socialist party, published a pamphlet proposing a Basic Income as a means of reducing working hours and therefore unemployment, but the idea attracted little attention. The following year 'Agalev', the Flemish-speaking ecology party, published a proposal to replace Belgium's social security system with a Basic Income, and in 1985 a conference organized by Flemish-speaking elements of the labour and ecology movements discussed 'uncoupling labour and income', and was addressed by Greetje Lubbi, Chair of the Voedingsbond FNV, a Dutch trade union that was already advocating a Basic Income (Van Trier, 1988: 279–80).

At the end of 1982, a young academic, Philippe Van Parijs, had discussed the same idea with Ecolo, Agalev's French-speaking equivalent; and in 1984, in response to an invitation from the King Baudouin Foundation to submit scenarios about the future of work, Van Parijs wrote an essay on behalf of the Collectif Charles Fourier: a group of academics and trades unionists that he had initiated. The essay asked its readers to imagine that each month the Government should pay to each citizen an 'allocation universelle', a 'universal grant', sufficient to cover the basic needs of an individual, whatever their employment status, household structure, or income, and that this regular income should replace existing social insurance and means-tested benefits, state pensions, student grants, employment subsidies and state aid to industry. 'Do all of that and see what happens.' The essayists predicted that the allocation universelle would put an end to mass unemployment by encouraging work-sharing and improving the intrinsic quality of paid work (Duverger, 2018: 92–4). In 1985, the essay was republished in a widely read monthly journal accompanied by other articles from the Collectif Charles Fourier on the same subject.

For forty years Van Parijs has remained central to the European and now global debate about Basic Income. A particularly important contribution was his 1995 book *Real Freedom for All: What (if anything) can justify capitalism?* (Van Parijs, 1995), in which he argues for the highest sustainable Basic Income subject to a constraint of 'undominated diversity' (Van Parijs, 1995: 59–60). John Rawls had objected to the idea of a Basic Income because it provided an unconditional income for individuals who could support themselves if they wished to do so but who had decided to spend every day surfing instead, to which Van Parijs responded that jobs are assets for which those with jobs should pay rent to those without them. This, and every other argument in *Real Freedom for All*, relied on a conception of social justice as the sustainable maximization of the 'real freedom' of those least free to choose how to conduct their lives.

Hundreds of articles, interviews, books and edited collections have followed, culminating in Van Parijs's 2017 book, written with Yannick Vanderborght, *Basic Income: A radical proposal for a free society and a sane economy* (Van Parijs and Vanderborght, 2017): a book that discusses the history of Basic Income, its ethical justification, funding options, pilot projects, political feasibility, and the national, regional and global levels at which Basic Incomes could be paid.

Perhaps the most important consequence of the essay winning a prize in 1985 was that the money was used to fund a conference in 1986 at the University of Louvain-la-Neuve. About sixty academics, trades unionists, and a variety of others interested in Basic Income, came from several European countries to attend the event, and a significant outcome was the birth of the Basic Income European Network (BIEN: now the Basic Income Earth Network) (Van Parijs, 2020).

An interesting question is whether Van Parijs's early personal dominance of the Basic Income debate on the Continent, and the fact that he was secretary of BIEN for the period 1994 to 2004, distracted attention from the necessity for the specifically Belgian organization that would have been required if Belgium was to see the kind of constant and diverse activity experienced by the UK during the past forty years. As it is, Belgium has seen only occasional disconnected Basic Income incidents: support from the country's two Green parties during the 1980s; and in 1997 the millionaire Roland Duchâtelet founded a political party, VIVANT, with Basic Income at the heart of its programme, which in 1999 gained 2 per cent of the votes in elections but now appears to be moribund. At the time of writing, nothing has been posted on its website since 2017 (Vanderborght, 2000; Vivant, 2020). The Belgian organization registered with BIEN was founded in 2012, experienced a brief flurry of activity during the 2013 European Citizens' Initiative (see below), achieved a pro-Basic Income documentary on Belgium's major television channel, and then became as moribund as VIVANT. At the time of writing, the organization's website was entirely composed of adverts for personal loans (Belgian Network for Basic Income, 2020; Jacobson, 2021).

The Hoover Chair (Chaire Hoover d'éthique économique et sociale) at the University of Louvain, which Philippe Van Parijs directed from its creation in 1991 until 2016, hosted BIEN's secretariate until 2004, and still hosts the BIEN archive. It has promoted research and debate on Basic Income, in particular by hosting post-doctoral fellows or doctoral visitors, many of whom have gone on to play major roles in the promotion of Basic Income, including Juliana Bidadanure (Stanford), Yannis Varoufakis (Athens), François Blais (Québec), Karl Widerquist (Georgetown), Michael Howard (Maine), Simon Birnbaum (Stockholm), David Casassas (Barcelona) and Jurgen De Wispelaere (Tampere).

FRANCE

For the ecosocialist theoretician André Gorz, the choice was not simply between the State and the market, between socialists and liberals, but between the State, the market and the 'autonomous sphere'—that sphere of work that is neither controlled by the State nor by the market: such activity as bringing up children, caring work, voluntary community activity and so on—so the choice was socialism, liberalism, and 'ecosocialism' (Van Parijs, 2009). Gorz saw that a significant problem preventing automation from enabling the autonomous sphere to take its rightful place in the triad was that full-time employment was normally the only route to sufficient money to live on. What was required was

> le droit de chacun et de chacune de gagner sa vie en travaillant, mais en travaillant de moins en moins, de mieux en mieux, tout en recevant sa pleine part de la richesse socialement produite. (Gorz, [1990] 2013)

> [the right of each person to earn a living by working, but by working less and less, and better and better, while still receiving their full share of the socially produced wealth.]

When he wrote that in 1990, Gorz was still convinced that income had to be inextricably connected with work (Gorz, 1992): but by 1997 he had changed his mind (Van Parijs, 2009; Van Trier, 2019):

> Le revenu social garanti n'était plus un salaire. [Cette formule] était cohérente avec l'appropriation et la maîtrise du temps. Mais elle n'était pas cohérente avec les perspectives ouvertes et les changements introduits par le postfordisme. Je l'abandonne donc … Défense de l'inconditionnalité … (Gorz, 1997: 24)

> The guaranteed social income was no longer a wage. [This formula] was consistent with taking back, and gaining control of time. But it was not consistent with the perspectives opened up, and the changes brought about, by post-Fordism. I am therefore abandoning it … In defence of unconditionality … (Gorz, 1999: 85)

André Gorz's writings on the place of work in society, and particularly his conversion experience in relation to Basic Income, have been an important motivator for debate on Basic Income debate in France and beyond; and it was Gorz's more recent writings, along with careful lobbying by two Basic Income organizations in France, the MFRB and AIRE (see below), that inspired Benoît Hamon to study Basic Income and then to include in his election manifesto a Revenu Universel d'Existence (RUE): a Universal Existence Income (Jacobson, 2021; Masquelier, 2019). By the time Hamon declared himself a candidate in the Socialist Party's primary elections for presidential candidate, Basic Income was becoming slightly better known in France, partly because of the publicity about the new European Citizens' Initiative about Basic Income (on which, see later in this chapter), the collection of signatures for it, and the new organization that had been established to collect statements of support: the Mouvement Français pour un Revenu de Base (MFRB) (French Movement for a Basic Income). Hamon's proposal was that the RUE should be approached by stages by making a series of changes to France's existing tax and benefits systems. He maintained a commitment to Basic Income during the primary campaign, which he won, but during the presidential election campaign in 2017 he sidelined both the universality and the employment unconditionality of his initial proposal, and what emerged was something closer to a conditional

Negative Income Tax, with the final shape of the benefit put off to a conference sometime after the presidential election. Hamon received 6.36 per cent of the votes in the first round of the election and so was eliminated from the race.

Gorz's political theory has not been the only facilitator of the Basic Income debate in France. An early advocate of an 'allocation universelle', 'universal grant', was Yoland Bresson, Professor of Economics at the University of Paris-Val-de-Marne. He attended the first BIEN congress in Louvain-la-Neuve in 1986, and continued to argue for a Basic Income on the basis that it would reduce economic exclusion and therefore social exclusion (Bresson and Guilhaume, 1986: 78).

By the 1980s, most countries in Europe had developed both social insurance schemes to cover such contingencies as unemployment, sickness and old age, and means-tested safety nets to ensure that household disposable incomes would reach something like subsistence level. An interesting exception was France, where no national safety net existed, although a variety of local experiments had taken place. Negative Income Tax proposals had been discussed, mainly in neoliberal circles and (therefore) criticized elsewhere on the political spectrum (Van Parijs and Vanderborght, 2017: 95–6), and what emerged was the Revenu Minimum D'Insertion (RMI), a 'minimum insertion income': a means-tested income conditional on the recipient signing an individual 'insertion contract' that imposed activities designed to 'insert' people into employment.

In 1989, Yoland Bresson helped to found AIRE, Association pour l'Instauration du Revenu d'Existence (Association for the Implementation of an Existence Income): but the RMI had been established the year before, and public and political debate about it quickly submerged any emerging interest in Basic Income. During the 1990s, discussion about benefits reform in France became somewhat diffuse, not to say confused, because 'unconditional' came to mean 'not work-tested' rather than 'not work-tested or means-tested' (Duverger, 2018: 99–111). In 2014, Bresson died, and Marc de Basquiat took over the presidency of AIRE. He has ensured that AIRE has become more engaged with the global Basic Income debate, and has actively involved the organization with think tanks and politicians.

Following the implementation of the RMI, a variety of proposals were made for its improvement, some of them in the directions of unconditionality and universality (Euzéby, 2000). In 2009, the RMI was replaced by the Revenu de Solidarité Active (RSA) (Active Solidarity Income), with a lower marginal deduction rate than the RMI (Van Parijs and Vanderborght, 2017: 162) and designed to provide a Minimum Income Guarantee for both unemployed and employed workers.

In 2016, the Département de la Gironde (the Gironde region) planned a number of experiments with benefits with different characteristics, including a Basic Income. Unfortunately, that was the aspect of the experiment that in the end did not happen. The closest was an income-tested revenu de base ciblé (targeted Basic Income), and so not a Basic Income at all. Genuine Basic Incomes have been received for a year by a few French participants in the German Basic Income lottery organized by Mein Grundeinkommen, Basic Incomes in a local currency have been tried in a handful of agricultural communities, and further Départements have now asked to be permitted to conduct local experiments mirroring the original intention in la Gironde.

The 2017 presidential election was won by Emmanuel Macron, whose government is now planning to combine the RSA and a number of other means-tested programmes into a single means-tested benefit in much the same way as the UK has combined several means-tested benefits into 'Universal Credit'. Macron is calling his new benefit a Revenu Universel d'Activité (RUA) (Universal Activity Income): but French debate about Basic Income and similar incomes is far from moribund. The Institut des Politiques Publiques (Institute of Public Policy) has simulated the effects of a variety of Basic Income schemes and of steps towards them; and at the time of writing, the island of Corsica has asked for permission to implement a Negative Income Tax (de Basquiat, 2020; Duverger, 2018: 115–18) and the French National Assembly has recently debated a similar measure (Generation Libre, 2020; Assemblée Nationale, 2020).

SPAIN

Red Renta Básica, Spain's Basic Income Network, was established in 2001, and for twenty years has promoted debate on a genuine Basic Income. Basic Income achieved rather more visibility ten years later when the Indignados (15M) movement in Spain, which launched demonstrations against the Spanish Government's austerity policies in 2011, added a Basic Income to their demands (Martinez Lopez and San Juan, 2014: 11), and since 2014, as in other parts of Europe, public understanding of Basic Income has grown rapidly. That year a Popular Legislative Initiative for a Basic Income was launched by Isabel Franco, a Podemos Member of Parliament, and was supported by a variety of organizations advocating a Basic Income for Spain. The initiative expired, but it had raised the level of debate (Junta Electoral Central, 2014). The same year, Podemos proposed a Basic Income (Navas, 2014), subsequently joined a coalition with Izquierda Unida, a radical left-wing party which had also proposed a Basic Income, and in 2019 found itself in Spain's coalition government (Rincón, 2020b): except that by then what was still being called a 'renta básica' (Basic Income) was not one: it was an income-tested and household-based benefit (El Español, 2019). As Pablo Iglesias, the leader of Podemos and Spain's Deputy Prime Minister, explained in 2020:

> We are currently working—together with the Ministry of Inclusion and Social Security and the Ministry of Labour—to launch a basic income for those households that, as a consequence of the crisis, have run out of income and are not entitled to unemployment benefits. It is not for all households, only for those without income.
> Our proposal is to give an allowance of around 500 euros a month to an adult who lives alone, which would reach up to 1,000 euros per month in the case of a home with two adults and two children. … by guaranteeing this basic income for households that lose their earnings, we will facilitate the recovery and, with that, the return to economic growth. The best way to reduce debt is to restore growth as soon as possible. … this basic income should remain once we overcome the current crisis. We do not propose the implementation of a universal basic income, but rather a guaranteed income scheme that supplements the income of poor households. (Mason, 2020)

The shift from Basic Income to Minimum Income Guarantee had occurred because when it became clear that Podemos might become a significant political force, the party's proposal for a Basic Income came under sustained media attack. Both a consultation exercise, and Podemos members' preference for a Minimum Income Guarantee, led to the policy change, and subsequently to other political parties developing their own Minimum Income Guarantee proposals (Noguera, 2018: 291–2). Until now, Spain has had no national scheme for maintaining household incomes, only regional ones; so a proposal for a national Minimum Income Guarantee might have looked like a step in the right direction. The Government launched its new 'Basic Income' in May 2020, and by August its administration had seized up (TheLocalES, 2020).

José Noguera follows his account of Podemos's journey from Basic Income to a variant of a Minimum Income Guarantee by quoting OECD research (OECD, 2017) that found that one particular Basic Income scheme would worsen poverty, and wrongly concludes that Basic Income would therefore worsen poverty. This failure of logic is found rather too often in articles by otherwise knowledgeable academics who do not understand that financially feasible Basic Income schemes exist that would substantially reduce poverty (Rothstein, 2018; Torry, 2020b). Noguera suggests that Basic Income advocates should accept Minimum Income Guarantee schemes as 'stepping stones' in the right direction, without recognizing that means-tested systems tend to remain means-tested (Noguera, 2018: 297). A significant problem that Noguera does not tackle is that the Minimum Income Guarantee is still called a 'Basic Income' when it is not one (Rincón, 2020a).

At least the experiments that took place in Barcelona between 2017 and 2019 did not call themselves Basic Income experiments.

The *B-MINCOME, combining a minimum guaranteed income with active social policies in deprived urban areas of Barcelona,* is a pilot project that aims to fight poverty and social exclusion. (Ajuntament de Barcelona, 2019: 5: italics in the original)

B-MINCOME was an experiment carried out and evaluated by a substantial consortium that included the Ajuntament de Barcelona (Barcelona City Council), Ivàlua (Catalan Institute for Evaluation of Public Policies), NOVACT (International Institute for Nonviolent Action), the Institute of Government and Public Policies (UAB), The Young Foundation, and the Data Management Group (UPC), alongside ICTA (Institute of Environmental Science and Technology), with financial assistance from the European Union and participation from Urban Innovative Actions, a European Union agency (Ajuntament de Barcelona, 2019). One thousand households from some of Barcelona's most deprived communities received additional incomes with a variety of conditions attached; 450 households received a means-tested benefit with no other conditions, with 200 of them having their benefits withdrawn euro for euro as earned income rose, and 250 having their benefits withdrawn more slowly. The other 550 households were divided into four groups to which different activities were allocated: training and employment activities; assistance with forming cooperatives and other social enterprises; housing renovation; and community participation and organizing. Each of the groups was again divided, with half of each group being required to participate in the projects, and the other half joining in if they wished to. All of these 550 households received means-tested benefits that were withdrawn gradually as earned income rose. The terminology employed by the project had meanings specific to the project: slow withdrawal of the income was labelled 'unlimited', withdrawal euro for euro was labelled 'limited', 'conditional' meant that participants were obliged to join in the projects allocated to the group, and 'unconditional' meant that they could join in if they wished (Bollain, 2019). Two reports were issued in the autumn of 2019: one about the role of social workers in relation to participation in the different projects:

The shift that happened over the course of the BMINCOME pilot's implementation meant a shift of social support from office-led to people-led, changing the perspective from the bureaucratic towards more peer-to-peer, participative and community-based work. ... The separation of the management of economic subsidies from social work: without the economic pressures, social workers could deal with other critical aspects of beneficiaries' lives; (Colini, 2019: 15) and the other containing results from the first year of the project:

> B-MINCOME has led to a reduction in material deprivation indices and, conse-
> quently, increased satisfaction with the financial situation of households. ... Again,
> in line with the expected results, B-MINCOME has reduced the sensation of finan-
> cial uncertainty ... the non-conditional and unlimited participation modalities show
> better results on average than others. ... The impact on the employment situation
> is very small and, in the majority of cases, not statistically significant. ... there
> is a slight negative impact on finding employment, especially in the conditional
> participation groups. ... this phenomenon (lock-in effect) may respond to the fact
> that taking part in the active policies (or in similar programmes) takes time away
> from and modifies people's preferences, expectations and strategies when it comes
> to looking for work in the short and medium term. ... a reduction of 9 percentage
> points is detected in the risk of contracting mental illness, as well as a major
> improvement in quality of sleep. These two results could be due to a reduction in
> the level of general stress associated with reducing financial difficulties in meeting
> basic needs ... In relation to the community dimension, a positive effect is observed
> on the probability of undertaking volunteering among those taking part in an active
> policy ... In aggregate across the ten participant neighbourhoods, general satisfac-
> tion with life has increased by 27%, going from 5 to 6.45 points ... those partici-
> pating in the active training and employment policy, report happiness 9.5% higher
> than the general average, while the limited SMI group shows a 5% lower response
> than the unlimited one. ... In general, it seems that the factors with the most positive
> impact on satisfaction with life and general happiness are income, being in full-time
> employment and having financial stability, while those that have a more negative
> impact are age, poor health and reserved or introverted personality. ... a strong
> increase in wellbeing and confidence for the future ... was ... observed. ... the
> improvement in these indicators could be explained by three factors: a) reduced
> stress as a result of having more resources; b) the possibility of spending more time
> with family; and c) improving social relations. (Laín, 2019: 37–9)

The Barcelona City Council summarized the results of the first year of the
project:

> [T]he fact that a significant impact on certain dimensions has already been detected
> leads us to think that, on finishing the project, the results will be even more sig-
> nificant. In line with the hypotheses posed, positive impacts are observed in the
> majority of indicators and dimensions analyzed, as summarised below. (Ajuntament
> de Barcelona, 2019: 37)

Results relating to the second year, and for the experiment as a whole, were
still awaited at the time of writing.

It is a pity that in the midst of the substantial diversity of the B-MINCOME
experiment room was not found for a group receiving a genuine Basic Income:
a completely unconditional and nonwithdrawable income. Logic would
suggest that as the results relating to the different configurations appear to
represent a correlation between increasing unconditionality and more positive

outcomes, we would expect to see an entirely unconditional option delivering even better results.

ITALY

Early on, Italy looked as if it might match the Netherlands for the extent and depth of its Basic Income debate. The Lega Nazionale Cooperative e Mutue (National Co-operative League) was at the heart of the debate; there was debate and disagreement among trades unions (Saconi, 1992); and Italy hosted the third BIEN congress in Florence in 1990. The debate then went through quite a quiet period until in 2008 the national organization BIN Italia (Basic Income Network Italia) was founded, and since when it has run an active website and has involved itself in the European Citizens' Initiatives (Basic Income Network Italia, 2021).

The recent history of the political debate in Italy mirrors that in Spain. The 2018 General Election resulted in a hung Parliament, and after months of negotiation a coalition government was formed between the Five Star Movement and the Lega ('League'). The Five Star Movement had promised a Basic Income (BBC, 2018), but what eventually emerged in 2019 was an income-tested and work-tested benefit (Giuffrida, 2019; Jessoula et al., 2019). In itself this might not have been a problem, except that the benefit was called a Reddito di Cittadinanza, 'Citizenship Income', and this was too often interpreted as a Basic Income when it was not one (O'Neal, 2019).

THE NETHERLANDS

In 1935, Jan Tinbergen, joint winner of the first Nobel Memorial Prize in Economic Sciences in 1969, argued unsuccessfully for a Basic Income to be included in a Dutch Labour Plan prepared by the Social Democratic Party (Don, 2019), but his was a lone voice, and it was not until forty years later that the idea made any headway in the Netherlands. In 1975, Jan Pieter Kuiper, a professor of social medicine in Amsterdam, read Robert Theobald's *Free Men and Free Markets* (1963) and wrote the first of a number of articles that recommended that income and work should be uncoupled in order to promote personal autonomy. To that end he asked for a 'guaranteed income', by which he meant an unconditional income: although he did not specify how it would be funded or implemented. Kuiper's ideas took root among Christian socialists, and also among people involved in the ecology movement because they could see that uncoupling income and work could promote individual emancipation and allow non-polluting activities to flourish and polluting activities to decline: but trades unions were generally dismissive. Kuiper's ideas functioned as a critique of the work/income relationship current at the time, rather than as a potentially implementable social policy.

The economic crisis of the early 1980s increased unemployment in the Netherlands from 6 per cent to 12 per cent, and in that context, in 1981, the food workers' trade union, Voedingsbond FNV, published a paper that promoted the idea of a Basic Income as a means of redistributing paid employment: a rare example of a trade union leading a campaign for Basic Income, although there was less enthusiasm for Basic Income among the membership of the union than among its leadership (Henderson and Quiggin, 2019: 496; Van Oijen, 1988: 269–70; Van Parijs and Vanderborght, 2017: 174). Most trades unions disagreed with Voedingsbond FNV, arguing that a Basic Income would compromise the right to work, cause the erosion of social insurance benefits, and require increased taxation which would increase production costs and damage exports.

The Voedingsbond FNV paper stimulated a debate about Basic Income among organizations belonging to the national council of claimants' organizations (Landelijk Beraad Uitkeringsgerechtigden: LBU), and in 1986, the LBU published a discussion document in which a Basic Income accompanied by additional benefits for those with higher than average expenses was argued for on the basis of a right to a liveable income, a right to economic independence, and a right to access to a variety of different kinds of work (Hogenboom and Janssen, 1988). Voedingsbond FNV's initiative had given rise to the nearest thing to a public debate about Basic Income that Europe had experienced up till then (Van Parijs, 2020).

As the economic crisis lengthened, the Social Democratic Party, influenced by the Voedingsbond FNV, adopted Basic Income as a policy in 1983 (Van der Veen, 1988: 298), and a report by the government-supported Scientific Council for Government Policy took Basic Income seriously as a policy option. Advocates became more pragmatic, arguing that a Basic Income would simplify an over-complex social security system, encourage care and voluntary labour, and incentivize improvements in employment conditions. And then in 1985, another report by the Scientific Council for Government Policy took Basic Income even more seriously as a policy option, this time in the form of a small Basic Income alongside enhanced social insurance and means-tested systems. A funding package composed of environmental and production taxes was proposed, but no details were provided. What was provided was an administrative method: employers would pay the Basic Income to their employees and then deduct the cost from company tax liabilities. The Basic Income would therefore function as a direct wage subsidy rather than as an indirect one, and at the same time it would protect employees' incomes and reduce employee income inequality. As council members saw it, the Basic Income would enable the statutory minimum wage to be abolished without compromising employees' net incomes, and the Scientific Council argued in defence of their plan that the combination of Basic Income and the abolition of the statutory minimum wage would make part-time employment more feasible for both industry and workers, and that the combination of the Basic Income and part-time employment would take a lot of households off means-tested benefits. Unfortunately, rejection of the report and its highly pragmatic approach was almost unanimous. Trades unions, and even Voedingsbond FNV, rejected it, perhaps because the administrative mechanism had made it clear that unions would end up negotiating over only a proportion of an employee's income rather than over the whole of it, as well as because the report envisaged the abolition of the statutory minimum wage. The lack of costings in a context of austerity, the proposal to abolish the statutory minimum wage, the failure to acknowledge a widespread desire to see a mandatory shorter working week, and an attempt to make changes to every part of the tax and benefits systems at the same time, were all problematic. Everyone could find some reason to object to elements of the complex package, so everyone could find reasons to reject the package as a whole. The main lesson that Groot and van der Veen draw from this episode is that detailed costings, and a clear description of effects on households, are essential elements of any proposal that wants to be taken seriously (Groot and van der Veen, 2000: 200–206; van Berkel, 1994a; 1994b: 4). Detailed costings have appeared in the Netherlands since then, although it is unfortunate that the Central Planning Board's 2006 research exercise simulated a Basic Income and single flat tax proposal and on that basis declared that 'a basic income is not efficient as a redistributive system' (de Mooij, 2006: 68), which of course it would not be. A properly scientific approach would have set feasibility criteria and then simulated a wide variety of Basic Income schemes to see if one could be found that conformed to the criteria (Torry, 2020b; 2020e). A further research exercise by the Central Planning Board in 2015 to discover the employment market effects of a variety of tax and benefit reforms again simulated the effects of a Basic Income and single flat tax scheme and found that employment market activity would fall by 5 per cent (Jongen et al., 2015: 10–11). Again, a properly scientific approach would have set feasibility criteria for employment market activity and then simulated a wide variety of Basic Income schemes to see if one could be found that fitted the criteria. It is always unfortunate when effort is expended on research that is conducted using unscientific methods.

In 1987, fourteen organizations, including trade union sections, political parties, claimants' unions, and voluntary organizations, established the Workshop on Basic Income, which became the Vereniging Basisinkomen (Basic Income Association) in 1991. Its thrice-yearly newsletter, work on costed Basic Income schemes by Paul de Beer, who worked alongside Robert van der Veen, and discussion of the differences between Basic Income,

Negative Income Tax and a variety of alternative structures, represent a strategy remarkably similar to that of the Basic Income Research Group in the UK: a similarity already represented in the small Basic Income accompanied by means-tested benefits recommended in a paper presented at the first BIEN conference in 1986 (Douben and Dekkers, 1988), and by the staged process for the implementation of a Basic Income recommended by Alexander De Roo at the second BIEN conference in 1988 (De Roo, 1990). During the early 1990s, the Basic Income debate in the Netherlands saw occasional stimulus provided by the publication of reports by a variety of organizations, including a report in 1992 by the Central Planning Bureau (van Berkel, 1994b: 6); and then in 1995 both the Minister of Economic Affairs and the Minister of Finance, members of a 'social liberal' coalition government, expressed sympathy for the idea of a Basic Income: but again path dependency resulted in tinkering with the existing social security system. Subsidized jobs and employment requirements were central elements of the reform that followed.

The late 1990s saw some important debates: for instance, over whether the provision of a Basic Income would incentivize less secure employment and therefore discourage skills development and human capital formation among young adults. The response offered was that the Basic Income would help to pay for higher education, meaning that loans would not be required to the same extent; and the higher taxation required to pay for Basic Incomes would reduce net earned incomes, so net foregone earned income would be lower and higher education therefore incentivized. Perhaps not sufficiently recognized was that a further effect of the Basic Income could be less tax revenue being spent on higher education because tax revenue would be needed to fund the Basic Income, meaning that the overall effect might be ambiguous (Atkinson, 1995: 135). In any case, as Groot and van der Veen suggest, the norm of full-time employment has already been eroded, and working hours are already declining, so the kind of employment scenario that would require a Basic Income is already beginning to occur; and similarly, more women are now in the employment market, so the former problem of Basic Income schemes costing too much because non-employed women would have to receive Basic Incomes and would not be contributing to them might no longer exist to the same extent (Groot and van der Veen, 2000: 207–13).

During the mid- to late-1990s, a variety of proposals more or less like a Basic Income were made by the Green Left Party (GroenLinks) and trades unions, including a 'basic benefit', 'basisuitkering', proposed by the Trade Union Federation, that looked remarkably like Tony Atkinson's Participation Income (see Chapter 7). The aim was to take account of what Groot and van der Veen refer to as 'the most entrenched of all conditionalities, the "reciprocity" requirement of willingness to do (un)paid work' (Groot and van der Veen, 2000: 214). No account seems to have been taken of the near impossibility of administering such an income. At the same time, the Labour Party was moving in a similar direction by proposing that the definition of 'work' should encompass unpaid community and care activity, and that the benefits system should facilitate the shift (Groot and van der Veen, 2000: 213–15).

Of particular interest in the Dutch context are the tax credits paid since 2001. These are Negative Income Taxes that are calculated using rather complicated formulae not dissimilar to those used to calculate the Earned Income Tax Credit in the USA. The only substantial difference is that in the Netherlands the tax credits are managed by the employer if there is one, whereas in the US the payments are made annually following the submission of tax returns. An important motive for the Dutch scheme is that the system increases the incentive for the partner of an employee to seek employment. The complication is that when the tax credits were introduced they were stated to be a form of Basic Income by individuals involved in the Dutch Basic Income debate: understandable because the tax credits are not conditional on employment status and are paid to the individual rather than to the household (Groot and van der Veen, 2000: 199, 216). However, the complexity of the formulae for calculating the General Tax Credit (algemene heffingskorting) and the Labour Tax Credit (arbeidskorting), both of which are income-tested, and the fact that the Labour Tax Credit is only available to people in employment, mean that it is difficult to see how they can be aligned very closely with Basic Income. Very different are the Netherlands child benefit, paid unconditionally for every child, and the old age pension, paid unconditionally to every older person who satisfies a residency condition. These are real Basic Incomes according to the definition (Belastingdienst, 2020; Groot and van der Veen, 2000: 200).

Of particular contemporary interest is a series of local experiments taking place in the Netherlands. Like the 2001 tax credits, these have had the label 'Basic Income experiments' attached to them, which they are not. The incomes being tested are household-based; they are being tested only on current social assistance recipients; they exclude people in full-time or part-time employment or self-employment; and they are means-tested. In this respect they are not dissimilar to the B-MINCOME experiment described above; and like the Barcelona experiment, they are of interest simply because they are happening. Before 2001, social assistance benefits were regulated by the central government, but since then local authorities have been allocated budgets for social assistance and have been permitted to adapt benefits to their local employment market circumstances. Since the 2015 'Participation Act', local authorities have been permitted to vary what claimants have to do in order to retain their benefits, and some local authorities have taken advantage of the invitation to innovate offered by article 83 of the Act: hence the experiments that began in 2017 and 2018 in Utrecht, Tilburg, Wageningen, Groningen, Deventer and Nijmegen.

The experiments were designed to test the effects of varying the work-related conditions related to social assistance benefits, with different cities using different conditions, but with a consistent evaluation process being used to ensure that the results in the different cities could be compared. Comparisons were sought between the effects of the current regime, with its sanctions for not seeking employment and not accepting it if it was offered; a regime that reduces the level of benefit more slowly as earned income rises; a regime with no work-related requirements; and a regime with intensive case-worker involvement with each participant. All of the experiments were with means-tested benefits, so no Basic Income was being tested. The evaluation will be studying the levels of social participation, individual wellbeing, reintegration into paid work, the cost of each scheme, the financial situations of claimants, and caseworker evaluations of the schemes.

The choice of treatments during the two-year experiments has been motivated by a variety of kinds of research: firstly, research that shows that poverty reduces cognitive functioning (Mani et al., 2013; Mullainathan and Shafir, 2013), and that dealing with complex and intrusive bureaucracy can exacerbate the effect, leading to the hypothesis that reducing conditionalities might increase cognitive capacity; secondly, research that suggests that people can be motivated by fairness (Fehr and Schmidt, 2003), meaning that a generous context can result in reciprocal generosity, and harm can generate revenge, which in turn suggests that punitive sanctions might have the opposite effect to that intended; and thirdly, research on the importance of intrinsic motivation and the ways in which it can be compromised by attempts at extrinsic motivation (Ryan and Deci, 2000). All of this research suggests that better outcomes, on a range of measures, might be expected if benefit conditionality is reduced (Groot and Verlaat, 2019); and it would of course have been better if a genuine Basic Income had been tested alongside the various conditional benefits, because then the effects of the extreme case of no conditionality whatsoever could have been evaluated (Groot, 2004: 93).

A review of the history of the debate about Basic Income in the Netherlands finds that the debate started out with an emphasis on the idea's emancipatory possibilities in a time of relative economic prosperity during the 1970s; that political, press and academic interest rose during the period of high unemployment during the mid-1980s; and that during the 1990s emphasis shifted towards how a Basic Income could enable the poor to escape from the poverty trap. Throughout, most of the resistance to the idea has been related to its unconditionality in relation to employment. A spectrum of advocacy methods has been in evidence in sequence: argument for a sizeable Basic Income on the basis of its emancipatory and redistributive possibilities; argument for a smaller Basic Income on the basis that it could solve many of the problems faced by the current benefits system, particularly during periods of high unemployment; and a recognition that steps that loosen the connection between income and paid work are steps towards a Basic Income: although the authors caution that by this route the Netherlands might end up with 'something like a basic income, though by then no one may remember what the term was supposed to mean' (Groot and van der Veen, 2000: 197, 217, 219).

The Netherlands Basic Income debate has been of particular interest because of its diversity over time, and the ways in which it continues to embrace new directions at the same time as retaining its historic approaches. Alexander de Roo, a Dutch Green Party Member of the European Parliament (MEP), has been at the more campaigning end of the European Basic Income debate for forty years; Robert van der Veen has been at the heart of the academic debate for a similar length of time; Hilde Latour and others have ensured that the Netherlands has been at the heart of the organization UBI Europe and its European Citizens' Initiatives, and heavily engaged in debates about the relationship between cryptocurrencies and Basic Income; and the Netherlands are heavily involved in the wave of experiments now taking place. While the conditionality-reducing experiments in the Netherlands were not themselves Basic Income pilot projects, the results that emerge will no doubt be a significant element in the ongoing debate about the entirely unconditional Basic Income.

A similarly diverse debate has emerged in Germany, where the ability of Basic Income to broaden the definition of work beyond paid employment has also been an important element in the debate (Duverger, 2018: 94–5; Sloman, 2019: 228–9).

GERMANY

In 1978, the artist Joseph Beuys published an Aufruf zur Alternative, 'Call for an Alternative', in which he called for an income separated from work and no longer of a 'dependent size', but instead 'guaranteed' as an 'elemental human right', an 'original right'. While the terminology is not entirely clear, the combination of the resetting of the relationship between work and income that Beuys asks for, and the fact that the income would not have depended on work (or on anything else presumably), means that Beuys had a Basic Income in mind (Beuys, [1978] 2019).

During the 1980s and 1990s, books and articles about Basic Income were written, and German scholars were well integrated into the European debate. An important figure was the sociologist Claus Offe, one of the first two co-chairs of the Basic Income European Network, whose earlier contributions on the subject emphasized the way in which a Basic Income would release individuals for a variety of kinds of work, but who eventually agreed with Tony Atkinson that a first step should be a Participation Income that would require participation conditions to be fulfilled before an income could be paid (Offe, 1992; 2000).

During the 1980s, political parties were sometimes content to debate Basic Income: but following the fall of the Berlin Wall, and the massive cost of German reunification, discussion of social policy reform almost disappeared, and the story was one of tax cuts and continuing means-testing (Lessenich, 2000: 247–50; Liebermann, 2012: 180–81). Unemployment was far more of a political concern than poverty, so any discussion of benefits reform, including in the direction of a Basic Income, was framed in relation to how it would facilitate the low wage employment seen as necessary to competing in the global marketplace (Lessenich, 2000: 253). Such a context is not an easy one for debate about a Basic Income that would have uncoupled income and work: so although elements of the German Basic Income debate continued to emphasize the broadening of the definition of work that a Basic Income would facilitate, more central to practical policymaking were ideas that cohered with an existing work ethic about paid employment (Duverger, 2018: 94–5; Lessenich, 2000: 247; Sloman, 2019: 228–9). Among these ideas was the Bürgergeld, 'citizen's income': but not 'Citizen's Income' as a synonym for Basic Income. The Bürgergeld proposal was for an integration of means-tested benefits into one single means-tested benefit that would have functioned rather like a Negative Income Tax, would have reduced the total marginal deduction rate related to current means-tested benefits so as to incentivize employment, and would have functioned 'as a wage-supplementing income ... reliable, indiscretionary, easy to administer, needs-oriented, and without time limits' (Mitschke, 2000: 111). The household-based and income-tested Bürgergeld would in fact have been far from easy to administer (see Chapter 1), and it is fortunate that the idea failed to gather political support because of the perceived political cost of trying to change too many parts of the tax and benefits system all at the same time (Lessenich, 2000: 251–2).

During the last twenty years, Germany has seen a lively debate about a genuine Basic Income, beginning with a poster campaign in 2003. In 2004, Netzwerk Grundeinkommen (Basic Income Network), was founded, and since then it has provided a focus for German Basic Income campaigning. Think tanks and policymakers began to take an occasional interest, and videos were made and distributed; and then in 2005, during a radio interview, Götz Werner, founder and former CEO of the drugstore chain DM, advocated a Basic Income funded by taxing consumption. As he put it, this would be an income in order to be able to work, rather than work in order to have an income. In 2010 he proposed a Basic Income of €1,000 per month (Werner and Goehler, 2010). Also in 2010 a government commission met to discuss a petition asking for a Basic Income and signed by over 50,000 people (Liebermann, 2012: 175–80).

There has been something of a history in Germany of using the term Grundeinkommen to describe a variety of different mechanisms, including a Negative Income Tax and a Minimum Income Guarantee (Liebermann, 2012: 181); and in 2016, Maximilian Sommer published what he called a 'Basic Income scheme for Germany' (Sommer, 2016), which was not a Basic Income scheme at all: it was a Negative Income Tax of a particularly complicated variety; and when Sommer looked as if he was about to discuss the administrative differences between Basic Income and Negative Income Tax, he simply suggested that 'this is a question of the actual implementation of a specific scheme and exceeds the scope of this paper' (Sommer, 2016: 61). Unfortunately, the title of his book is *A Feasible Basic Income Scheme for Germany*, so one might have thought that discussion of whether the scheme would be feasible to administer would have been at the heart of the discussion (Citizen's Basic Income Trust, 2016a). Germany, like the United States and the UK, has been fortunate not to have found itself attempting to implement a Negative Income Tax.

One unique aspect of the German Basic Income debate is Mein Grundeinkommen, founded in 2014 by Michael Bohmeyer, a successful young entrepreneur. Mein Grundeinkommen is an independent crowd-funded organization that pays genuine Basic Incomes for short periods of time to individuals chosen by a lottery. The aim is to discover how people's lives change in the context of a Basic Income (Duverger, 2018: 123; Van Parijs and Vanderborght, 2017: 138). At the time of writing, almost 500 one-year Basic Incomes had been awarded (Liebermann, 2020: 213) and the scheme was due to be scaled up into a pilot project paying €1,200 per month to 120 individuals for a period of three years. The German Institute for Economic Research is involved with the project, and a randomized controlled trial is intended (Mein Grundeinkommen, 2020). While Grundeinkommen does not always mean a Basic Income, Mein Grundeinkommen certainly does.

A further interesting development in Germany was the foundation of a new political party, the Bündnis Grundeinkommen (Basic Income Alliance), in 2016. The party has gained no more than 0.2 per cent of the votes in the various elections for which it has presented candidates, and unfortunately in 2017 the Social Democratic Party used the name Solidarisches Grundeinkommen (Solidarity Basic Income), to describe a work-tested and means-tested benefit (Liebermann, 2020: 214–15). Misnaming of benefits has always been a strategy available to governments to obfuscate the true nature of their policies, and it is unfortunate that the even worse tactic of employing a term that already means something else is becoming more common. The last but one UK Government called an increased National Minimum Wage a 'National Living Wage'. 'Living Wage' already meant a subsistence wage that a successful campaign was persuading an increasing number of employers to pay to their employees, and for the Government to use 'living wage' language was not only disingenuous, because the increased National Minimum Wage was not enough to live on, but it also took the wind out of the Living Wage campaign, which might have been the reason for doing it. It is not impossible that the German misnaming was intended to deflate the growing campaign for a genuine Basic Income.

In spite of the difficulties, lively and diverse debate continues in Germany (Liebermann, 2020: 216–25), and also in Austria, both facilitated by jointly run German language conferences (Liu, 2020: 237). Significant elements of those debates are an understanding that a Basic Income could both reduce poverty and contribute to personal freedom; a recognition that a Basic Income, particularly if funded by a resource tax, could make a significant contribution to a postgrowth economy and society and the reduction of damaging climate change; and multiple detailed Basic Income and Minimum Income Guarantee proposals made by Nongovernmental Organizations, political party working groups and academics (Blaschke, 2017; Howard et al., 2019; Schachtschneider, 2020).

SWITZERLAND

An event that in its own terms had to be regarded as a failure was in hindsight one of the most important events of the recent Basic Income debate.

In 2006, Enno Schmidt, an artist, and Daniel Häni, Managing Director of the largest coffee house in Switzerland, the 'Unternehmen Mitte' in the centre of Basel, began to campaign for a Basic Income for Switzerland. Discussion about Basic Income was not new to Switzerland: an organization affiliated to the Basic Income Earth Network (BIEN) had been founded in 2001 and along with the International Labour Organization had helped to organize BIEN's 2002 congress in Geneva (Basic Income Earth Network—Switzerland, 2020): but Schmidt's and Häni's campaigning style was something new: a well-designed and engaging website (Initiative Grundeinkommen, 2020); a ten-day event at the coffee house; and a high-quality full-length film about Basic Income, 'Grundeinkommen: Ein Kulturimpuls' (Basic Income: A cultural imperative)—'an income is like the wind beneath your wings' (Schmidt and Häni, 2008). Other people joined in, and Christian Müller and Daniel Straub from Zürich suggested that a Federal Popular Initiative should be attempted. Popular Initiatives are a unique aspect of Switzerland's democracy. If, during a period of eighteen months, 100,000 signatures can be collected in public places for a legislative proposal, then the Swiss Federal Government has to hold a nation-

wide referendum, and if a majority is achieved then the proposal becomes law.
The initiative was launched in 2012 with this proposal:

Federal Popular Initiative 'For an unconditional basic income':
The Federal Constitution of 18 April 1999 is amended as follows:
Art. 110a (new) unconditional basic income
(1)   The Confederation shall ensure the introduction of an unconditional basic
        income.
(2)   The basic income should enable the entire population to live in dignity and
        participate in public life.
(3)   The law regulates in particular the financing and the amount of the basic
        income. (Schmidt, 2019: 429)

In October 2013, 126,000 valid signatures were submitted to the Federal
Chancellery. To mark the occasion, the initiators poured eight million 5 rappen
coins onto the Federal Square in Bern in front of the Federal Palace and the
National Bank, and swept them into a carpet of money to represent a floor for
the life and work of the whole of Swiss society (Switzerland has a population
of eight million) (BBC, 2013; Schmidt, 2020). The image triggered widespread debate around the world.

The Federal Popular Initiative having succeeded, the Federal Government
was obliged to hold a referendum, and to prepare for this various ministries
were asked to assess the Initiative's demands. During the autumn of 2015 the
Federal Council, Switzerland's governing body, recommended that Parliament
should oppose the Initiative and recommend that citizens should reject it.
As the referendum approached, every household in Switzerland received
a booklet containing arguments for and against a Basic Income; and the initiators themselves publicized the referendum by distributing 10 franc notes with
stickers about the vote attached to them.

On 30 April 2016, the day before Labour Day, the campaign team dressed
as robots, paraded through Zürich's main shopping street, and declared 1
May to be Basic Income Day; and then on 14 May the campaign displayed
a huge poster on Switzerland's largest square, the Plainpalais in Geneva. The
poster was 8,115.53 square metres in area—a Guinness World Record—and
it read: 'What would you do if your income were taken care of?' (Initiative
Grundeinkommen, 2016). The referendum took place on 5 June 2016. Out of
the 46.4 per cent of the electorate voting, 23.1 per cent voted for the proposition. The majority voted against.

Although the proposition itself had been clear that the level of the Basic
Income and its funding mechanism were to be decided by the Swiss Parliament
and further referenda, it might not have helped the campaign that in 2012
Müller and Straub had suggested an illustrative Basic Income scheme that
would have given 2,500 Swiss francs per month to every adult and 625

Swiss francs per month for every child (Müller and Straub, 2012: 47, 56–65). In monetary terms this was the equivalent of £1,765 per month (Agence France-Presse, 2016), but because of Switzerland's high cost of living some people thought that the figure was about right, and some that it was too little (Schmidt, 2020). However, it was still a substantial sum, and those opposed to the Popular Initiative proposal were able to claim that it would make the Basic Income unaffordable. The more academic discussion of financing possibilities for a Basic Income published in 2010 by Basic Income Earth Network— Switzerland/BIEN-CH (Dommen-Meade, 2010) received nothing like the same publicity, perhaps understandably.

In spite of the setback, Schmidt and his collaborators remain positive. As Schmidt says, 'the subject is on the table' (Schmidt, 2019: 430), and the Popular Initiative can take a lot of the credit for that. There is still a high level of debate about Basic Income in Switzerland (Liu, 2020: 236–7); after the vote, 69 per cent of the Swiss population expected a second referendum on Basic Income to be held; and a second Popular Initiative on Basic Income has now been launched.

The impact of the campaign and the referendum was felt well beyond Switzerland. On the day of the referendum the world's press was gathered around the campaign headquarters in Basel, and the publicity that had sur- rounded the four-year campaign had already generated debate about Basic Income throughout Europe and beyond (Schmidt, 2019: 430; 2020). This was, after all, the first time that an entire country's population had debated Basic Income and been asked to make a decision about it. Switzerland's direct democracy is an educational process, and not only for Switzerland.

SCANDINAVIA

Scandinavia's benefits systems exhibit characteristics that take them close to practical universalism: that is, a combination of characteristics, such as funding from general taxation, a rights-based approach, social insurance with high replacement rates, minimal use of means-testing, and well-resourced public services, particularly in relation to childcare, mean that the vast majority of the population can feel secure that their incomes and the services available to them will be fairly secure and will be sufficient for social inclusion as well as for subsistence (Esping-Andersen, 1990). These characteristics have been somewhat eroded during the past thirty years, particularly by an 'activation' agenda that privileges a 'paid work' norm above other social values, but Scandinavian benefits systems are still sufficiently different from those of other European countries for the term 'Scandinavian model' to continue to make sense.

Until the mid-1990s, for anyone who was a member of a government-subsidized unemployment insurance fund and had been employed for 26 weeks, Danish Unemployment Benefit could be claimed for anything between seven and nine years: an experience not dissimilar from that of a Basic Income. Since then, the qualifying period has lengthened, the claim period has shortened, availability for work is no longer sufficient to qualify, and active steps to find employment are now required. Similarly, a social assistance system designed simply to replace lost income was replaced during the 1990s by a system with activation policies at its heart. The state pension and child allowances that were once unconditional are now means-tested (Christensen and Loftager, 2000: 257–61). Christensen and Loftager conclude that now 'the status of citizenship is considered as being conditioned by the ability to meet obligations to work' (Christensen and Loftager, 2000: 261).

During the 1970s, a number of Danish authors proposed a Basic Income, and in particular Villy Sørensen, Niels Meyer and Krisen Helveg Petersen, in their *Oprør fra midten* in 1978 (later translated into English as *Revolt from the Centre*), which gave birth to an ongoing social movement campaigning for the implementation of a Basic Income; although in his presentation to the first BIEN congress in Louvain-la-Neuve in 1986 it became clear that the 'Basic Income' that Meyer had in mind for young adults was in fact an income-tested benefit (Meyer, 1988).

And then, during the mid-1990s, a further period of grass-roots campaigning met rejection of the idea of a Basic Income from political parties, government ministers and civil servants. Some political actors were opposed to Basic Income because they believed that changed employment market behaviour might make the proposal unaffordable in the long run, but the most common objections were moral: that a Basic Income would create a passive and State-dependent citizenry, both in terms of the employment market and in other ways. The evidence of Basic Income pilot projects and of similar experiments is that the opposite would be the case, and the objection took no account of the fact that it was in fact the activation trends related to existing benefits systems that were creating a passive and State-dependent citizenry.

During the mid-1990s, the one political party that did take an interest in Basic Income was the Radical Liberals, which often held the balance of power in the Danish Parliament: but a commission report then declared a large Basic Income to be too expensive and a smaller one not as useful. The report's conclusions were challenged, but both political and public interest had already evaporated (Christensen and Loftager, 2000: 261–5).

As Christensen and Loftager put it, 'Basic Income has never seriously been on the Danish agenda of practical politics. On the contrary, … the idea has been outright rejected, and political leaders have been careful to dissociate themselves from it' (Christensen and Loftager, 2000: 257). At the same time, the 'activation' agenda has added to the conditionality of the existing system and moved it even further from the unconditionality of Basic Income. However, the foundations exist in the Danish welfare state for a more positive attitude towards Basic Income. The welfare state as a whole has a 'human development' character. Education policy prioritizes personal and social development; employment incentives are still as important as sanctions; and 'cooperative values and practices tend to be inculcated and governed through socialisation rather than compulsion' (Haagh, 2019b: 304). This means that there are social forces pulling in two directions, both towards and away from the kind of universalism and unconditionality represented by Basic Income. As Haagh suggests: 'The direction of basic income debate and transformation in Denmark therefore remains to be seen' (Haagh, 2019b: 314).

Why has Basic Income been 'almost a non-issue' in Norway and Sweden? It's not that there haven't been authors proposing Basic Income: there have been, although some proposals, such as that of the Swede Gunnar Adler-Karlsson during the 1970s, have included an employment condition, and so have not been proposals for Basic Incomes. Occasional newspaper articles about Basic Income in Sweden have met with no response, and means-testing remains the default position for all of the political parties, although in both Sweden and Norway child allowances remain unconditional. Any consideration given to Basic Income regards it as a utopian idea that might happen in the future, but certainly not now.

One reason for the lack of interest has been the success of the Swedish and Norwegian welfare states in protecting their populations' living standards; and in Sweden the dominance of the Social Democratic Party, which has always rejected the idea of a Basic Income on the basis that means-testing is the best way to provide for those with no other source of income, that social policy's goal should be full employment, and that members of society have an obligation to work, by which is normally meant paid employment (Andersson, 2000: 224–7, 233–4).

FINLAND

Finland is the Nordic outlier in relation to the Basic Income debate, witnessing frequent academic interest, occasional political interest and a significant experiment (Halmetoja et al., 2019). In 1971, the writer Samuli Paronen proposed a genuine Basic Income, and numerous other authors have followed his lead, often seeing Basic Income as a promise of time for creativity and of an ability to leave poor-quality jobs and therefore of higher job quality. Some of the proposals have been for entirely feasible genuine Basic Incomes—often called a 'Citizen's Wage' or a 'Citizen's Income'—that would not be sufficient to live on, but would provide sufficient for subsistence if paid alongside a low-wage job or existing means-tested benefits. Other proposals have been for short-term 'sabbatical' Basic Incomes; for incomes that would have been a Basic Income if they had been based on the individual rather than on the household; and for a Negative Income Tax. At the end of the 1980s, the Green Party took an interest: but then a serious depression hit Finland and the idea of a Basic Income disappeared from view. As the depression subsided during the mid-1990s, think tank research caused Basic Income to become the dominant option in the social security reform debate (De Wispelaere et al., 2019: 394; Halmetoja et al., 2019). A variety of reform proposals emerged, some of which were for Basic Income schemes, but others were for a Participation Income, or for a work-tested but otherwise unconditional income. Somewhat unscientifically, social policy researchers during this period were sometimes rather dismissive of Basic Income, as were employers' organizations and trades unions, who were asking for incremental changes to means-tested benefits in order to ameliorate poverty traps. Objectors to Basic Income schemes were concerned that the cost would mean less money for public services; and objectors to a Participation Income recognized that 'work' might be 'constructed' by organizations in order to give people access to the benefit (Andersson, 2000: 227–32).

As Jan-Otto Andersson shows, Finland's political parties have been willing to discuss Basic Income since the 1980s, although often preferring a Negative Income Tax. In 2000, Osmo Soininvaara, an influential member of the Green Party who had written positively about Basic Income in 1980, became Minister of Social Affairs. Only the Social Democratic Party has consistently rejected Basic Income as an idea worth pursuing, but unlike in Sweden, the Social Democratic Party in Finland normally has to govern as part of a coalition, or it finds itself in opposition to a Centre Party that has often supported more universal benefits. Importantly, Basic Income schemes recommended both by the Green Party and by the Left Alliance have been fully evaluated by microsimulation, thus stimulating a debate about feasibility and not just about Basic Income's desirability (De Wispelaere et al., 2019: 393).

A further reason for Finland's historically more positive attitude to Basic Income is that Finland has seen rather more mass unemployment than Sweden, and its welfare state is younger. Yet another reason is a cultural difference, with Finland's culture being more individualistic, and Sweden's more collectivist. History might also be a factor. Finland has faced significant disruptions until relatively recently, largely because it is sandwiched between Sweden and Russia. Rapid response to new situations is therefore part of the national psyche. It is no accident that Finland was an early adopter of mobile phone technology and was the birthplace of Nokia. Sweden has a more stable history, and tends to work more by consensus-building and evolution (Andersson, 2000: 233–5). Given this background, it is not entirely surprising that Finland hosted a small experiment in something close to a Basic Income for two years from January 2017 to December 2018.

In 2015, in a context of heightened interest in Basic Income generated by the Swiss referendum on the subject, the newly elected Centre-Right coalition government, led by Juha Sipilä, promised to hold a Basic Income experiment in Finland. In 2016, a consortium of Finnish universities, research institutes and think tanks, led by Olli Kangas of the Finnish Social Insurance Institution Kela, published a report outlining a number of options (Kansaneläkelaitos Kela/Social Insurance Institution of Finland Kela, 2016):

> The basic income experiment is one of the policy measures designed to reform the Finnish social security system to better correspond with the changes in working life, to make social security more participatory and diminish work-disincentives, reduce bureaucracy and simplify the overly complex benefit system. (Kansaneläkelaitos Kela/Social Insurance Institution of Finland Kela, 2016: 5)

In December 2016, following scrutiny by parliamentary committees, the Finnish Parliament passed by a majority of 170 to 30 legislation that allowed the experiment to go ahead (Ministry of Social Affairs and Health, 2016). The Centre Party's support both for evidence-based policy and for Basic Income had persuaded the party's coalition partners to permit the experiment to proceed, but their resistance was an important reason for the focus on the employment market and for the refusal of an extension once the two-year experiment had been held. Long-term supporters of Basic Income, such as the Green Party and the Left Alliance, objected to the narrow focus of the project, but their support for Basic Income as an idea meant that they did not object to the legislation (De Wispelaere et al., 2019: 393; Stirton et al., 2017). As always, particular political circumstances both permitted an initiative to occur and determined its character.

A significant influence on the character of the experiment when it was held was a report published by the think tank Tänk (Forss and Kanninen, 2014), which had suggested a random selection of individuals and obligatory participation, but the final design process was coordinated by a consortium containing Kela, the Finnish social insurance organization; the universities of Helsinki, Tampere, Turku and Eastern Finland; a research funding body; Tänk; the Federation of Finnish Enterprises; and the Association of Finnish Local and Regional Authorities. Initially a variety of models were to be tested, including a Negative Income Tax, and different methods were to be employed, including randomly selected individuals and a saturation site, but in the end only one scheme was chosen: making the main unemployment benefit unconditional for a period of two years for 2,000 individuals randomly selected from the entire national population. This was partly because decisions about the character of the experiment were taken by government ministers and civil servants and submitted for consultation before the consortium had published its final report (De Wispelaere et al., 2019: 396). The plan had to be put to the Constitutional Law Committee to discover whether it was constitutional, and the Committee permitted the project to go ahead because even though it required differential treatment of individuals, which was not normally permitted, nobody would have ended up worse off, and the project would have benefited society as a whole (Kalliomaa-Puha et al., 2016). This has set an important precedent, and should ensure that questions should not arise over the constitutional legitimacy of future Basic Income experiments in Finland and possibly elsewhere.

The experiment was the first nationwide randomized controlled trial designed to pay a genuine Basic Income, in the sense that the income paid for two years was based on the individual, was not means-tested, and was not work-tested. The selection being nationwide rather than localized meant that no effects of relationships between individuals receiving the Basic Income could be measured (Forget, 2011; Calnitsky, 2016), but it did mean that a huge database of individuals was available to Kela both for the random selection of individuals who would have their benefits made unconditional and for the selection of a control group. An advantage of the mandatory participation required by the legislation was that the project's administrators could ensure that the sample was representative of the unemployed population of Finland; but a significant disadvantage of the design was that the sample group was entirely composed of individuals who on 1 December 2016 had been between the ages of twenty-five and fifty-eight and who on 30 November 2016 were in receipt of Finland's basic unemployment benefit or its labour market subsidy, and so not a group representative of the population as a whole. These decisions were entirely motivated by cost and administrative considerations. Another and considerable disadvantage of the experimental design was that it would have been unaffordable to pay the unconditional benefits to every member of Finland's population without at the same time making adjustments to the tax and benefits systems that were not made during the experiment, thus seriously compromising the experiment's status as a Basic Income pilot project: a point made by Osmo Soininvaara (2017). There were two reasons for the tax system not being altered for the experiment participants in the way in which it would have to be altered for a feasible nationwide Basic Income: the practical difficulty of doing so for 2,000 randomly selected individuals; and the Minister of Finance's lack of engagement with the experiment (De Wispelaere et al., 2019: 400–401). The lesson to draw is that in any country with a tax and benefits system as complex as Finland's, an experiment will need consistent commitment across all relevant government departments and among all relevant government ministers if it is to be a genuine Basic Income pilot project.

One decision largely imposed by the context of the experiment was that of the level at which the unconditional incomes would be paid: €560 per month for each randomly selected individual. This matched the level of basic unemployment benefit and labour market subsidy, thus ensuring that nobody in either the test sample or the control group would be better off than someone in the other (Kalliomaa-Puha et al., 2016): except, of course, that someone in the test sample who found employment would keep their unconditional income as well as their earned income, whereas someone in the control group would not. Any Basic Income pilot project will inevitably suffer from this injustice. A further significant disadvantage of the project's design was that the experiment was to be for only two years. This is probably too short a time for behavioural change to emerge, simply because participants will be thinking about the period following the end of the experiment before it even starts. This means that while wellbeing might improve due to the lower stress levels that would accompany the unconditional incomes, employment market change might be more difficult to detect (Forget, 2011). The short time span was again motivated by cost and political concerns: the political motivation here being the need to see results before the end of the election cycle (De Wispelaere et al., 2019: 401).

Because Kela managed much of Finland's existing unemployment benefit and labour market subsidy, and because it has offices throughout the country, it was the obvious choice to administer the project. The problem was that Kela was only appointed to evaluate the project as well as administer it in June 2018, meaning that no baseline survey was taken with which wellbeing and health measurements taken later in the project could be compared. However, as this was a randomized controlled trial, it was at least possible to compare outcomes for the test sample and for the control group. Interim results published in February 2019 reported employment market results for the first year of the experiment and some other results for both years. After the first year of the experiment no significant employment market effects were in evidence, although there was a small upswing at the end of the year. This result was of course interpreted in two directions (Dent, 2019; Lehto, 2019). Because the €560 per month was not withdrawn when someone found employment, it might have been expected that employment market activity would have increased. On the other hand, because someone with low living costs and no dependents might be able to live on €560 per month, it might have been expected that employment market activity would have decreased. The only conclusion to draw from there having been no overall employment market effects was either that neither factor was operating to any significant extent, perhaps because a year was too short a time for either effect to occur, or that the effects of both factors had on average balanced out across the sample as a whole (Citizen's Basic Income Trust, 2019; Kela, 2019). When the final results were published, it was found that after two years there had been a small increase in employment market activity: 'During the observation period from November 2017 to October 2018, days in employment increased, on average, about six days more in the group that received basic income than in the control group' (Kangas et al., 2020: 188). Larger increases had been experienced by families with children, and by individuals whose mother tongue was not Finnish.

Unfortunately the Finnish Government had done what should never be done half way through an experiment: it had changed the context of the experiment by increasing the conditionality related to unemployment benefits—although given that the significant difference between the incomes received by the test sample and the control group was that they were unconditional for the former and work-tested and means-tested for the latter, it might be that changes in the work conditionality of unemployment benefit would have had only a small effect on the results, if any.

What was totally clear from the research data based on questionnaires and interviews with participants was that individuals in the test sample experienced better wellbeing, less stress, less depression, less bureaucracy, less financial stress, better cognitive functioning, a higher rate of trust in others, more trust in their futures, and more trust in politicians, than individuals in the control group, and that €560 per month was experienced as a more adequate income in the pilot group than in the control group even though the Basic Income was at the same level as the means-tested benefit received by the control group. Some recipients of the Basic Income had experienced a wider variety of participation in society outside employment, and a sense of autonomy had increased (Kela, 2019; Kangas et al., 2020: 188).

As we have recognized throughout this account, both political and practical realities heavily influenced most of the design and implementation character-istics of the experiment, suggesting that this will be true of future experiments. As De Wispelaere et al. (2018) suggest, this should be no surprise given that Basic Income experiments function firmly within the political arena.

A significant factor in relation to any practical experiment will always be the electoral cycle. A government could reckon on getting a Basic Income experiment planned and carried out within the five or so years permitted by the cycle. Agreeing, planning and implementing a nationwide Basic Income might look rather more daunting: except, of course, that large-scale tax and benefits reforms can be carried out across more than one parliament if cross-party agreement can be obtained.

De Wispelaere points out that political interest in Basic Income can be 'cheap': that is, it can have no connection with either an ability or a willing-ness to implement a Basic Income scheme; or it can be 'superficial': that is, the engagement with Basic Income can be in purely general terms that mask divisions over the specifics of Basic Income schemes (De Wispelaere, 2016a). In the case of the Finnish Government, the desire to understand the likely employment market effects of Basic Income was probably genuine, but the lack of deep commitment across government departments meant that even if the experiment did generate useful results, those results could not tell us what effects a nationwide Basic Income scheme would have. There has to be a suspicion, therefore, that promising and carrying out an experiment was a way of delaying having to decide anything at all significant about Basic Income: but that does not mean that Basic Income researchers and advocates should refuse the offer of a pilot project. As De Wispelaere et al. have put it, if all that is on offer is an experiment of some kind then 'basic income advocates may have little choice but to grab the opportunity that is on offer, warts and all' (De Wispelaere et al., 2019: 404).

Even if flawed in terms of its design, a Basic Income experiment will always increase the level of debate about Basic Income, and possibly the level of understanding of what a Basic Income is and of its likely effects. An interesting outcome of the planning process for the Finnish experiment was the fake news that it accidentally generated. In the UK and elsewhere the idea circulated that Finland was about to pay a Basic Income to every member of its population. This was never true, but fake news generally continues to circulate no matter how many knowledgeable individuals and organizations attempt to deny its truth, and in this case the error gave birth to radio and television interviews about Basic Income, a whole radio programme about it, and numerous press articles (Torry, 2020c: 190).

Positive lessons learnt from the Finland experiment are that if possible broad political commitment should be obtained, broad-based planning and evaluation teams must be constructed, that even from experiments that some might regard as far from ideal some very useful results can emerge, and that everyone involved in the Basic Income debate in a country planning and carrying out an experiment should remain engaged with the experiment throughout, and constantly use the opportunity that the experiment offers to educate the public about Basic Income (De Wispelaere et al., 2019: 404).

PAUSED DEBATES

In 2017, the United Nations Development Programme office in Serbia began work with a number of local researchers, academics and advisers to construct Basic Income proposals that might be feasible within the Serbian context. Advice was taken from the team planning the Finland pilot project, and a plan was drawn up for a similar two-year experiment that would have paid a flat-rate income to at least 1,000 low-income individuals selected from the population of Niš, the country's third largest city. The income paid would have been a Basic Income if it had not been restricted to poor families. Monitoring was planned to continue for between two and five years after the two-year period of the experiment in order to measure labour market behaviour change, changes in health outcomes, and changes in household financial situations (Tahiraj, 2021).

In Serbia, discussion of such a plan was not easy to conduct because of the deeply embedded tendency to add exclusion criteria to the existing system rather than to make it more universal and less conditional. Younger government employees were interested and enthusiastic, but disinterest elsewhere meant that nothing has come of the plans. Similar discussions have taken place in Slovenia, where there is more clearly articulated support for Basic Income among the general public, including among trades unions: but still nothing practical has occurred.

An important reason for the lack of interest in changing the benefits system in the Western Balkan states is ubiquitous experimentation fatigue brought on by thirty years of post-communist transition and accompanying short-term projects carried out by Western European institutions (Tahiraj, 2019). A reason for resistance to unconditional incomes in particular is that the idea sounds rather communist and is rejected for that reason; and any suggestion that implementation might begin with poor households, and therefore with a means-tested and non-work-tested benefit, makes it unappealing for anyone not poor to engage with it. This means that either of the ways of introducing the idea of a Basic Income that might work in other contexts is problematic from the start in the Western Balkans. A further and perhaps even more important reason for it proving difficult to get almost any social policy issue on the public and political agenda is that that agenda is already so dominated by matters concerning national, ethnic and religious identities, that there is rarely room for anything else (Currion, 2020).

EUROPEAN CITIZENS' INITIATIVES

The most significant pan-European initiative to have been undertaken in relation to Basic Income has been the European Citizens' Initiatives. Since 2012, it has been possible for citizens of the European Union (EU) to employ a mechanism contained in the Lisbon Treaty of 2007 that enables them to petition the European Union institutions. A successful petition results in a response from the European Commission and a debate in the European Parliament. However, the conditions relating to the petition are stringent, to say the least. Seven individuals from different European Union countries must submit a proposal, which has to be within the competence of the European Union institutions: and so, for instance, a proposal could not ask for a European Basic Income to be established, because tax and benefits policy is reserved to national governments. Once the proposal has been approved as legitimate by the European Commission, one million statements of support from European Union voters in at least seven EU countries have to be collected in the prescribed form, with minimum thresholds in the different countries (European Commission, 2019).

In January 2013, the Commission agreed to an initiative in the following form:

> Asking the Commission, to encourage cooperation between the Member States (according to Art 156 TFEU) aiming to explore the Unconditional Basic Income (UBI) as a tool to improve their respective social security systems.
>
> In the long run the objective is to offer to each person in the EU the unconditional right as an individual, to having his/her material needs met to ensure a life of dignity as stated by the EU treaties, and to empower participation in society supported by the introduction of the UBI.
>
> In the short term, initiatives such as 'pilot-studies' (Art 156 TFEU) and examination of different models of UBI (EP resolution 2010/2039(INI) §44) should be promoted by the EU. (European Commission, 2014)

A new organization, Unconditional Basic Income Europe, was established, along with national organizations in different European Union countries, for the purpose of collecting statements of support (for instance, Basic Income UK). Over 300,000 statements of support were collected, which was a considerable achievement, but nowhere near the required overall threshold, so the initiative failed. However, the campaigning relating to the collection of statements of support had raised the profile of Basic Income in the European Union; UBI Europe has affiliated to BIEN and continues to hold Europe-wide conferences and to campaign on a European basis; and UBIE's various affiliated national organizations continue to campaign effectively in their own countries, often working alongside other Basic Income organizations: and so, for instance, in the UK Basic Income UK and the Citizen's Basic Income Trust have worked well together for nearly a decade.

At the time of writing, a new European Citizens' Initiative has just been launched:

> Subject Matter: Our aim is to establish the introduction of unconditional basic incomes throughout the EU which ensure every person's material existence and opportunity to participate in society as part of its economic policy. This aim shall be reached while remaining within the competences conferred to the EU by the Treaties.
>
> Objectives: We request the EU Commission to make a proposal for unconditional basic incomes throughout the EU, which reduce regional disparities in order to strengthen the economic, social and territorial cohesion in the EU. This shall realize the aim of the joint statement by the European Council, the European Parliament and the European Commission, stated in 2017, that 'the EU and its member states will also support efficient, sustainable and equitable social protection systems to

guarantee basic income' in order to combat inequality. (European Commission, 2020)

The collection of statements of support began on 25 September 2020 and will cease on the same date in 2021. During the 2013 initiative, Basic Income UK was an active participant. One of the casualties of Brexit is the UK's inability to participate in the new initiative.

THE BASIC INCOME EUROPEAN NETWORK (BIEN)

At the beginning of this chapter there is an account of the conference that took place in 1986 at Louvain-la-Neuve that gave birth to the Basic Income European Network (BIEN). A committee was established, with Peter Ashby from the UK and Claus Offe from West Germany as co-chairs, and Walter Van Trier as secretary, and proceedings of the conference were published (Miller, 1988: vi). At the heart of the organization's activities for the thirty-five years of its existence have been the dissemination of news and research, and the regular gathering of interested individuals from all over Europe, and subsequently from around the world, for the sharing of knowledge and experience. News and research were first of all disseminated through a regular newsletter posted to a growing membership (Basic Income Research Group, 1986a; Sloman, 2019: 228–9), and from 2000 onwards through an emailed 'Newsflash' that referred readers to the now highly active website full of news, research and opinion articles. Congresses were held once every two years in a variety of European cities: Antwerp in 1988, Florence in 1990, Paris in 1992, London in 1994, Vienna in 1996, Amsterdam in 1998, Berlin in 2000, Geneva in 2002 and Barcelona in 2004. Then things began to change. In 2004, in response to an increasing number of individual members and affiliated organizations joining from around the world, BIEN became the Basic Income Earth Network: 'Earth', not 'Global', so that it could keep the BIEN acronym; and congresses began to oscillate between Europe and the rest of the world. The 2006 congress was held in Cape Town, 2008 in Dublin, 2010 in São Paulo, 2012 in Münich, 2014 in Montreal and 2016 in Seoul. Because by then the Basic Income debate was increasing in both extent and diversity, the decision was taken to hold congresses annually. In 2017, the congress was in Lisbon, in 2018 in Tampere and in 2019 in Hyderabad. If the pandemic had not caused its cancellation, the 2020 congress would have been held in Brisbane. At the time of writing, the plan is to hold the 2021 congress online and organised in Glasgow, and in 2022 Brisbane will be the host. A postal vote held in 2020 confirmed the decision to hold congresses annually.

Proceedings of the congresses—usually the timetable and those congress papers that had then been submitted for publication by their authors—were published in hard copy until 1998, and in 2004 papers from the 2002 congress in Geneva formed much of a book (Standing, 2004). From 1998 onwards, papers submitted by their authors were published on BIEN's website. All three days of the congress in Louvain-la-Neuve in 1986 contained both parallel sessions at which papers were presented and plenary sessions for open discussion, a panel discussion, reports on the state of the debate in different countries, and a public lecture. The papers presented covered terminology, objections to Basic Income, Basic Income and women, Basic Income and young people, Basic Income and social change, Basic Income and the claimants' movement, working time reduction, unemployment and job insecurity, small businesses, Basic Income's relationships with a variety of political ideologies, Basic Income and trades unions, Basic Income and the commons, theories of justice, Basic Income as an inheritance, Basic Income's relationships with existing welfare states, the financial feasibilities and redistributive and employment effects of illustrative Basic Income schemes, and implementation strategies. From the 1988 conference onwards, each event was given a theme. It is not insignificant that in 1988 the theme was 'problems of implementation' (Van Trier, 1990), a question that has seen diverse levels of attention during the past thirty-five years, and that is now firmly on the agenda.

From the 1996 Vienna congress onwards, BIEN congresses have usually been preceded or followed by a one-day event to which congress participants are invited and also a wide variety of people from the country in which the congress is held. The aim is to discuss the state of the Basic Income debate in the host country, so in 2019 the congress began with a day dedicated to India's national debate on Basic Income and to different initiatives in different provinces. Most of the following three-day congress was divided between plenary panel discussions and parallel sessions. As there were five or six parallel sessions on each occasion, and most of the sessions consisted of five papers, it would be tedious to list all of the subjects tackled by the presenters, but a list of the overall topics tackled by the panel and parallel sessions might be instructive: employment, freedom and community, pilot projects, political action and the implementation of Basic Income, campaigning for Basic Income, the commons and public inheritance, sovereign wealth funds, blockchain technology, Basic Income and women, post-conflict scenarios, mental health, a caring economy and society, financial feasibility, Basic Income and the environment, modelling of illustrative Basic Income schemes, poverty and shame, definitions, complementary currencies, secular, religious, and other perspectives on Basic Income, and the state of the Basic Income debate in Asia, Africa, North America and South America.

A survey of the proceedings of all of the congresses reveals that those topics that appear in both the 1986 and 2019 lists of subjects all appear regularly in the programmes of all nineteen congresses. As we can see, there is little that was discussed in 1986 that was not discussed in 2019; and the additions in 2019 are divided between those that we might have expected to appear, such as pilot projects and ecological concerns, and those that we might not have done: but once we see such subjects as post-conflict scenarios and cryptocurrencies, it is obvious why they are there.

The congresses have been superlative educational events, but above all they have enabled experience to be shared and collaborations to develop. It is not impossible that during the next couple of years congresses might have to go wholly or partially online, which means that although congresses will remain educational events, opportunities for networking and collaboration might not be so prominent: but hopefully physical meetings of academics and activists from all over the world will continue to be possible, because such gatherings have been highly significant for the global debate.

BIEN has fulfilled a variety of functions since its foundation in 1986: the congresses; the publication of news, opinion, and research; the affiliation of existing national Basic Income organizations; and the encouragement of new organizations that could then affiliate (Van Parijs and Vanderborght, 2017: 206–7). An increasingly important function as the global debate continues to evolve will be BIEN's co-ordinating role: not an attempt to control the now highly diverse Basic Income debate, because that would be both undesirable and impossible, but the important task of ensuring that everyone knows what everyone else is doing so that the maximum amount of useful collaboration can occur.

An important dynamic underlying the evolution of BIEN as a communication hub for the global Basic Income debate has been the increasingly globalized academic and social policy worlds that have provided BIEN with some of its most active members and officers, partly because BIEN has provided a more appropriate institutional home for them than any of the national Basic Income organizations in the countries in which they have lived and worked. Guy Standing, a British academic who worked for the International Labour Organization (ILO) in Geneva, and was subsequently attached to the University of Bath and then London University's School of Oriental and African Studies (SOAS), was a co-chair of BIEN from its beginnings to 2008. He has lived in Geneva since working for the ILO, but has frequently worked elsewhere in the world, whether managing Basic Income pilot projects in Namibia and India or lecturing on the subject-matter of his many books. Perhaps the most extreme example of the globalized academic community is Jurgen De Wispelaere, a Belgian who has lived in Belgium, the UK, Ireland, Canada, and now Chile, and who has worked in all of those and in Finland as well. He organized the BIEN congress in Montreal in 2014 and then the congress in Finland in 2018.

BIEN congresses have tended to be like other academic conferences, with plenary lectures and papers given in parallel sessions. This was entirely appropriate during the first twenty-five years or so of the modern Basic Income debate. However, with the increasingly worldwide character of the debate during the new millennium, and the increasingly diverse membership of BIEN, with now probably the majority of active members seeing themselves more as campaigners than as academic researchers, a change in emphasis has clearly been appropriate. An important signal of that change was the election of a new Chair in 2020. Louise Haagh, Professor of Politics at the University of York (Haagh, 2019a), decided not to stand again for election as Chair, and the membership elected Sarath Davala, the Chair of INBI, the Indian Network for Basic Income. Davala was a lecturer in sociology at an Indian business school, and subsequently worked for trades unions, was instrumental in organizing the Indian Basic Income pilot project, and then organized the 2019 BIEN congress in Hyderabad. This congress departed somewhat from the previous academic format and instead focused on diverse panels discussing topics important to the Basic Income debate (Davala et al., 2015). For BIEN to have as its chair someone who is both an academic and an active campaigner seems entirely appropriate for the current stage both of the global Basic Income debate and for BIEN's role within it. It is also appropriate that this account in which we have seen a Europe-wide Basic Income organization become a global organization should close this chapter on continental Europe, as it could equally well have been the first section of the chapter that follows on the now worldwide nature of the Basic Income debate.

CONCLUSIONS

Europe during the second half of the twentieth century was struggling to reconcile relatively free markets with social protection, a struggle that was to become even more acute during the current century; and as Duverger suggests, the Basic Income debate 'interacts with the question of the political community' (Duverger, 2018: 8) and offers a perspective on the choices available to governments. It also raises a significant question: to what extent would the implementation of Basic Incomes in the countries of Europe, or even a Eurodividend to serve the whole of the European Union, be a useful response to the multiple crises afflicting the continent: the aftermath of the financial crisis and accompanying austerity policies; employment market change resulting from globalization and technological change; increasingly insecure incomes; the climate crisis; migration; the social divisions and more extreme political movements and parties resulting from all of that; and now the coronavirus pandemic that has both revealed and exacerbated the poverty, inequality and social rifts all across Europe, and that has therefore made even more obvious the advantages that a Basic Income would offer? Clearly, no Basic Income would provide the solution to all of those interconnected crises, but it is clear that it could be a useful response to some elements of them, and therefore to the whole. This is particularly true of the element of income security that a Basic Income could provide following the disruptions to household incomes caused by the pandemic. Although increasing conditionality, and in particular increasingly sanction-infested work conditionality, have been a common government response, there has been occasional movement in another direction. In the midst of the financial crisis, it was something of a surprise to find Greece implementing a new near-universal pension (Matsaganis and Leventi, 2011); and it was hardly predictable that a centre-right government in Finland would hold the experiment that it did. If momentum is to be maintained, then the research, education and active campaigning represented in this chapter will have to continue to occur, and to occur across the Continent.

But the crises listed here are not purely European: they are global as well. To match this situation, the Basic Income debate is now also worldwide and global. What we have here is a double reality. The Basic Income debate is now found everywhere: that is, it is worldwide; and the interconnectedness of the world means that there is now a single debate as well as there being multiple separate national debates: that is, the debate is global. The two chapters that follow represent this double reality. Chapter 9 charts the way in which the debate has become worldwide; and Chapter 10 the way in which the debate is now a single global debate.

9. A worldwide Basic Income debate

INTRODUCTION

Continental Europe is not the only place to have experienced forerunners of Basic Income schemes. We have discussed in Chapter 5 the birth of unconditional Family Allowance, and then Child Benefit, in the UK. New Zealand implemented a similarly unconditional scheme at the same time, although this was replaced in 1992 by an income-tested benefit (Rankin, 2012: 207, 209). Other countries followed. In 2012, Mongolia became the first developing country to implement such a scheme. Europe was not the first continent to implement an unconditional pension: that honour also goes to New Zealand, which implemented one in 1938. Denmark, Finland, Sweden and the Netherlands all followed during the following two decades; and to all intents and purposes Kenya's Inua Jamii Senior Citizens' Scheme is a Citizen's Pension, because it is based on the individual and paid to every individual apart from those already in receipt of a civil service pension. Namibia implemented an unconditional pension in 1992; in 2002, a government commission put Basic Income on the agenda; and from 2008 to 2009 the country hosted the first Basic Income pilot project. Bolivia implemented an unconditional pension in 2008 (International Labour Office, 2019; O'Connell, 2004; Rankin, 2012: 204–5; St John, 2016; Van Parijs and Vanderborght, 2017: 159–60). Apart from Denmark's pension, which is no longer paid to the highest earners, all of these pensions and child allowances remain Basic Incomes for particular age groups.

Although during the earlier period of the modern Basic Income debate activity was concentrated in the UK, and then also in continental Europe and North America, from the 1990s onwards lively debate has emerged in South America (Lo Vuolo, 2013a; 2020), Australasia (Klein et al., 2019; Luccioni, 2020; Mays et al., 2016: 10; Rankin, 2012; Tomlinson, 2012), Africa (Haarmann et al., 2019; Seekings and Matisonn, 2012), and Asia (Davala, 2019; Davala et al., 2015; Mehta, 2019; Vanderborght and Yamamori, 2014). There was a lull in the debate in the US and Canada during the final years of the twentieth century, but in 2002 the United States Basic Income Guarantee (USBIG) Network was founded with the aim of putting Basic Income and similar ideas back on the political agenda (Widerquist and Sheahen, 2012: 23), which it has succeeded in doing, with assistance from the various experiments discussed later in this chapter, and from Andrew Yang's presidential campaign in 2020 in which Basic Income was at the heart of his pitch for support.

It is at this point in the book that selection of material becomes extremely difficult, as during the past twenty years or so Basic Income debates with similar characteristics have occurred in dozens of countries. Readers will find in this chapter those distinctive events and debates that simply had to be included (for instance, Iran's accidental implementation of something very close to a Basic Income, and Namibia's and India's pilot projects), and also descriptions of a selection of regional and national debates that seem to the author to be somehow representative of the worldwide debate or to have important distinctive characteristics.

SOUTH AMERICA

Brazil

There is a strong case to be made that the globalization of the Basic Income debate, following its previous Europeanization, began in Brazil in 1991 when Senator Eduardo Matarazzo Suplicy of the Workers' Party (PT: Partido dos Trabalhadores) proposed a law that would grant a Minimum Income Guarantee by means of a Negative Income Tax. The plan was to introduce the Negative Income Tax slowly, starting with older residents, with a view to full implementation by 2002. The law was passed to the Chamber of Deputies and remained there for ten years without being voted on (Suplicy, 2003: 408–9). What did happen was a variety of local Bolsa Escola (School Allowance) programmes that paid means-tested benefits to poor families whose children attended school regularly; and in 1997 a law was passed that enabled the federal government to contribute 50 per cent of the funds needed by such municipal programmes. The federal government then provided the administrative infrastructure required (Suplicy, 2003: 410). Further conditional schemes followed, benefiting the children whose parents are incentivized to send them to school rather than subjecting them to child labour, and benefiting both poor families and local economies more generally as increased household incomes were spent on goods and services (Suplicy, 2003: 411–13).

In 2002, Luiz Inacio Lula da Silva won the presidential election for the Workers' Party, and in his programme for government he proposed a Minimum Income Guarantee with a view to a transition to a Basic Income. Suplicy understood that a Basic Income would promote the kind of employment-based society that President Lula wanted to see and would be simpler to administer and more effective than conditional cash transfers and other Minimum Income Guarantee options. In 2002, Suplicy introduced a draft bill to implement a Renda Básica de Cidadania (Citizenship Basic Income): an unconditional income for every Brazilian and anyone of another nationality resident in Brazil for five years, with implementation being by stages from 2005 onwards, starting with the poorest. The draft was approved by the Senate at the end of 2002 and by the National Congress in 2003, and the resulting Law no. 10,835 was approved by President Lula on 8 January 2004 (Silva and Lima, 2019: 321; Suplicy, 2003: 408, 414–16). Whilst no national Basic Income has been implemented, by 2002 forty-five municipalities had implemented experiments of various kinds, and eleven state experiments had covered 1,131 of the then 5,561 Brazilian municipalities; and then in 2003, as the first stage in the implementation process for the Renda Básica de Cidadania, the Bolsa Família (Family Allowance) was created, which unified four existing federal programmes: Bolsa Escola (School Allowance), Bolsa Alimentação (Food Allowance), Auxílio-Gás (Gas Subsidies) and Cartão Alimentação (Food Card). Unlike the Benefício de Prestação Continuada (BPC: Continued Cash Benefit, for the elderly over sixty-five years of age and those with disabilities), all of these income transfer programmes required families to fulfil conditions related to health and education (Silva and Lima, 2019: 320–21). Families can register for the Bolsa Família if their incomes fall below specified levels, and they receive incomes from the fund if their children maintain an average school attendance of 86 per cent for six- to fifteen-year-olds and 75 per cent for sixteen- and seventeen-year-olds; if children under seven years old are vaccinated; and if pregnant women undergo prenatal examinations. Failure to keep to the rules can mean suspension or loss of the benefit. As Silva and Lima suggest, the Bolsa Família functions as a concession rather than as a right, so it is difficult see this kind of benefit as a step towards the Renda Básica de Cidadania envisaged by Law no. 10,835/2004 (Coêlho, 2012: 62–8; Silva and Lima, 2019: 323–4). According to the law, the transition from the Bolsa Família to a Renda Básica de Cidadania was supposed to begin in 2005, but no steps have been taken, perhaps because of anxiety that to move towards unconditional incomes for everyone might be too costly, diminish government control over the lives of the poor, disincentivize work (which it would not), and inspire demands for further social and economic rights (Silva and Lima, 2019: 324–5). A more pessimistic view is that because

> BF [Bolsa Família] is the antithesis of a CI [Citizen [Basic] Income: Renda Básica de Cidadania] ... it cannot be seen as a starting point toward a universal and unconditional income, nor does it even show the way to reach the point of departure that was left behind ... The prospects are not promising for Brazil to make a CI a reality. One path to reach it has been lost. This potential legacy has been ignored, and the odds of remaining forgotten are great. (Lavinas, 2013: 44)

Similarly, Coêlho finds that 'there is no prospect that the two programmes will converge' (Coêlho, 2012: 79). However, the Government's unwillingness to move towards a Renda Básica de Cidadania has not prevented municipalities from undertaking experiments in universality and unconditionality, with the most developed, and the closest to a Basic Income, being the non-work-tested Programa Social Bolsa Mumbuca, established in 2013 in a local currency, the mumbuca, in Maricá, a municipality in the state of Rio de Janeiro: first of all to poorer members of the community with total household income less than one minimum wage (which means that the income is means-tested), but with an intention to include every resident. And then in 2015 the programme was expanded to families with incomes less than three minimum wages per household; and at the same time a law was passed to pay a Renda Básica de Cidadania, Citizen's Basic Income, to all individuals born in Maricá and resident there for at least a year, to other Brazilians resident for two years, and to foreigners resident for five years, but with implementation in stages, again beginning with poorer households, with an aim of universality by 2022. A further extension of the Programa Social Bolsa Mumbuca took place in 2019 (Rocha, 2020; Silva and Lima, 2019: 327). Just as local programmes paved the way for the Bolsa Família, so we might one day see local Basic Income programmes inspire the federal government to implement a genuine Renda Básica de Cidadania (Coêlho, 2012: 79).

Elsewhere in South America

A similar story to Brazil's can be told about Mexico City, where discussion about Basic Income goes even further back to the 1970s, but with a somewhat different outcome. In 2000, in a complex political context in which both the federal government and local governments run cash transfer programmes (Yanes, 2013), Mexico City's government, led by Andrés Manuel López Obrador, implemented and enshrined in law an unconditional, universal and individual pension for every Mexico City resident aged seventy years or over, later reduced to sixty-eight years. The Renta Dignidad in Bolivia is of the same character (Arza, 2013: 95–7).

In 2017, Mexico City's government was discussing a new constitution, the first draft of which contained a proposal to establish a Basic Income, beginning with a means-tested but not work-tested income for the poorest households:

Every person has a right to a standard of living that is adequate for them and their family, as well as a continued improvement of their conditions of existence. The right to a basic income is guaranteed, with priority for people in situations of poverty and those who cannot fulfill their material needs by their own means, as well as priority attention groups. In order to access basic income, this will defer to the common dispositions in this article. (Mexico City, 2017)

The proposal achieved a majority of 57 per cent, but not the 66 per cent required by the Assembly rules for inclusion in the constitution. Negotiations continued, and new wording achieved the required majority:

> Article 9. Dignified Life … 2. Every person is entitled to a minimum vital figure to ensure a dignified life by the terms of this Constitution. (Mexico City, 2017)

The following year, Andrés Manuel López Obrador won Mexico's presidential election with a promise to extend the unconditional pension to the whole country, and although this has not happened, the commitment suggests that Mexico City's Basic Income for elderly people is secure (Yanes, 2019). Steps towards a Basic Income for working-age adults will have to wait.

At the time of writing, Chile's national debate about its future constitution overlaps with discussion of Basic Income. The Red Chilena de Ingreso Básico, Chilean Basic Income Network, was founded in 2020; opposition Members of Parliament have presented to Parliament proposals to include the introduction of a Basic Income in the country's constitution (Drago, 2020); and a lively academic discussion is evolving (Cabaña, 2019; 2020; Radio JGM, 2020; Solimano, 2011; Zúñiga Fajuri, 2017). Colombia, too, is seeing a lively Basic Income debate fuelled by proposals made by parliamentarians and others (Linares, 2020).

Argentina has seen a lively academic debate about Basic Income for something like thirty years. The Centro Interdisiplinario para el Estudio de Políticas Públicas (CIEPP), Interdisciplinary Centre for the Study of Public Policy, has taken a leading role (Lo Vuolo, 1995); and Red Argentina de Ingreso Ciudadano, the Argentine Citizen's Income Network, was founded in 2003. In 1997, a proposal was made in Parliament for a universal income for children (Lo Vuolo, 2002), but what happened instead was the Asignacion Universal por Hijo para Protección Social: a child allowance for parents who are unemployed. As with Brazil's Bolsa Família, the expressed intention was that the Asignacion Universal por Hijo para Protección Social would be progressively extended until it was universal, but that has not happened; and although the scheme has been extended from the families of unemployed workers to the families of unemployed and informal workers, the benefit is income-tested, and part of the payment is conditional on behavioural conditionalities being met. The income is far from universal (Gasparini and Cruces, 2010; Lo Vuolo, 2013b: 55; Roca, 2010: 18). Other schemes have also become more conditional on attendance at school or on undergoing health checks (Barrientos,

2011; Lund, 2011; Standing, 2011b). Like Lavinas in relation to Brazil's Bolsa Família, Lo Vuolo suggests that

> conditional and focalized assistance programs … cannot be considered a step toward the gradual implementation of a CI [Citizen's Income] in the region [whereas] a Childhood CI could form a strong base from which the state can proceed toward the legitimacy of a CI for other age groups. (Lo Vuolo, 2013b: 62–3)

This is not to say that the Conditional Cash Transfers cannot be useful. They can be. Research by the International Labour Organization has found that the Latin American Conditional Cash Transfers established in a number of countries for families with children result in numerous positive outcomes for recipients, including new economic activity (Standing, 2017a: 228–9), higher net incomes, less child labour (Orton, 2009), increased school attendance, higher educational achievement, increasing productive activity, and better nutrition: but research has also shown that short-term results might be more positive than longer term ones; that for the children involved the schooling conditionality does not necessarily result in better life-chances; and that the programmes make little impact on intergenerational poverty transmission (Jones, 2016). Conditional Cash Transfers are now common, particularly in South America, and they have been subjected to a great deal of research (Cobham, 2014). The problem is that there are far fewer genuinely unconditional transfers, and in particular not enough for working-age adults, which means that research is difficult to carry out (Torry, 2018a: 135–6). However, as Orton suggests, 'the results of social pensions and a number of other unconditional transfers support the expectation that a [Basic Income] could generate similarly positive social and micro-economic effects' (Orton, 2011: 6); and evidence on Bolivian cash transfers that are not dependent on employment status has supported the view that unconditional cash transfer schemes can generate as much additional school attendance as conditional ones (Standing, 2017a: 228). Following a survey of cash transfers with varying degrees of conditionality, Standing concludes that

> now conditional cash transfers are legitimized. But the flaws of all forms of targeting, selectivity and conditionality, as well as their unnecessary costs, are making more people question the need for them. What we can say is that only universalistic transfers, … where they have been tried, including in some of the world's poorest countries, … have proved an effective means to combat poverty and income insecurity while promoting livelihoods and work. (Standing, 2017a: 228)

The research conducted by UNICEF reported at the end of the next section corroborates this finding.

However the patchwork of different conditional and unconditional incomes across Latin America now evolves, whether towards genuine country-wide Basic Incomes as Senator Suplicy had hoped, or towards an even more complex network of incomes to which various conditionalities are attached, it is into this complex situation that any future genuine Basic Income will have to fit (Van Parijs and Vanderborght, 2017: 69).

NAMIBIA

South Africa is where interest in Basic Income first emerged in southern Africa. In 1997, the Congress of South African Trade Unions (COSATU) commissioned research on a comprehensive social security system for the country (Haarmann and Haarmann, 1998; Seekings, 2020). The researchers modelled and suggested a Basic Income to address widespread poverty and redress the economic injustices of the apartheid era, and COSATU then took the proposal to a Jobs Summit in 1998. Initially the Minister for Social Development publicly supported the idea, but enthusiasm was short-lived, and it ended when the Minister of Finance and the President rejected the proposal (Haarmann and Haarmann, 2020).

In 2001, the representative bodies of churches and Nongovernmental Organizations (NGOs) and COSATU formed the Basic Income Grant Coalition, with the trades unions arguing for a Basic Income on the grounds that it would stimulate economic growth and job creation and also reduce poverty. The African National Congress (ANC) government discussed and rejected the idea, and trade union interest declined. The 2006 Basic Income Earth Network (BIEN) congress was held in Cape Town, but the initiative had already passed to Namibia (Henderson and Quiggin, 2019: 496; Van Parijs and Vanderborght, 2017: 175; Seekings and Matisson, 2012).

By the turn of the millennium, a debate about cash transfers was already taking place in Namibia (Haarmann and Haarmann, 2007) because it was a resource-rich country with a small population; there was substantial poverty, inequality and unemployment; and there was already a universal pension. In 2001, the Namibian Government established the Namibian Tax Commission (NAMTAX), which in 2002 decided that the best way to reduce poverty and inequality would be to make the tax system more progressive and use the proceeds to pay for a Basic Income.

Claudia Haarmann had written her PhD thesis on the COSATU Basic Income proposal, and it was her supervisor at the University of the Western Cape, Professor Pieter le Roux, who suggested that Namibia should follow the same model (Haarmann and Haarmann, 2020). NAMTAX's modelling of what it regarded as a feasible scheme would have meant 85 per cent of Namibians experiencing net disposable income gains (Haarmann et al., 2019: 358–9). In

2004, six civil society organizations—the Council of Churches, the National Union of Namibian Workers, the Namibian NGO Forum, the Namibian Network of AIDS Service Organisations, the National Youth Council and the Church Alliance for Orphans—formed a Basic Income Grant Coalition. Trade union involvement resulted from some of their members understanding that a Basic Income would better enable workers to thrive in the context of increasingly flexible employment markets, but commitment to the project was not always consistent. Neither did global organizations offer the kind of constructive interest that they might have done. The International Monetary Fund (IMF) objected to the universality of the proposal, and asked for a 'targeted cash grant' to be rolled out gradually instead; and it also objected to what it said would be an unaffordable cost of 5.5 per cent of Gross Domestic Product (GDP). The organization eventually retracted its objections both to Basic Income's universality and to the cost. Its figure of 5.5 per cent of GDP had included the cost of the existing universal pension and did not take account of the increased higher tax rate that would have accompanied the implementation of the Basic Income. They had made the classic mistake of complaining about the gross cost of the unconditional incomes rather than recognizing that what mattered was the net cost of the scheme as a whole, which in this case would have been 3.5 per cent of GDP (Haarmann and Haarmann, 2006; Insight, 2006a; 2006b). But the IMF was not the only organization to cause problems for the project. Guy Standing, then of the International Labour Organization, had assisted with a survey that sought public opinion about Basic Income, but the results were never evaluated or published because of opposition from the United Nations Development Programme, which worried that the results might encourage the implementation of a Basic Income. The Evangelical Lutheran Church in the Republic of Namibia was rather more constructive: Bishop Zephania Kameeta enthusiastically promoted Basic Income as a solution to Namibia's poverty, and Claudia and Dirk Haarmann, responsible for the Church's Desk for Social Development, facilitated the coalition (Haarmann et al., 2019: 359–60). In 2006, the Basic Income Earth Network (BIEN) Congress in Cape Town heard Bishop Kameeta's enthusiasm for a pilot project; and the same year Otjivero-Omitara, a deprived community of mainly displaced farm workers, was chosen for the experiment, and fund-raising began.

From January 2008 to December 2009 each of the 1,000 inhabitants in the villages were paid a 'Basic Income Grant'—that is, a Basic Income—of N$100 (US$12) a month (Haarmann et al., 2019: 357–8). The costs were borne by donors, and the project was watched by the World Bank. A benchmark survey was carried out in November 2007, an interim survey in July 2008, and a final survey in November 2008 (so much inward migration had occurred by the end of the project in 2009 that only qualitative data and case studies were collected during the final year of the project) (Haarmann and Haarmann, 2020). As well as the collection of data on 398 individuals in 52 households, records were kept of the weights and heights of children, clinic attendance, household incomes, and educational and crime statistics, and a photo archive was maintained. This was not a randomized controlled trial, so the comparisons drawn were between the different sets of survey results relating to the same community. Results listed in a report published by the researchers were as follows:

- Household poverty dropped. In November 2007, 76 per cent of residents of the two villages fell below a food poverty line. Within a year, this was reduced to 37 per cent. Those households that were not joined by family members from outside the project villages (an understandable migration) saw poverty levels reduced from 76 per cent to just 16 per cent;
- The proportion of people engaged in economic activity rose from 44 per cent to 55 per cent, often through own-account work of various kinds, and especially through such initiatives as the tending of vegetable plots and the building of latrines, which directly led to an increase in the community's health;
- Far from leading to idleness and a decrease in economic activity, the economic security that a Basic Income offered to people gave them the confidence to take the economic risks necessary for new productive activity;
- Child malnutrition fell. Children's weight-for-age improved in just six months from 42 per cent of underweight children to just 10 per cent;
- Before the pilot project, almost half of the villages' children did not attend school regularly. Pass rates were at 40 per cent, and drop-out rates were high. This was mainly because parents had to pay fees for their children to attend school. By the end of the project, 90 per cent of parents were paying school fees, and most children were attending school. Drop-out rates fell from 40 per cent to almost zero during the project;
- The clinic, like the school, is funded by attendees' payments. During the project, residents could pay the attendance fee, use of the clinic increased six-fold, and the income of the clinic increased fivefold;
- During the first year of the project, average household debt fell from N$1,215 to N$772. Savings increased, as did ownership of livestock;
- Crime rates fell by 42 per cent during the project. Theft of stock fell by a similar amount, giving people the confidence to invest in assets;
- The Basic Income gave to women a new economic independence, and paid-for sex was reduced accordingly;
- There was no evidence that the Basic Income led to an increase in alcoholism;
- Administrative costs were just 3 to 4 per cent of the total outlay. (Basic Income Grant Coalition, 2009: 13–17)

The following results were reported by Professor Guy Standing at a seminar at SOAS (School for Oriental and African Studies) in the University of London on 27 January 2009:

- The villages of their own volition elected an advisory committee of eighteen residents, and among its achievements were the opening of a post office, the establishment of savings accounts, and the closure of shebeens (drinking houses) on the day of the monthly distribution of the grants;
- New shops were opened;
- The number of people experiencing daily food shortages fell from 30 per cent to 12 per cent of the population in just six months;
- The number of people who rarely experienced food shortages rose from 20 per cent to 60 per cent of the population;
- Economic activity rose fastest among women;
- Average income rose in every earnings quintile, and proportionately more for lower quintiles;
- Average income rose a staggering 200 per cent in the lowest quintile *excluding* the N$100 (US$12) Basic Income, because people could now purchase the means for making an income, and they did;
- Low-wage employment was in many cases replaced by better-paid self-employment;
- The Basic Income was not inflationary;
- Women's economic status rose relative to men's; and
- The Basic Income was more effective than conditional transfers partly because it could not be removed by a local bureaucrat if someone had fallen out with them, as a conditional cash transfer could be; and also because there was almost no opportunity for bureaucratic skimming of Basic Incomes, whereas conditional services and cash transfers require administration and therefore risk being skimmed. (Torry, 2018a: 131–3)

Some of the common objections to Basic Income had therefore been answered: the Basic Income increased enterprise rather than encouraging idleness; it increased labour supply rather than reducing it; it encouraged productive use of resources rather than wastage; it was spent on goods and services that enhanced wellbeing rather than being wasted on undesirable goods and services; and far from being unaffordable, if the Basic Incomes paid during the project had been paid to the whole of the Namibian population, then they would have cost just 2.2 per cent to 3.8 per cent of the country's GDP, and the economic activity generated would probably have paid the entire cost.

The researchers had wanted the project to test a hypothesis: that poverty is a lack of money, so what is required is a means of providing economic security that is not paternalistic, is based on rights and not on charity, most benefits the most disadvantaged, encourages ecological practices, and facilitates dignified work (Casassas and Baílon, 2007). The pilot project supported the hypothesis: it was not paternalistic; it was based on rights and not charity; it benefited most the most disadvantaged; it facilitated dignified work; and the activity that it promoted tended not to damage the environment. Following the end of the two-year pilot project, additional small unconditional grants had similar effects (Standing, 2017a: 232).

Namibia's Government showed no interest in the results, and the Prime Minister offered the usual objection that money should not be given to people who do nothing. Guy Standing speculates that one reason why governments might not like the idea of Basic Income is because it is emancipatory: it allows people to make their own decisions, and prevents politicians and officials from interfering in people's lives (Standing, 2015). Initially the National Union of Namibian Workers joined the Government in its criticism of Basic Income, and withdrew from the consortium that had planned and managed the project: but a fierce reaction among its members provoked the union's leadership into at least nominal reengagement, and for the first time the trades unions found themselves in opposition to the Government. Subsequently, a greater degree of political interest was shown, particular by Hage Geingob, Namibia's first Prime Minister who had recently re-entered politics; and in 2015, when Geingob became Namibia's President, he included a Basic Income as an option in his anti-poverty strategy, and appointed Bishop Kameeta to head a new Ministry for Poverty Eradication and Social Welfare. No practical action on Basic Income followed. Instead, military spending increased, as did the number of government ministers and departments (Haarmann and Haarmann, 2012; Haarmann et al., 2019: 367–9; Standing, 2017: 232; Torry, 2018a: 133). In 2019, the Namibian Government issued a draft social protection policy that recognized the efficiency of universal and unconditional transfers and then proposed a targeted unemployment benefit (Basic Income Grant Coalition, 2019: 57).

One audience that did show an interest in the results was the participants in the seminar held at SOAS in January 2009. This was composed mainly of academics and representatives of NGOs. The most hostile questioning came from the staff members of NGOs that provided goods and services in Africa and elsewhere, who asked whether it would not be better to build facilities for people rather than giving them money. The answer was 'no', because the evidence of the pilot project was that if members of a community are given money unconditionally then they will build the facilities that they need, which might not be the ones that people outside the situation think that they should have (Torry, 2018a: 130–33).

A significant aspect of the Namibian pilot project was the controversy that erupted over its methodology. Both the involvement of Claudia and Dirk

Haarmann in both managing the project and conducting the research, and the lack of a control community, were criticized. In fact, an international advisory group had been appointed, and independent academics were involved in analysing the data and publishing the results. The reasons that no control community was sought were that it was thought to be unethical to ask a community to participate in the quite onerous surveys if it was not experiencing the benefits of a Basic Income, and that finding a community with the same characteristics as Otjivero-Omitara would have been difficult. A further criticism was that the improvements in child nutrition and the reduction in poverty might have reflected general improvements across Namibia. There certainly had been general improvements, but during the period of the experiment there had been no increase in either GDP or per capita income, and probably a deterioration in child nutrition, suggesting that the improvements in Otjivero-Omitara really were the result of the pilot project (Haarmann et al., 2019: 363–5; Osterkamp, 2013a; 2013b). One question that Claudia and Dirk Haarmann and Nicoli Nattrass ask themselves is whether the fact that the pilot project was being watched by local and global organizations meant that effects were generated that would not occur if a Basic Income were to be rolled out nationwide. For instance, knowing that a common criticism of Basic Income is that poor people might spend the money on alcohol might have inspired the local democracy that evolved in Otjivero-Omitara and the subsequent closure of shebeens on the days on which the Basic Incomes were distributed: an effect that might not occur to the same extent with a permanent nationwide Basic Income (Haarmann et al., 2019: 366).

Research for the World Bank has evaluated both conditional and unconditional schemes in Africa and has discovered how effective unconditional schemes can be (Garcia and Moore, 2012: 8); and more recent research by UNICEF has drawn the same conclusion:

> Taking eight experimental and quasi-experimental evaluations on large-scale government UCTs [Unconditional Cash Transfers] in subSaharan Africa (SSA), conducted in collaboration with the Transfer Project, we summarize evidence around six common perceptions associated with cash transfer programmes in resource-poor settings. Specifically we investigate if transfers: 1) Induce higher spending on alcohol or tobacco; 2) Are fully consumed (rather than invested); 3) Create dependency (reduce participation in productive work); 4) Increase fertility; 5) Lead to negative community-level economic impacts (including price distortion and inflation); and 6) Are fiscally unsustainable. We present evidence refuting each of these claims. We complement our evidence with summaries of other review papers and prominent literature, which has examined these questions, both in SSA, and globally. We conclude that these perceptions are myths, and that they present a distorted picture of the potential benefits of these programmes. Since such perceptions are utilized—or inform underlying assumptions—in policy debates, they

constrain governments' policy decisions in the area of poverty reduction. (Handa et al., 2017: 6)

The Namibian pilot project has added to our understanding of the usefulness of unconditional cash transfers, and interviews conducted ten years after the completion of the project found that even though the Basic Income had ceased to be paid at the end of 2009, significant effects continued (Basic Income Grant Coalition, 2019); but we are still waiting for the permanent unconditional cash transfer programmes for working-age adults that will tell us whether a Basic Income can create the long-term change in poverty levels hoped for but imperfectly achieved by conditional schemes (Papadopoulos and Velázquez Leyer, 2016).

While the Basic Income debate in South Africa was somewhat eclipsed by the pilot project in Namibia, interest is now reviving. A Basic Income experiment is planned for a single community (Jooste, 2020), and there is a growing debate among academics: but neither a rights-based nor a developmental agenda has so far achieved traction in relation to public opinion (Seekings, 2020: 268–9).

INDIA

In 2008, the Self-Employed Women's Association (SEWA), a large trade union that organizes street vendors, home-based workers, agricultural workers, domestic workers and construction workers, and is a significant political player in India, began planning for a rural Basic Income pilot project to see if Basic Incomes might be better for women than the existing welfare schemes; and subsequently the Indian Government worked with SEWA to organize an urban project as well. The urban project in West Delhi's Raghubir Nagar slum began first, in 2010, and the project in eight rural villages in Madhya Pradesh began in 2011. The projects were supported and funded by the Government of Delhi, the United Nations Development Programme, and UNICEF India.

In the Madhya Pradesh villages, each adult received 200 rupees a month (about 30 per cent of subsistence income) and 100 rupees a month was paid for each child under the age of fourteen, with the amounts being raised to 300 rupees and 150 rupees per month after the first year of the project. In West Delhi, one hundred households received 1,000 rupees per month (about US$22) and were deprived of permission to use the subsidized ration shops; another one hundred households received bank accounts and continued to use the ration shops; a third group of 150 families received neither cash nor a bank account, and continued to use the ration shops; and a fourth group of 150 families expressed a wish not to receive the cash transfers. The cash transfers were genuine Basic Incomes, because they were unconditional, without means test, and without work test, and they were paid to individuals, with the children's transfers being paid to the mother. The payments were made into individual bank accounts, or, in the case of women who were members of SEWA, into their accounts with the SEWA credit co-operative society. A further project for two tribal villages was added later. Because SEWA wanted to know what effect its own organizing might have on communities involved in the pilot project, in both the rural and urban contexts some of the pilot communities experienced SEWA organizing activity, and some did not. The experiment was a genuine randomized controlled trial, because in each of the urban, rural and tribal contexts each pilot community was matched with a control community with similar characteristics, and the outcomes in both the pilot and control communities were evaluated in the same way, with baseline surveys, interim surveys, final surveys, and then follow-up surveys being carried out. Case studies were researched; key respondents were interviewed; community-wide surveys were carried out to discover community-wide effects; children's weights were measured, and their ages recorded; and school attendance figures were collected (Davala, 2019: 374; Davala et al., 2015: 34–46; Sewa Bharat, 2015).

It is unfortunate that the pilot project faced significant opposition. Representatives of NGOs involved with existing welfare schemes distributed leaflets in the West Delhi slum communities warning residents that the pilot project might lead to the ration shops being closed, and they disrupted meetings held by SEWA (Standing, 2012a). Where personal and organizational interests are threatened by the possibility of Basic Incomes being paid, it is not surprising that reactions might occur. Basic Incomes are far more difficult to corrupt than many of India's existing complex welfare schemes (Davala et al., 2015: 1–18), and particularly the subsidized ration shops and the make-work schemes.

Interim results of the experiments were announced at the 2012 Basic Income Earth Network (BIEN) Congress in Munich, and final results in a report (Davala et al., 2015). The researchers found that households spent their Basic Incomes mainly on food, healthcare and education. School attendance increased threefold, school performance twofold, and more girls attended secondary school. Spending on alcohol declined, and did not increase as might have been expected (Davala et al., 2015: 96, 113, 134, 154). In the Madhya Pradesh villages, food sufficiency increased, particularly for the tribal villages and for vulnerable households; the proportion of children with normal weight for age increased from 39 per cent to 58 per cent, with a 25 percentage point increase for girls; consumption of milk and fresh vegetables rose; one fifth of households in the Basic Income villages reported an increase in earned income; debt levels declined for 73 per cent of the Basic Income households; within four months of the start of the project 95.6 per cent of individuals had bank or co-operative accounts, substantially increasing the level of financial inclusion; and the number of illnesses declined, more households were able to buy necessary medicines and healthier diets, and use of private doctors and hospitals increased. In the tribal villages, small farmers were spending more time on their own farms and less on wage labour (Davala, 2019: 375–8; Sewa Bharat, 2015: 4). An interesting result in Madhya Pradesh was that more families turned to private schooling for their children. As the researchers point out, this is not a reason for regarding Basic Income as a possible substitute for public services: rather, it is a reason for improving public education and other public services (Sewa Bharat, 2015: 20).

Especially where SEWA was involved, communities pooled some of their new incomes to create roads, water supplies, drains and toilets for the benefit of the whole community; and SEWA's health education work increased the healthcare effects of the Basic Incomes (Davala, 2019: 377; Davala et al., 2015: 73, 76, 92–5). Throughout the pilot communities, economic activity increased, new businesses were started, and households co-operated with each other to improve their accommodation (Davala et al., 2015: 153–5). A particularly significant effect of the experiment was the empowerment of women in the communities receiving the Basic Incomes. Many of them started their own businesses for the first time, so that they were no longer dependent on their husbands for income—a development experienced as much by wealthier women as by poorer ones (Davala et al., 2015: 158–80). An important emancipation for many of the households was the ability that the Basic Incomes gave them to escape from debt, a particularly widespread problem in India (Devala et al., 2015: 69–70; Standing, 2017a: 236).

The project concluded in 2013, and in 2017 a legacy survey carried out in the tribal villages found that many of the effects discovered during the project had persisted, mainly because assets developed during the experiment had enabled income generation to continue. Healthcare and educational practices developed during the experiment had also continued, as had the reduced consumption of alcohol. Where significant illnesses had occurred after the pilot project ended, the men in the household had often fallen back into debt bondage. There were thus momentum effects; persistence effects, which might tail off; and drop-back effects, which returned households to their position before the experiment. The conclusion to draw is that a Basic Income paid for a short time can have a permanently transformative effect on communities (Davala, 2019: 379–81; Davala et al., 2017: 2–3).

SEWA was of course particularly interested in the significant empowerment of women that Basic Income represented. The Indian Government's interest in the project was different: to see if a Basic Income might be able to replace the many inefficient and corrupt welfare programmes. The results of the project suggested that it could do so (Standing, 2012b; 2013). Throughout the project, the research team maintained contact with both the national and the state governments: but then in 2014 the Congress Party was replaced in government by the Bharatiya Janata Party, meaning that contacts had to be rebuilt, not only with new government ministers, but also with new civil servants. The researchers found the new Chief Economic Advisor, Arvind Subramanian, to be sympathetic to the idea of cash transfers, and in 2016 a team constituted by the Government engaged with the India Network for Basic Income (INBI), which those interested in Basic Income in India had founded in 2015. In January 2017, Subramanian included a chapter on Basic Income in his annual Economic Survey, in which he wrote that Basic Income is a 'powerful idea whose time even if not ripe for implementation is ripe for serious discussion' (Liu and Nemana, 2020: 278–9). An intense public and political debate followed (Mehta, 2019: 14–16), with fears being expressed that the implementation of a Basic Income would lead to the abolition of the existing welfare system, along with the common objections that the idea was unaffordable, and that giving poor people money would make them lazy. Arguments offered for Basic Income tended to be based on its administrative efficiency and on India's need for social justice. To facilitate the national and parliamentary debate, INBI and SEWA held a national conference at which senior politicians from two states were present: but so far no further movement on Basic Income has emerged from the Indian Government.

A significant question is now being asked as part of the Basic Income debate in India: given that India has a population of 1.3 billion, would it be wise to initiate a Basic Income for the whole population all in one go? If not, might it be better to implement a non-work-tested but means-tested benefit to start with? INBI does not regard this suggestion as diluting the concept of a Basic Income, which remains an entirely unconditional income for every individual, but sees it as a step in the right direction. Alternative proposals have been for non-means-tested but still not universal incomes for particular castes, for scheduled tribes, or for women, on the basis that these tend to be the poorer members of society. This approach Davala has termed 'targeted universalism' (Davala, 2019: 384), which he sees as a practical response to political realities, and as a promise of a genuine Basic Income in the future. An interesting new development occurred in Telengana in 2018: an entirely unconditional 8,000 rupees (US$120) per acre for every farmer. Arvind Subramanian has called the scheme a 'Quasi Universal Basic Income' (Subramanian, 2018). Importantly, the scheme is not perceived as welfare payments, but as investment, and its unconditionality and 'universality within a category' are viewed as a paradigm shift that could provide the conditions required for the implementation of a genuine Basic Income. In January 2019, the scheme for farmers was extended to the whole of India by the Indian Government (Mehta, 2019: 16–18), and in the same year the small state of Sikkim in North India promised a Basic Income: but the Sikkim Government then changed and nothing happened. Perhaps one day something will (Davala, 2019: 382–6). Those who witnessed the projects suggest that Basic Income could be transformative for India, and the results of the project bear out that verdict (Davala, 2019: 378; Davala et al., 2015: 195–214; Standing, 2017a: 237).

Liu and Nemana (2020) suggest that India's competitive democracy, activist civil society organizations and government economists, the State's significant administrative capacity, the pilot projects, widespread economic insecurity, the inefficiency of the current welfare state, and increasing concern about inequality, mean that India is ripe for further lively debate about Basic Income and possibly for implementation.

EVALUATION OF THE NAMIBIAN AND INDIAN PILOT PROJECTS

The first thing to say about the Namibian and Indian pilot projects is that they were both significant achievements. For the first time, whole communities received genuine Basic Incomes for sufficient lengths of time for a variety of positive effects to be evidenced. A legitimate conclusion to draw from the diverse results obtained is that 'the basic income's emancipatory value exceeds the monetary value, and as such could be expected to have a bigger impact on other issues than might be imagined from just considering the modest amount that was paid out' (Davala et al., 2015: 69). The second thing to say is that many of the criticisms that have been offered in relation to the experiments, including Osterkamp's criticisms of the experiment in Namibia, were and still are easily countered. None of them compromise the value of the two projects.

However, the value of the experiments does not mean that we should not be careful how we employ the results. Firstly, the effects generated by a two-year experiment will not match the effects that a permanent Basic Income implemented in the same place would generate, and it is difficult to know the extent to which the effects would be the same and the extent to which they would be different. During a pilot project, employment market decisions would be likely to be made in the light of the likely situation following the end of the project, rather than in the light of the worker's situation during the experiment. It is even more the case that the effects generated by the pilot projects would not match those that would be generated by any realistic Basic Income scheme implemented in a country with an economy more developed than those of Namibia and India. The sums supplied to residents of Otjivero-Omitara, Madhya Pradesh and Delhi came from outside the situation, and constituted small proportions of average per capita GDP, and in total small proportions of total national GDP. For the experiments to be genuinely pilot projects, the organizers would have had to ask themselves where the money would come from to fund permanent Basic Incomes, and then would have had to ask themselves how the funding mechanism would impact the Basic Income recipients' household disposable incomes. If the Basic Incomes had been funded from within each of the communities then the results might have been rather different.

And then there is the even more difficult question as to how these experimental results might apply in other parts of the world. To be meaningful, Basic Incomes implemented in countries with more developed economies than those of Namibia and India would have to be larger proportions of average per capita GDP for each individual, and a larger proportion of national GDP in total, and the more developed economy's more complex existing tax and benefits systems would have to be adjusted when the Basic Incomes were implemented. The effects generated would be the result of a combination of the Basic Incomes and the tax and benefits system changes that occurred at the same time. This situation would be so different from the situations in Namibia and India that comparison is surely not possible between the Namibian and Indian pilot projects and what might happen in Europe, the US, or Canada, if genuine Basic Incomes were to be implemented. In Namibia and India, some of the effects would have been the result of additional money being supplied to local economies, so applying the results to situations in which the funding of Basic Incomes would have to be generated internally will be bound to be difficult, and difficult to justify (Van Parijs and Vanderborght, 2017: 139–40).

But having said all of that, the pilot projects in Namibia and India were significant achievements, and they will rightly be seen as important steps towards the implementation of national Basic Incomes in Namibia and India whenever that occurs.

IRAN

There are many complex causes of social policy change. Sometimes there might be more of an orderly rational process, with a social problem being understood, possible solutions being sought and tested, a rational choice among the options being made, and then legislation and implementation. But sometimes it does not happen like that. The United Kingdom ended up with an unconditional Family Allowance after the Second World War because Eleanor Rathbone wrote a book about it (Rathbone, [1924] 1986), William Beveridge read the book and tried out the idea on the staff at the London School of Economics, where he was Director, and when he was appointed to chair a committee tasked with sorting out the UK's social insurance and social assistance systems he wrote an unconditional benefit for children into the preface. The Treasury watered it down, but Members of Parliament with different political views found that they could support it, so it happened (see Chapter 5).

In 2010, Iran experienced its own policy accident. The subsidy programme was in desperate need of reform. Fuel and food were being purchased in Iran and smuggled over its borders; the low prices meant that food and fuel were being wasted; and 70 per cent of the value of the subsidies was being enjoyed by 30 per cent of the population. The Government planned to replace the subsidies with a means-tested benefit, which it called a 'cash subsidy', so that poorer households would be able to pay the higher prices that would result from the subsidy withdrawal. In 2008, in preparation for the reform, seventeen million households filled in claim forms for the new benefit. The means test was not of the normal variety: instead of calculating what a household would receive by deducting a proportion of earned and investment income from a specified income level, proxy indicators of earned incomes were used to allocate each household to one of three categories: one category in which households would receive the whole cash subsidy; a second in which they would receive less; and a third in which no cash subsidy would be paid. So many people protested about their category assignments that the Government decided to withdraw the results of the exercise and to allocate everyone to the group that would receive the whole of the subsidy (Tabatabai, 2011b: 10–11). Because the price increases due to the withdrawal of food and fuel subsidies affected everyone, there was little opposition to wealthy individuals claiming the cash subsidy; and because there was no longer any risk of incomes having to be revealed, wealthier households were happy to apply. Because the payments were neither means-tested nor work-tested, two essential characteristics of a Basic Income were fulfilled. The payments were even based on the individual and not on household structure, so a couple received twice the amount for an individual: again, a necessary characteristic of a Basic Income. The only respect in which the payments were not Basic Incomes was that the household's Basic Incomes were paid to the head of the household, which is hardly surprising in the Iranian context, and also logical in relation to a context in which the head of the household is responsible for paying household bills. Largely by accident, Iran had found itself paying something like a Basic Income of 455,000 rials per month (approximately US$45 in 2010) for every individual; and 96 per cent of the population were found to be receiving the payments. One group not receiving the payments was Afghan refugees, many of whom had lived in Iran for decades, and they, like everyone else, were experiencing the higher prices for food and fuel consequent on the withdrawal of subsidies. Whether the exclusion of this group from receiving the cash subsidy compromises its categorization as a Basic Income is an important question (De Wispelaere, 2016b: 625; Karshenas and Tabatabai, 2019: 339–45; Salehi-Isfahani, 2014; Tabatabai, 2011a; 2011b; 2012a: 295; 2012b; 2021).

Initially, the cash transfers were worth something like two thirds of the minimum wage. The plan had been to pay the cash subsidies out of revenue raised from the higher food and fuel prices, but because more people than originally intended were now receiving the incomes, the Government had to provide additional funds. There was therefore a question as to whether the payments could be sustained if oil revenues declined. The question has now lost some of its salience because inflation resulting from international sanctions and government policy choices from 2011 onwards has eroded the real value of the cash transfers. There have been suggestions that the transfers themselves have contributed to inflation, but this appears not to have been the case. In 2011, the substantial increases in the prices of fuel, food and some other items caused a brief spike in inflation, but the inflation rate then fell back to what it had been before the subsidies were withdrawn and the cash transfers paid. It would therefore appear that the transfers themselves have not been inflationary (Karshenas and Tabatabai, 2019: 349–51).

Another question related to the sustainability of the scheme concerns the fact that it was implemented largely by accident and not in the context of a government commitment to social and economic rights. Both the Government and the population regard the cash transfers as a pragmatic measure and not necessarily as a permanent fixture: but because the transfers were and are a necessary corollary to the reduction in price subsidies, it is difficult to envisage the scheme being abolished and the public revenue involved being diverted to other purposes, however worthy. In 2016, the Government attempted to remove 6 per cent of residents from the list of individuals receiving the cash subsidy, but again administrative chaos supervened, and more than half of them had to be restored. Whether the still popular transfers, which have been enshrined in law, will themselves generate a rights discourse in Iran is a further interesting question (De Wispelaere, 2016b: 625; Karshenas and Tabatabai, 2019: 340, 344–5; Tabatabai, 2012b).

In 2017, the payments were at the same nominal level as in 2010 but were worth 70 per cent less in real terms. They must now be worth a lot less than that (Karshenas and Tabatabai, 2019: 352). This has made it difficult to carry out research on how something very like a Basic Income has affected long-term employment patterns, social cohesion, poverty, inequality and a variety of other factors. In Namibia and India, women experienced an increase in their autonomy, but there would have been no evidence of this in Iran because women only receive the payments if they are regarded as the head of a household, which usually they are not: and there is evidence that male heads of households receiving the cash subsidies for all household members might have strengthened Iran's patriarchal gender norms (Karshenas and Tabatabai, 2019: 349; Salehi-Isfahani, 2014). It is also a pity that so many changes have occurred in Iranian society and in Iran's economy since 2010. This makes it difficult to determine which changes have been caused by the cash subsidies and which by other factors. Changes that can only have been caused by the cash subsidies are the rapid increase in the number of households with bank accounts in preparation for their implementation, and a general sense among the population that providing something like a subsistence income is a proper task for a government. Research has found no increase in the purchase of temptation goods due to the cash transfers. It is also clear that the cash subsidies caused significant increases in household disposable income during 2011: 28 per cent in the case of a household of four individuals with median income; and they also constituted large proportions of household expenditure: an average of 14.2 per cent in urban areas, and 26.1 per cent in rural areas. Although some prices rose, households saw net gains, and both poverty and inequality declined between 2010 and 2011, suggesting that the increase in household disposable incomes as a result of the cash transfers was having a greater effect than the price increases due to the withdrawal of subsidies. However, recent increases in the price of fuel, and the continuing devaluation in real terms of the cash transfers, mean that poverty and inequality levels are now back to where they were in 2010.

What is not clear is whether for some households the cash subsidies resulted in employment market withdrawal, because not as much had to be earned to sustain the same standard of living; and whether in other households the additional income has facilitated investment in income generation potential, and therefore an increase in earned income. The research that has been possible has shown that in most age groups employment market activity did not change during 2011, but that young adults were more likely to substitute continuing education for employment, which, as the researchers suggest, should be counted as an investment effect (Karshenas and Tabatabai, 2019: 346–9, 351–3; Salehi-Isfahani and Mostafavi-Dehzooei, 2017).

Karshenas and Tabatabai's interpretation of Iran's cash subsidies is that the rapid reduction in fuel subsidies that gave rise to them was in effect the imposition of a carbon tax, which means that the cash subsidy scheme is evidence for the viability of carbon taxes as a means of paying for a Basic Income, but also evidence for the necessity of alternative sources of funding as carbon fuel use declines. They also suggest that the scheme is evidence that almost any government has the capacity to roll out a Basic Income; and also that it is evidence that widespread understanding of and debate about Basic Income are not a prerequisite for the implementation of a Basic Income: and maybe that public ignorance of the concept might actually aid the idea's implementation (Karshenas and Tabatabai, 2019: 346, 353–4).

Small though it now is in real terms, the Iranian scheme is important because it is the closest that a country has ever come to paying to almost the whole of its population an unconditional income; because it is yet another example of a policy accident; and because it tells us that we cannot predict where a genuine Basic Income, fulfilling all of its criteria, will first be implemented.

THE REPUBLIC OF KOREA (SOUTH KOREA)

[Korean names can be written in two different orders. In this section, a 'given name followed by family name' convention is followed.]

Korea's welfare state is relatively young, the work ethic is strong, and family solidarity is a significant aspect of Korean society, so although a national pension was established in 1988, and in 2000 a National Basic Living Security System (NBLSS) defined a national minimum income, implemented the means-tested benefit that the national minimum required, and established social security benefits as a right, the system remains fairly rudimentary. In particular, the priority of family obligation means that if there is a family member who can care for someone in need, then NBLSS benefits will not be available (Nam and Park, 2020: 219). In spite of the fact that some on the right of Korean politics regard Basic Income as a means of dismantling other aspects of the welfare state, the weakness of the current benefits system, and the growth of employment precarity and income insecurity, have led many on the left to embrace the idea. Two individuals who had studied in Germany and returned to Korea (Nowan Kwack to an academic post and Min Geum to be a left-wing politician) have been particularly influential. Geum promised that he would implement a Basic Income if he was elected president. He lost, but as with Andrew Yang's run for president of the United States, the campaign raised the profile of Basic Income. In 2007, Geum's Socialist Party made Basic Income a policy commitment, and although it then merged with the New Progressive Party in 2012, and the new party changed its name to the Labor Party in 2013, Basic Income remains a policy commitment. In 2009, the Korean Confederation of Trade Unions issued a positive report on Basic Income along with costings for a feasible scheme; and the same year the Basic Income Korean Network (BIKN) was founded, with Nam-Hoon Kang as its chair. In 2010, BIKN held a conference to which it invited significant Basic Income scholars from around the world. The same year, it affiliated to the Basic Income Earth Network; became a membership organization and formed local chapters; and conducted further research on feasible Basic Income schemes for Korea. In 2019, it clarified its purpose as seeking the realization of a 'Basic Income', understood to mean an 'income that is paid to all, unconditionally, individually, regularly, in cash as a share based on the rights of all members of society to the common wealth' (Yi, 2020). Meanwhile, the *Green Review* introduced the idea of a Basic Income to its readers, which meant that when a Green party was founded in Korea its members were already knowledgeable about the idea. By then the most significant practical turn in the Basic Income debate had already occurred: in 2016, Jae-myung Lee, Mayor of Seongnam City, close to Seoul, implemented a Youth Dividend (Ahn and Kang, no date).

The Youth Dividend is an unconditional quarterly income for all 10,000 of the twenty-four-year-olds who have lived in Seongnam City for at least three years. The four payments during the year are made in a local currency, the 'Seongnam Gift Certificate' (Seongnamsalangsangpumkkwon) that has to be spent in the City, and they amount to an annual value of about US$900. The Youth Dividend is universal for the age group, unconditional, and individual. Apart from the fact that it is not paid in cash that can be spent anywhere, this is a Basic Income; and the payment being in a local currency means that the local economy benefits, thus increasing public support for Basic Income. The Dividend was the Mayor's initiative, it was funded from the City's budget, and it was approved by a majority of just two votes in the City Council after a vigorous debate during which many of the normal arguments for and against Basic Income were heard. Objectors said that rich young people did not need it; poverty would be reduced more by giving the money just to the poor; it would be better to provide jobs than money; and people would waste it. Supporters framed the Dividend as a right; argued that if it went to everyone then everyone would be interested in the amount and in the age range of recipients growing; suggested that autonomy rather than paternalism would result in wise consumption; claimed that the Dividend would enable young people to prepare for good jobs, which would be better than giving them not so good jobs; and also claimed that the Dividend would stimulate the local economy, which would create jobs.

Although the Council had agreed to pay the Youth Dividend, President Park's government objected to it and threatened to cut the local grant by the same amount as the total cost of the dividend. The Dividend was launched at half the promised amount in order to prove the City's case, and then in 2017 President Geun-hye Park was impeached, which led people to question the Government's neoliberal economic policies and drew attention to alternatives such as Basic Income. The new government supported the Seongnam City Youth Dividend.

No control group was surveyed when the Dividend was first paid, but in April 2016 both the recipients and some of the City's businesses were asked their opinions; 96.3 per cent of recipients surveyed said that they found the Dividend helpful, with higher support registered in poorer areas of the City; and recipients were found to be more interested in politics than they had been before receiving the Dividend. Sales in local businesses rose by 20 per cent, thus increasing support for the Youth Dividend among the normally conservative business owners (Ahn and Kang, no date). In July 2016, a further survey, conducted at fifteen community service centres, and to which 498 recipients responded, established that 95.3 per cent of recipients had found the payments helpful, and 84.5 per cent agreed with the unconditionality of the payments (Yi, 2019: 419).

An interestingly significant event that also occurred in 2016 was the world's number one Go player Sedol Lee's defeat four nil by AlphaGo, Google's artificial intelligence Go-playing computer. Anxiety about the future of employment rose during the match. And then during the General Election campaign in April 2016 both the Labour Party and the Green Party included Basic Income among their campaign promises, with different accompanying policies and phase-in methods. Neither of these parties gained seats in the National Assembly, but their campaigns had raised public interest in Basic Income, and when the 2016 Basic Income Earth Network (BIEN) Congress was held in Seoul, Jongin Kim, provisional chair of the Democratic Party, spoke at the opening session. No further action followed, but it was of interest that such a prominent politician had recognized the importance of Basic Income as a policy option, and equally of interest that the press and other media paid so much attention to the congress. During the congress the Swiss referendum and the successful pilot projects in Namibia and India were of course discussed, so those received publicity in Korea, which further raised understanding of Basic Income; and then in 2017 Jae-myung Lee was an unsuccessful candidate in the presidential election, and his proposal for a small Basic Income paid for by a land tax became a matter for public debate.

During the local elections in 2018, the idea of a Basic Income received considerable attention. Jae-myung Lee became Governor of Gyeonggi Province, the largest province in South Korea, with a promise to introduce a province-wide Youth Dividend; and many of the new governors in rural areas have promised an unconditional income for farmers. The province-wide Youth Dividend was implemented in 2019 with a regional currency. Of the 3,500 recipients who responded to an online survey, 80.6 per cent stated satisfaction with the Dividend. Reasons for dissatisfaction were that the dividend was only paid to twenty-four-year-olds; the local currency could not be spent in supermarkets, department stores and entertainment stores; and separate applications had to be made each quarter (Gyeonggi Research Institute Basic Income Research Group, 2019: 16; see also Ahn and Kang, no date).

City-led and province-led initiatives are not the only examples of unconditional incomes in Korea. A farming community wanting to reduce the average age of its inhabitants is paying an unconditional income to young adults for a year, and in some cases longer, to encourage them to stay in the area; a church is collecting donations from its members in order to pay equal incomes to every member in order to replicate the experience of the early Christians, who pooled and distributed their wealth; and a variety of projects, inspired by Germany's 'Mein Grundeinkommen', 'My Basic Income', are crowdfunding six-month Basic Incomes for winners of lotteries (Yi, 2019: 420–21). In the political sphere, a Basic Income party was established in 2020, from which Hye-in Yong was elected to the National Assembly, and she and other representatives have submitted bills asking for research and discussion about Basic Income, with the most recent bill asking for a parliamentary committee to be established with the purpose of encouraging public debate. Both 'carbon tax and dividend' and 'land tax and dividend' models are now significant elements of that debate, as is what claims to be the first ever data dividend now being paid in local currency in Gyeonggi Province (Gnews, 2020; National Assembly of the Republic of Korea, 2020; News1, 2020; Yi, 2020).

In just ten years, from a low base, the Republic of Korea has seen a most rapid increase in both practical Basic Income experiments and public, academic and political debate about Basic Income. The Basic Income Korean Network had hoped to host the 2021 BIEN Congress, and was initially the only bid, but a late bid from Scotland won a majority at BIEN's General Assembly at the end of the 2019 congress. A large international conference and national Basic Income festival planned for February 2020 in Suwon City had to be cancelled because of the coronavirus pandemic, and only a one-day online event was possible the following September. In the context of Korea's practical experience of Basic Income and its brief but intense debate on the subject, such setbacks are a problem, but the hope must be that the highly capable individuals and organizations now engaged in that debate will be able to maintain momentum. South Korea has a history of innovation, and it would not be a complete surprise if it were to become the first country to implement a Basic Income for every working-age adult, perhaps first in Gyeonggi Province and then nationwide. The Republic of Korea would then reap the benefits of doing that, and other countries would follow.

EXPERIMENTS AND PILOT PROJECTS ELSEWHERE

As well as the various projects discussed in this chapter, we have already discussed past, existing and planned experiments in Finland (Chapter 8), the Netherlands (Chapter 8), and Scotland (Chapter 7). In 2017, GiveDirectly, a US non-profit organization, began a large Basic Income randomized controlled trial that pays small Basic Incomes to 20,000 individuals in 197 rural Kenyan villages. A further 100 villages act as a control group. Entire communities are involved, and a variety of types of income: lump-sum transfers, long-term Basic Incomes designed to last for twelve years, and short-term Basic Incomes. Results have been similar to those obtained in Namibia and India, with a variety of changes more pronounced in the villages looking forward to twelve-year Basic Incomes. A similar small-scale experiment has been carried out in a village in Uganda by a Belgian NGO, 'Eight', again with similar results; and a comparable project is soon to begin in the Democratic Republic of Congo (Banerjee et al., 2020; Douillard, 2017; Duverger, 2018: 127; Eight, 2021; GiveDirectly, 2020; 2021).

In 2009, thirteen homeless men in London were given £3,000 each, and most of them used it to turn their lives around (Bregman, 2017: 25–7). In 2016, three British families were each given £26,000 on condition that they came off unemployment benefit, and television cameras followed their progress. A second series followed a new group of people. Results were mixed, but in many ways more positive than might have been expected (IMDb, 2017).

Sometimes, a natural experiment—that is, a condition experienced by a community that either was not experienced before or is not experienced by another identical community—can provide results that tell us something about the effects of a Basic Income. An annual distribution of casino profits to Cherokee Indians has delivered health and education benefits similar to those experienced during the Indian and Namibian pilot projects, along with a significant increase in the quality of parenting (Akee et al., 2015; Van Parijs and Vanderborght, 2017: 152).

A pilot project planned in 2016 for Oakland, California (Altman, 2016), by the start-up funder Y-Combinator, never got off the ground (Duverger, 2018: 128; Tiku, 2018), but a project in Stockton, California, has happened, and is funded by the Economic Security Project, an organization founded by Chris Hughes, a co-founder of Facebook and an advocate for the US's Earned Income Tax Credit being turned into a Minimum Income Guarantee (Hughes, 2018: 160–80). One hundred and twenty randomly selected residents from poorer neighbourhoods have been receiving $500 per month, and the experiment has been extended into 2021 on the basis of an additional private donation (Emison, 2020). Wealthy entrepreneurs sometimes understand that it is their automation of previously labour-intensive industries that is causing a future of unemployment, and some of them recognize that a Basic Income might be essential to provide households with a subsistence income and to provide the purchasing power to maintain their own industries and profits. Mark Zuckerberg endorsed Guy Standing's most recent book, *Battling Eight Giants: Basic Income now* (Duverger, 2018: 128; Standing, 2020). Experiments similar to Stockton's are now running in St. Paul, Minnesota; Compton, California; and Richmond, Virginia (Kingson, 2021).

It is becoming increasingly difficult to keep up with Basic Income initiatives around the world. There are more planned, and there will be more still (Standing, 2017a: 260–74). Few of them are or will be unproblematic. Only a permanent, universal, regular and unconditional income is a Basic Income, and only that kind of income will have the effects of a Basic Income; and because any experiment or pilot project will have an end-point, it will never entirely replicate the effects of a real Basic Income (Widerquist, 2018). It is encouraging that a longer-term project is now being tried in Kenya, and it would no doubt be helpful for longer-term Basic Incomes to be trialled in countries with more developed economies (GiveDirectly, 2020; 2021).

The experiments discussed in this chapter have been for unconditional incomes, but it should also be said that any experiment, even with incomes with conditions attached, will provide useful information, as long as it is recognized that the further an experiment's characteristics are from those of a genuine Basic Income, the less reliable will be the results as predictors of a Basic Income's effects. Perhaps the most problematic factor is that of affordability. Any experiment that could not be permanently rolled out across a whole country in an affordable way should not be regarded as a Basic Income pilot project simply because the Basic Income being tested would not be feasible to implement. This would appear to apply to the current Stockton experiment, and also to the Alaskan and Cherokee Indian annual distributions, because none of them could be rolled out across the whole country.

CONCLUSIONS

The Basic Income debate is now truly worldwide, and it was no surprise when the authors of a recent international handbook were drawn from five different continents (Torry, 2019b). It is also no surprise that in our inter-connected world so much of what happens in the Basic Income debate now happens all over the planet, and not just in one country or another: so here we must begin to use the word 'global', because we are now discussing a single global Basic Income debate. The Basic Income Earth Network (BIEN) is the longest standing example of such global activity. More recent examples are the International Basic Income Week now held each September; the Basic Income March that now occurs as part of that week in many parts of the world (Basic Income Earth Network, 2020; Basic Income March, 2020); and 'UBI Advocates', a gathering of Basic Income campaigners who organize working groups for particular projects, such as a letter to the Secretary General of the United Nations and a survey of Basic Income organizations around the world.

It is to the character of the now global Basic Income debate that we turn in the next chapter.

10. A global Basic Income debate

INTRODUCTION

As Van Parijs and Vanderborght have put it,

> Since the mid-1980s, the history of basic income is no longer a set of isolated national developments, completely independent and mostly ignorant of each other. Thanks to the existence of an international network, to the power of the internet, and to the spreading of the idea, new initiatives around basic income are now happening every day and are being echoed worldwide. (Van Parijs and Vanderborght, 2017: 98)

Chapter 9 has revealed the worldwide character of the Basic Income debate, but what is truly global about the contemporary debate is that so many of its aspects are not restricted to one country or to one continent, but are found throughout the world. This chapter will choose just a few of those aspects: trade union attitudes to Basic Income; Basic Income and the status of women; questions about feasibility, funding options, and the level at which a Basic Income would be paid; and the diverse debate across what we might call the worldview spectrum, politically from the left to libertarians, among Green parties and in relation to climate change, and, to take just one religious perspective, among Christians.

The aim is to provide a partial anatomy of today's global debate about Basic Income. Others might have made different selections of the aspects of the debate to be covered, and might have given the aspects chosen different amounts of attention, so readers should treat this chapter as an invitation to offer their own interpretations of the current stage of the global Basic Income debate.

Trades Unions

Throughout the history recorded here we have discovered occasional trade union interest—for instance, in the Netherlands, South Africa, and Namibia—and Henderson and Quiggin have found that more recently occasional trades unions have supported the idea, but that the major trend, both among trades unions as organizations, and in the labour movement in general, has been disinterest and rejection, even though trade union members have recorded levels of approval similar to those of other participants in opinion surveys (Henderson and Quiggin, 2019: 497–8; Van Parijs and Vanderborght, 2017: 174–5). A recent survey of trade union opinion has discovered that in relation to the level of a trade union's level of support for Basic Income there are

> four causal channels. First, unions' propensity to support a UBI depends on the degrees of socio-economic insecurity. In contexts characterized by high levels of poverty, unemployment and precariousness, UBI proposals look more attractive in the eyes of union leaders. Secondly, welfare regime generosity is a strong explanans of trade unions' support. Less encompassing welfare systems encourage trade unionists to regard UBI as a legitimate policy alternative. Third, trade unions' attachment to the work ethic and the insurance principle affects their preferences for unconditionality and universality in policy settings. Fourth, their role in the industrial landscape, and their degree of organisational inclusivity, have a strong influence on UBI support. (Cigna, 2020)

Given that a Basic Income would increase workers' bargaining power relative to their employers, it might seem strange that unions have been either hostile or indifferent to Basic Income. Common objections are easily countered: for instance, it would be possible to implement a Basic Income scheme that abolished national minimum wages and a variety of aspects of the welfare state, but all that needs to be said is that the kind of financially feasible Basic Income scheme that would be likely to be implemented would work happily alongside existing national minimum wages, social insurance benefits, means-tested benefits and public services, and would provide precisely the layer of security that workers need.

However, rejection is understandable during a period in which trades unions are seeing membership numbers collapse, putting them on the defensive; and it cannot help that Basic Income is sometimes recommended on the basis that technological change is inevitable, jobs will disappear and full employment will never return. It is equally problematic that, depending on the details of the Basic Income scheme as a whole, a Basic Income might look as if it would reduce the proportion of a worker's disposable income over which trade union officers would be able to negotiate with employers, thus reducing unions' usefulness to their members: although a more careful understanding of the situation would recognize that there would still be just as much of a wage to negotiate over as before, because the Basic Income would not be funded by reducing the wage itself but rather by increasing the tax paid on it, or by some other method; and a broader perspective would recognize that a Basic Income would make every worker, and therefore all workers, more able to resist poor employment conditions and low pay, suggesting that trade union support for Basic Income might be more rational than rejection of the idea. But having said that, a worker's possession of a Basic Income would reduce their union's hold over them, just as it would reduce their employer's hold over them. Trade union leaders ought not to object to such enhanced individual freedom, but we can see why they might.

An argument is sometimes put that a Basic Income would act as a subsidy to wages, and would therefore cause employers to reduce them. This would be a fair point in countries with no existing means-tested benefits. Means-tested benefits function as dynamic subsidies: that is, they rise as wages are reduced, thus providing employers with a significant incentive to lower wages. A Basic Income would be a static subsidy, and would not rise if wages fell, which means that in any country with means-tested benefits a Basic Income would generate less of a subsidy effect than the existing system and ought to be supported by trades unions (Van Parijs and Vanderborght, 2017: 176–81).

Union leaderships might also feel that any campaign for a Basic Income might distract attention from campaigns for higher national minimum wages and better working conditions. However, trades unions have traditionally taken a broad view of their members' interests, and it is this tradition that has generated the occasional support expressed for Basic Income, in the Netherlands, Germany, the UK, South Africa, Namibia and a variety of other countries (Henderson and Quiggin, 2019: 498–500; Van Parijs and Vanderborght, 2017: 181).

What might persuade trade union leaderships to understand the benefits of Basic Income for their members and for their unions as organizations? Henderson and Quiggin suggest a Basic Income scheme that combines a 'Basic Income, with minimum wages at a realistic level, and a commitment to full employment: that is, the availability of jobs for all those willing and able to work' (Henderson and Quiggin, 2019: 501). While a job guarantee can cause 'lock in', that is, workers get locked in to the created jobs and find it difficult to enter the normal employment market, and while job guarantee schemes can suffer from a variety of other problems (Szlinder, 2019), Henderson and Quiggin suggest that there should be no obligation to be gainfully employed, but that jobs should be available for those who want them. A combination of Basic Income and job guarantee would put workers and their trades unions in a strong bargaining position (Henderson and Quiggin, 2019: 502–4). However, as we have seen, a Basic Income on its own would do that as well. What is clearly required is research, education and wide consultation with trade union leaders.

THE POLITICAL SPECTRUM

The Left

'The left' has a somewhat flexible meaning, encompassing any combination of the following: working democratically for an elected government that nationalizes major industries and redistributes the profits in the form of incomes and public services; permitting an oligopoly to control the means of production on behalf of a population; local control of the means of production; a network of co-operative enterprises; workers managing industries; and Karl Marx's 'From each according to his ability, to each according to his need' (Marx, [1891] 1970). Underlying all of these meanings lies the conviction that we are all equally members of the human race, and that that equality needs to be given effect in social arrangements.

A significant fact about the current global Basic Income debate is that it is located not just across much of the political spectrum, but also in a variety of ways across the more socialist end of it. In Chapter 4, we found the UK's Labour Party discussing but then rejecting the State Bonus League's proposal during the early 1920s, and in Chapter 7, we discovered the Labour Party's Social Justice Commission treating seriously the possibility of a Basic Income. We have also found individuals on the left of the political spectrum, such as James Meade and G.D.H. Cole, advocating the implementation of a Basic Income. Given these early diverse views of Basic Income on the leftward segment of the political spectrum in the UK, it might be helpful to continue to study the left in the UK as an example of how diverse attitudes on the left persist and of how a slow shift is taking place towards a more positive assessment of Basic Income.

During the past five years, left-leaning think tanks in the UK have been divided on the issue. In 2016, the Director of the Institute for Public Policy Research (IPPR) wrote an article that called Basic Income a 'universal basic mistake' because

> it would discourage work, perpetuate inequality, would be expensive and politically extremely unpopular. Supporters see no social obligation arising from a universal income, and fall back on the notion that individuals, having received universal income, would take it upon themselves to do socially useful things. This is utopian in the extreme. … It is also antithetical to the values of most British people, who believe in the value of work; in the dignity that comes with self-sufficiency; in the pride that comes with purposeful activity. There is overwhelming evidence that having a job is crucial to good mental and physical health. It provides a sense of purpose and a vital set of relationships and social networks. (Cruddas and Kibasi, 2016)

The authors had not recognized that both logic and empirical evidence suggest that a Basic Income would incentivize and reward paid employment for many households currently on means-tested benefits, and that it would stimulate new economic and other productive activity.

Two years later, the IPPR published a report that proposed a citizens' wealth fund that would pay a single unconditional lump sum dividend to every twenty-five-year-old (Roberts and Lawrence, 2018).

In a report published in 2019, the New Economics Foundation suggested that

> whereas universal benefits such as healthcare or unemployment payments are pro-
> vided to all who need it, UBI is provided to all regardless of need. Inevitably it is not
> enough to help those in severe need but is a generous gift to the wealthy who don't
> need it. It is the expenditure equivalent of a flat tax and as such is regressive. But the
> consequences are more than a question of principle. The estimates of funds required
> to provide a UBI at anything other than token levels are well in excess of the entire
> welfare budget of most countries. If we were able to build the political movement
> required to raise the massive extra funds would we chose to return so much of it to
> the wealthiest, or would it be better spent on targeted measures to reduce inequality
> and help the neediest? (Coote and Yazici, 2019)

The authors quote without comment a feasible illustrative Basic Income scheme published by this author that disproves every statement that they make in this paragraph except the one that a Basic Income would be paid regardless of need; and adding to confusion, just one month earlier the same organization had published a report suggesting that the UK's Income Tax Personal Allowance should be turned into a National Weekly Allowance: a regular cash payment for every working age adult. The researchers proposed that anyone earning over £100,000 per annum should have their National Weekly Allowance withdrawn on a taper, with no withdrawal at £100,000 per annum and complete withdrawal at earnings of £125,000 per annum. If it weren't for this withdrawal, the proposal would be for a Basic Income.

Between them, the IPPR and the New Economics Foundation represent well the ambivalence about Basic Income frequently found across the leftward end of the political spectrum. Given the deep historical connections between trades unions, political parties and think tanks on the left, this ambivalence should not surprise us. What is of interest is the movement towards proposals remarkably similar to Basic Income but with different names. This might be a recognition first of all that there are now substantial reasons for political parties and think tanks on the left to argue for Basic Income, and in particular to argue for Basic Income schemes that would be redistributive and would retain existing welfare state provision in order to counter increasing interest in rather different Basic Income schemes proposed by extreme libertarians; and secondly, that the terms 'Basic Income' and 'Universal Basic Income' might still be toxic on the left, so different terminology is required. A working group established by the Citizen's Basic Income Trust to create draft Basic Income legislation for the UK suggested that the unconditional income enshrined in the legislation should be called a Fair Allowance (Citizen's Basic Income Trust, 2018b). Such terminology might assist the left to come together around a feasible Basic Income scheme that would threaten neither national minimum wages nor aspects of the welfare state.

A somewhat different and far more positive engagement with Basic Income is now in evidence on the left: one that is well represented by the UK think tank Compass. In 2016, Compass published a report arguing for a Basic Income:

> Central to the case for a UBI is the way it would help prepare us for a world in which the new technological revolution, driven by artificial intelligence and robotics, will, over time, transform the nature of work and the type and number of jobs. A UBI offers a powerful way of protecting all citizens from the great winds of change to be ushered in by the fourth industrial age, and of sharing the potentially massive productivity gains that it will bring. (Reed and Lansley, 2016: 8)

The report included two potentially feasible Basic Income schemes, and proposed to fund them either from within the current income tax system or by employing the dividends from a citizens' wealth fund. A follow-up report offered more detail, and included a foreword by Baroness Ruth Lister, a left-leaning academic who had herself been on a journey from significant scepticism about Basic Income to seeing that it could be useful in a more turbulent era (Lansley and Reed, 2019; Lister, 2017). Compass is now hosting a 'Basic Income Conversation' with two paid staff members.

Like left-leaning think tanks, the UK's parliamentary Labour Party, and probably the party more generally, is divided on Basic Income. There are many Members of Parliament who would agree with Jon Cruddas MP's rejection of the idea (Cruddas and Kibasi, 2016); and many, including the previous Shadow Chancellor, John McDonnell MP, are in favour. The Labour Party was well represented among the 110 Members of Parliament and members of the House of Lords who recently wrote to the Chancellor of the Exchequer asking for a Recovery Basic Income to help the UK to recover from the coronavirus pandemic (Basic Income Conversation, 2020).

Elsewhere in the world, Senator Eduardo Matarazzo Suplicy, a cofounder with Luiz Inacio Lula da Silva of the Partido dos Trabalhadores (Workers' Party) in Brazil, persuaded the party to pass legislation that required the Government to implement a Basic Income by gradual steps (see Chapter 9). In the Netherlands, the Partij van de Arbeid (Labour Party) had for twenty years experienced a similar division of opinion as the UK's Labour Party, but in 2016 its membership voted to include Basic Income experiments in the party's manifesto for the 2017 General Election. The Swiss socialist party was divided on Basic Income during the period of the national referendum on the issue in 2016 (see Chapter 8); and in other European countries it tends to be very small left-wing parties, or occasional high-profile individuals in the larger parties, who advocate for the implementation of a Basic Income or for Basic Income pilot projects. Sometimes commitment to Basic Income is briefly high but then slides into support for means-tested benefits, as has happened in the radical left-wing Podemos in Spain; and sometimes what is being called a Basic Income is not one, as has also happened in Spain (Coelho, 2015; Rincón, 2020a). Since 2003, Germany's Die Linke (The Left) has seen significant interest in Basic Income, although as in the UK this interest is controversial within the parliamentary party.

As Van Parijs and Vanderborght point out, the importance of paid employment on the left of the political spectrum is to be expected, both in theory and in practice: but this 'labourist' mindset has always been challenged to a greater or lesser extent by the more 'socialist' demand, in the Paine and Spence tradition, for an equal distribution of resources (Van Parijs and Vanderborght, 2017: 189–94). A point of contention between the two viewpoints is that labourism assumes that labour is a commodity, and that the worker should therefore seek the highest possible value for their labour in an employment market, whereas socialism seeks the decommodification of labour: that is, that someone's labour should no longer be regarded as a commodity to be bought and sold in a market, but should instead be a means of freely chosen production and reproduction, with workers collectively or individually owning the means of production.

> Freedom and social emancipation require the reconquest of the value of flexible (paid and/or unpaid) work … Basic Income does not inevitably pave the way to post-capitalist social scenarios, but it can firmly disarm one of the main disciplining mechanisms within capitalist societies: the obligatory nature of wage-earning work—hence its anti-capitalist strength. (Casassas et al., 2019: 468, 472)

A Basic Income represents social provision for universal needs, and therefore ought to be an attractive policy for socialists, in the same way that the universal franchise and universal public services are givens on the left of the political spectrum (Flora, 1981: 358–9; Hill, 1990: 165): a tendency that we already see in relation to support for universal child allowances and pensions. A Basic Income would contribute to this universalizing socialist process and, as Callinicos puts it, such a development could also be attractive to the labourist part of the left-wing spectrum:

> The basis of capital's power lies … in its control of production, not in the financial markets. One of the attractions of the idea that every citizen be granted as of right

a basic income set, say, at a level that would allow them to meet their socially recognized subsistence needs, is that it could help to emancipate workers from the dictatorship of capital. Such a basic income would radically alter the bargaining power between labour and capital, since potential workers would now be in a position, if they chose, to pursue alternatives to paid employment. Moreover, because all citizens would receive the same basic income (perhaps with adjustments for economic handicaps such as age, disability, and dependent children), its introduction would be an important step towards establishing equality of access to advantage. (Callinicos, 2003: 134)

Even further to the left we can find Basic Income advocated as an essential accompaniment to the abolition of capitalism as we know it (Breitenbach et al., 1990: 33; Shutt, 2010: 122–7).

We have recognized the importance of such public services as healthcare and education to individuals and organizations on this section of the political spectrum; and here we have suggested that the provision of public services equally available to everyone might suggest that a similar approach should be taken in relation to incomes: but what we find is individuals and organizations on the left opposing universal services and Basic Income to each other on the basis that the country could not afford both at the same time, and that public services do more to reduce inequality than a Basic Income would do (Coote and Percy, 2020: 51–6, 125–6). In pursuit of this cause, authors such as Coote and Percy have sometimes chosen to reference Basic Income schemes that could be unaffordable and could increase inequality, rather than financially feasible Basic Income schemes that would reduce inequality and would be eminently affordable: but Andrew Percy himself has now recognized that it could be perfectly feasible to implement both a Basic Income and additional universal public services (Percy, 2019: 222), as of course it could be. The two proposals are entirely compatible as ideas, and potentially compatible in relation to cost if appropriate schemes are chosen. There is no need for the left to divide into supporters of Basic Income and supporters of additional public services.

One of the understandable objections that labourists offer is that a Basic Income would be a 'subsidy to wages … Employers should be compelled to meet the costs of employing the labour from which they derive a benefit' (Esam et al., 1985: 53). Those who offer such objections seem not to recognize that a tax allowance—which they intend to retain—also operates as a subsidy to wages; that profits have only a partial relationship to wages paid to workers; and that means-tested benefits function as an even more damaging subsidy because the benefits rise if wages fall. A major factor that has driven the contemporary Basic Income debate is changes in the employment market brought about by a combination of technological change and globalization (Brynjolfsson and McAfee, 2014: 232–3; Cholbi and Weber, 2020; Greve,

2017: 94–7; Parker, 1991): and the most obvious outcome has been the division of the working class into a shrinking group of employed and unionized workers and a rapidly growing 'precariat': workers without stable jobs, occupations, or incomes, a group that now includes significant elements of the middle class as well as the working class (Jordan, 1987; Standing, 2011a). University lecturers are now increasingly subject to short-term or zero-hour contracts: no longer is this a problem associated only with delivery drivers. In Chapter 7 we encountered the UK's claimants' unions of the 1970s. More recently, similar movements have occurred in other countries, and particularly in France (Van Parijs and Vanderborght, 2017: 184–5); and now the 'Occupy' movement has given voice to elements of the precariat: but such associations possess little political leverage, and are themselves quite precarious. It is not insignificant that Guy Standing has been both an important voice for the precariat and a high-profile advocate for Basic Income (Standing, 2011a).

By recognizing the meeting of need as a universal requirement, a Basic Income could reconcile the precariat with what is left of the organized working class without compromising trades unions' ability to enable their members to extract as much as possible from the proceeds of production. As we have already recognized, because a Basic Income would mean that part of every individual's subsistence income would be secure, workers would be more able to decline undesirable employment, thus increasing trades unions' bargaining power (Jordan, 1987: 161). There is as much reason for labourists to argue for the implementation of a Basic Income as there is for socialists to do so (Sherman and Judkins, 1996; Torry, 2013: 214–16). As the global Basic Income debate continues to evolve, and as the employment market becomes even more precarious for even more people, it would not be a surprise if labourists and socialists around the world were to join forces to argue for Basic Income, to insist that the scheme implemented must be redistributive, and to be clear that the Basic Income must be accompanied by realistic national minimum wages and by well-funded public services. If this does not occur, then those on the left of the political spectrum might have to stand and watch while rather less attractive Basic Income schemes are implemented.

Libertarians

I have divided the political spectrum somewhat naively between the left and libertarians because political configurations in different countries are so very different that any other division would have been even more problematic. By 'libertarians' here I mean everything from the UK's Liberal Democratic Party, for which individual liberty is a vital political value, but which sometimes espouses policies to the left of the Labour Party, to the neoliberal pro-market position occupied by academics such as Charles Murray in the United States

(Murray, 1984; 1994; 1996; 2008). Positions along this part of the political spectrum are not necessarily averse to the public provision of incomes and services because the Lockean Proviso, that any private enclosure of resources must leave 'enough and as good' for others (Chapter 2), is not in principle opposed to property rights or individual liberty (Fleischer and Lehto, 2019: 442, 444–5; Locke, [1690] 1884: 207).

Close to one end of the 'libertarian' spectrum lies neoliberalism, or the 'New Right', which Giddens describes in terms of

> minimal government, autonomous civil society, market fundamentalism, moral authoritarianism (plus strong economic individuation), a labour market that clears like any other, acceptance of inequality, traditionalist nationalism, the welfare state as a safety net, linear modernization, low ecological consciousness ... . (Giddens, 1998: 8, 13)

There are a wide variety of reasons why liberal and neoliberal politicians, academics and journalists might propose the implementation of a Basic Income (Fleischer and Lehto, 2019), although they often prefer a Negative Income Tax (Fleischer and Lehto, 2019: 441), perhaps because its administration would continue to distinguish between recipients and providers, which a Basic Income would not. Where either of these is advocated it will be because it would be preferable to means-tested benefits, which are a 'deterrent to hard work' (Joseph and Sumption, 1979: 19; Minford, 2002); it would facilitate a free market in labour because earned income would no longer need to provide for the whole of a household's subsistence income; it might enable wages to fall to their market-clearing levels (Fitzpatrick, 1999: 84); it might enable statutory minimum wages to be dispensed with (on which, see below); and it would enable working-age adults to provide for themselves and their families in the context of a free market economy because it would place as few disincentives as possible in the way of people seeking employment, progressing in employment, and improving their skills. Perhaps the most significant driver of New Right enthusiasm for Basic Income is the fear of 'dependency at the bottom of society' (Mead, 1992: ix). As Charles Murray puts it: during the 1960s and 1970s, the USA 'tried to provide more for the poor and produced more poor instead. We tried to remove the barriers to escape poverty, and inadvertently built a trap' (Murray, 1984: 9). Unemployment and dependence on benefits were

> rational responses to changes in the rules of the game of surviving and getting ... Compulsory transfers from one person to another are uncomfortably like robbery ... If we are even a little bit wrong about the consequences of the transfer, we are likely to do great injustices to people who least deserve to bear the burden ... Social programs in a democratic society ... tend to have enough of an inducement to produce

bad behavior and not enough of a solution to produce good behavior ... . (Murray, 1984: 155, 204, 218)

The answer was to scrap 'the entire federal welfare and income-support structure for working-age persons' in order to force people to seek and retain employment, with an unemployment insurance scheme designed purely to fill in short-term gaps (Murray, 1984: 227, 230; 1996: 50; 2006). Murray recommended a Negative Income Tax (Murray, 1996: 125), and then, from 2006 (Murray, 2006), what he calls a 'Guaranteed Income', by which he means a Basic Income (Murray, 2008). This would remove the incentive to apply for other cash benefits; would not disincentivize employment; and would ensure that no family would end up destitute (Murray, 2008). Above all, it would remove government interference from people's lives. Murray proposes an amendment to the Constitution of the United States of America:

> Henceforth, federal, state, and local governments shall make no law nor establish any program that provides benefits to some citizens but not to others. All programs currently providing such benefits are to be terminated. The funds formerly allocated to them are to be used instead to provide every citizen with a cash grant beginning at age 21 and continuing until death ... . (Murray, 2008: 4)

However, while a Basic Income would provide some proportion of the costs of everyone's basic needs, it would not be able to provide for such particular needs as disability or for varying housing costs, so a Basic Income would never be sufficient on its own: but Murray's positive argument for Basic Income is fully coherent both with neoliberalism and with the Lockean Proviso, and strongly echoes Juliet Rhys Williams' reasons for advocating a Basic Income (see Chapter 5).

Just as the implementation of a Basic Income would not require the abolition of other publicly provided services or incomes, and successful implementation of a Basic Income might require them to be retained, so the implementation of a Basic Income would not require the abolition of statutory minimum wages and might require their retention. There is a risk that a Basic Income of significant size would disincentivize employment in low-wage sectors, so wages would have to rise, potentially rendering a statutory minimum wage unnecessary: but there is also a possibility that the existence of an unconditional foundational income might cause additional automation in low-wage sectors, causing more unemployment, and that wages in some sectors would fall because they would no longer have to provide the full subsistence costs of a family. In this situation a continuing statutory minimum wage would be required. Whether we would need a statutory minimum wage would depend on the level of the Basic Income and on a variety of other contingent factors, meaning that nobody should argue for or against the retention of a statutory minimum wage in general terms: only particular arguments relating to particular contexts would be valid.

Not everyone towards the libertarian end of the political spectrum is keen on Basic Income. This is mainly because it is counterintuitive to recognize that an unconditional income would provide a higher employment incentive than a means-tested one. Something unconditional sounds more 'something for nothing' than something means-tested, even though the opposite is the case: and so at the UK's Conservative Party's annual conference in 2010 the Chancellor of the Exchequer announced that households containing at least one higher rate taxpayer would be deprived of their otherwise unconditional Child Benefit. It did not work out like that because the Chancellor would very soon have been told that the UK possesses no database connecting Child Benefit recipients with higher rate taxpayers: so the result was a new question in everyone's annual tax return, and an additional tax for anyone receiving Child Benefit or living with someone who was receiving it. But what was interesting was that when the policy was announced, members of the audience expressed the view that 'They don't need it' and 'The money should be targeted on the poor'. Nobody seemed to understand that an unconditional income was already targeted on the poor, because it constitutes a higher proportion of the disposable income of a poor household than of a wealthier household, and nobody seemed to understand that it did not matter if the rich received Child Benefit because they were in any case paying more in Income Tax than they were receiving. It was and remains efficient to give the money to everyone: precisely the argument for Basic Income.

A close relative of neoliberalism is what we might call classical liberalism: the idea that individual liberty is the highest human aspiration. It is to the left of neoliberalism because it generally recognizes that people working together can create the conditions for individual liberty. As Samuel Brittan, a former *Financial Times* journalist, has put it: 'It is individuals who feel, exult, despair and rejoice. Any statements about group welfare are a shorthand way of referring to such individual effects' (Brittan, 1998: 11). Regulation is often required to ensure that the economy best serves individual liberty; and the State, far from being a hindrance to individual liberty, is an essential instrument for promoting it, because only the State can control some aspects of society or the economy that conflict with an individual's freedom. In relation to incomes, the high rates at which means-tested benefits are withdrawn as earned income rises restricts the resources available to the worker and therefore compromises their liberty. A Basic Income would not be withdrawn, so any household taken off means-tested benefits by their Basic Incomes would experience an increase in its ability to improve its net income and would thus see an increase in liberty. 'If we are serious about pursuing real freedom for all ... what we have to go for is the highest *unconditional* income for all' (Van Parijs, 1995: 1, 33: italics in the original). As Brittan sees it, 'it is positively desirable that people should have a means of subsistence independent of needs', because this would 'separate the libertarian, free choice aspects of capitalism from the puritan work ethic'. So a Basic Income should be seen 'not as a handout, but as a property right' and as a 'return on the national capital' (Brittan and Webb, 1990: 2–3). In his view, a Basic Income would be

> a superior alternative to the minimum wage ... Minimum wages represent just that kind of interference with markets which does most harm. ... Those most likely to suffer are just the people whom the proponents of minimum wages say they most want to help. They include those on the fringes of the labour market or on the borderline of disablement or other incapacity ... and all the others who face a choice between low pay and no pay. Minimum wages are a denial of the human right to sell one's labour to a willing buyer and to make one's own decision about whether or not to take paid work at going rates. (Brittan and Webb, 1990: 7)

As we continue to move leftwards on the political spectrum, classical liberalism merges into what Fleischer and Lehto term left-libertarianism, which 'combines a defence of robust self-ownership ... with a defence of the egalitarian ownership of natural resources' (Fleischer and Lehto, 2019: 452). At the heart of this tradition is the 'real libertarianism' or 'real freedom' (Van Parijs, 1995) discussed by Philippe Van Parijs: freedom that is real because the individual's Basic Income enables them to live their freely chosen way of life.

> To understand what real-freedom-for-all truly means, and to be able to assess what it is worth, it is essential to spell out its specific institutional implications. ... Most strikingly, an unconditional income for all. ... If real freedom is a matter of means, not only of rights, people's incomes are obviously of great importance. But the real freedom we are concerned with is not only the freedom to purchase or consume. It is the freedom to live as one might like to live. Hence the importance of granting this purchasing power irrespective of people's work or willingness to work. (Van Parijs, 1995: 30)

Within the same tradition is Karl Widerquist's 'indepentarianism' or 'republican freedom':

> the effective power to make and to refuse active cooperation with other willing people. To have this power a person must have independence, freedom from directly and indirectly forced service to others. Independent people require civil and political rights, control of their persons, and access to a sufficient amount of resources so that they can meet their basic needs without serving anyone else's interests. (Widerquist, 2013: 187–8)

Widerquist argues that the best way to provide the freedom not to be dominated by employers, governments, or anyone else in a modern society, is to provide everyone with a Basic Income (Widerquist, 2013).

There is often a balance to be struck: while the taxation necessary to pay for a Basic Income might compromise taxpayer liberty, the taxpayer ought to want to see tax revenue spent on a liberty-enhancing Basic Income rather than on non-liberating means-tested systems (Munger, 2011). Dominic Hobson and Alan Duncan, who call themselves 'modern Conservatives' but are probably better described as classic liberals, ask how we might implement a national Minimum Income Standard so as best to promote 'liberty, property and prosperity' (Hobson and Duncan, 1995a; 1995b). They find means-tested benefits to be detrimental to all three, and so align themselves with Samuel Brittan to recommend a Basic Income (Hobson and Duncan, 1995b).

The only argument against a Basic Income from a liberal perspective that I have been able to discover is from Johannes Richardt: that a Basic Income is

> underpinned by a negative image of humankind as weak, vulnerable and isolated. The basic thrust of this sentiment is that people cannot cope within the harsh environment of globalized capitalism without state assistance. (Richardt, 2011)

Because society, the economy, and in particular the employment market, are increasingly turbulent, it is increasingly true that 'people cannot cope within the harsh environment of globalized capitalism', and that we are 'vulnerable'. Richardt's argument is an argument for Basic Income.

We have seen how the US and the UK have generated arguments for Basic Income across the non-left part of the political spectrum. The UK's Liberal Democrats included Basic Income in their election manifestos in 1989 and 1994 and were then persuaded to abandon the proposal because the leadership decided that it was too difficult to sell it on the doorstep, which perhaps it was. In the Netherlands, a party on the same political territory advocated for and then dropped Basic Income during the same period. At its 2014 congress, the same party voted in favour of Basic Income experiments, and the UK's Liberal Democrats are again discussing the idea. From 1996 onwards, small Austrian parties towards the libertarian end of the spectrum, but not the far right, have argued for a Negative Income Tax; and in Ireland the centre-right Fianna Fáil has recently shown substantial interest in Basic Income. As we saw in Chapter 8, it was a centre-right coalition that gave birth to Finland's recent Basic Income experiment, and in Chapter 9 we have seen how a single politician has not only generated considerable debate about Basic Income in South Korea, but also how a genuine provincial Basic Income has been implemented for a single year age cohort. Japan has seen political discussion, but not action (Van Parijs and Vanderborght, 2017: 194–6).

As with the leftward end of the political spectrum, the more libertarian end has seen recent think tank activity in relation to Basic Income in France, the US, and elsewhere; and in the UK, the Adam Smith Institute published a paper on Negative Income Tax in 2015, and another on Basic Income in 2018 (Lehto, 2018; Story, 2015; Van Parijs and Vanderborght, 2017: 196–7). Where politically we should locate US business leaders' financial support of experiments in the US and Kenya is an interesting question. Van Parijs and Vanderborght suggest that the connection between that support and think tank and political interest among libertarians is a Basic Income's administrative and economic efficiency (Van Parijs and Vanderborght, 2017: 197): but a further reason might be concern that the unemployment and employment market turbulence caused by their companies' innovations and the consequent loss of employment income will mean fewer people buying their products, so they have a personal interest in new ways of distributing purchasing power. The fact that the equality enshrined in Basic Income might make it look rather socialist is no problem to those further towards the libertarian end of the spectrum who can see that the proposal could well serve their own more capitalist agenda.

Basic Income on the Political Spectrum

'Basic Income' always means a regular unconditional income paid to every individual without means test or work test: but there could be many different Basic Income schemes: that is, different schemes constituted by Basic Incomes at different levels, different funding methods, different accompanying changes to existing tax and benefits systems, and so on. As we have seen, arguments for Basic Income can be found right across the mainstream political spectrum. As the global debate continues to evolve, and particularly as individual countries move from simply thinking about Basic Income or carrying out experiments and pilot projects to planning for implementation, we shall see controversy about Basic Income as an idea give way to controversy over the character-istics of Basic Income schemes: how is the country's new Basic Income to be funded? Should the statutory minimum wage be retained? Should other benefits be retained, and, if so, how should they adapt to the new Basic Income context? How redistributive should the scheme be? The kind of scheme that will emerge in each context will depend largely on the extent to which policy-makers and legislators have engaged positively with the Basic Income debate. Those parts of the political spectrum in which engagement in the debate is non-existent, conflicted or non-committal, could find that in other parts of the spectrum there might be consistent engagement and co-ordinated planning for Basic Income schemes of a particular kind.

Green Parties, and the Relationship Between Basic Income and Climate Change

Green party enthusiasm for Basic Income has been widespread and consistent, but it was never inevitable, because there is no clear and unambiguous connection between Basic Income and the ecological concerns at the heart of Green party interests. A variety of arguments are offered in support of Basic Income: for instance, the Paine and Spence argument that the planet and its resources belong to everyone, so those who now 'own' the land and its resources should pay an equal rent to everyone for their occupation of them; and the argument that a Basic Income would break the link between income and employment, and so might reduce employment and therefore economic growth as measured by Gross Domestic Product, and might therefore deliver a 'post-productivist' and 'sustainable post-capitalist world' that would mitigate climate change (Fitzpatrick, 1999: 186; Van Parijs and Vanderborght, 2017: 201–2; Widerquist et al., 2013: 259–310). However, a Basic Income could reduce marginal deduction rates, increase net incomes and therefore *increase* consumption, which would increase carbon emissions and make it more difficult to tackle climate change (Sovacool et al., 2014: 3). A further factor would operate if a Basic Income scheme were to reduce inequality. Any reduction in inequality, even in the absence of economic growth, would be likely to increase carbon emissions, because a poorer household's propensity to consume is on average higher than that of a wealthier household, so any Basic Income scheme that reduced inequality would be likely to increase carbon emissions (Sager, 2017). However, that is not the whole story, because any illustrative Basic Income scheme must specify the funding method as well as the levels of Basic Incomes for different age groups. If a Basic Income were to be funded by implementing a carbon tax, then the Basic Incomes would increase household disposable incomes and increase carbon emissions, and the carbon tax would reduce carbon emissions but would impact household disposable incomes, with the disposable incomes of poorer households being particularly hard hit because they spend a higher proportion of their disposable incomes on transport and heating than wealthier households do. If balances could be struck so that the entire package of Basic Income and carbon taxes were to reduce carbon emissions and increase household disposable incomes, particularly for poorer households, then a virtuous outcome would have been achieved (Fitzpatrick, 1999: 201; Howard et al., 2019: 126–7). As carbon use declined, the tax base would shrink, and so would the revenue available to fund the Basic Income. Additional funding would then have to be found.

But perhaps the main reason for the connection between Green concerns and Basic Income is not to be found in the field of policies and reasons, but in relation to personal characteristics. Someone who values nature and therefore the time to enjoy it and be creative within it might join a Green party and also campaign for a Basic Income because of its capacity to reduce employment hours: hence the connection. An increasing understanding of the physical limits of growth is likely to enhance this motive and thus both a commitment to Basic Income and active involvement in Green politics (Van Parijs and Vanderborght, 2017: 201–2).

Throughout this book we have found Green parties engaging positively with the Basic Income debate. In Chapter 7, we have discussed recent UK Green Party interest: interest that goes back to when the Green Party was the Ecology Party during the late 1970s. The Green Party of England and Wales' single Member of Parliament, Caroline Lucas, continues to work with MPs from other parties to promote interest in Basic Income in Parliament.

In the United States, the Green Party has advocated for a genuine Basic Income; and consistently with its normal understanding of 'Basic Income' as an income-tested benefit, the Canadian Green Party has at various points campaigned for a Minimum Income Guarantee and a Negative Income Tax. In the Netherlands, GroenLinks (Green Left), has called for Basic Income experiments, and, as we saw in Chapter 8, the Netherlands is now hosting a variety of experiments in benefits with some characteristics similar to those of a Basic Income. In Germany, Die Grünen (The Greens) hosted BIEN's annual congress in 2000, and in 2004 helped to establish the Netzwerk Grundeinkommen (the German Basic Income Network). A poster campaign about Basic Income had already contributed to debate on the 'Hartz IV' proposals that took the German welfare state towards more stringent work-testing, and the network's launch was followed by high profile Basic Income campaigns by Götz Werner, founder of dm-drogerie markt, a drugstore chain, and Katja Kipping, the leader of Die Linke (The Left). Books followed, including Werner's own *€1000 Euros für Jeden (€1000 for Everyone)*, written with Adrienne Goehler (Van Parijs and Vanderborght, 2017: 207; Werner and Goehler, 2010).

Advocacy for Basic Income is consistently found among Green party memberships in Germany, France, Belgium, Switzerland and elsewhere, and among Green party leaderships and candidates when there is little likelihood of entering government: but Green party representatives in regional and national assemblies and governments have frequently been divided on the issue, and have often found the proposal to have been submerged by other coalition partners' commitments to work-tested and means-tested benefits. As Van Parijs and Vanderborght put it (2017: 206): 'In the case of green parties … the intensity and clarity of their endorsements seem to be inversely correlated with the probabilities of their governmental participation'; and De Wispelaere and Noguera (2012: 22) suggest that 'expressed support without either the commitment or the capacity to engage in the necessary political action to build a sustainable coalition around the policy of granting each citizen an unconditional basic income is "cheap"'. This is a little unfair. Junior partners in coalition governments often occupy only subsidiary ministerial positions, have little control over policy direction, and have to spend their time attempting to mitigate what they see as the worst aspects of policies pursued by the majority party. Only if a Green party were to be the majority party in a parliament would we know whether Green party support for Basic Income was in fact 'cheap'. What we have found is that both in Finland (Chapter 8) and in South Korea (Chapter 9) Green party advocacy for Basic Income has been at least partially instrumental in keeping Basic Income on the political agenda, so that when a political opportunity for the implementation of a local or provincial Basic Income or a Basic Income experiment has emerged there has already existed a foundation of interest and understanding to build on (Van Parijs and Vanderborght, 2017: 197–201).

The Christian Connection

There are three respects in which the Christian religion has been and might remain an element in the global Basic Income debate. First of all, the Christian Faith and Basic Income are in many ways natural partners; secondly, and connectedly, many Christians have been and are involved in the Basic Income debate; and thirdly, political parties with an explicitly Christian history have sometimes played roles in the Basic Income debate.

Firstly, Basic Income reflects many of the aspects of the Christian Faith. Briefly, a Basic Income would celebrate God-given abundance, be an act of grace (that is, of unconditional generosity), recognize our individuality, recognize God's equal treatment of us, provide for the poor, constantly forgive, never judge, ensure that workers would be paid for their work, be the basis of a covenant, inspire us to be co-creators, understand both our original righteousness and our original corruption, recognize our mutual dependency, facilitate a more just society, promote liberty, both relativize and enhance the family, facilitate the duty to serve, be welcoming and hospitable, and be an act of love (Torry, 2016b).

Secondly, these connections probably help to motivate large numbers of practising Christians to participate actively in the Basic Income debate. This is particularly true of Quakers, for whom practical application of the Christian Faith in the public sphere has always been important; but members of other denominations have also been involved: for instance, it is the Justice Commission of the Conference of Religious of Ireland, staffed by Seán Healy and Brigid Reynolds, both members of Roman Catholic religious orders, that for thirty years has driven the Irish Basic Income debate; and the same two individuals now run the independent Social Justice Ireland (Reynolds and Healy, 1994; 1995; 2016; Van Parijs and Vanderborght, 2017: 203–4).

The South African Council of Churches was active in the Basic Income Grant Coalition established in South Africa in 2002; and, as we have seen (in Chapter 9), the Lutheran Church in Namibia was a major player in inspiring and staffing the pilot project there. Books, chapters and articles have been written from a variety of Christian perspectives (Meireis, 2004; Preston, 1992; Reynolds and Healy, 1994; 1995; 2016; Torry, 2016b), although sometimes these have not been sufficiently clear in their terminology for them to be able to draw distinctions between Basic Income and a Minimum Income Guarantee (Tanner, 2005; Wogaman, 1968). Understandably, questions have been asked as to whether other faith traditions have been as connected to the Basic Income debate as has the Christian tradition. The answer to that is that of course large numbers of members of other faiths have participated in the global Basic Income debate and continue to do so, but the kind of ideas-based relationship with Basic Income that we have discovered in relation to the Christian Faith does not appear to be replicated in relation to other faiths. It is not insignificant that when for the first time at a BIEN congress a session on the different faiths' relationships to Basic Income was planned in Hyderabad in highly multi-faith India in 2019, only a Christian could be found to discuss the connections between a faith tradition and Basic Income. There is clearly work to be done.

Thirdly, Van Parijs and Vanderborght discuss the '(more or less secularized) Christian-democratic parties' (Van Parijs and Vanderborght, 2017: 203) in which they have found very little evidence of interest in Basic Income apart from occasional individual members attempting to promote debate about it. However, it is not just those parties with 'Christian' in their names that have a Christian heritage. Many trades unions and political parties on the left, such as the British Labour Party, possess a distinctively Christian heritage, and in them we find both an enthusiasm for means-tested and work-tested benefits that coheres with an over-generalized interpretation of Paul's 'Anyone unwilling to work should not eat' (2 Thessalonians 3:10, New Revised Standard Version) and with a more Calvinist stream of Christian thought, and also advocacy for unconditional incomes based on the centrality that Christian Faith gives to God's unconditional love (Van Parijs and Vanderborght, 2017: 205–6). As we have seen, the secular evolution of this bifurcation into the current labourist and socialist tendencies on the left of the political spectrum is one of the reasons for continuing ambivalence towards Basic Income among trades unions and left-wing political parties.

The Status of Women

During the course of this history we have frequently found ourselves discussing the ways in which Basic Income would affect women. Bertrand Russell pondered on the value of an unconditional income for women (Chapter 4);

Juliet Rhys Williams' proposal would have treated women and men more equally than Beveridge's 1942 report, but not necessarily equally (Chapter 5); the US and Canadian experiments during the 1970s had particular effects on the employment market behaviour of women (Chapter 6); the 'wages for housework' campaign can be understood as a precursor to advocacy for Basic Income (Chapter 7); research on the effects that Basic Income would have on the lives of women has been a frequent feature of debate on Basic Income in the UK (Chapter 7; Carlson, 1997; Parker, 1993); the feminist economist Ailsa McKay was prominent in the Basic Income debate in Scotland (Chapter 7; Campbell and Gillespie, 2016: 3–12); women's increasing involvement with the employment market is improving the financial feasibility of Basic Income (Chapter 8); and the pilot projects in Namibia and India have revealed the emancipatory potential of Basic Income for women (Chapter 9). In this chapter, we have discussed the precariat. There has always been a precariat, and historically most of it has been occupied by women.

However differently some proposed Basic Income schemes have treated women differently from men (Chapters 3 and 5), in relation to the Basic Incomes themselves, the definition of Basic Income insists on equal treat-ment, which suggests that in a world in which women are often treated less favourably than men, women would be bound to support the implementation of a genuine Basic Income. However, the matter is not simple, and certainly not in countries with more developed and formal economics, because in that context a Basic Income could enable women more easily to say 'no' to undesirable jobs, to say 'yes' to voluntary caring or community roles, or both, and to leave the employment market: or they might choose to reduce their employment hours in order to spend more time caring for children and other dependents, thus reducing further their ability to secure positions of influence in social and economic institutions (Van Parijs and Vanderborght, 2017: 186–7). In a context of social norms that more easily assume that caring work is women's work rather than men's work, the dilemma—Wollstonecraft's dilemma—is real. Bambrick points out that if a Basic Income were to replace the gendered aspects of the UK's social security system (for instance, the continuing assumption of a 'male breadwinner' model, and the requirement for one individual, usually the man, to claim means-tested benefits on behalf of the household), then the unconditional income would

offer all citizens a choice in how they spend their time—caring, in employment or at leisure, without the threat of destitution and/or exploitation. Moreover, in placing this choice with individuals, Wollstonecraft's Dilemma becomes obsolete—women will be incorporated into the state on the basis of their citizenship alone; thereafter their role will be a private decision rather than a public issue. (Bambrick, 2006: 5)

However, during the 1970s, elements of the Claimants' Union movement and of the new Women's Liberation Movement argued that 'wages for housework' would perpetuate a gendered division of labour (Miller et al., 2019: 138–42). Only if women and men were treated equally and as individuals by the State, and only if men were to take up the opportunity that a Basic Income would offer them to participate equally in caring and domestic work, would women escape from being burdened with an unfair share of such unpaid work. Only if that were to happen would gender equality become possible.

> Fewer women than men fit exclusively into either ['worker' or 'caring'] category, and less so over time. Rather, large numbers combine the breadwinner and caregiver roles. A [Basic Income] extends the opportunity to make this work-care mix the norm for men as well as women. Should this opportunity be seized, Wollstonecraft's dilemma of how the state should incorporate women into its policies would be resolved. That is, no longer will it have to integrate women according to how their behaviour relates to that of men, since men will now be in a position to behave the same as women. (Bambrick, 2006: 9)

As Miller et al. point out, only the implementation of a genuine Basic Income will be able to resolve the question as to whether it would solve Wollstonecraft's dilemma: but the various experiments that have been held in the US, Canada, Namibia and India suggest that a Basic Income would indeed be emancipatory for women, particularly in a context of sufficiently high Basic Incomes for children (Miller et al., 2019: 134–6, 147).

A further dilemma relates to a Basic Income's effect on household dissolution. While the news that the Negative Income Tax experiments in the United States during the 1970s had facilitated a rapid rise in the divorce rate proved to be largely fake (Chapter 6), it is still true that providing an unconditional income for every woman might enable some to leave failed or abusive relationships which their previous financial dependence on their partners might not have permitted them to do. Whether in this context an increase in relationship dissolutions is a good thing or a bad thing must be a matter of opinion, especially when there are children involved in a break-up: but perhaps it might be said that if the only thing holding a relationship together is financial dependence of one partner on another then maybe the relationship ought to end (Van Parijs and Vanderborght, 2017: 185–6).

What will matter is the context in which a Basic Income influences the decisions that women make. In relationships characterized by equality and individual autonomy, a Basic Income would provide women with more freedom to make new decisions about how they divide their time between employment, caring work and voluntary community work; and it would provide enhanced opportunities for decision-making for men as well. The decisions that those individuals would make, whatever they might be, would be the result of the enhanced freedom provided by their Basic Incomes. All one can say about the objection that women's decisions might hamper their progress in the employment market is that it would be far better to have available the freedom to make those decisions in the context of a Basic Income than for that freedom to be severely restricted by current means-tested systems or complete financial dependence on a spouse (Van Parijs and Vanderborght, 2017: 188–9).

In an increasingly globalized world, these debates, like debate about Basic Income more generally, are becoming global debates. Discussion about women's status in global society and in every country will from now on have to take account of the global Basic Income debate, and the Basic Income debate will have to take account of the highly diverse social and economic contexts of women around the world.

FEASIBILITY

Until about 2013, the Basic Income debate was generally about the question 'Would it be a good idea?' That is, what might be the advantages and disadvantages of Basic Income. But then, as the global debate has rapidly developed in both extent and depth, rather different questions have come to the fore, and particularly questions about feasibility and implementation. Questions relating to desirability have not gone away, but attention has shifted, so today the three interconnecting questions, about desirability, feasibility and how a Basic Income would be implemented, are ubiquitous in the global debate (Torry, 2016c; 2018a).

In a country with a developing economy, it might be possible to implement a Basic Income without making other changes to existing taxes and benefits—for instance, by employing royalties from resource extraction: but in the context of a more developed economy a Basic Income would be unlikely to be implemented on its own. Existing tax and benefits systems would have to be changed, and what would be implemented would be a Basic Income scheme: with the levels of Basic Income specified for different age groups, and changes to existing taxes and benefits specified in detail. The question would not be 'Is Basic Income feasible?' but 'Is there a feasible Basic Income scheme?': that is, is there a Basic Income at particular levels for different age groups, and accompanied by particular changes to current tax and benefits systems, that would be feasible?

Then of course we have to ask what we might mean by 'feasible'. What in practice policymakers would be looking for would be a series of different feasibilities, the list of which would look something like this, although there might be differences in different contexts:

- Is the Basic Income scheme financially feasible? This question can be asked with two different senses: (i) Can the Basic Incomes be paid for? (ii) Will the scheme as a whole impose disposable income losses on low-income households, or unmanageable losses on any households?
- Is the Basic Income scheme psychologically feasible? That is, is the idea of a Basic Income understood, and is it understood to be desirable?
- Is the Basic Income scheme administratively feasible? Given the simplicity of a Basic Income, this test would generally be the easiest one to pass, although some initial work might be required to construct the database required to ensure that every legal resident would receive their Basic Income.
- Is the Basic Income scheme behaviourally feasible? This is a difficult feasibility to test, because the question is asking whether a Basic Income would have the effects promised for it: for instance, in terms of employment market behaviour, social cohesion, improvements in mental health, and so on. This can only be tested after a genuine Basic Income scheme has been implemented, although experiments and pilot projects that have already taken place can offer a certain amount of evidence on which a tentative initial assessment might be made about behavioural feasibility. Perhaps if a Basic Income scheme were to be implemented for a particular age bracket before moving on to further implementations then behavioural feasibility could be tested for the Basic Income recipients and this would inform the psychological feasibility experienced by other age groups.
- Is the Basic Income scheme politically feasible? That is, does it cohere with the political ideologies of the Government and political parties who would have to implement the scheme?
- Is the Basic Income scheme policy process feasible? Policy process feasibility is related to political feasibility, but it is not the same. The question to be asked is this: is it possible for the Basic Income scheme to navigate its way from idea to implementation through the complex policy process of a country? And, in particular, is it possible for the scheme to navigate its way from idea to implementation with the Basic Income remaining a genuine Basic Income? (Torry, 2016a; 2019c).

While it is important to recognize that it might be necessary for a Basic Income scheme to pass all of those tests in some kind of explicit fashion before the policy change could be implemented, things do not always work out like that. Accidents happen (Torry, 2016a: 238–9). An example of a policy accident can be found in Chapter 5, where we discuss the implementation of the UK's unconditional Family Allowance after the Second World War. Eleanor Rathbone wrote a book (Rathbone, [1924] 1986); in 1924 William Beveridge read the book, liked the idea, and tried the idea on the staff of the London School of Economics (Harris, 1977: 343); and when he was asked to chair a committee on the reform of social insurance and social assistance, he inserted an unconditional child allowance into the preface of his report (Harris, 1977: 390), so that when the UK Parliament debated the report it had to debate an unconditional child allowance and Members of Parliament from different parties all had their own reasons for voting for it. If any one of those accidental steps had not occurred, then the UK would not now have an unconditional Child Benefit. A further policy accident can be found in Chapter 9. Iran had intended a means-tested benefit to replace its fuel and food subsidies, but the outcome of the means test met with considerable public disapproval, so the incomes were given to every household. While the incomes were paid to the head of the household and not to individuals, they were in every other respect a Basic Income implemented by accident. The Iranian Government had never budgeted for a universal income, and its value has been massively reduced because the income has not been uprated even though inflation has been rapid: but Iran still has an otherwise unconditional income paid to household heads but calculated in relation to the number of individuals in the household. Whether we shall see other Basic Income schemes implemented by policy accident is an interesting question.

The question of feasibility will remain a live issue in every country where Basic Income is debated, and therefore throughout the global debate. An essential requirement will therefore be constant and detailed research on feasibility in every country: in every country because every context is different, which means that a Basic Income scheme that might be feasible in one country would be unlikely to be feasible in another. In order for the feasibility of Basic Income schemes to be tested, every one of the different feasibilities will have to be tested in every country, and the best available methods will have to be used. In relation to financial feasibility, we discussed in Chapter 7 the importance of microsimulation for testing the two different kinds of financial feasibility: both the affordability of a Basic Income scheme as a whole, and the requirement that low-income households should not suffer disposable income losses, and that no household should suffer unmanageable losses. Methods that rely on calculating gains and losses for particular household types are still in use in the UK and elsewhere (Rankin, 2012: 202–4), as is a method that calculates the net costs of schemes using national accounts and census data, but these will never provide an overall picture of household net gains and losses, nor will they be able to tell enquirers whether poverty and inequality would be increased or decreased by illustrative schemes. Only microsimulation can prove that a Basic Income scheme would reduce and not increase poverty, and would reduce and not increase inequality: surely two essential requirements for a Basic Income scheme to be psychologically and politically feasible. It will therefore be essential for researchers in any country that already possesses microsimulation facilities to use them; and equally essential that where those facilities do not exist researchers should collaborate with others to create them so that they can be used to test the feasibility of Basic Income schemes.

Equally important will be research into all of the other feasibilities, again separately in each country. But while conclusions drawn in relation to the feasibility tests in one country might not be transferable to another, it will still be important for researchers in different countries to collaborate with each other, particularly in relation to research methods. While conclusions drawn about feasibilities might not be transferable between countries, research methods might well be.

FUNDING BASIC INCOME

Related to questions of feasibility is the question as to how Basic Incomes should be funded: a question that is becoming a significant factor in the global debate. There are multiple options:

- *From within the current tax and benefits system*: This is the most likely funding method for an initial Basic Income in a country with a more developed economy simply because it would require the smallest number of policy changes and so the package as a whole would be most likely to find its way through the complexities of a country's policy process. It is also the method for which it is easiest to predict the effects of implementing the Basic Income scheme. Microsimulation calculations can only be trusted if the scheme that is being tested is revenue neutral: that is, the net cost is zero after the Basic Incomes have been paid and changes have been made to existing taxes and benefits. Any other funding method is bound to introduce uncertainties. For instance, if there is a funding gap, and a proposal is made to fill the gap by charging a carbon tax, then the new tax will impact household disposable incomes, and particularly those of low-income households; and because the effects of a carbon tax cannot be microsimulated (because the data that the programme employs cannot include the net annual costs of fuel price rises for each individual household) any microsimulation calculations previously made are bound to be inaccurate by an unpredictable degree.
- *Revenues from natural resources*: In Chapter 6, we studied the Alaskan Permanent Fund, built up from the royalties collected by the State of Alaska from companies extracting oil from its territory; in Chapter 9, we discussed the unconditional income accidentally implemented by Iran on

the basis of a reduction in food and fuel subsidies, and so indirectly on the basis of revenues from oil extraction; and earlier in this chapter we have discussed the possibility of paying a Basic Income by implementing a tax on the use of carbon-based fuel, and recognized that the Basic Income would ameliorate the disposable income challenges that a carbon tax would impose on low income households (Barnes, 2014; Piketty, 2020: 1004–7; Van Parijs and Vanderborght, 2017: 150–52). Any or all of these methods could be employed to fund a Basic Income: but as we have already recognized, it would be difficult to predict the financial and possibly other effects of such a funding method, so either microsimulation programmes would need to be enhanced to enable reliable estimates to be made of the effects of carbon taxes on the disposable incomes of low income households, or pilot projects would have to be held in which the households of a community would have to be charged extra for their fuel consumption at the same time as being paid a Basic Income. What can be said with a degree of confidence is that any country with a relatively undeveloped economy and significant natural resources should be able to use resource extraction revenue to fund a Basic Income without causing any difficulties for low-income households. An obvious example is Namibia (Chapter 9).

A somewhat different proposal, but in fact in the same field, is the suggestion that data should be taxed. Our data belongs to us, but it is mined by private companies who then make money by using and selling it. There is an argument that not only could the proceeds from taxing data be used to fund a Basic Income, but that that is how they should be used (Andrade, 2019).

- *Land Value Tax*: As we discovered in Chapter 2, the basis of Thomas Paine's and Thomas Spence's arguments for paying unconditional incomes was that in principle the land belongs to everyone, so those occupying it owe a land rent to everyone. We have also studied the similar arguments offered by John Locke (Chapter 2) and by Henry George (Chapter 3; Fleischer and Lehto, 2019: 452–3). There are several advantages to employing this method to fund Basic Incomes. First of all, every country has land: indeed, every country is land; so Land Value Tax is a resource tax that any country could use to fund a Basic Income (Torry, 2018a: 128; Van Parijs and Vanderborght, 2017: 149–50). Secondly, apart from occasional coastal erosion and the increasing problem of inundation due to climate change, the amount of land is a fixed quantity. This makes land an ideal tax base. Many tax bases reduce in extent as the tax rate rises: and so, for instance, as an income tax rate rises, hours in employment are worth less to the worker, so hours spent on other purposes might be substituted for hours spent in employment, thus reducing the tax base and the revenue raised. If land were to be the tax base, then the tax base could never be reduced, so the revenue raised would be predictable. Thirdly, a land tax could be so organized as to protect low-income households, because they tend to occupy relatively small amounts of land. A significant difficulty relating to Land Value Tax would be its administration, because the value of each plot of land has to be evaluated separately: but this would not be an insuperable difficulty as long as the value of the land and the value of any improvements were to be evaluated together rather than separately (Dye and England, 2010: 25).

- *A financial transaction tax*: A tax on financial transactions, with financial transactions in this context understood as currency exchanges, would reduce the incentive to speculate on currency movements and so would stabilize economies (Tobin, 1978: 155); and the tax revenue could be used to fund a Basic Income. An objection to the idea might be that because financial transactions can take place anywhere in the world, a financial transaction tax in one country could simply drive speculative currency trades to countries without such a tax. However, both the UK and the US already charge low rates of tax on share transactions, but share transactions still take place in those jurisdictions because of their other advantages, such as reliable legal systems and market concentration. A financial transaction tax at a low enough rate would therefore be a possibility: but a low enough rate might enable only a very small Basic Income to be funded. A further difficulty with a financial transaction tax is that many currency exchanges take place in order to facilitate international trade: so there would be an argument for trying to exclude such transactions from the tax, which would complicate administration and reduce the tax base. A possible solution might be a financial activity tax: that is, a very small tax on all financial transactions. This would not be difficult to administer, and could be employed to fund a larger Basic Income than a tax purely on currency exchanges (Adam et al., 2011: 151–3, 195–215; Torry, 2018a: 163; Van Parijs and Vanderborght, 2017: 154).

- *Sovereign money*: Since the financial crisis of 2008, we have seen the frequent employment of 'quantitative easing': governments creating new money in order to buy back government debt. Bond price inflation and the further enrichment of bondholders have been predictable and unfortunate results of injecting liquidity into the economy in this way. Less problematic would be the creation of new money to fill the gap between employment income and Gross Domestic Product (GDP), as Major Douglas suggested (Chapter 4) and as Geoff Crocker suggests today (Crocker, 2019; 2020). Care would have to be taken not to breach the GDP limit, as doing so could generate inflation: which means that a government's ability to create new money might diminish over time. At the time of writing, research in this area is taking place at the University of Bath in the UK (Torry, 2018a: 164–5; Van Parijs and Vanderborght, 2017: 153).

- *Consumption taxes*: A significant problem with consumption taxes is that they are regressive: that is, they fall most heavily on low-income households because low income households spend a higher proportion of their income on immediate consumption than wealthier households do. However, research has shown that in many countries a package that included consumption taxes and a Basic Income would be both financially and socially feasible (Dommen-Meade, 2010); and in the longer term a shift from income taxation to consumption taxes might in any case be required. If automation continues to reduce the need for employment, then the income tax base will decline, and the profits of production will go increasingly to capital. It will therefore become essential to tax company profits and to use the proceeds to pay incomes, and perhaps Basic Incomes, out of the proceeds. (In Chapter 9 we encountered an interesting example of this process in relation to casino profits being used to pay dividends to Cherokee Indians.) The problem with taxing declared profits is that many companies can choose to declare profits in low-tax jurisdictions. A useful alternative might be to tax the value of a company's products in the country in which they are sold. Provided the proceeds were to be used to fund a Basic Income, the increase in disposable household incomes that would result would enable households to pay the price increases that the new tax might generate (Torry, 2018a: 164; Van Parijs and Vanderborght, 2017: 154–7).
- *A sovereign wealth fund*: A sovereign wealth fund could be built up, from resource extraction revenues, as in Alaska (Chapter 9), from the profits of State-owned companies, or in other ways, and the dividends could be employed to fund a Basic Income. Because it would take some decades for such a fund to be built up, this could only be a longer-term funding option (Lansley, 2016; 2019).
- *A wealth tax*: Rather than taxing income in order to pay for Basic Incomes, perhaps wealth should be taxed instead (Piketty, 2014: 515–34; 2020: 975–1004; Van Parijs and Vanderborght, 2017: 148–9). Because wealth is more unequally distributed than income, such a tax could be more progressive than an income tax. However, disadvantages that we have already encountered would apply. Whereas in most cases it is clear where an individual has earned their income, it is often not clear how much wealth they possess or where it is. It is easy to move capital between jurisdictions, so to tax wealth, rather than the income from wealth, could result in wealth being moved to low-tax environments. As discussed above, the only substantial form of wealth that cannot be moved is land: hence the argument for a Land Value Tax.

• *Cryptocurrency*: A relatively new element of the Basic Income debate is the idea that cryptocurrencies (such as Bitcoin) might be used to pay Basic Incomes, and small-scale experiments are already taking place. However, 'mixing two socially, economically and even psychologically disruptive concepts, and then trying to get acceptance for them, is always going to be tough' (Mermelstein, 2019).

It might appear from the way in which the text is set out on these pages that all of these potential means of paying for a Basic Income, and perhaps others as well, exist on a conceptual level playing field: that is, they really are alternatives, and all or any of them could be used to fund a Basic Income scheme in any country. However, particularly in countries with more developed economies, there is a significant difference related to the first method listed: paying for a Basic Income by changing the existing tax and benefits system of a country. The reason that this is different from the other methods is that all of the other revenue-raising methods could be used to fund something other than a Basic Income, whereas if the tax and benefits system of a country is changed so as to generate additional revenue, then only if that revenue is used to fund a Basic Income or some other kind of personal income by recycling the proceeds back into household incomes would it be possible to ensure that no average loss to disposable household incomes would occur, no unmanageable losses for any households, and no losses at all for low-income households; and, just as importantly, that it would be possible to predict the financial effects, and therefore the feasibility, of the Basic Income scheme (because only in relation to a revenue neutral Basic Income scheme can microsimulation results achieve credibility). Perhaps equally important is policy process feasibility. Any Basic Income scheme will require changes to be made to a developed economy's tax and benefits system, and it would be more difficult to navigate a Basic Income, the accompanying income tax and benefits changes, and a new funding method, through the policy process, than to navigate a Basic Income with accompanying income tax and benefits changes through it. Policy process feasibility really matters (Torry, 2016a: 195–236). Different factors would apply in countries with less-developed benefits and personal income tax systems, because here there would be fewer existing systems to change, and in this context resource extraction revenue, if it exists, might be the most obvious funding source for Basic Incomes.

Whatever the advantages and disadvantages of the many different funding methods discussed here, we can be sure that all of them will remain elements of the Basic Income debate as it continues to evolve: and there will no doubt be further alternative methods proposed in the future. What will be essential if rational debate about the different methods is to occur is to ensure careful definition of the different funding methods, and that the best available research methods will be applied to them.

HOW MUCH SHOULD THE BASIC INCOME BE?

As we discovered in our discussion of the definition of Basic Income in Chapter 1, the UK's Citizen's Basic Income Trust (CBIT) defines a Basic Income as

> an unconditional, automatic and nonwithdrawable income for each individual as a right of citizenship,

and the Basic Income Earth Network (BIEN) defines it as

> a periodic cash payment delivered to all on an individual basis, without means test or work requirement.

Neither definition mentions the amount of the Basic Income: but the definitions of some other Basic Income organizations do. Here would appear to be the one factor over which Basic Income organizations disagree: the amount of the payment. For some national organizations, only an unconditional, nonwithdrawable, regular and individual income at 'subsistence level' can qualify as a Basic Income, whereas for other organizations an unconditional, nonwithdrawable, regular and individual income of any amount can count as one. A survey of organizations affiliated to BIEN found that

- some affiliated organizations did not mention the issue, suggesting that the amount to be paid is not integral to the definition;
- some said that a democratic process would be used to decide the amount;
- one mentioned a particular amount (South Africa);
- and some offered a description of the kind of life that the Basic Income would be expected to fund ('subsistence', 'dignity', 'participation', 'poverty line') in relation to the national context, but without specifying the relevant level of Basic Income (Torry, 2017b).

This particular diversity is likely to remain an aspect of the Basic Income debate. What is most important is that as far as possible this should be the only diversity relating to the definition. This diversity does not compromise the unconditional nature of Basic Income, a useful test of which is that at whatever the level at which a Basic Income would be paid it could be turned on at someone's birth and turned off at their death, with no active administration being required in between. Any variations in the definition that did compromise unconditionality (such as varying amounts for different household structures, or amounts varying in relation to other income) would mean that a Basic Income would no longer be being discussed. But whatever the differences between different definitions of Basic Income—whether they compromise unconditionality and therefore conflict with the definition, or suggest that a particular level of Basic Income should be integral to the definition—those differences should always be clearly stated so that participants in a debate, readers of research results, and so on, are always clear about what is being discussed.

CONCLUSIONS

In this chapter we have encountered just some of the aspects of the current stage of the Basic Income debate: a debate that is now a single global debate as well as being a worldwide one.

The one line that I can remember from Peter Gabriel's music for the central highwire show at the Millennium Exhibition at the Millennium Dome in London during the year 2000 is 'The one thing that I'm sure about is the accelerating rate of change'. We can be even more sure of that today. As the world changes, the Basic Income debate will continue to change. What must not change is the definition of a Basic Income.

11. Conclusions: where now for Basic Income?

DIVERSE ARGUMENTS

Peter Sloman has shown that during the 1980s and 1990s, three main arguments were employed to advocate for a Basic Income: firstly, that a Basic Income would provide a secure layer of income as other income sources become less secure in the context of a more flexible employment market; secondly, that existing benefits systems were degrading, divisive, opaque and complicated, whereas a Basic Income would carry no stigma, would facilitate social cohesion and would be simple to administer and easy to understand; and thirdly, that a Basic Income would provide every individual with the freedom to exercise their autonomy and creativity (Sloman, 2019: 230–31). In fact, these arguments go back in one way or another to the very beginning of the debate during the late eighteenth century.

As we have recounted the history of Basic Income, we have of course encountered diversity both across time and across the planet: both historically and geographically. Duverger offers a useful summary: during an agricultural era, Thomas Paine and Thomas Spence sought a solution to poverty by tackling the private occupation of land; during the industrial era, the proceeds of industry and various aspects of developing economies were the focus of the Basic Income debate; and during a post-industrial age, the complexity of employment and other markets has drawn attention to Basic Income's ability to distribute work and income (Duverger, 2018: 131–5).

While it is true that the Basic Income debate has been diverse throughout its history, and that it is now in many ways far more diverse than it ever was, and while it is also true that questions relating to feasibility and implementation might now be more important than they once were, we can identify considerable commonalities across time, and this is one of them: that the three areas of argument identified by Sloman remain at the centre of the debate. A further commonality across time has been the definition of Basic Income. Although there has been some diversity, particularly in Canada and the US, where household- and income-tested benefits can be called 'Basic Income', and where 'Basic Income Guarantee' contains 'Basic Income' and has rather too flexible a definition, the definition of Basic Income has remained fairly consistent both across time and across the planet. It is the character of Basic Income that generates its advantages and therefore the arguments for it, and it is because the character of Basic Income has remained consistent across time and space that both the advantages and therefore the arguments have remained consistent. And what appear to be new elements in the debate might not be as new as we might think. Whilst questions relating to feasibility and implementation might now appear to be more important than they once were, this might be because they are more central to the debate than they were twenty years ago. Thomas Paine and Thomas Spence were at pains to show how their proposals would be paid for, and the Milners' costings were as detailed as many that have appeared during the past couple of decades. Perhaps there really is nothing entirely new: merely changes of emphasis in relation to diverse and changing circumstances, and the availability of research methods not available to earlier Basic Income proponents.

BEYOND NATIONAL BASIC INCOMES

The whole of this history, and most of the Basic Income literature, assumes that any Basic Income that was actually implemented would be a national one. This is understandable because it is mostly national governments that determine tax and benefits policies. In countries with more federal structures, such as the USA, Canada, India and South Korea, a regional approach would be possible, as we have seen in relation to the US, Canadian, Indian and Korean experiments. However, in the longer term, somewhat broader approaches might be possible. And so, for instance, a global Basic Income at a relatively low level and paid for by taxing countries in proportion to Gross Domestic Products would contribute significantly to global justice by shifting resources from wealthier countries to poorer ones (Van Parijs and Vanderborght, 2017: 217–18, 226–30; World Basic Income, 2020). Unfortunately, there are no global institutions with the competence to establish the kind of taxation mechanisms that would be required, so a global Basic Income must be some way off. In the meantime, might a more regional approach be possible?

As early as 1975, Brandon Rhys Williams MP was advocating a Basic Income for the whole of what was then the European Community (now the European Union), and during the 1990s James Meade, who had for a long time recommended a Social Dividend (Chapter 5), suggested that a European Social Dividend could be a useful method for both maintaining household incomes and moving resources from wealthier European regions to poorer ones (Meade, 1991: 24–9). Philippe Van Parijs has continued to argue for a 'Eurodividend' for the same reasons (Sloman, 2019: 229; Van Parijs and Vanderborght, 2017: 23–41). Again, there is an institutional problem: tax and benefits policy remains the preserve of EU national governments, and they are unlikely to hand this competence to EU institutions in anything like the near future. Although it is not impossible that national governments might be able to agree to such new taxation as a tax on fossil fuels mined in or entering the European Union, and for the proceeds to be spent on an initial Eurodividend, obtaining such agreement could well be problematic. A proposal for a regional Basic Income for Central America would no doubt encounter similar problems (Krozer and Lo Vuolo, 2013).

So we are left with national and subnational possibilities. A possible scenario is that a country or a state within a country might implement a genuine Basic Income. Other countries would then see the social and economic advantages experienced by countries in which Basic Incomes were being paid, so they would follow: and as the number of countries with Basic Incomes grew, so pressure might build for a Eurodividend, and EU governments might then see the point of Europeanizing their own Basic Incomes, probably by agreeing to co-ordinate the rates at which their national Basic Incomes were being paid, and perhaps seeing the project as a whole as a way of encouraging citizens to remain in their own countries and not add to politically problematic immigration figures. It is not impossible that the same motive might one day inspire the implementation of a global Basic Income. This is not to suggest that national Basic Income schemes would increase immigration (Van Parijs and Vanderborght, 2017: 218–26), because countries that attract immigration already have means-tested benefits systems, and it is unlikely that a Basic Income scheme would be implemented that would significantly increase the generosity of the combination of a Basic Income and retained and recalculated means-tested benefits. It is also unlikely that any national Basic Income scheme would be implemented without a residence condition being implemented (Citizen's Basic Income Trust, 2016b). It should therefore be both safe and useful for the European Union's institutions to propose a Europe-wide Basic Income project, and for national governments to respond constructively; and also for governments to construct their own national Basic Income schemes as an interim measure.

THE CORONAVIRUS PANDEMIC

During the closing stages of the research and writing of this history of Basic Income, the world has been struggling with the impact of a coronavirus pandemic. Readers will have noticed occasional mentions of it in the last four chapters of the book, and in particular in Chapter 7 a discussion of how the Basic Income debate in the UK has evolved in the context of the pandemic. No attempt has been made to provide a systematic discussion of how the pandemic has influenced the history of the Basic Income debate around the world. First of all, that history is very recent, so objective evaluation would be even more difficult than usual; and secondly, how the pandemic has influenced the debate would be a huge subject in itself, so it deserves a book of its own. The eventual author of that book might find this history of Basic Income helpful as a starting point.

THE FUTURE OF THE BASIC INCOME DEBATE

It would be foolish to predict in any detail how the Basic Income debate will evolve in the future. However, just one prediction should now be safe to make that we might not have been able to make a few years ago: that the Basic Income debate is not going to go away. We might see occasional dips in interest in particular places, but now that the debate is a global debate we are unlikely to see the idea disappear from view as it sometimes has in the past. We can also fairly safely predict that the debate will continue to possess both similar characteristics across the planet and diverse aspects in different contexts. What we cannot predict is when the first country will implement a genuine Basic Income, or which country that will be. Iran got close. What is required is for a country, or a province of a federal country, to implement an unconditional income for every individual, without means test and without work test, the same amount of money every week or every month for everyone of the same age. That country would be the first to reap the advantages of a Basic Income. Other countries would follow. And perhaps one day there really will be a global Basic Income.

Bibliography

Abel-Smith, Brian and Peter Townsend (1966), *The Poor and the Poorest: A new analysis of the Ministry of Labour's Family Expenditure Surveys of 1953–54 and 1960*, London: Bell.

Académie Française, *Dictionnaire de l'Académie Française*, accessed 9 January 2021 at https://www.dictionnaire-academie.fr.

Adam Smith Institute (2018), accessed 9 January 2021 at https://www.adamsmith.org/.

Adam, Stuart et al. (eds) (2011), *Tax by Design: The Mirrlees Review*, Oxford: Oxford University Press.

Agence France-Presse (2016), 'Swiss voters reject proposal to give basic income to every adult and child', *The Guardian*, 5 June 2016, accessed 9 January 2021 at https://www.theguardian.com/world/2016/jun/05/swiss-vote-give-basic-income -every-adult-child-marxist-dream.

Ahn, Hyosang and Namhoon Kang (no date), 'Trajectory of Basic Income movement in South Korea', unpublished paper.

Ajuntament de Barcelona (2019), *Report on the Preliminary Results of the B-MINCOME Project (2017–2018)*, Barcelona: Barcelona City Council, accessed 6 January 2021 at https://ajuntament.barcelona.cat/dretssocials/sites/default/files/arxius-documents/ results_bmincome_eng.pdf.

Akee, Randall, Emilia Simeonova, E. Jane Costello and William Copeland (2015), *How Does Household Income Affect Child Personality Traits and Behaviors?*, Cambridge, MA: National Bureau of Economic Research, accessed 9 January 2021 at http://www.nber.org/papers/w21562.pdf.

Alaska Department of Revenue (2020), 'Permanent Fund Dividend Division: Summary of dividend applications and payments', accessed 9 January 2021 at https://pfd .alaska.gov/Division-Info/Summary-of-Applications-and-Payments.

Alaska Permanent Fund Corporation (2021), 'Frequently asked questions', accessed 4 February 2021 at https://apfc.org/frequently-asked-questions/.

Alston, Philip (2018), 'Statement on visit to the United Kingdom, by Professor Philip Alston, United Nations Special Rapporteur on extreme poverty and human rights', Geneva: Office of the United Nations Commissioner on Human Rights, accessed 9 January 2021 at https://www.ohchr.org/EN/NewsEvents/Pages/DisplayNews.aspx ?NewsID=23881&LangID=E.

Altman, Sam (2016), 'Basic Income', YCombinator, accessed 9 January 2021 at https:// blog.ycombinator.com/basic-income/.

Andersson, Jan-Otto (2000), 'The History of an idea: Why did Basic Income thrill the Finns, but not the Swedes?', in Robert van der Veen and Loek Groot (eds), *Basic Income on the Agenda: Policy objectives and political chances*, Amsterdam: Amsterdam University Press, pp. 224–37.

Andrade, Julio (2019), 'Funding a UBI by digital royalties', in Malcolm Torry (ed.), *The Palgrave International Handbook of Basic Income*, Cham: Palgrave Macmillan, pp. 185–8.

Aperghis, G. (2013), 'Athenian mines, coins and triremes', *Historia: Zeitschrift für Alte Geschichte*, **62** (1), 1–24.

Archbishop of Canterbury's Commission on Urban Priority Areas (1985), *Faith in the City: A call for action by church and nation*, London: Church House Publishing.

Arza, Camila (2013), 'Basic pensions in Latin America: Toward a rights-based policy?', in Rubén Lo Vuolo (ed.), *Citizen's Income and Welfare Regimes in Latin America*, New York: Palgrave Macmillan, pp. 87–112.

Ashby, Peter (1984), *Social Security after Beveridge—What next?*, London: National Council for Voluntary Organisations.

Ashdown, Paddy (1989), *Citizens' Britain*, London: Fourth Estate.

Assemblée Nationale (2020), 'Session ordinaire de 2020–2021: Compte rendu integral, Premier séance du jeudi 26 novembre 2020', accessed 1 January 2021 at https://www.assemblee-nationale.fr/15/cri/2020-2021/20210095.asp#P2328908.

Atkinson, A.B. (1969), *Poverty in Britain and the Reform of Social Security*, Cambridge: Cambridge University Press.

Atkinson, A.B. (1973), *The Tax Credit Scheme and the Redistribution of Income*, London: Institute for Fiscal Studies.

Atkinson, Tony (1992), 'Towards a European social safety net?', *Fiscal Studies*, **13** (3), 41–53.

Atkinson, Tony (1993), 'Participation Income', *Citizen's Income Bulletin*, no. 16, July 1993, pp. 7–11.

Atkinson, Tony (1995), *Public Economics in Action: The Basic Income/Flat Tax proposal*, Oxford: Clarendon Press.

Atkinson, A.B. (1996), 'The case for a Participation Income', *The Political Quarterly*, **67** (1), 67–70.

Atkinson, Tony (2011), 'The case for universal child benefit', in Alan Walker, Adrian Sinfield and Carol Walker (eds), *Fighting Poverty, Inequality and Injustice: A manifesto inspired by Peter Townsend*, Cambridge: Polity Press, pp. 79–90.

Atkinson, Anthony B. (2015), *Inequality: What can be done?* Cambridge, MA: Harvard University Press.

Atkinson, Anthony B., Chrysa Leventi, Brian Nolan, Holly Sutherland and Iva Tasseva (2017), 'Reducing poverty and inequality through tax-benefit reform and the minimum wage: The UK as a case-study', *Journal of Economic Inequality*, **15**, 303–23.

Atkinson, A.B. and H. Sutherland (1984), *A Tax Credit Scheme and Families in Work*, Tax, Incentives and the Distribution of Income no. 54, London: London School of Economics.

Atkinson, A.B. and Holly Sutherland (1988), *Integrating Income Taxation and Social Security: Analysis of a partial Basic Income*, London: London School of Economics.

Bambrick, Laura (2006), 'Wollstonecraft's Dilemma: Is a Citizen's Income the answer?', *Citizen's Income Newsletter*, issue 2 for 2006, pp. 3–10.

Bambrough, Renford (1969), *Reason, Truth and God*, London: Methuen.

Banerjee, Abhijit, Michael Faye, Alan Krueger, Paul Niehaus and Tavneet Suri (2020), *Effects of a Universal Basic Income During the Pandemic*, Washington, DC: Innovations for Poverty Action, accessed 25 September 2020 at https://www.poverty-action.org/publication/effects-universal-basic-income-during-pandemic.

Banting, Keith G. (1979), *Poverty, Politics and Policy: Britain in the 1960s*, London: Macmillan.

Barnes, Peter (2014), *With Liberty and Dividends for All: How to save our middle class when jobs don't pay enough*, San Francisco: Berrett-Koehler Publishers.

Barr, Nicholas and Fiona Coulter (1991), 'Social Security: Solution or problem?', in John Hills (ed.), *The State of Welfare: The Welfare State in Britain since 1974*, Oxford: Clarendon Press, pp. 274–337.

Barrientos, Armando (2011), 'Conditions in antipoverty programmes', *Journal of Poverty and Social Justice*, **19** (1), 15–26.

Bartlett, Randall, James Davies and Michael Hoy (2005), 'Can a Negative Income Tax system for the United Kingdom be both equitable and affordable?' in Karl Widerquist, Michael Anthony Lewis and Steven Pressman (eds), *The Ethics and Economics of the Basic Income Guarantee*, Aldershot: Ashgate, pp. 293–315.

Basic Income Canada Network (2021), accessed 9 January 2021 at https://www.basicincomecanada.org/.

Basic Income Conversation (2020), '110 MPs and Peers call on the Chancellor to introduce a Recovery Universal Basic Income (UBI) in response to the coronavirus crisis', London: Compass/Basic Income Conversation, accessed 9 January 2021 at https://www.basicincomeconversation.org/recovery-ubi.

Basic Income Conversation (2021), accessed 9 January 2021 at https://www.basicincomeconversation.org/.

Basic Income Earth Network (2020), 'International Basic Income Week 2020', accessed 9 January 2021 at https://basicincome.org/news/2020/09/international-basic-income-week-2020/.

Basic Income Earth Network (2021), accessed 9 January 2021 at https://basicincome.org/.

Basic Income Earth Network—Switzerland (2020), 'Who are we? What do we want?', Geneva: Basic Income Earth Network—Switzerland, accessed 9 January 2021 at https://bien.ch/en/page/who-are-we-what-do-we-want.

Basic Income Grant Coalition (2009), *Making the Difference: The BIG in Namibia: Basic Income Grant Pilot Project: Assessment report*, Namibia: Namibia NGO Forum, accessed 9 January 2021 at http://www.bignam.org/Publications/BIG_Assessment_report_08b.pdf.

Basic Income Grant Coalition (2019), 'Basic Income Grant: Otjivero, Namibia—20 years later', Namibia: Economic and Social Justice Trust, accessed 1 January 2021 at http://www.bignam.org/Publications/BIG_ten_years_later_report_2019.pdf.

Basic Income Ireland (2020), 'Programme for Government Commitment to trial Universal Basic Income welcomed by Basic Income Ireland', Dublin: Basic Income Ireland, accessed 9 January 2021 at https://basicincome.ie/ireland-programme-for-government-ubi/.

Basic Income March (2020), '2020 Basic Income March', accessed 9 January 2021 at https://www.basicincomemarch.com/.

Basic Income Network Italia (2021), 'BIN Italia', accessed 19 January 2021 at https://www.bin-italia.org/.

Basic Income Research Group (1986a), 'BIRG progress report, September 1986', unpublished document.

Basic Income Research Group (1986b), 'Basic Incomes and elderly people', *BIRG Bulletin*, no. 6, Autumn 1986, pp. 5–10.

Basic Income Research Group (1986–93), Minutes of meetings.

Basic Income UK (2018), accessed 9 January 2021 at https://www.basicincome.org.uk/about_us.

BBC (2013), 'Swiss campaigners dump eight million coins', 17 December 2013, accessed 9 January 2021 at https://www.bbc.co.uk/news/av/business-25415922.

BBC (2018), 'Italy budget: Parliament passes budget after EU standoff', *BBC News*, accessed 26 January 2021 at https://www.bbc.co.uk/news/world-europe-46710472.

Beer, M. (1920), *The Pioneers of Land Reform*, London: G. Bell and Sons Ltd.

Belastingdienst (2020), 'Werk en inkomen: Hoe zit het met de belasting over uw loon, pensioen of uitkering?', Netherlands: Belastingdienst, accessed 9 January 2021 at https://www.belastingdienst.nl/wps/wcm/connect/nl/werk-en-inkomen/werk-en -inkomen.

Belgian Network for Basic Income (2020), 'Basic Income', accessed 9 January 2021 at https://www.basicincome.be/.

Berry, Christine (2018), 'Beyond Mont Pelerin: How does a movement prepare for power?', *Renewal*, **26** (4), 5–11.

Beuys, Joseph (2019), 'Aufruf zur Alternative', *Frankfurter Rundschau*, 23 December 1978, quoted in Philip Kovce and Birger P. Priddat (2019), *Bedingungsloses Grundeinkommen: Grundlagentexte*, Berlin: Suhrkamp Verlag, p. 291, first published in 1978.

Beveridge, Sir William (1942), *Social Insurance and Allied Services*, Cmd 6404, London: Her Majesty's Stationery Office.

Beveridge, William (1949), 'Epilogue', in Eleanor Rathbone, *Family Allowances*, London: George Allen and Unwin, pp. 269–77 (a new edition of *The Disinherited Family* with an epilogue by William Beveridge).

BIEN (2021), accessed 9 January 2021 at https://basicincome.org/about-basic-income/.

Blaschke, Ronald (2017), 'Grundeinkommen und Grundsicherungen—Modelle und Ansätze in Deutschland. Eine Auswahl', accessed 9 January 2021 at https://www.grundeinkommen.de/wp-content/uploads/2017/12/17-10-%C3%9Cbersicht -Modelle.pdf.

Blatchly, Cornelius (1817), 'Some causes of popular poverty, derived from the enriching nature of interests, rents, duties, inheritances, and church establishments, investigated in their principles and consequences, and agreement with the scriptures', in Thomas Branagan, *The Pleasures of Contemplation*, Philadelphia: Eastwick and Stacy, pp. 195–220 (pp. 175–204 in the second edition).

Block, Fred and Margaret Somers (2005), 'In the shadow of Speenhamland: Social policy and the old poor law', in Karl Widerquist, Michael Anthony Lewis and Steven Pressman (eds), *The Ethics and Economics of the Basic Income Guarantee*, Aldershot: Ashgate, pp. 13–54.

Bollain, Julen (2019), 'Barcelona: B-Mincome', in Malcolm Torry (ed.), *The Palgrave International Handbook of Basic Income*, Cham: Palgrave Macmillan, pp. 421–5.

Bonnett, Alastair (2014), 'Introduction', in Alastair Bonnett and Keith Armstrong (eds), *Thomas Spence: The poor man's revolutionary*, London: Breviary Stuff, pp. 1–6.

Booker, H.S. (1946), 'Lady Rhys Williams' proposals for the amalgamation of direct taxation with social insurance', *The Economic Journal*, **56**, 230–43.

Borcherding, Thomas E., Patricia Dellon and Thomas D. Willett (1998), 'Henry George: Precursor to public choice analysis', *The American Journal of Economics and Sociology*, **57** (2), 173–82.

Boulanger, Paul-Marie (1988), 'Simulating the impact of Basic Income on the Belgian labour market: Results and difficulties', in Anne Miller (ed.), *First International Conference on Basic Income: Proceedings, 1986*, Antwerp: Basic Income European Network, pp. 196–207.

Bradshaw, Jonathan and Fran Bennett (2011), 'National Insurance: Past, present, and future?', *Journal of Poverty and Social Justice*, **19** (3), 207–9.

Breemersch, Koen, Jože P. Damijan and Jozef Konings (2017), *Labour Market Polarization in Advanced Countries: Impact of global value chains, technology, import competition from China and labour market institutions*, OECD Social, Employment and Migration Working Papers, No. 197, Paris: OECD Publishing, accessed 9 January 2021 at https://www.oecd-ilibrary.org/employment/labour -market-polarization-in-advanced-countries_06804863-en.

Bregman, Rutger (2017), *Utopia for Realists: And how we can get there*, London: Bloomsbury.

Brehmer, Elwood (2020), 'Alaska Permanent Fund rebounds to pass $70 billion as stock markets rally', *Anchorage Daily News*, 9 December 2020, accessed 11 January 2021 at https://www.adn.com/business-economy/2020/12/09/alaska-permanent -fund-rebounds-to-pass-70-billion-as-stock-markets-rally/#.

Breitenbach, Hans, Tom Burden and David Coates (1990), *Features of a Viable Socialism*, New York: Harvester Wheatsheaf.

Bresson, Yoland and Philippe Guilhaume (1986), *Le Participat: Réconcilier l'écomonomique et le social*, Paris: Chotard et Associés Editeurs.

Briggs, Asa and Anne Macartney (1984), *Toynbee Hall: The first hundred years*, London: Routledge and Kegan Paul.

Brittan, Samuel (1998), *Towards a Humane Individualism*, London: John Stuart Mill Institute.

Brittan, Samuel and Steven Webb (1990), *Beyond the Welfare State: An examination of Basic Incomes in a market economy*, Aberdeen: Aberdeen University Press.

Browne, James and Herwig Immervoll (2018), *Mechanics of Replacing Benefit Systems with a Basic Income: Comparative results from a microsimulation approach*, EUROMOD Working Paper EM8/18, Colchester: Institute for Social and Economic Research, University of Essex, accessed 9 January 2021 at www.iser.essex.ac.uk/ research/publications/working-papers/euromod/em8-18.

Brownson, Orestes (1840), *The Laboring Classes: An article from the Boston Quarterly Review*, third edition, Boston: Benjamin H. Greene.

Brownson, Orestes (1978), *The Laboring Classes (1840) with Brownson's Defence of the Article on the Laboring Classes*, New York: Scholars' Facsimiles and Reprints, first published in 1840.

Brownson, Orestes (2007), 'Equality', in Orestes Brownson, *Works in Political Philosophy*, volume II, 1828–1841, Wilmington, DE: ISI Books, pp. 85–8, first published in 1829.

Bryan, James B. (2005), 'Targeted programs v. the Basic Income Guarantee: An examination of the efficiency costs of different forms of redistribution', *The Journal of Socioeconomics*, **34** (1), 39–47.

Brynjolfsson, Erik and Andrew McAfee (2014), *The Second Machine Age: Work, progress, and prosperity in a time of brilliant technologies*, New York: W.W. Norton.

Burczak, Theodore (2013), 'A Hayekian Case for a Basic Income', in Guinevere Liberty Nell (ed.), *Basic Income and the Free Market: Austrian economics and the potential for efficient redistribution*, New York: Palgrave Macmillan, pp. 49–64.

Butler, Gregory S. (1992), *In Search of the American Spirit: The political thought of Orestes Brownson*, Carbondale and Edwardsville, IL: Southern Illinois University Press, 1992.

Cabaña, Gabriela (2019), 'Dignidad es cuidado. Hacia una nueva forma de integración social', *Intervención*, **9** (2), accessed 9 January 2021 at https://intervencion .uahurtado.cl/index.php/intervencion/article/view/79.

Cabaña, Gabriela (2020), correspondence with the author.

Cain, Glen G. and Douglas A. Wissoker (1990), 'A reanalysis of marital stability in the Seattle-Denver Income Maintenance Experiment', *American Journal of Sociology*, **95** (5), 1235–69.

Callan, Tim, Cathal O'Donoghue, Holly Sutherland and Moira Wilson (1999), *Comparative Analysis of Basic Income Proposals: UK and Ireland*, Cambridge: Department of Applied Economics, University of Cambridge.

Callender, Rosheen (1988), 'Basic Income in Ireland: The debate to date', in Anne Miller (ed.), *First International Conference on Basic Income: Proceedings, 1986*, Antwerp: Basic Income European Network, pp. 288–95.

Callinicos, Alex (2003), *An Anti-Capitalist Manifesto*, Cambridge: Polity Press.

Calnitsky, D. (2016), '"More normal than welfare": The Mincome experiment, stigma, and community experience', *Canadian Review of Sociology/Revue Canadienne de Sociologie*, **53** (1), 26–71.

Campbell, Jim and Morag Gillespie (2016), *Feminist Economics and Public Policy: Reflections on the work and impact of Ailsa McKay*, London: Routledge.

Cappelen, Cornelius and Jørgen Pedersen (2018), 'Just wealth transfer taxation: Defending John Stuart Mill's scheme', *Politics, Philosophy and Economics*, **17** (3), 317–35.

Carlile, R. (1825), 'To Allen Davenport', *The Republican*, **11** (2), 57–8.

Carlson, Judith (1997), *Is a Basic Income Woman Friendly? A feminist assessment of the problems and prospects associated with Basic Income schemes*, Hertford: University of Hertfordshire Business School.

Casassas, David and Sandra González Bailón (2007), 'Corporate watch, consumer responsibility, and economic democracy: Forms of political action in the orbit of a Citizen's Income', *Citizen's Income Newsletter*, issue 3 for 2007, pp. 8–12.

Casassas, David, Daniel Raventós and Maciej Szlinder (2019), 'Socialist arguments for Basic Income', in Malcolm Torry (ed.), *The Palgrave International Handbook of Basic Income*, Cham: Palgrave Macmillan, pp. 459–76.

Centre for Social Justice (2009), *Dynamic Benefits: Towards welfare that works*, London: The Centre for Social Justice, accessed 9 January 2021 at https://www.centreforsocialjustice.org.uk/library/dynamic-benefits-towards-welfare-works.

Charlier, Joseph (1848), *Solution du Problème Social ou Constitution Humanitaires, Basée sur la Loi Naturelle et Précédée de l'Exposé des Motifs ...* , Marrickville: Wentworth Press.

Charlier, Joseph (2004), 'Solution of the social problem or humanitarian constitution, based upon natural law, and preceded by the exposition of reasons', trans. John Cunliffe and Guido Erreygers, in John Cunliffe and Guido Erreygers (eds), *The Origins of Universal Grants: An anthology of historical writings on Basic Capital and Basic Income*, Basingstoke: Palgrave Macmillan, pp. 103–20, first published in 1848.

Chase, Malcolm (1988), *'The People's Farm': English radical agrarianism 1775–1840*, Oxford: Clarendon Press.

Chase, Malcolm (2004), 'Davenport, Allen', *Oxford Dictionary of National Biography*, accessed 9 January 2021 at https://www.oxforddnb.com/view/10.1093/ref:odnb/9780198614128.001.0001/odnb-9780198614128-e-47111.

Chase, Malcolm (2016), '"The real rights of man": Thomas Spence, Paine and Chartism', *Miranda*, accessed 9 January 2021 at https://journals.openedition.org/miranda/8989.

Cholbi, Michael and Michael Weber (2020), *The Future of Work, Technology, and Basic Income*, New York: Routledge.

Christensen, Erik and Jørn Loftager (2000), 'Ups and downs of Basic Income in Denmark', in Robert van der Veen and Loek Groot (eds), *Basic Income on the Agenda: Policy objectives and political chances*, Amsterdam: Amsterdam University Press, pp. 257–67.

Cigna, Luca Michele (2020), 'Looking for a North Star? Trade unions' positions in the Universal Basic Income debate', Paris: Sciences Po School of Public Affairs, accessed 9 January 2021 at https://www.sciencespo.fr/public/sites/sciencespo.fr.public/files/Lucas%20CIGNA%20(autorisation%20OK%20%2B%20web).pdf.

Citizens' Basic Income Feasibility Study Steering Group (2020), *Assessing the Feasibility of Citizens' Basic Income Pilots in Scotland*, Scotland: Basic Income Scotland, accessed 9 January 2021 at https://basicincome.scot/2020/06/10/draft-final-report-cbi-feasibility-study/.

Citizen's Basic Income Trust (2016a), 'Review: Maximilian Sommer, *A Feasible Basic Income Scheme for Germany*', London: Citizen's Basic Income Trust, accessed 9 August 2021 at https://citizensincome.org/book-reviews/maximilian-sommer-a-feasible-basic-income-scheme-for-germany/.

Citizen's Basic Income Trust (2016b), 'Who should receive a Citizen's Basic Income?', London: Citizen's Basic Income Trust, accessed 9 January 2021 at https://citizensincome.org/research-analysis/who-should-receive-a-citizens-basic-income/.

Citizen's Basic Income Trust (2018a), *Citizen's Basic Income: A brief introduction*, London: Citizen's Basic Income Trust.

Citizen's Basic Income Trust (2018b), 'Illustrative draft legislation for a Citizen's Basic Income', London: Citizen's Basic Income Trust, accessed 9 January 2021 at https://citizensincome.org/news/illustrative-draft-legislation-for-a-citizens-basic-income/.

Citizen's Basic Income Trust (2019), 'Results of the Finnish Basic Income Experiment', London: Citizen's Basic Income Trust, accessed 9 January 2021 at https://citizensincome.org/news/preliminary-results-of-the-finnish-basic-income-experiment/.

Citizen's Basic Income Trust (2020), 'CBIT evidence to a House of Lords Inquiry', accessed 9 January 2021 at https://citizensincome.org/news/cbit-evidence-to-a-house-of-lords-inquiry/.

Citizen's Income Trust (1993–2001), Minutes of meetings.

Citizen's Income Trust (2007), 'Both the House of Commons and the House of Lords support a Citizen's Income approach to the reform of tax and benefits', *Citizen's Income Newsletter*, London: Citizen's Income Trust, issue 2 for 2007, pp. 1–2.

Citizen's Income Trust (2010), 'A response to *21st Century Welfare*', *Citizen's Income Newsletter*, issue 3 for 2010, pp. 3–9.

Citizen's Income Trust (2015), 'Book review: *Inequality*, by Anthony B. Atkinson', accessed 9 January 2021 at http://citizensincome.org/book-reviews/inequality-by-anthony-b-atkinson/.

Claeys, Gregory (1989), *Thomas Paine: Social and political thought*, Boston: Unwin Hyman.

Clark, Charles M.A. (2002), *The Basic Income Guarantee: Ensuring progress and prosperity in the 21st century*, Dublin: The Liffey Press.

Clark, Charles M.A. and John Healy (1997), *Pathways to a Basic Income*, Dublin: CORI Justice Commission.

Clinton, David, Michael Yates and Dharminder Kang (1994), *Integrating Taxes and Benefits?*, London: Institute for Public Policy Research.

CNBC (2018), 'US states with the highest levels of income inequality', Englewood Cliffs, NJ: CNBC, accessed 9 January 2021 at https://www.cnbc.com/2018/03/12/us-states-with-the-highest-levels-of-income-inequality.html.

Cobham, Alex (2014), 'Unconditional: The limits of evidence', *Citizen's Income Newsletter*, issue 3 for 2014, pp. 8–10.

Coelho, André (2015), 'Spain: Podemos introduces a conditional grant in its electoral program', Basic Income Earth Network, accessed 9 January 2021 at https://basicincome.org/news/2015/11/spain-podemos-reintroduces-basic-income-in-its-electoral-program/.

Coêlho, Denilson Bandeira (2012), 'Brazil: Basic Income—A new model of innovation and diffusion', in Matthew C. Murray and Carole Pateman (eds), *Basic Income Worldwide: Horizons of reform*, Basingstoke and New York: Palgrave Macmillan, pp. 59–80.

Cohen, Wilbur J. and Milton Friedman (1972), *Social Security: Universal or selective?*, Washington, DC: American Enterprise Institute.

Cole, G.D.H. (1929), *The Next Ten Years in British Social and Economic Policy*, London: Macmillan and Co.

Cole, G.D.H. (1935), *Principles of Economic Planning*, London: Macmillan and Co.

Colini, Laura (2019), *The B-MINCOME Project Journal No. 5*, Lille: Urban Innovative Actions, accessed 9 January 2021 at https://www.uia-initiative.eu/sites/default/files/2020-03/Barcelona_BMINCOME_Journal_5.pdf.

Colombino, Ugo, Marilena Locatelli, Edlira Narazani and Cathal O'Donoghue (2010), 'Alternative Basic Income mechanisms: An evaluation exercise with a microeconometric model', *Basic Income Studies*, **5** (1), accessed 9 January 2021 at https://www.degruyter.com/view/journals/bis/5/1/article-bis.2010.5.1.1162.xml.xml.

Commission on Social Justice (1994), *Social Justice: Strategies for national renewal*, London: Vintage.

Compass (2018), accessed 9 January 2021 at http://www.compassonline.org.uk/.

Coote, Anna and Andrew Percy (2020), *The Case for Universal Basic Services*, Cambridge: Polity Press.

Coote, Anna and Edanur Yazici (2019), *Universal Basic Income: A union perspective: Full report*, London: New Economics Foundation, accessed 9 January 2021 at http://www.world-psi.org/sites/default/files/documents/research/en_ubi_full_report_2019.pdf.

Creedy, John (1998), *Pensions and Population Ageing*, Cheltenham, UK and Lyme, NH, USA: Edward Elgar Publishing.

Creedy, John and Richard Disney (1985), *Social Insurance in Transition*, Oxford: Clarendon Press.

Crocker, Geoff (2015), 'Keynes, Piketty, and Basic Income', *Basic Income Studies*, **10** (1), 91–113.

Crocker, Geoff (2019), 'Funding Basic Income by money creation', in Malcolm Torry (ed.), *The Palgrave International Handbook of Basic Income*, Cham: Palgrave Macmillan, pp. 180–85.

Crocker, Geoff (2020), *Basic Income and Sovereign Money: The alternative to economic crisis and austerity policy*, Cham: Palgrave Macmillan.

Cruddas, Jon and Tom Kibasi (2016), 'A Universal Basic Mistake', *Prospect*, 16 June 2016, accessed 9 January 2021 at https://www.prospectmagazine.co.uk/magazine/a-universal-basic-mistake.

Cunliffe, John and Guido Erreygers (2001), 'The enigmatic legacy of Charles Fourier: Charles Fourier and Basic Income', *History of Political Economy*, **33** (3), 459–84.

Cunliffe, John and Guido Erreygers (eds) (2004), *The Origins of Universal Grants: An anthology of historical writings on Basic Capital and Basic Income*, Basingstoke: Palgrave Macmillan.

Currion, Paul (2020), 'Building a path to UBI for Serbia', accessed 9 January 2021 at https://medium.com/@paulcurrion/building-a-path-to-ubi-for-serbia-e204e3140338.

Daugareilh, Isabelle, Christophe Degryse and Philippe Pochet (2019), *The Platform Economy and Social Law: Key issues in comparative perspective*, Brussels: European Trade Union Institute, accessed 9 January 2021 at https://www.etui.org/Publications2/Working-Papers/The-platform-economy-and-social-law-Key-issues-in-comparative-perspective.

Davala, Sarath (2019), 'Pilots, evidence and politics: The Basic Income debate in India', in Malcolm Torry (ed.), *The Palgrave International Handbook of Basic Income*, Cham: Palgrave Macmillan, pp. 373–87.

Davala, Sarath (2020), correspondence with the author.

Davala, Sarath, Renana Jhabvala, Soumya Kapoor Mehta and Guy Standing (2015), *Basic Income: A transformative policy for India*, London: Bloomsbury.

Davala, Sarath, Renana Jhabvala, Guy Standing and Nina Badgaiyan (2017), *Piloting Basic Income: A legacy study: Final report*, Sewa Bharat, accessed 8 January 2021 at https://sewabharat.org/wp-content/uploads/2019/02/Legacy-Study-Final-Report-a.pdf.

Davenport, Allen (1824), 'Agrarian Equality—To Mr. R. Carlile, Dorchester Gaol', *The Republican*, **10** (13), 390–411, with Richard Carlile's reaction in footnotes.

Davenport, Allen (1826), 'Co-operation', *Co-operative Magazine and Monthly Herald*, **1** (11), 356–7.

Davenport, Allen (no date), *Life, Writings and Principles of Thomas Spence*, London: Wakelin.

Davis, Abigail, Donald Hirsch, Matt Padley and Claire Shepherd (2018), *A Minimum Income Standard for the UK 2008–2018: Continuity and change*, York: Joseph Rowntree Foundation, accessed 9 January 2021 at https://www.jrf.org.uk/report/minimum-income-standard-uk-2018.

de Basquiat, Marc (2020), 'The Corsica Assembly votes for a Negative Income Tax with a notional basic income', accessed 9 January 2021 at https://basicincome.org/news/2020/05/the-corsica-assembly-votes-for-a-negative-income-tax-with-a-notional-basic-income/.

de Jager, Nicole E.M., Johan J. Graafland and George M.M. Gelauff (1994), *A Negative Income Tax in a Mini Welfare State: A simulation with MIMIC*, The Hague: Central Planning Bureau.

De Keyser, Napoleon (2004), 'Natural law, or justice as a new governance for society according to the destiny of man', trans. John Cunliffe and Guido Erreygers, in John Cunliffe and Guido Erreygers (eds), *The Origins of Universal Grants: An anthology of historical writings on Basic Capital and Basic Income*, Basingstoke: Palgrave Macmillan, pp. 56–72, first published in 1854.

Delattre, Lucas and Malcolm Torry (2017), 'Would a Citizen's Basic Income pilot project in the UK be possible?', *Citizen's Income Newsletter*, Issue 4 for 2017, pp. 2–4.

de Mooij, Ruud (2006), *Reinventing the Welfare State*, The Hague: Centraal Planbureau/Bureau for Economic Policy Analysis, accessed 7 January 2021 at https://www.cpb.nl/sites/default/files/publicaties/download/reinventing-welfare-state.pdf.

Dent, Anna (2019), 'Free money wouldn't make people lazy—but it could revolutionise work', *The Guardian*, 12 February 2019, accessed 9 January 2021 at https://www.theguardian.com/commentisfree/2019/feb/12/universal-basic-income-work-finland-experiment-payments.

Department for Work and Pensions (2011), *A State Pension for the 21st Century*, Cm 8053, London: The Stationery Office.

De Potter, Agathon (1874), *Économie Sociale*, two volumes, Bruxelles: Chez les Principaux Libraires.

De Potter, Agathon (1886), *La Révolution Sociale Prédite*, Bruxelles: A. Manceaux. [Translations by Malcolm Torry.]

De Potter, Agathon (1897), *La Justice et sa Sanction Religieuse*, Bruxelles: A. Manceaux. [Translations by Malcolm Torry.]

De Potter, Agathon (2004), 'Social Economics', trans. John Cunliffe and Guido Erreygers, in John Cunliffe and Guido Erreygers (eds), *The Origins of Universal Grants: An anthology of historical writings on Basic Capital and Basic Income*, Basingstoke: Palgrave Macmillan, pp. 73–8, first published in 1874.

De Roo, Alexander (1990), 'How to create a Basic Income scheme in Holland', in Walter Van Trier (ed.), *Second International Conference on Basic Income: Basic Incomes and problems of implementation*, Antwerp: Basic Income European Network, pp. 25–41.

De Wispelaere, Jurgen (2016a), 'The Struggle for strategy: On the politics of the Basic Income proposal', *Politics*, **36** (2), 131–41.

De Wispelaere, Jurgen (2016b), 'Basic Income in our time: Improving political prospects through policy learning?', *Journal of Social Policy*, **45** (4), 617–34.

De Wispelaere, Jurgen, Antti Halmetoja and Ville-Veikko Pulkka (2018), 'The rise (and fall) of the Finnish Basic Income Experiment', *CESifo Forum*, **19**, 15–19, accessed 9 January 2021 at https://www.ifo.de/DocDL/CESifo-Forum-2018-3-de-wispelaere-halmetois-pulkka-unconditional-basic-income-september.pdf.

De Wispelaere, Jurgen, Antti Halmetoja and Ville-Veikko Pulkka (2019), 'The Finnish Basic Income Experiment: A primer', in Malcolm Torry (ed.), *The Palgrave International Handbook of Basic Income*, Cham: Palgrave Macmillan, pp. 389–406.

De Wispelaere, Jurgen and José Antonio Noguera (2012), 'On the political feasibility of Universal Basic Income: An analytic framework', in Richard Caputo (ed.), *Basic Income Guarantee: International experiences and perspectives on the viability of Income Guarantee*, New York: Palgrave Macmillan, pp. 17–38.

De Wispelaere, Jurgen and Lindsay Stirton (2004), 'The many faces of Universal Basic Income', *Political Quarterly*, **75** (3), 266–74.

De Wispelaere, Jurgen and Lindsay Stirton (2008), 'Why Participation Income might not be such a great idea after all', *Citizen's Income Newsletter*, issue 3 for 2008, pp. 3–8.

Dilnot, A.W., J.A. Kay and C.N. Morris (1984), *The Reform of Social Security*, Oxford: Clarendon Press.

Dommen-Meade, Bridget (ed.) (2010), *Le Financement d'un Revenu de Base Inconditionnel*, Zürich: Seismo, for BIEN-Suisse.

Don, F.J.H. (2019), 'The influence of Jan Tinbergen on Dutch Economic Policy', *De Economist*, **167**, 259–82.

Douben, Nic and Jos Dekkers (1988), 'The Future of Basic Income: A Dutch proposal', in Anne Miller (ed.), *First International Conference on Basic Income: Proceedings, 1986*, Antwerp: Basic Income European Network, pp. 211–22.

Douglas, C.H. (1920), *Economic Democracy*, New York: Harcourt, Brace and Howe.

Douglas, C.H. (1933), *Social Credit*, London: Eyre and Spottiswoode.
Douglas, C.H. (1951), *The Monopoly of Credit*, third edition, Liverpool: K.R.P. Publications Ltd.
Douillard, Austin (2017), 'New study published on results of Basic Income pilot in Kenya', Basic Income Earth Network, accessed 9 January 2021 at http://basicincome .org/news/2017/03/us-kenya-new-study-published-results-basic-income-pilot -kenya/.
Downes, Amy and Stewart Lansley (2018), *It's Basic Income*, Bristol: Policy Press.
Drago, Giorgio Jackson (2020), 'Modifica la Carta Fundamental para incorporar una prestación monetaria fiscal, a la que tendrá derecho toda persona mayor de edad, denominada renta básica universal', accessed 1 January 2021 at https://www.camara .cl/verDoc.aspx?prmTipo=SIAL&prmID=53300&formato=pdf.
Duverger, Timothée (2018), *L'Invention du Revenu de Base: La fabrique d'une utopie démocratique*, Bordeaux: Éditions le Bord de l'Eau. [Translations into English by Malcolm Torry.]
Dye, Richard F. and Richard W. England (2010), *Assessing the Theory and Practice of Land Value Taxation*, Cambridge, MA: Lincoln Institute of Land Policy, accessed 9 January 2021 at https://www.lincolninst.edu/sites/default/files/pubfiles/assessing -theory-practice-land-value-taxation-full_0.pdf.
Eight (2021), 'Eight', accessed 8 January 2021 at https://www.eight.world/En/.
El Español (2019), 'Podemos propone una renta básica de 600 a 1.200 euros con un coste de 12.000 millones al año', *El Español*, 31 March 2019, accessed 6 January 2021 at https://www.elespanol.com/espana/politica/20190331/podemos-propone -renta-basica-euros-coste-millones/387461482_0.html.
Elliott, Larry (2014), 'Would a Citizen's Income be better than our benefits system?', *The Guardian*, 11 August 2014, accessed 9 January 2021 at https://www.theguardian .com/business/2014/aug/10/tax-benefits-citizens-income-self-employment.
Emison, Linnea Feldman (2020), 'The promising results of a citywide Basic Income experiment', *New Yorker*, 15 July 2020, accessed 9 January 2021 at https://www .newyorker.com/news/news-desk/the-promising-results-of-a-citywide-basic-income -experiment.
Esam, Peter and Richard Berthoud (1991), *Independent Benefits for Men and Women: An enquiry into options for treating husbands and wives as separate units in the assessment of social security*, London: Policy Studies Institute.
Esam, Peter, Robert Good and Rick Middleton (1985), *Who's to Benefit? A radical review of the social security system*, London: Verso.
Esping-Andersen, Gøsta (1990), *The Three Worlds of Welfare Capitalism*, Cambridge: Polity Press.
European Commission (2014), 'Unconditional Basic Income (UBI)—Exploring a pathway towards emancipatory welfare conditions in the EU', accessed 9 January 2021 at https://europa.eu/citizens-initiative/initiatives/details/2013/000001_en.
European Commission (2019), *Guide to the European Citizens' Initiative*, Brussels: European Commission, accessed 9 January 2021 at https://op.europa.eu/en/ publication-detail/-/publication/8abe3729-640f-11ea-b735-01aa75ed71a1.
European Commission (2020), 'Start Unconditional Basic Incomes (UBI) throughout the EU', accessed 9 January 2021 at https://europa.eu/citizens-initiative/initiatives/ details/2020/000003_en.
Euzéby, Chantal (1994), 'From "insertion" income to "existence" income', *Citizen's Income Bulletin*, no. 17, January 1994, pp. 14–18.

Euzéby, Chantal (2000), 'What reforms are needed for the Minimum Insertion Income (RMI) in France?', in Robert van der Veen and Loek Groot (eds), *Basic Income on the Agenda: Policy objectives and political chances*, Amsterdam: Amsterdam University Press, pp. 268–75.

Expert Working Group on Welfare (2014), *Re-thinking Welfare: Fair, personal and simple*, Edinburgh: Expert Working Group on Welfare, accessed 9 January 2021 at https://www.webarchive.org.uk/wayback/archive/3000/https://www.gov.scot/Resource/0045/00451915.pdf.

Fairer Fife Commission (2015), *Fairness Matters*, Fife: Fairer Fife Commission, accessed 9 January 2021 at https://www.carnegieuktrust.org.uk/publications/fairness-matters.

Farley, Martin (2017), 'Why Land Value Tax and Universal Basic Income need each other', *Progress*, accessed 9 January 2021 at https://www.progress.org/articles/why-land-value-tax-and-universal-basic-income-need-each-other.

Fehr, Ernst and Klaus M. Schmidt (2003), 'Theories of fairness and reciprocity: Evidence and economic applications', Advances in Economics and Econometrics, Econometric Society Monographs, Eighth World Congress, Vol. 1, pp. 208–57, accessed 9 January 2021 at http://web.mit.edu/14.193/www/WorldCongress-IEW-Version6Oct03.pdf.

Feloni, Richard (2019), 'Nearly everyone living in Alaska gets about $2,000 a year from the state's $65 billion fund. We asked 9 Alaskans how they spend it', *Business Insider*, accessed 9 January 2021 at https://www.businessinsider.com/alaskans-spend-permanent-fund-dividend-2019-2.

Ferdosi, Mohammad, Tom McDowell, Wayne Lewchuk and Stephanie Ross (2020), *Southern Ontario's Basic Income Experience*, Hamilton: McMasters University Labour Studies, accessed 9 January 2021 at https://labourstudies.mcmaster.ca/documents/southern-ontarios-basic-income-experience.pdf.

Fevre, Ralph (2016), *Individualism and Inequality: The future of work and politics*, Cheltenham, UK and Northampton, MA, USA: Edward Elgar Publishing.

Field, Frank (1982), 'Three political pieces' and 'Killing a commitment: The cabinet v the children (1976)', in Frank Field, *Poverty and Politics: The inside story of the Child Poverty Action Group's campaigns in the 1970s*, London: Heinemann, pp. 93, 108–13.

Fitzgerald, Rory (2017), 'Survey reveals young people more likely to support Universal Basic Income, but it's not a Left-Right thing', *The Conversation*, accessed 9 January 2021 at https://theconversation.com/survey-reveals-young-people-more-likely-to-support-universal-basic-income-but-its-not-a-left-right-thing-87554.

Fitzpatrick, Tony (1999), *Freedom and Security: An introduction to the Basic Income debate*, Basingstoke: Macmillan.

Fleischer, Miranda Perry and Otto Lehto (2019), 'Libertarian perspectives on Basic Income', in Malcolm Torry (ed.), *The Palgrave International Handbook of Basic Income*, Cham: Palgrave Macmillan, pp. 439–58.

Flora, P. (1981), 'Solution or source of crises? The Welfare State in historical perspective', in W.J. Mommsen, *The Emergence of the Welfare State in Britain and Germany, 1850–1950*, London: Croom Helm, pp. 343–89.

Floyd, David (2020), 'The long weird history of Basic Income: And why it's back', *Investopedia*, accessed 9 January 2021 at https://www.investopedia.com/news/history-of-universal-basic-income/.

Forget, Evelyn (2011), 'The town with no poverty: The health effects of a Canadian Guaranteed Annual Income field experiment', *Canadian Public Policy/Analyse de Politiques*, **37** (3), 283–305.

Forss, Mikko and Ohto Kanninen (2014), *Miten testata perustulon vaikutuksia? Kenttäkoekulttuurin lyhyt oppimäärä*, Helsinki: Tänk.

Fourier, Charles (1829), *Le Nouveau Monde Industriel et Sociétaire*, Quebec: University of Quebec, accessed 9 January 2021 at http://classiques.uqac.ca/classiques/fourier_charles/nouveau_monde/fourier_nouveau_monde_1.pdf.

Fourier, Charles (1874), *Lettre de Fourier au Grand Juge*, edited by Charles Pellarin, Paris: Galerie D'Orleans et Librairie des Sciences Sociales, first published in 1803.

Fourier, Charles (2004), 'Letter to the High Judge', trans. Jonathan Beecher and Richard Bienvenu, in John Cunliffe and Guido Erreygers (eds), *The Origins of Universal Grants: An anthology of historical writings on Basic Capital and Basic Income*, Basingstoke: Palgrave Macmillan, pp. 99–102, first published in 1803.

Fox Piven, Frances and Richard Cloward (1966), 'The weight of the poor: A strategy to end poverty', *The Nation*, 2 May 1966, accessed 9 January 2021 at https://www.tandfonline.com/doi/abs/10.1080/07393148.2011.591906.

Frankel, Sid (2020), 'Basic Income advocacy in Canada: Multiple streams, experiments and the road ahead', in Richard Caputo and Larry Liu (eds), *Political Activism and Basic Income Guarantee*, Cham: Palgrave Macmillan, pp. 139–62.

Fraser, Derek (1984), *The Evolution of the British Welfare State: A history of social policy since the industrial revolution*, second edition, Basingstoke: Macmillan.

Friedman, Milton (2002), *Capitalism and Freedom*, Chicago: University of Chicago Press, first published in 1962.

Galbraith, John Kenneth (1970), *The Affluent Society*, second edition, Harmondsworth: Penguin.

Garcia, Marito and Charity M.T. Moore (2012), *The Cash Dividend: The rise of cash transfer programs in sub-Saharan Africa*, Washington, DC: The World Bank.

Gasparini, Leonard and Guillermo Cruces (2010), 'Las Asignaciones por Hijo en Argentine' ['Child Benefits in Argentina'], *Económica*, La Plata, **61**, 105–46.

Generation Libre (2020), 'Comprendre le "socle citoyen"—un revenu universel pour 2021', accessed 1 January 2021 at https://www.generationlibre.eu/medias/comprendre-le-socle-citoyen-un-revenu-universel-pour-2021/.

George, Henry (1884a), *Social Problems*, London: Kegan Paul, Trench and Co.

George, Henry (1884b), *Scotland and Scotsmen*, Glasgow, Bradford and London: Land Values Publication Department.

George, Henry (1888), *Land and People*, London: Williams Reeves.

George, Henry (1907), *Progress and Poverty*, New York: Doubleday, Page and Co., first published in 1879.

George, Henry (1932), *The Science of Political Economy*, London: The Henry George Foundation, first published in 1898.

George, Henry (1947), *The Condition of Labour: An open letter to Pope Leo XIII*, London: Land and Liberty Press, first published as *The Condition of Labor* in 1891.

Giddens, Anthony (1998), *The Third Way: The renewal of social democracy*, Cambridge: Polity Press.

Ginn, Jay (1996), 'Citizens' pensions and women', *Citizen's Income Bulletin*, no. 21, February 1996, pp. 10–12.

Giuffrida, Angela (2019), 'Italy rolls out "citizens' income" for the poor amid criticisms', *The Guardian*, 6 March 2019, accessed 26 January 2021 at https://www

.theguardian.com/world/2019/mar/06/italy-rolls-out-citizens-income-for-the-poor -amid-criticisms.
GiveDirectly (2020), 'The definitive guide to Universal Basic Income', GiveDirectly, accessed 9 January 2021 at https://www.givedirectly.org/basic-income/.
GiveDirectly (2021), 'Launch a Basic Income', GiveDirectly, accessed 8 January 2021 at https://www.givedirectly.org/ubi-study/.
Gnews (2020), 'The world's first data dividend! Experience data sovereignty. Gyeonggi-do data dividend review', accessed 2 January 2021 at https://gnews.gg.go .kr/news/news_detail.do?number=202003041146073570C094&s_code=C094.
Goldsmith, Scott (2012), 'The economic and social impacts of the Permanent Fund Dividend on Alaska', in Karl Widerquist and Michael W. Howard (eds), *Alaska's Permanent Fund Dividend*, New York: Palgrave Macmillan, pp. 49–64.
Goodhart, William and Hermione Parker (1994), 'To BI or not to BI? An exchange of letters between Sir William Goodhart QC and Hermione Parker', *Citizen's Income Bulletin*, no. 18, July 1994, pp. 9–12.
Goodwin, Stephen (1994), 'Liberal Democrats' Conference: Citizen's income plan dropped', *The Independent*, 22 September 1994, accessed 9 January 2021 at www .independent.co.uk/news/uk/liberal-democrats-conference-citizens-income-plan -dropped-1450315.html.
Gorz, André (1992), 'On the difference between society and community, and why Basic Income cannot by itself confer full membership of either', in Philippe Van Parijs (ed.), *Arguing for Basic Income: Ethical foundations for a radical reform*, London: Verso, pp. 178–84.
Gorz, André (1997), 'Sortir de la société salariale', extraits de *Misères du Present Richesse du Possible*, chapter IV, Editions Galilée, accessed 4 January 2021 at https://www.millenaire3.com/content/download/850/9332.
Gorz, André (1999), *Reclaiming Work: Beyond the wage-based society*, trans. Chris Turner, Cambridge: Polity Press.
Gorz, André (2013), 'Revenue garanti, une utopie à portée de main; A reculons', *Le Monde Diplomatique*, 1 May 2013, accessed 18 January 2021 at http://ezproxy .staffs.ac.uk/login?url=https://www-proquest-com.ezproxy.staffs.ac.uk/newspapers/ revenu-garanti-une-utopie-à-portée-de-main/docview/1346233780/se-2?accountid= 17254, first published in 1990.
Gough, Ian (2017), *Heat, Greed and Human Need: Climate change, capitalism and sustainable wellbeing*, Cheltenham, UK and Northampton, MA, USA: Edward Elgar Publishing.
Goulden, Chris (2018), 'Universal Basic Income—Not the answer to poverty', York: Joseph Rowntree Foundation, accessed 9 January 2021 at https://www.jrf.org.uk/ blog/universal-basic-income-not-answer-poverty.
Grayling, A.C. (1988), *Wittgenstein*, Oxford: Oxford University Press.
Green Party (2015), *For the Common Good: General Election Manifesto 2015*, London: The Green Party of England and Wales.
Green Party (2019), *If not now, when? Manifesto 2019*, London: Green Party, accessed 9 January 2021 at https://www.greenparty.org.uk/assets/files/Elections/ Green%20Party%20Manifesto%202019.pdf.
Greve, Bent (2017), *Technology and the Future of Work: The impact on labour markets and welfare states*, Cheltenham, UK and Northampton, MA, USA: Edward Elgar Publishing.
Groot, L.F.M. (2004), *Basic Income, Unemployment and Compensatory Justice*, Boston: Kluwer Academic Publishers.

Groot, Loek (2020), correspondence with the author.

Groot, Loek and Robert van der Veen (2000), 'Clues and leads in the policy debate on Basic Income in the Netherlands', in Robert van der Veen and Loek Groot (eds), *Basic Income on the Agenda: Policy objectives and political chances*, Amsterdam: Amsterdam University Press, pp. 197–223.

Groot, Loek and Timo Verlaat (2019), 'Local experiments in the Netherlands', in Malcolm Torry (ed.), *The Palgrave International Handbook of Basic Income*, Cham: Palgrave Macmillan, pp. 408–13.

Gyeonggi Research Institute Basic Income Research Group (2019), *1Q 2019 Satisfaction Survey Report on the Youth Basic Income in Gyeonggi Province*, accessed 9 January 2021 at https://basicincomekorea.org/eng-paper_1q-2019-satisfaction-survey-report -on-gyeonggi-youth-basic-income/.

Haagh, Louise (2019a), *The Case for Universal Basic Income*, Cambridge: Polity Press.

Haagh, Louise (2019b), 'The developmental social contract and Basic Income in Denmark', *Social Policy and Society*, **18** (2), 301–17.

Haarmann, Claudia and Dirk Haarmann (1998), *Towards a Comprehensive Social Security System in South Africa*, Cape Town: Congress of South African Trade Unions (COSATU).

Haarmann, Claudia and Dirk Haarmann (2006), Letter to the editor, *Insight*, 5 July 2006.

Haarmann, Claudia and Dirk Haarmann (2007), 'From survival to decent employment: Basic Income security in Namibia', *Basic Income Studies*, **2** (1), 1–7.

Haarmann, Claudia and Dirk Haarmann (2012), 'Namibia: Seeing the sun rise—The realities and hopes of the Basic Income Grant Pilot Project', in Matthew C. Murray and Carole Pateman (eds), *Basic Income Worldwide: Horizons of reform*, New York: Palgrave Macmillan, pp. 33–58.

Haarmann, Claudia and Dirk Haarmann (2020), correspondence with the author.

Haarmann, Claudia, Dirk Haarmann and Nicoli Nattrass (2019), 'The Namibian Basic Income Grant pilot', in Malcolm Torry (ed.), *The Palgrave International Handbook of Basic Income*, Cham: Palgrave Macmillan, pp. 357–72.

Hall, Christopher (1988), 'The Future of Basic Income in Great Britain', in Anne Miller (ed.), *First International Conference on Basic Income: Proceedings, 1986*, Antwerp: Basic Income European Network, pp. 309–13.

Halliday, R.J. (1976), *John Stuart Mill*, London: George Allen and Unwin.

Halmetoja, Antti, Jurgen De Wispelaere and Johanna Perkiö (2019), 'A policy comet in Moominland? Basic Income in the Finnish Welfare State', *Social Policy and Society*, **18** (2), 319–30.

Hammond, Jay S. (1994), *Tales of Alaska's Bush Rat Governor*, Kenmore, WA: Epicenter Press.

Handa, Sudhanshu, Silvio Daidone, Amber Peterman, Benjamin Davis, Audrey Pereira, Tia Palermo and Jennifer Yablonski (2017), *Myth-busting? Confronting six common perceptions about Unconditional Cash Transfers as a poverty reduction strategy in Africa*, Florence: UNICEF Office of Research—Innocenti, accessed 9 January 2021 at https://www.unicef-irc.org/publications/pdf/IWP_2017_06.pdf.

Hansard (2016), 'Universal Basic Income, 14 September 2016', accessed 9 January 2021 at https://hansard.parliament.uk/commons/2016-09-14/debates/1B16BDDC -5BB5-40AB-93E0-A78D0A39BF5B/UniversalBasicIncome.

Hansard (2017), 'Work and Pensions Committee. Oral evidence: Universal Basic Income, HC793, Thursday 12 January 2017', accessed 9 January 2021 at http://data

.parliament.uk/writtenevidence/committeeevidence.svc/evidencedocument/work
-and-pensions-committee/universal-basic-income/oral/45336.html.

Harris, José (1977), *William Beveridge: A biography*, Oxford: Clarendon Press.

Harris, J. (1981), 'Some aspects of social policy in Britain during the Second World War', in W.J. Mommsen (ed.), *The Emergence of the Welfare State in Britain and Germany, 1850–1950*, London: Croom Helm, pp. 247–62.

Harrop, Andrew (2012), *The Coalition and Universalism*, London: The Fabian Society, accessed 9 January 2021 at https://fabians.org.uk/publication/the-coalition -and-universalism/.

Harrop, Andrew (2016), *For Us All: Redesigning social security for the 2020s*, London: Fabian Society.

Harrop, Andrew and Cameron Tait (2017), *Universal Basic Income and the Future of Work*, London: Fabian Society.

Hattersley, C. Marshall (1922), *The Community's Credit: A consideration of the principle and proposals of the Social Credit Movement*, London: Credit Power Press.

Hattersley, C.M. (1931), *Men, Machines and Money*, second edition, Mexborough: The Times Printing Co. Ltd.

Hattersley, C. Marshall (1937), *Wealth, Want and War: Problems of the power age*, Mexborough: Social Credit Co-ordinating Centre.

Hattersley, C. Marshall (1942), *Now—or Never? Financial principles in relation to present requirements: A survey, with certain proposals*, Mexborough: Social Credit Co-ordinating Centre.

Hayek, Friedrich A. (2008), *The Road to Serfdom*, in *The Collected Works of F.A. Hayek*, volume 2, ed. Bruce Caldwell, London and New York: Routledge, first published in 1944.

Healy, Seán (2021), correspondence with the author.

Healy, Seán and Brigid Reynolds (2000), 'From concept to Green Paper: Putting Basic Income on the agenda in Ireland', in Robert van der Veen and Loek Groot (eds), *Basic Income on the Agenda: Policy objectives and political chances*, Amsterdam: Amsterdam University Press, pp. 238–46.

Healy, Seán and Brigid Reynolds (2012), 'Ireland: The prospects for Basic Income reform', in Matthew C. Murray and Carole Pateman (eds), *Basic Income Worldwide: Horizons of reform*, Basingstoke and New York: Palgrave Macmillan, pp. 151–72.

Henderson, Troy and John Quiggin (2019), 'Trade unions and Basic Income', in Malcolm Torry (ed.), *The Palgrave International Handbook of Basic Income*, Cham: Palgrave Macmillan, pp. 493–505.

Her Majesty's Government (1972), *Proposals for a Tax-Credit System*, Cmnd. 5116, London: Her Majesty's Stationery Office.

Hill, Michael (1990), *Social Security Policy in Britain*, Aldershot, UK and Brookfield, VT, USA: Edward Elgar Publishing.

Hirsch, Donald (2015), *Could a 'Citizen's Income' Work?*, York: Joseph Rowntree Foundation, accessed 10 January 2021 at www.jrf.org.uk/publications/could-citizens -income-work.

Hirsch, Donald (2019), *A Minimum Income Standard for the United Kingdom in 2019*, York: Joseph Rowntree Foundation, accessed 9 January 2021 at https://www.jrf.org .uk/report/minimum-income-standard-uk-2019.

Hobson, Dominic and Alan Duncan (1995a), *Saturn's Children: How the state devours liberty and prosperity*, London: Sinclair-Stevenson.

Hobson, Dominic and Alan Duncan (1995b), 'Every citizen a rentier', *Citizen's Income Bulletin*, no. 19, February 1995, pp. 9–10.

Hogenboom, Erik and Raf Janssen (1988), 'Basic-Income and the Claimants' Movement in the Netherlands', in Anne Miller (ed.), *First International Conference on Basic Income: Proceedings, 1986*, Antwerp: Basic Income European Network, pp. 237–55.

Hollander, Samuel (1985), *The Economics of John Stuart Mill*, volume II: 'Political Economy', Oxford: Basil Blackwell.

House of Commons Select Committee on Tax-Credit (1973), *Report and Proceedings of the Committee*, Session 1972–73, Volume I, report no. 341–I, London: Her Majesty's Stationery Office.

House of Commons Treasury and Civil Service Committee Sub-Committee (1982), *The Structure of Personal Income Taxation and Income Support: Minutes of Evidence*, HC 331–ix, London: Her Majesty's Stationery Office.

House of Commons Treasury and Civil Service Committee (1983), *Enquiry into the Structure of Personal Income Taxation and Income Support*, Third Special Report, Session 1982–3, London: Her Majesty's Stationery Office, section 13.35, quoted in Hermione Parker (1989), *Instead of the Dole: An enquiry into integration of the tax and benefit systems*, London: Routledge, p. 100.

House of Commons Work and Pensions Committee (2007), *Benefit Simplification*, the Seventh Report of Session 2006–2007, HC 463, London: The Stationery Office.

House of Commons Work and Pensions Committee (2018), *Benefit Sanctions*, The Nineteenth Report of Session 2017–19, HC 955, London: The Stationery Office, accessed 9 January 2021 at https://publications.parliament.uk/pa/cm201719/cmselect/cmworpen/955/955.pdf.

Howard, Michael W., Jorge Pinto and Ulrich Schachtschneider (2019), 'Ecological effects of Basic Income', in Malcolm Torry (ed.), *The Palgrave International Handbook of Basic Income*, Cham: Palgrave Macmillan, pp. 111–32.

Hughes, Chris (2018), *Fair Shot: Rethinking inequality and how we earn*, London: Bloomsbury.

IMDb (2017), 'The great British benefits handout', accessed 8 January 2021 at https://www.imdb.com/title/tt5455122/.

Immervoll, Herwig, Cathal O'Donoghue and Holly Sutherland (1999), *An Introduction to Euromod*, Cambridge: Department of Applied Economics, University of Cambridge.

Initiative Grundeinkommen (2016), 'Die größte Frage der Welt kommt nach Berlin', accessed 9 January 2021 at http://www.grundeinkommen.ch/die-groesste-frage-der-welt-kommt-nach-berlin/.

Initiative Grundeinkommen (2020), 'Grundeinkommen: Nach der Abstimmung ist vor der Abstimmung', Basel: Initiative Grundeinkommen, accessed 9 January 2021 at http://www.grundeinkommen.ch/.

Insight (2006a), 'Indefinite article: International Monetary Fund', *Insight*, 13 June 2006.

Insight (2006b), 'The head and the heart', *Insight*, 7 December 2006.

International Labour Office (2019), 'Inua Jamiii Senior Citizens' Scheme', Geneva: International Labour Office, accessed 8 January 2021 at https://www.developmentpathways.co.uk/wp-content/uploads/2019/05/Inua-Jamii-Country-Brief-1.pdf.

International Labour Organization (2010), *Effects of Non-contributory Social Transfers in Developing Countries: A compendium*, Geneva: International Labour Organization, accessed 9 January 2021 at https://www.research.manchester.ac.uk/portal/files/32800126/FULL_TEXT.pdf.

Ipsos MORI (2017), *Poll Conducted for University of Bath—Institute for Policy Research: Universal Basic Income Research*, London: Ipsos MORI.

Jacobson, Barb (2021), correspondence with the author.

Jessoula, Matteo, Marcello Natili and Michele Raitano (2019), *Italy: Implementing the new minimum income scheme*, Brussels: European Commission, accessed 26 January 2021 at https://ec.europa.eu/social/BlobServlet?docId=19024&langId=en.

Jones, Damon and Ioana Marinescu (2018), 'The labor market impacts of Universal and Permanent Cash Transfers: Evidence from the Alaska Permanent Fund', Chicago: University of Chicago, accessed 9 January 2021 at https://home.uchicago.edu/~j1s/Jones_Alaska.pdf.

Jones, Hayley (2016), 'More education, better jobs? A critical review of CCTs and Brazil's *Bolsa Família* programme for long-term poverty reduction', *Social Policy and Society*, **15** (3), 465–78.

Jongen, Egbert, Henk-Wim de Boer and Peter Dekker (2015), *De Effectiviteit van Fiscaal Participatiebeleid*, CPB Policy Brief 2015/02, Den Haag: Centraal Planbureau, accessed 7 January 2021 at https://www.cpb.nl/sites/default/files/publicaties/download/cpb-policy-brief-2015-02-de-effectiviteit-van-fiscaal-participatiebeleid.pdf.

Jooste, Karen (2020), *RightFulShare*, Karen Jooste.

Jordan, Bill (1987), *Rethinking Welfare*, Oxford: Basil Blackwell.

Jordan, Bill (1988), 'Basic Incomes and the Claimants' Movement', in Anne Glenda Miller (ed.), *First International Conference on Basic Income: Proceedings, 1986*, Antwerp: Basic Income European Network, pp. 257–68.

Jordan, Bill, Phil Agulnik, Duncan Burbidge and Stuart Duffin (2000), *Stumbling Towards Basic Income: The prospects for tax-benefit integration*, London: Citizen's Income Trust.

Joseph, Keith and Jonathan Sumption (1979), *Equality*, London: John Murray.

Junta Electoral Central (2014), 'Proposición de Ley por la Renta Básica Estatal', accessed 6 January 2021 at http://www.juntaelectoralcentral.es/cs/jec/ilp/legislaturas/Legislatura?idDocNumExp=22&p=1379061558559&sIdLeg=10&template=ILP/JEC_DetalleBD.

Kalliomaa-Puha, Laura, Anna-Kaisa Tuovinen and Olli Kangas (2016), 'The Basic Income Experiment in Finland', *Journal of Social Security Law*, **23** (2), 75–88.

Kangas, Olli (2016), 'The Finnish Basic Income Experiment—"A foolish and outrageously expensive travesty"?', *Tutkimusblogi*, Helsinki: Kela, accessed 9 January 2021 at http://blogi.kansanelakelaitos.fi/arkisto/3316.

Kangas, Olli, Signe Jauhiainen, Miska Simanainen and Minna Ylikännö (2020), *Suomen Perustulokokeilun Arviointi*, Helsinki: Sosiaali-ja terveysministeriö, accessed 9 January 2021 at http://julkaisut.valtioneuvosto.fi/bitstream/handle/10024/162219/STM_2020_15_rap.pdf (in Finnish, with English summary).

Kansaneläkelaitos Kela/Social Insurance Institution of Finland Kela (2016), 'From idea to experiment: Report on Universal Basic Income experiment in Finland', Helsinki: Kela, accessed 9 January 2021 at https://helda.helsinki.fi/handle/10138/167728.

Karshenas, Massoud and Hamid Tabatabai (2019), 'Basic Income by default: Lessons from Iran's "Cash Subsidy" programme', in Malcolm Torry (ed.), *The Palgrave International Handbook of Basic Income*, Cham: Palgrave Macmillan, pp. 339–55.

Kay, John (2017), 'The basics of Basic Income', *Intereconomics*, **52** (2), 69–74.

Kela (2019), 'Experimental study on a Universal Basic Income: Preliminary results of the Basic Income experiment: Self-perceived wellbeing improved, during the first year no effects on employment', Helsinki: Kela, accessed 9 January 2021 at http://newsletter.kela.fi/a/s/87958914-52f6e3ad50430ae1102afd040b9e1a93/2953840.

Keynes, John Maynard (1936), *The General Theory of Employment, Interest, and Money*, London: Macmillan and Co. Ltd.

Kingson, Jennifer (2021), 'Guaranteed income programs are proliferating', *Axios*, accessed 22 January 2021 at https://www.axios.com/guaranteed-income-programs-cities-8fffc3a0-e203-4aa9-919e-e27782c5d315.html.

Kitchenman, Andrew (2019), 'PFDs, state funding at risk if Alaska Permanent Fund earnings reserve falls to zero, board hears', Anchorage: Alaska Public Media, accessed 9 January 2021 at https://www.alaskapublic.org/2019/12/08/pfds-state-funding-at-risk-if-alaska-permanent-fund-earnings-reserve-falls-to-zero-board-hears/.

Klein, Elise, Jennifer Mays and Tim Dunlop (2019), *Implementing a Basic Income in Australia: Pathways forward*, Cham: Palgrave Macmillan.

Kovce, Philip and Birger P. Priddat (2019), *Bedingungsloses Grundeinkommen: Grundlagentexte*, Berlin: Suhrkamp Verlag.

Krozer, Alice and Rubén Lo Vuolo (2013), 'A Regional Citizen's Income to reduce poverty in Central America', in Rubén Lo Vuolo (ed.), *Citizen's Income and Welfare Regimes in Latin America*, New York: Palgrave Macmillan, pp. 113–37.

Kurer, O. (1998), 'John Stuart Mill and the Welfare State', in G.W. Smith (ed.), *John Stuart Mill's Social and Political Thought*, London and New York: Routledge, pp. 338–54.

Labour Party (1921), *Report of the Twenty-first Annual Conference, held in the Dome, Brighton, London, 1921*, quoted in Walter Van Trier (1995), *Every One a King*, Leuven: Departement Sociologie, Katholieke Universiteit Leuven, pp. 125–7.

Laín, Bru (2019), *Report on the Preliminary Results of the B-MINCOME Project (2017–18): Combining a guaranteed minimum income and active social policies in deprived urban areas of Barcelona*, Ajuntament de Barcelona/Barcelona City Council, accessed 9 January 2021 at https://ajuntament.barcelona.cat/dretssocials/sites/default/files/arxius-documents/results_bmincome_eng.pdf.

Land, Hilary (1975), 'The introduction of Family Allowances: An act of historic justice?', in Phoebe Hall, Hilary Land, Roy Parker and Adrian Webb, *Change, Choice and Conflict in Social Policy*, London: Heinemann, pp. 157–230.

Lansley, Stewart (2016), *A Sharing Economy: How social wealth funds can reduce inequality and help balance the books*, Bristol: Policy Press.

Lansley, Stewart (2019), 'The People's Stake: Basic Income and Citizen's Wealth Funds', in Malcolm Torry (ed.), *The Palgrave International Handbook of Basic Income*, Cham: Palgrave Macmillan, pp. 177–80.

Lansley, Stewart and Joanna Mack (1983), *Breadline Britain*, London: London Weekend Television.

Lansley, Stewart and Joanna Mack (2015), *Breadline Britain: The rise of mass poverty*, London: Oneworld Publications.

Lansley, Stewart, Duncan McCann and Steve Schifferes (2018), *Remodelling Capitalism: How social wealth funds could transform Britain*, London: City University/Friends Provident Foundation.

Lansley, Stewart and Howard Reed (2019), *Basic Income for All: From desirability to feasibility*, London: Compass, accessed 9 January 2021 at http://www.compassonline.org.uk/basic-income-for-all/.

Lapati, Americo D. (1965), *Orestes A. Brownson*, New York: Twayne Publishers Inc.

Lavinas, Lena (2013), 'Brazil: The lost road to Citizen's Income', in Rubén Lo Vuolo (ed.), *Citizen's Income and Welfare Regimes in Latin America*, New York: Palgrave Macmillan, pp. 29–49.

Lawrence, Mathew and Neal Lawson (2017), 'Basic Income: A debate', *Renewal*, **24** (4), 69–79.

Layman, Daniel (2011), 'Locke on Basic Income', *Basic Income Studies*, **6** (2), article 7, 1–12.

Leff, Benjamin (2019), 'The US Earned-Income Tax Credit', in Malcolm Torry (ed.), *The Palgrave International Handbook of Basic Income*, Cham: Palgrave Macmillan, pp. 225–9.

Legein, Thomas, Audrey Vandeleene, Pauline Heyvaert, Julien Perrez and Min Reuchamps (2017), *The Basic Income Debate in Belgium—An experimental study on the framing impact of metaphors on the opinion formation process*, Louvain: University of Louvain, accessed 9 January 2021 at https://dial.uclouvain.be/pr/boreal/object/boreal%3A193660/datastream/PDF_01/view.

Lehto, Otto (2018), *Basic Income Around the World: The unexpected benefits of unconditional cash transfers*, London: Adam Smith Institute, accessed 9 January 2021 at https://www.adamsmith.org/research/basic-income-experiments.

Lehto, Otto (2019), 'Schrödinger's Basic Income: What does the Finnish UBI experiment really show?', London: Adam Smith Institute, accessed 9 January 2021 at https://www.adamsmith.org/blog/schrdingers-basic-income-what-does-the-finnish-ubi-experiment-really-show.

Lerner, Abba P. (1944), *The Economics of Control*, New York: Macmillan.

Lessenich, Stephan (2000), 'Short cuts and wrong tracks on the long march to Basic Income: Debating social policy reform in Germany', in Robert van der Veen and Loek Groot (eds), *Basic Income on the Agenda: Policy objectives and political chances*, Amsterdam: Amsterdam University Press, pp. 247–56.

Levy, Horacio, Manos Matsaganis and Holly Sutherland (2013), 'Towards a European Union Child Basic Income? Within and between country effects', EUROMOD Working Paper EM6/13, Colchester: Institute for Social and Economic Research, University of Essex, accessed 9 January 2021 at http://www.iser.essex.ac.uk/research/publications/working-papers/euromod/em6-13.

Lewis, Judy L. (2020), 'The USA's modern Civil Rights Movement and Basic Income Guarantee', in Richard Caputo and Larry Liu (eds), *Political Activism and Basic Income Guarantee*, Cham: Palgrave Macmillan, pp. 115–37.

Ley, Henry W. (1888), *Land Nationalisation: Who shows the way? Henry George, Thomas Spence, Thomas Paine, or Alfred Russel Wallace?* London: W. Reeves.

Liebermann, Sascha (2012), 'Germany: Basic Income in the German debate', in Matthew C. Murray and Carole Pateman (eds), *Basic Income Worldwide: Horizons of reform*, Basingstoke and New York: Palgrave Macmillan, pp. 173–99.

Liebermann, Sascha (2020), 'From marginal idea to contested alternative: Recent developments and main arguments in the German debate', in Richard Caputo and Larry Liu (eds), *Political Activism and Basic Income Guarantee*, Cham: Palgrave Macmillan, pp. 209–27.

Linares, Julio (2020), correspondence with the author.

Lipsky, Michael (1980), *Street-level Bureaucracy: Dilemmas of the individual in public services*, New York: Russell Sage Foundation.

Lister, Ruth (2017), 'Coming off the fence on UBI?', London: Compass, accessed 9 January 2021 at https://www.compassonline.org.uk/universal-basic-income-coming-off-the-fence/.

Liu, Larry (2020), 'Universal Basic Income activism in Switzerland and Austria', in Richard Caputo and Larry Liu (eds), *Political Activism and Basic Income Guarantee*, Cham: Palgrave Macmillan, pp. 229–51.

Liu, Larry and Vivekananda Nemana (2020), 'From trials to election promises: The politics of Basic Income in India', in Richard Caputo and Larry Liu (eds), *Political Activism and Basic Income Guarantee*, Cham: Palgrave Macmillan, pp. 273–93.

Locke, John (1884), *Two Treatises on Civil Government*, London: George Routledge and Sons, first published in 1690.

Locke, John (1997), 'An essay on the Poor Law', in Mark Goldie (ed.), *Locke: Political Essays*, Cambridge: Cambridge University Press, pp. 182–98, first published in 1697.

Long, Huey (1934), 'Share our wealth: Every man a king', radio broadcast transcript, accessed 9 January 2021 at https://www.senate.gov/artandhistory/history/common/generic/Speeches_Long_EveryManKing.htm.

Long, Huey (1935), 'Statement of the Share Our Wealth movement', accessed 9 January 2021 at http://web.mit.edu/21h.102/www/Primary%20source%20collections/The%20New%20Deal/Long,%20Share%20Our%20Wealth.htm.

Lord, Clive (1993), *A Guide to the Green Party's Basic Income Scheme*, Batley: Clive Lord.

Lo Vuolo, Rubén (ed.) (1995), *Contra la Exclusión: La propuesta del ingreso ciudadano*, Buenos Aires: Miño y Dávila editors.

Lo Vuolo, Rubén M. (2002), 'The Basic Income debate in the context of a systemic crisis: The case of Argentina', paper presented at the 2002 BIEN Congress in Geneva, accessed 9 January 2021 at https://basicincome.org/bien/pdf/2002LoVuolo.pdf.

Lo Vuolo, Rubén (ed.) (2013a), *Citizen's Income and Welfare Regimes in Latin America*, New York: Palgrave Macmillan.

Lo Vuolo, Rubén (2013b), 'The Argentine "Universal Child Allowance": Not the poor but the unemployed and informal workers', in Rubén Lo Vuolo (ed.), *Citizen's Income and Welfare Regimes in Latin America*, New York: Palgrave Macmillan, pp. 51–66.

Lo Vuolo, Rubén (2020), correspondence with the author.

Luccioni, Loriana (2020), 'UBI activism and advocacy in Australia: The present', in Richard Caputo and Larry Liu (eds), *Political Activism and Basic Income Guarantee*, Cham: Palgrave Macmillan, pp. 163–84.

Lund, Francie (2011), 'A step in the wrong direction: Linking the South Africa Child Support Grant to school attendance', *Journal of Poverty and Social Justice*, **19** (1), 5–14.

Mackenzie, John, Siobhan Mathers, Geoff Mawdsley and Alison Payne (2016), *The Basic Income Guarantee*, Edinburgh: Reform Scotland, accessed 9 January 2021 at https://reformscotland.com/wp-content/uploads/2016/02/The-Basic-Income-Guarantee-1.pdf.

Macnicol, John (1980), *The Movement for Family Allowances, 1918–1945: A study in social policy development*, London: Heinemann.

Mani, Anandi, Sendhil Mullainathan, Eldar Shafir and Jiyaing Zhao (2013), 'Poverty impedes cognitive function', *Science*, **341** (6149), 976–80.

Martinelli, Luke (2017a), *The Fiscal and Distributional Implications of Alternative Universal Basic Income Schemes in the UK*, Bath: Institute for Policy Research, accessed 9 January 2021 at http://www.bath.ac.uk/ipr/policy-briefs/working-papers/

the-fiscal-and-distributional-implications-of-alternative-universal-basic-income
-schemes-in-the-uk.html.

Martinelli, Luke (2017b), *Exploring the Distributional and Work Incentive Effects of Plausible Illustrative Basic Income Schemes*, Bath: Institute for Policy Research, accessed 9 January 2021 at http://www.bath.ac.uk/ipr/publications/reports/work -incentive-effects-on-basic-income.html.

Martinelli, Luke (2017c), *Assessing the Case for a Universal Basic Income in the UK*, Bath: Institute for Policy Research, accessed 9 January 2021 at http://www.bath.ac .uk/publications/assessing-the-case-for-a-universal-basic-income-in-the-uk/.

Martinez Lopez, Miguel A. and Elena Domingo San Juan (2014), 'Social and political impacts of the 15M movement in Spain', accessed 6 January 2021 at https://www .miguelangelmartinez.net/?Social-and-political-impacts-of.

Marx, Karl (1970), *Critique of the Gotha Programme*, Moscow: Progress Publishers, first published in 1891, accessed 9 January 2021 at https://www.marxists.org/ archive/marx/works/1875/gotha/.

Mason, Paul (2020), 'Pablo Iglesias on Spain's plan to introduce a basic income to fight the economic crisis', *New Statesman*, 9 April 2020, accessed 9 January 2021 at https://www.newstatesman.com/world/europe/2020/04/pablo-iglesias-spains-plan -introduce-basic-income-fight-economic-crisis.

Masquelier, Charles (2019), 'French Left-libertarianism and Benoît Hamon's socialist vision', *Hard Times*, **103** (1), 45–54, accessed 18 January 2021 at https://hard-times -magazine.org/index.php/Hardtimes/article/view/51/43.

Mathews, Cheyenne (2020), 'Permanent fund Dividend amount announced at $992', *KTUU*, 12 June 2020, accessed 11 January 2021 at https://www.alaskasnewssource .com/content/news/Permanent-Fund-Dividend-amount-announced-571226441.html #.

Matsaganis, Manos and Chrysa Leventi (2011), 'Pathways to a Universal Basic Pension in Greece', *Basic Income Studies*, **6** (1), 1–20.

Mays, Jennifer, Greg Marston and John Tomlinson (2016), 'Neoliberal frontiers and economic insecurity: Is Basic Income a solution?', in Jennifer Mays, Greg Marston and John Tomlinson (eds), *Basic Income in Australia and New Zealand: Perspectives from the neoliberal frontier*, Basingstoke: Palgrave Macmillan, pp. 1–25.

McFarland, Kate (2016), 'Glasgow, Scotland: Citizen's Basic Income Network Scotland launch event (Nov 26)', London: Basic Income Earth Network, accessed 9 January 2021 at https://basicincome.org/news/2016/11/glasgow-scotland-citizens -basic-income-network-scotland-launch-event-nov-26/.

McGovern, George (1972), 'George McGovern: On taxing and redistributing income', with an introduction by Wassily Leontief, *New York Review of Books*, accessed 9 January 2021 at https://www.nybooks.com/articles/1972/05/04/george-mcgovern -on-taxing-redistributing-income/.

McKay, Ailsa (2005), *The Future of Social Security Policy: Women, work and a Citizen's Basic Income*, Abingdon: Routledge.

McKnight, Abigail, Magali Duque and Mark Rucci (2016), *Creating More Equal Societies: What works? Evidence review*, Brussels: European Commission, accessed 9 January 2021 at https://op.europa.eu/en/publication-detail/-/publication/0a351db5 -e6b9-11e6-ad7c-01aa75ed71a1/language-en.

Mead, Lawrence (1992), *The New Politics of Poverty: The non-working poor in America*, New York: Harper Collins.

Meade, J.E. (1938), *An Introduction to Economic Analysis and Policy*, Oxford: Oxford University Press, first published in 1936.

Meade, J.E. (1945), 'Mr. Lerner on "The Economics of Control"', *Economic Journal*, **55** (217), 47–69.

Meade, J.E. (1948), *Planning and the Price Mechanism: The Liberal-Socialist solution*, London: George Allen and Unwin.

Meade, James (1964), *Equality and the Ownership of Property*, London: George Allen and Unwin.

Meade, J.E. (1971), *The Controlled Economy*, London: George Allen and Unwin.

Meade, J.E. (1972), *Poverty in the Welfare State*, Oxford Economic Papers, **24** (3), Oxford: Clarendon Press.

Meade, J.E. (1975), *The Intelligent Radical's Guide to Economic Policy: The mixed economy*, London: George Allen and Unwin.

Meade, J.E. (1984), 'Full employment, new technologies and the distribution of income', *Journal of Social Policy*, **13** (2), 129–46.

Meade, J. E. (1989), *Agathotopia: The economics of partnership*, Aberdeen: Aberdeen University Press for the David Hume Institute.

Meade, James (1990), 'Topsy-turvy nationalisation', *Samizdat no. 5* (July/August 1989), reprinted in *BIRG Bulletin*, no. 10, Autumn/Winter 1990, pp. 3–4.

Meade, J.E. (1991), *The Building of the New Europe: National diversity versus continental uniformity*. Edinburgh: The David Hume Institute.

Meade, J.E. (1995), *Full Employment Regained? An Agathotopian dream*, University of Cambridge Department of Applied Economics, Occasional Paper no. 61, Cambridge: Cambridge University Press.

Meade, James (2016), 'Outline of economic policy for a Labour Government', in Susan Howson (ed.), *The Collected Papers of James Meade*, vol. 1, 'Employment and Inflation', London: Routledge, pp. 33–78, first published in 1935.

Mehta, Vanya (2019), *The Great Indian Basic Income Debate*, Hyderabad: India Network for Basic Income.

Mein Grundeinkommen (2020), 'Pilot project Grundeinkommen: How does a Basic Income change our society?', accessed 9 January 2021 at https://www.pilotprojekt -grundeinkommen.de/english.

Meireis, Torsten (2004), '"Calling": A Christian argument for Basic Income', in Guy Standing (ed.), *Promoting Income Security as a Right: Europe and North America*, London: Anthem Press, pp. 145–61.

Mermelstein, Daniel (2019), 'Basic Income and cryptocurrency', London: Citizen's Basic Income Trust, accessed 9 January 2021 at https://citizensincome.org/opinion/ basic-income-and-cryptocurrency/.

Mexico City (2017), 'Mexico City Constitution Project', unpublished paper.

Meyer, Niels I. (1988), 'Gradual implementation of a Basic Income in Denmark', in Anne Miller (ed.), *First International Conference on Basic Income: Proceedings, 1986*, Antwerp: Basic Income European Network, pp. 223–7.

Mill, John Stuart (1924), *Autobiography of John Stuart Mill*, New York: Columbia University Press, first published in 1873.

Mill, John Stuart (1965), *Chapters on Socialism*, in *Collected Works of John Stuart Mill*, edited by J.M. Robson, volume V, Toronto and London: University of Toronto Press and Routledge and Kegan Paul, first published in 1879.

Mill, John Stuart (1965), *Principles of Political Economy with Some of their Applications to Social Philosophy*, in *Collected Works of John Stuart Mill*, edited by J.M. Robson, volume II, Toronto and London: University of Toronto Press and Routledge and Kegan Paul, first published in 1848.

Mill, John Stuart (2001), *Utilitarianism*, second edition, edited by George Sher, Indianapolis: Hackett Publishing Company, Inc., first published in 1861.

Miller, Anne (1983), *In Praise of Social Dividends*, Edinburgh: Heriot-Watt University.

Miller, Anne (ed.) (1988), *First International Conference on Basic Income: Proceedings, 1986*, Antwerp: Basic Income European Network.

Miller, Annie (2017), *A Basic Income Handbook*. Edinburgh: Luath Press.

Miller, Annie (2019), 'Why Scotland?', in Malcolm Torry (ed.), *The Palgrave International Handbook of Basic Income*, Cham: Palgrave Macmillan, pp. 425–8.

Miller, Annie, Toru Yamamori and Almaz Zelleke (2019), 'The gender effects of a Basic Income', in Malcolm Torry (ed.), *The Palgrave International Handbook of Basic Income*, Cham: Palgrave Macmillan, pp. 133–53.

Milner, Dennis (1920), *Higher Production by a Bonus on National Output: A proposal for a minimum income for all varying with national productivity*, London: George Allen and Unwin.

Milner, E. Mabel and Dennis Milner (1918), *Scheme for a State Bonus*, Darlington: North of England Newspaper Co. Ltd.

Milner, E. Mabel and Dennis Milner (1920), *Labour and a Minimum Income for All*, Darlington: Echo Printing Works, for the Minimum Income League, London.

Minford, Patrick (2002), '"Basic Income" that could prove an escape route from the benefits trap', *Daily Telegraph*, 13 May 2002.

Minister of Supply and Services (1985), *Report of the Royal Commission on the Economic Union and Development Prospects for Canada*, chapter 19, 'The Income-Security System', Canada: Canadian Government Publishing Centre, accessed 4 February 2021 at http://publications.gc.ca/collections/collection_2014/bcp-pco/Z1-1983-1-2-6-eng.pdf.

Ministry of Social Affairs and Health (2016), 'Legislative proposal on basic income experiment submitted to Parliament', accessed 9 January 2021 at https://stm.fi/en/-/lakiehdotus-perustulokokeilusta-eduskunnan-kasiteltavaksi.

Mirowski, Philip and Dieter Plehwe (2015), *The Road from Mont Pelerin: The making of the neoliberal thought collective*, Cambridge, MA: Harvard University Press.

Mitschke, Joachim (2000), 'Arguing for a Negative Income Tax', in Robert van der Veen and Loek Groot (eds), *Basic Income on the Agenda: Policy objectives and political chances*, Amsterdam: Amsterdam University Press, pp. 107–20.

More, Thomas (1995), *Utopia*, edited by George Logan et al., Cambridge: Cambridge University Press, first published in 1516.

Morgan, Gareth (2016), 'Some typical household effects of a Citizen's Income scheme', *Citizen's Income Newsletter*, Issue 3 for 2016, p. 7.

Morley, Kate Rose (2020), 'Historical UK inflation rates and calculator', accessed 9 January 2021 at http://inflation.iamkate.com/.

Mullainathan, Sendhil and Eldar Shafir (2013), *Scarcity: Why having too little means so much*, London: Macmillan.

Müller, Christian and Daniel Straub (eds) (2012), *Die Befreiung der Schweiz: Über das bedingungslose Grundeinkommen*, Zürich: Limmat Verlag.

Munger, Michael (2011), 'Basic Income is not an obligation, but it might be a legitimate choice', *Basic Income Studies*, **6** (2), 1–13.

Murray, Charles (1984), *Losing Ground: American social policy, 1950–1980*, New York: Basic Books.

Murray, Charles (1994), *Underclass: The crisis deepens*, London: Institute of Economic Affairs.

Murray, Charles (1996), *Charles Murray and the Underclass: The developing debate*, London: Institute of Economic Affairs (contains 'The Emerging British Underclass', first published in 1989, and 'Underclass: The Crisis Deepens', first published in 1994).

Murray, Charles (2006), *In Our Hands: A plan to replace the welfare state*, Washington, DC: AEI Press.

Murray, Charles (2008), 'Guaranteed Income as a replacement for the Welfare State', *Basic Income Studies*, **3** (2), 1–12.

Nam, Jaehyun and Hyungjohn Park (2020), 'The 2015 welfare reform of the National Basic Livelihood Security System in South Korea: Effects on economic outcomes', *International Journal of Social Welfare*, **29**, 219–32.

National Assembly of the Republic of Korea (2020), 'A bill on the establishment and operation of the Basic Income Public Debate Committee', accessed 2 January 2021 at http://likms.assembly.go.kr/bill/billDetail.do?billId=PRC_V2Q0A1V2Q1 W4M1H3X3M6U2P7V0C2I6.

National Association of Pension Funds (2002), *Pensions—Plain and Simple*, London: National Association of Pension Funds.

Navas, Jose A. (2014), 'Las propuestas de Podemos: Crear un salario máximo, renta básica universal y jubilación a los 60 años', *El Mundo*, 26 May 2014, accessed 6 January 2021 at https://www.elmundo.es/espana/2014/05/26/53830a6c268e3e 28488b456c.html.

News1 (2020), 'Yong Hye-in initiates the Basic Income Public Debate Act … 21 members of the opposition party', accessed 2 January 2021 at https://www.news1 .kr/articles/?4157773.

New York Times (1978), 'Moynihan says recent studies raise doubts about "Negative Income Tax" Proposals', *New York Times*, 16 November 1978, accessed 5 August 2020 at https://www.nytimes.com/1978/11/16/archives/moynihan-says-recent -studies-raise-doubts-about-negative-income-tax.html.

Noguera, José A. (2018), 'The political debate on Basic Income and welfare reform in Spain', *Social Policy and Society*, **18** (2), 289–99.

O'Brien, J. Patrick and Dennis O. Olson (1991), 'The Alaska Permanent Fund and Dividend Distribution Program', *BIRG Bulletin*, no. 12, February 1991, pp. 3–6.

O'Connell, Alison (2004), *Citizen's Pension: Lessons from New Zealand*, London: Pensions Policy Institute, accessed 9 January 2021 at https://www.pensionspolic yinstitute.org.uk/media/2283/20040310-ppi-cp-lessons-from-new-zealand.pdf.

OECD (2017), 'Basic income as a policy option: Can it add up?', Policy Brief on the Future of Work, Paris: OECD Publishing, accessed 7 January 2021 at https://www .oecd.org/els/emp/Basic-Income-Policy-Option-2017.pdf.

OECD (2019), *OECD Employment Outlook 2019: The future of work*, Paris: OECD Publishing, accessed 9 January 2021 at https://doi.org/10.1787/9ee00155-en.

Offe, Claus (1992), 'A non-productivist design for social policies', in Philippe Van Parijs (ed.), *Arguing for Basic Income: Ethical foundations for a radical reform*, London: Verso, pp. 61–78.

Offe, Claus (2000), 'A Basic Income for all: Pathways from here', *Boston Review*, 1 October 2000, accessed 2 January 2021 at http://bostonreview.net/forum/basic -income-all/claus-offe-pathways-here.

O'Neal, Adam (2019), 'Italy institutes a Universal Basic Income. Is the U.S. next?', *Wall Street Journal*, 27 February 2019, accessed 26 January 2021 at https:// www.wsj.com/articles/italy-institutes-a-universal-basic-income-is-the-u-s-next -11551313085.

Ontario (2018), 'Ontario's Government for the People announces compassionate wind down of Basic Income Research Project', accessed 9 January 2021 at https:// news.ontario.ca/mcys/en/2018/08/ontarios-government-for-the-people-announces -compassionate-wind-down-of-basic-income-research-projec.html.

Ontario (2019), 'Archived—Ontario Basic Income Pilot', accessed 9 January 2021 at https://www.ontario.ca/page/ontario-basic-income-pilot.

Ontario (no date), 'Ontario's Basic Income Pilot: Studying the impact of a basic income', accessed 9 January 2021 at https://files.ontario.ca/170508_bi_brochure _eng_pg_by_pg_proof.pdf.

Orton, Ian (2009), 'The Citizen's Income and child labour: Two ships passing at night', *Citizen's Income Newsletter*, issue 1 for 2009, pp. 6–9.

Orton, Ian (2011), 'The International Labour Organisation's analysis of social transfers worldwide augurs well for a Citizen's Income in the context of middle and low-income countries', *Citizen's Income Newsletter*, issue 2 for 2011, pp. 4–8.

Osterkamp, Rigmar (2013a), 'Lessons from failure', *D+C: Development and Cooperation*, accessed 9 January 2021 at https://www.dandc.eu/en/article/ disappointing-basic-income-grant-project-namibia.

Osterkamp, Rigmar (2013b), 'The Basic Income Grant Pilot Project in Namibia: A critical assessment', *Basic Income Studies*, **8** (1), 71–90.

Paine, Thomas (1797), *Agrarian Justice opposed to Agrarian Law and to Agrarian Monopoly, being a plan for meliorating the condition of man ... etc.* (in the copy consulted the publisher's name and address had been covered by a press cutting).

Paine, Thomas (2006), *The Rights of Man*, Teddington: The Echo Library, first published in 1792.

Painter, Anthony and Chris Thoung (2015), *Report: Creative Citizen, Creative State—The principled and pragmatic case for a Universal Basic Income*, London: Royal Society of Arts, accessed 9 January 2021 at https://www.thersa.org/discover/ publications-and-articles/reports/basic-income (a review of the report can be found in *Citizen's Income Newsletter*, issue 2 for 2016, pp. 20–21).

Papadopoulos, Theodorus and Ricardo Velázquez Leyer (2016), 'Introduction: Assessing the effects of conditional cash transfers in Latin American societies in the early twenty-first century', *Social Policy and Society*, **15** (3), 417–20.

Parker, Hermione (1982), *The Moral Hazard of Social Benefits: A study of the impact of social benefits and income tax on incentives to work*, London: Institute of Economic Affairs.

Parker, Hermione (1985), 'Costing Basic Incomes', *BIRG Bulletin*, no. 3, Spring 1985, pp. 4–15.

Parker, Hermione (1988), 'Are Basic Incomes feasible?', *BIRG Bulletin*, no. 7, Spring 1988, pp. 5–7.

Parker, Hermione (1989), *Instead of the Dole: An enquiry into integration of the tax and benefit systems*, London: Routledge.

Parker, Hermione (1990), 'How to get a BI system in the UK: A personal viewpoint', in Walter Van Trier (ed.), *Second International Conference on Basic Income: Basic Incomes and problems of implementation*, Antwerp: Basic Income European Network, pp. 3–24.

Parker, Hermione (1991), *Basic Income and the Labour Market*, London: Basic Income Research Group.

Parker, Hermione (1993), *Citizen's Income and Women*, London: Citizen's Income Trust.

Parker, Hermione (1994), 'Citizen's Income', *Citizen's Income Bulletin*, no. 17, January 1994, pp. 4–12.

Parker, Hermione (1995), *Taxes, Benefits and Family Life: The seven deadly traps*, London: Institute of Economic Affairs.

Parker, Hermione and Andrew Dilnot (1988), 'Administration of integrated tax/benefit systems', *BIRG Bulletin*, no. 8, Autumn 1988, pp. 6–10.

Parker, Hermione and Holly Sutherland (1988), 'How to get rid of the poverty trap: Basic Income plus National Minimum Wage', *Citizen's Income Bulletin*, no. 25, February 1988, pp. 11–14.

Parker, Hermione and Holly Sutherland (1991), 'Child Benefit, Child Tax Allowances and Basic Incomes: A comparative study', *BIRG Bulletin*, no. 13, August 1991, pp. 6–13.

Parker, Hermione and Holly Sutherland (1994), 'Basic Income 1994: Redistributive effects of Transitional BIs', *Citizen's Income Bulletin*, issue 18, July 1994, pp. 3–8.

Parker, Hermione and Holly Sutherland (1995), 'Why a £20 CI is better than lowering Income Tax to 20%', *Citizen's Income Bulletin*, no. 19, February 1995, pp. 15–18.

Parker, Hermione and Holly Sutherland (1996), 'Earnings Top-up or Basic Income and a Minimum Wage', *Citizen's Income Bulletin*, no. 21, February 1996, pp. 5–8.

Parker, Hermione and Holly Sutherland (no date), *Child Tax Allowances? A Comparison of Child Benefit, Child Tax Reliefs, and Basic Incomes as Instruments of Family Policy*, London: Suntory-Toyota International Centre for Economics and Related Disciplines, London School of Economics and Political Science.

Pasma, Chandra and Jim Mulvale (2014), *Income Security for All Canadians: Understanding Guaranteed Income*, Legislative Assembly of the Northwest Territories/BIEN Canada, accessed 4 February 2021 at https://www.ntassembly.ca/sites/assembly/files/td_63-175.pdf and https://www.ntassembly.ca/sites/assembly/files/td_63-175.pdf.

Pateman, Carole (2003), 'Freedom and democratization: Why Basic Income is to be preferred to Basic Capital', in Keith Dowding, Jurgen De Wispelaere and Stuart White (eds), *The Ethics of Stakeholding*, Basingstoke: Palgrave Macmillan, pp. 130–48.

Penny, Laurie (2016), 'What might society look like with Universal Basic Income', *New Statesman*, 15 April 2016, accessed 9 January 2021 at https://www.newstatesman.com/politics/economy/2016/04/what-would-society-look-universal-basic-income.

Percy, Andrew (2019), 'Universal Basic Services', in Malcolm Torry (ed.), *The Palgrave International Handbook of Basic Income*, Cham: Palgrave Macmillan, pp. 219–22.

Pereira, Richard (ed.) (2017), *Financing Basic Income: Addressing the cost objection*, Cham: Palgrave Macmillan.

Piachaud, David (2016), *Citizen's Income: Rights and wrongs*, London: Centre for Analysis of Social Exclusion, London School of Economics, accessed 9 January 2021 at http://sticerd.lse.ac.uk/dps/case/cp/casepaper200.pdf.

Pickard, Bertram (1919), *A Reasonable Revolution: Being a discussion of the State Bonus Scheme—a proposal for a national minimum income*, London: George Allen and Unwin.

Pigden, Charles R. (2003), 'Bertrand Russell: Moral philosopher or unphilosophical moralist?', in Nicholas Griffin (ed.), *The Cambridge Companion to Bertrand Russell*, Cambridge: Cambridge University Press, pp. 475–506.

Piketty, Thomas (2014), *Capital in the Twenty-first Century*, Cambridge, MA: The Belknap Press of Harvard University Press.

Piketty, Thomas (2020), *Capital and Ideology*, Cambridge, MA: The Belknap Press of Harvard University Press.

Pitts, Frederick Harry, Lorena Lomardozzi and Neil Warner (2017), 'Speenhamland, automation and the basic income: A warning from history?', *Renewal*, **25** (3–4), 145–55.

Preiss, Joshua (2015), 'Milton Friedman on freedom and the Negative Income Tax', *Basic Income Studies*, **10** (2), 169–91.

Preston, Ronald (1992), 'A Christian slant on Basic Income', *BIRG Bulletin*, no. 15, July 1992, pp. 8–9, London: Basic Income Research Group, accessed 9 January 2021 at https://citizensincome.org/wp-content/uploads/2016/03/1992-Bulletin-15-July.pdf.

Price, R. Arnold (1920), *Economic Basis for an Ethical Solution of the Social Problem*, London: Watts and Co.

Psychologists for Social Change (2017), *Universal Basic Income: A psychological impact assessment*, London: Psychologists Against Austerity, accessed 9 January 2021 at http://www.psychchange.org/basic-income-psychological-impact-assessment.html.

Purdy, David (1990), 'The political feasibility of the transition to a Basic Income society', in Walter Van Trier (ed.), *Second International Conference on Basic Income: Basic Incomes and problems of implementation*, Antwerp: Basic Income European Network, pp. 45–64.

Quilley, Stephen (1994), 'What's Left? Citizen's Income and Thomas Paine (1737–1809)', *Citizen's Income Bulletin*, no. 17, January 1994, pp. 2–4.

Radio JGM (2020), 'Nueva constitución con perspectiva de género', accessed 1 January 2021 at https://radiojgm.uchile.cl/wp-content/uploads/2020/10/Nueva-Constitucion-Perspectiva-de-Genero.pdf.

Rae, Gilbert (1963), *Automated Incomes can End Unemployment*, London: Phelp Brothers and Weir.

Rankin, Keith (2012), 'New Zealand: Prospects for Basic Income reform', in Matthew C. Murray and Carole Pateman (eds), *Basic Income Worldwide: Horizons of reform*, Basingstoke and New York: Palgrave Macmillan, pp. 200–226.

Rathbone, Eleanor (1940), *The Case for Family Allowances*, Harmondsworth: Penguin.

Rathbone, Eleanor (1986), *The Disinherited Family*, Bristol: Falling Wall Press, first published in 1924.

Rawls, John (1971), *A Theory of Justice*, Cambridge, MA: The Belknap Press of Harvard University Press.

Reed, Howard and Stewart Lansley (2016), *Universal Basic Income: An idea whose time has come?*, London: Compass, accessed 9 January 2021 at http://www.compassonline.org.uk/publications/universal-basic-income-an-idea-whose-time-has-come/.

Reynolds, Brigid, S.M. and Seán Healy, S.M.A. (eds) (1994), *Towards an Adequate Income for All*, Dublin: Conference of Religious of Ireland.

Reynolds, Brigid, S.M. and Seán Healy, S.M.A. (eds) (1995), *An Adequate Income Guarantee for All: Desirability, viability, impact*, Dublin: Conference of Religious of Ireland.

Reynolds, Brigid, S.M. and Seán Healy, S.M.A. (eds) (2016), *Basic Income: Radical utopia or practical solution?*, Dublin: Social Justice Ireland.

Rhys Williams, Brandon (1967), *The New Social Contract*, London: Conservative Political Centre.

Rhys Williams, Brandon (1972), *From Status to Contract in Social Reform*, London: Brandon Rhys Williams.

Rhys Williams, Brandon (1989), *Stepping Stones to Independence: National Insurance after 1990*, Aberdeen: Aberdeen University Press.

Rhys Williams, Juliet (1943), *Something to Look Forward To: A suggestion for a new social contract*, London: MacDonald and Co.

Rhys Williams, Juliet (1953), *Taxation and Incentives*, London: William Hodge and Co.

Richardt, Johannes (2011), 'Basic Income, low aspiration', *The Sp!ked Review of Books*, issue 41, January 2011, accessed 9 January 2021 at https://www.spiked -online.com/2011/01/28/basic-income-low-aspiration/.

Rincón, Leire (2020a), 'Living Minimum Income in Spain: Very far from a UBI', London: Basic Income Earth Network, accessed 9 January 2021 at https://basicincome .org/news/2020/06/living-minimum-income-in-spain-very-far-from-a-ubi/.

Rincón, Leire (2020b), correspondence with the author.

Roberts, Carys and Mathew Lawrence (2018), *Our Common Wealth: A citizen's wealth fund for the UK*, London: Institute for Public Policy Research.

Roberts, Keith (1983), *Automation, Unemployment and the Distribution of Income*, Maastricht: European Centre for Work and Society.

Roca, Emilio (2010), [no title], in *Asignación Universal por Hijo*, Buenos Aires: Asociacion Argentina de Politicas Sociales, pp. 17–20.

Rocha, Thiago Santos (2020), 'Maricá one step from Universal Basic Income', London: Basic Income Earth Network, accessed 9 January 2021 at https://basicincome.org/ news/2020/06/marica-one-step-from-universal-basic-income/.

Rolls, James (2018), 'State of the pilot projects for CBI', *Citizen's Income Newsletter*, Issue 4 for 2018, pp. 5–11.

Rose, Dave and Charles Wohlforth (2008), *Saving for the Future: My life and the Alaska Permanent Fund*, Kenmore, WA: Epicenter Press.

Rothstein, Bo (2018), 'UBI: A bad idea for the welfare state', in Philippe Van Parijs (ed.), *Basic Income and the Left: A European debate*, Berlin: Social Europe, pp. 103–9.

Rudkin, Oliver D. (1927), *Thomas Spence and his Connections*, London: George Allen and Unwin.

Russell, Bertie and Keir Milburn (2018), 'What can an institution do? Towards public-common partnerships and a new common-sense', *Renewal*, **26** (4), 45–55.

Russell, Bertrand (1996), 'In praise of idleness', in Bertrand Russell, *In Praise of Idleness and Other Essays*, Abingdon: Routledge, pp. 1–16, first published in 1935.

Russell, Bertrand (2006), *Roads to Freedom*, Nottingham: Spokesman, first published in 1918.

Russell, Bertrand (2012), *Political Ideals*, New York: Start Publishing, first published in 1917.

Ryan, Alan (1987), *The Philosophy of John Stuart Mill*, second edition, Basingstoke: Macmillan.

Ryan, Anne B. and John Baker (2012), 'Reflections on Developing a National Campaign for Basic Income in Ireland', paper presented at the Basic Income Earth Network Congress held in Munich in September 2012, accessed 9 January 2021 at https://basicincome.org/bien/pdf/munich2012/Ryan_Baker.pdf.

Ryan, Richard M. and Edward L. Deci (2000), 'Self-determination theory and the facilitation of intrinsic motivation, social development, and well-being', *American Psychologist*, **55** (1), 68–78.

Ryan, Thomas R. (1976), *Orestes A. Brownson: A definitive biography*, Noll Plaza, NT: Our Sunday Visitor.

Saconi, Stefano (1992), 'An outline of the debate in Italy on the hypothesis of a Basic Income', unpublished paper.

Sager, Lutz (2017), *Income Inequality and Carbon Consumption: Evidence from environmental Engel curves*, London: Grantham Research Institute on Climate Change and the Environment, London School of Economics, accessed 9 January 2021 at https://www.lse.ac.uk/granthaminstitute/publication/income-inequality-and-carbon-consumption-evidence-from-environmental-engel-curves/.

Salehi-Isfahani, Djavad (2014), *Iran's Subsidy Reform: From promise to disappointment*, Policy Perspective no. 13, Egypt: Economic Research Forum, accessed 9 January 2021 at https://erf.org.eg/publications/irans-subsidy-reform-from-promise-to-disappointment/.

Salehi-Isfahani, Djavad and Mohammad H. Mostafavi-Dehzooei (2017), *Cash Transfers and Labor Supply: Evidence from a large-scale program in Iran*, Economic Research Forum Working Paper 1090, accessed 9 January 2021 at https://erf.org.eg/publications/cash-transfers-and-labor-supply-evidence-from-a-large-scale-program-in-iran/.

Salter, Tony (1997), 'Being realistic about pensions reform', *Citizen's Income Bulletin*, no. 24, July 1997, pp. 9–11.

Salter, Tony, Andrew Bryans, Colin Redman and Martin Hewitt (2009), *100 Years of State Pension: Learning from the past*, London: Institute of Actuaries.

Schachtschneider, Ulrich (2020), correspondence with the author.

Schmidt, Enno (2019), 'The Swiss referendum about Basic Income', in Malcolm Torry (ed.), *The Palgrave International Handbook of Basic Income*, Cham: Palgrave Macmillan, pp. 428–31.

Schmidt, Enno (2020), correspondence with the author.

Schmidt, Enno and Daniel Häni (2008), 'Grundeinkommen—Ein Kulturimpuls', film, accessed 9 January 2021 at http://grundeinkommen.tv/grundeinkommen-ein-kulturimpuls-2/.

Scottish Parliament (2017), *Official Report: Social security committee 09 March 2017*, accessed 9 January 2021 at http://www.parliament.scot/parliamentarybusiness/report.aspx?r=10836.

Seekings, Jeremy (2020), 'Basic Income activism in South Africa, 1997–2019', in Richard Caputo and Larry Liu (eds), *Political Activism and Basic Income Guarantee*, Cham: Palgrave Macmillan, pp. 253–72.

Seekings, Jeremy and Heidi Matisonn (2012), 'South Africa: The continuing politics of Basic Income', in Matthew C. Murray and Carole Pateman (eds), *Basic Income Worldwide: Horizons of reform*, Basingstoke and New York: Palgrave Macmillan, pp. 128–50.

Sewa Bharat (2012), *An Experimental Pilot Cash Transfer Study in Delhi: Final report*, Sewa Bharat, accessed 8 January 2021 at https://sewabharat.org/wp-content/uploads/2016/01/Final-Report-DCT.pdf.

Sewa Bharat (2015), *Madhya Pradesh Unconditional Cash Transfer Project: Executive summary*, Sewa Bharat, accessed 8 January 2021 at https://sewabharat.org/wp-content/uploads/2015/07/Executive-summary.pdf.

Sheahen, Allan (1983), *Guaranteed Income: The right to economic security*, Los Angeles: GAIN Publications.

Sheahen, Allan (2012), *Basic Income Guarantee: Your right to economic security*, New York: Palgrave Macmillan.

Sherman, Barrie and Phil Judkins (1996), 'Labour market effects of CI: A trade union standpoint', *Citizen's Income Bulletin*, no. 21, February 1996, pp. 2–4.

Shutt, Harry (2010), *Beyond the Profits System: Possibilities for a post-capitalist era*, London and New York: Zed Books.

Silva, Maria Ozanira da Silva e and Valéria Ferreira Santos de Almada Lima (2019), 'Citizen's Basic Income in Brazil: From *Bolsa Família* to pilot experiments', in Malcolm Torry (ed.), *The Palgrave International Handbook of Basic Income*, Cham: Palgrave Macmillan, pp. 319–39.

Skidmore, Thomas (1829), *The Rights of Man to Property! Being a proposition to make it equal among the adults of the present generation: and to provide for its equal transmission to every individual of each succeeding generation, on arriving at maturity*, New York: Alexander Ming.

Skorupski, John (1989), *John Stuart Mill*, London and New York: Routledge.

Sloman, Peter (2019), *Transfer State: The idea of guaranteed income and the politics of redistribution in modern Britain*, Oxford: Oxford University Press.

Sloman, Peter (2020), correspondence with the author.

Smith-Carrier, Tracy A. and Steven Green (2017), 'Another low road to Basic Income? Mapping a pragmatic model for adopting a Basic Income in Canada', *Basic Income Studies*, **12** (2), accessed 9 January 2021 at https://doi.org/10.1515/bis-2016-0020.

Social Justice Ireland (2002), *Basic Income: A green paper*, Dublin: Social Justice Ireland, accessed 9 January 2021 at https://www.socialjustice.ie/sites/default/files/attach/policy-issue-article/3304/16601.pdf.

Soininvaara, Osmo (2017), 'Why the tested Basic Income model is not the right one', blog, accessed 9 January 2021 at http://www.soininvaara.fi/2017/02/10/miksi-kokeilussa-oleva-perustulomalli-ei-ole-se-oikea/ (in Finnish).

Solimano, Andrés (2011), 'Un programa de dividend ciudadano del Cobre: Hacia un ingreso universal para los chilenos', accessed 1 January 2021 at https://ingresobasico.files.wordpress.com/2020/04/un-programa-de-dividendo-ciudadano-del-cobre-hacia-un-ingreso-universal-para-los-chilenos.pdf.

Sommeiller, Estelle, Mark Price and Ellis Wazeter (2016), *Income Inequality in the U.S. by State, Metropolitan Area, and County*, Washington, DC: Economic Policy Institute, accessed 9 January 2021 at http://www.epi.org/publication/income-inequality-in-the-us/.

Sommer, Maximilian (2016), *A Feasible Basic Income Scheme for Germany: Effects on labor supply, poverty, and income inequality*, Cham: Springer.

Sovacool, Benjamin K., Roman V. Sidortsov and Benjamin R. Jones (2014), *Energy Security, Equality, and Justice*, London: Routledge.

Sowels, Nicholas (2018), 'Economic inequalities in the United Kingdom since 2008', in David Fée and Anémone Kober-Smith, *Inequalities in the UK: New discourses, evolutions and actions*, Bingley: Emerald, pp. 9–37.

Spence, Thomas (1796), *The Meridian Sun of Liberty, or the whole rights of man displayed and most accurately defined*, London: T. Spence, at no. 8 Little Turnstile, High Holborn.

Spence, Thomas (1797), *The Rights of Infants*, London: T. Spence, at no. 9 Oxford Street, lately removed from no. 8 Little Turnstile.

Spence, Thomas (1882), *Nationalization of the Land*, London: E.W. Allen, first published in 1775.

Spence, Thomas (1893–95), 'A Lecture', in *Pigs' Meat*, vol. 1, London, p. 266, undated.

Spence, Thomas (1893–95), *Pig's Meat*, second edition, three volumes, London.

Spence, Thomas (1893–95), 'The real rights of man', in *Pigs' Meat*, second edition, vol. 3, pp. 220–29, first published in 1793.

Spence, Thomas (1893–95), 'The Rights of Man' (a song), in *Pigs' Meat*, second edition, vol. 2, pp. 102–6, first published in 1783, also accessed 5 January 2021 at https://www.marxists.org/history/england/britdem/people/spence/selections/rights .htm.

Spence, Thomas (2014), 'Property in land every one's right, proved in a lecture read at the Philosophical Society in Newcastle on the 8th November 1775', in Alastair Bonnett and Keith Armstrong (eds), *Thomas Spence: The poor man's revolutionary*, London: Breviary Stuff, pp. 7–11, first published in 1775.

Spencer, M.C. (1981), *Charles Fourier*, Boston: Twayne.

Spicker, Paul (2011), *How Social Security Works: An introduction to benefits in Britain*, Bristol: Policy Press.

Stafford, William (1998), *John Stuart Mill*, Basingstoke: Macmillan.

Standing, Guy (ed.) (2004), *Promoting Income Security as a Right: Europe and North America*, London: Anthem Press for the International Labour Organization.

Standing, Guy (2011a), *The Precariat: The new dangerous class*. London: Bloomsbury.

Standing, Guy (2011b), 'Behavioural Conditionality: Why the nudges must be stopped—an opinion piece', *Journal of Poverty and Social Justice*, **19** (1), 27–37.

Standing, Guy (2012a), 'Social insurance is not for the Indian open economy of the 21st century', *Citizen's Income Newsletter*, issue 1 for 2012, pp. 5–7.

Standing, Guy (2012b), *Cash Transfers: A review of the issues in India*, New Delhi: UNICEF India.

Standing, Guy (2013), 'Can Basic Income cash transfers transform India?', *Citizen's Income Newsletter*, issue 2 for 2013, pp. 3–5.

Standing, Guy (2015), 'Why Basic Income's emancipatory value exceeds its monetary value', *Basic Income Studies*, **10** (2), 193–223.

Standing, Guy (2017a), *Basic Income: And how we can make it happen*, London: Penguin Random House.

Standing, Guy (2017b), 'Why you've never heard of a charter that's as important as Magna Carta', *Open Democracy*, accessed 10 January 2021 at https://www .opendemocracy.net/uk/guy-standing/why-youve-never-heard-of-charter-thats-as -important-as-magna-carta.

Standing, Guy (2019a), *Basic Income as Common Dividends: Piloting a transformative policy: A report for the Shadow Chancellor of the Exchequer*, London: Progressive Economy Forum, accessed 10 January 2021 at https://progressiveeconomyforum .com/publications/basic-income-as-common-dividends-piloting-a-transformative -policy/.

Standing, Guy (2019b), *Plunder of the Commons: A manifesto for sharing public wealth*, London: Penguin Random House.

Standing, Guy (2020), *Battling Eight Giants: Basic Income now*, London: I.B. Taurus, endorsements accessed 10 January 2021 at https://www.bloomsbury.com/uk/battling -eight-giants-9780755600632/.

Steensland, Brian (2008), *The Failed Welfare Revolution: America's struggle over guaranteed income policy*, Princeton and Oxford: Princeton University Press.

Stern, Will (2020), 'The forgotten forbearer of UBI', *Medium*, 14 August 2020, accessed 22 January 2021 at https://medium.com/basic-income/the-forgotten-forbearer-of-ubi -ddead9ac5915.

Stevens, Matt and Isabella Grullón Paz (2020), 'Andrew Yang's $1,000-a-month idea may have seemed absurd before. Not now', *The New York Times*, 18 March 2020, accessed 4 February 2021 at https://www.nytimes.com/2020/03/18/us/politics/universal-basic-income-andrew-yang.html.

Stirling, Alfie and Sarah Arnold (2019), *Nothing Personal: Replacing the personal tax allowance with a weekly national allowance*, London: New Economics Foundation, accessed 10 January 2021 at https://neweconomics.org/2019/03/nothing-personal.

Stirton, Lindsay, Jurgen De Wispelaere, Johanna Perkiö and Joe Chrisp (2017), 'Modelling political parties' support for Basic Income in Finland, 1979–2016', paper presented at the 17th BIEN Congress, Lisbon, 25–27 September 2017.

St John, Susan (2016), 'Can older citizens lead the way to a Universal Basic Income?', in Jennifer Mays, Greg Marston and John Tomlinson (eds), *Basic Income in Australia and New Zealand: Perspectives from the neoliberal frontier*, Basingstoke: Palgrave Macmillan, pp. 95–114.

Story, Michael (2015), *Free Market Welfare: The case for a Negative Income Tax*, London: Adam Smith Institute, accessed 10 January 2021 at https://www.adamsmith.org/blog/tax-spending/free-market-welfare-the-case-for-a-negative-income-tax.

Subramanian, Arvind (2018), 'Quasi-UBI: Rythu Bandhu can be the social and agri policy template', *Financial Express*, 1 July 2018, accessed 10 January 2021 at https://www.financialexpress.com/opinion/quasi-ubi-rythu-bandhu-can-be-the-social-agri-poicy-template/1239581/.

Suplicy, Eduardo Matarazzo (2003), 'Legitimizing Basic Income in developing countries: Brazil, or "The answer is blowin' in the wind"', *Journal of Post Keynesian Economics*, **25** (3), 407–24.

Sutherland, Holly (2016), 'EUROMOD: Introducing the team', *EUROMOD News*, November 2016, issue 6, Colchester: Institute for Social and Economic Research.

Szlinder, Maciej (2019), 'The Job Guarantee', in Malcolm Torry (ed.), *The Palgrave International Handbook of Basic Income*, Cham: Palgrave Macmillan, pp. 222–5.

Tabatabai, Hamid (2011a), 'Iran's economic reforms usher in a de facto Citizen's Income', *Citizen's Income Newsletter*, issue 1 for 2011, pp. 1–2.

Tabatabai, Hamid (2011b), 'The Basic Income road to reforming Iran's price subsidies', *Basic Income Studies*, **6** (1), 1–24.

Tabatabai, Hamid (2012a), 'Iran: A bumpy road toward Basic Income', in Richard Caputo (ed.), *Basic Income Guarantee and Politics: International experiences and perspectives on the viability of Income Guarantee*, New York: Palgrave Macmillan, pp. 285–300.

Tabatabai, Hamid (2012b), 'Iran's Citizen's Income scheme and its lessons', *Citizen's Income Newsletter*, issue 2 for 2012, pp. 2–4.

Tabatabai, Hamid (2021), correspondence with the author.

Taekema, Dan (2020), 'People kept working, became healthier while on basic income: Report', CBC, 5 March 2020, accessed 10 January 2021 at https://www.cbc.ca/news/canada/hamilton/basic-income-mcmaster-report-1.5485729.

Tahiraj, Enkeleida (2019), 'Basic Income in the European periphery', in Malcolm Torry (ed.), *The Palgrave International Handbook of Basic Income*, Cham: Palgrave Macmillan, pp. 413–18.

Tahiraj, Enkeleida (2021), correspondence with the author.

Takamatsu, Rie and Toshiaki Tachibanaki (2014), 'What needs to be considered when introducing a new welfare system: Who supports Basic Income in Japan?', in Yannick Vanderborght and Toru Yamamori (eds), *Basic Income in Japan: Prospects for a radical idea in a transforming welfare state*, New York: Palgrave Macmillan, pp. 197–218.

Tanner, Kathryn (2005), *Economy of Grace*, Minneapolis: Fortress Press.

Ten, C.L. (1998), 'Democracy, socialism, and the working classes', in John Skorupski (ed.), *The Cambridge Companion to Mill*, Cambridge: Cambridge University Press, pp. 372–95.

Thane, Pat (1996), *Foundations of the Welfare State*, second edition, London: Longman.

Thane, Pat (2011), 'The making of National Insurance, 1911', *Journal of Poverty and Social and Justice*, **19** (3), 211–19.

TheLocalES (2020), 'Spain's basic income scheme hits backlog dead-end', *TheLocalES*, 30 August 2020, accessed 7 January 2021 at https://www.thelocal.es/20200830/ spains-basic-income-scheme-hits-backlog-dead-end.

Theobald, Robert (1963), *Free Men and Free Markets*, New York: Clarkson N. Potter, Inc.

Theobald, Robert (1968), 'The implications of American physical abundance', *The Annals of the American Academy of Political and Social Science*, **378**, 11–21.

Thomas Spence Society (2020), 'Thomas Spence', accessed 21 December 2020 at http://www.thomas-spence-society.co.uk/.

Tiku, Natasha (2018), 'Y Combinator learns Basic Income is not so basic after all', *Wired*, accessed 10 January 2021 at https://www.wired.com/story/y-combinator -learns-basic-income-is-not-so-basic-after-all/.

Titmuss, Richard (1962), *Income Distribution and Social Change*, London: Allen and Unwin.

Tobin, James (1978), 'A Proposal for International Monetary Reform', *Eastern Economic Journal*, **4** (3–4), 153–9.

Tobin, James, Joseph A. Pechman and Peter M. Mieszkowski (1967), 'Is a Negative Income Tax practical?', *The Yale Law Journal*, **77** (1), 1–27.

Tomlinson, John (2012), 'Australia: Basic Income—A distant horizon', in Matthew C. Murray and Carole Pateman (eds), *Basic Income Worldwide: Horizons of reform*, Basingstoke and New York: Palgrave Macmillan, pp. 227–49.

Torry, Malcolm (1996), Letter to Professor Tony Atkinson.

Torry, Malcolm (ed.) (2005), 'On Citizen's Income and related topics: A compilation of writings by James Meade', *Citizen's Income Newsletter: James Meade commemorative edition*, London: Citizen's Income Trust, accessed 10 January 2021 at https:// citizensincome.org/wp-content/uploads/2016/02/CIT_Newsletter_2005_4_James _Meade_commemorative_edition.pdf.

Torry, Malcolm (2013), *Money for Everyone: Why we need a Citizen's Income*, Bristol: Policy Press.

Torry, Malcolm (2014a), 'A Basic Income is feasible: But what do we mean by feasible?', Paper presented at the 2014 BIEN Congress in Montreal, 27–29 June 2014, accessed 9 January 2021 at https://basicincome.org/bien/pdf/montreal2014/ BIEN2014_Torry.pdf.

Torry, Malcolm (2014b), *Research Note: A Feasible Way to Implement a Citizen's Income*, EUROMOD Working Paper EM17/14, Colchester: Institute for Social and Economic Research, accessed 10 January 2021 at https://www.iser.essex.ac.uk/ research/publications/working-papers/euromod/em17-14.

Torry, Malcolm (2015a), 'Some options for reform of the UK's tax and benefits systems', a paper prepared for a consultation on options for reform of the benefits system organized by some of the UK's major charities in June 2015, and subsequently published as 'Alternatives to Citizen's Basic Income', London: Citizen's Basic Income Trust, January 2018, accessed 10 January 2021 at https:// citizensincome.org/research-analysis/alternatives-to-citizens-basic-income/.

Torry, Malcolm (2015b), *Two Feasible Ways to Implement a Revenue Neutral Citizen's Income Scheme*, EUROMOD Working Paper EM6/15, Colchester: Institute for Social and Economic Research, accessed 10 January 2021 at https://iser.essex.ac.uk/research/publications/working-papers/euromod/em6-15.

Torry, Malcolm (2016a), *The Feasibility of Citizen's Income*, New York: Palgrave Macmillan.

Torry, Malcolm (2016b), *Citizen's Basic Income: A Christian social policy*, London: Darton, Longman and Todd.

Torry, Malcolm (2016c), *How Might we Implement a Citizen's Income?*, London: Institute for Chartered Accountants of England and Wales, accessed 10 January 2021 at www.icaew.com/-/media/corporate/files/technical/sustainability/outside-insights/citizens-income-web---final.ashx?la=en.

Torry, Malcolm (2016d), *Citizen's Income Schemes: An amendment, and a pilot project*, EUROMOD Working Paper EM5/16a, Colchester: Institute for Social and Economic Research, accessed 10 January 2021 at https://www.iser.essex.ac.uk/research/publications/working-papers/euromod/em5-16a.

Torry, Malcolm (2016e), *An Evaluation of a Strictly Revenue Neutral Citizen's Income Scheme*, EUROMOD Working Paper EM5/16, Colchester: Institute for Social and Economic Research, accessed 10 January 2021 at https://www.iser.essex.ac.uk/research/publications/working-papers/euromod/em5-16.

Torry, Malcolm (2017a), '"Unconditional" and "universal": Definitions and applications', a paper presented at the Foundation for International Studies on Social Security conference, Sigtuna, 2017.

Torry, Malcolm (2017b), 'What's a definition? And how should we define "Basic Income"?', A paper for the BIEN Congress in Lisbon, 2017, accessed 10 January 2021 at http://basicincome.org/wp-content/uploads/2015/01/Malcolm_Torry_Whats_a_definition_And_how_should_we_define_Basic_Income.pdf.

Torry, Malcolm (2017c), *A Variety of Indicators Evaluated for Two Implementation Methods for a Citizen's Basic Income*, EUROMOD Working Paper EM12/17, Colchester: Institute for Social and Economic Research, accessed 10 January 2021 at https://www.iser.essex.ac.uk/research/publications/working-papers/euromod/em12-17.

Torry, Malcolm (2018a), *Why we Need a Citizen's Basic Income: The desirability, feasibility and implementation of an unconditional income*, Bristol: Policy Press.

Torry, Malcolm (2018b), 'Speenhamland, automation, and basic income: A response', *Renewal*, **26** (1): 32–5.

Torry, Malcolm (2018c), *An Update, a Correction, and an Extension of an Evaluation of an Illustrative Citizen's Basic Income Scheme: An addendum to working paper EM12/17*, EUROMOD Working Paper EM12/17a, Colchester: Institute for Social and Economic Research, accessed 10 January 2021 at https://www.iser.essex.ac.uk/research/publications/working-papers/euromod/em12-17a.

Torry, Malcolm (2018d), 'What is an Unconditional Basic Income? A response to Rothstein', in Philippe Van Parijs, *Basic Income and the Left: A European debate*, Berlin: Social Europe, pp. 110–15.

Torry, Malcolm (2019a), *Static Microsimulation Research on Citizen's Basic Income for the UK: A personal summary and further reflections*, EUROMOD Working Paper EM13/19, Colchester: Institute to Social and Economic Research, accessed 10 January 2021 at https://www.iser.essex.ac.uk/research/publications/working-papers/euromod/em13-19.pdf.

Torry, Malcolm (ed.) (2019b), *The Palgrave International Handbook of Basic Income*, Cham: Palgrave Macmillan.

Torry, Malcolm (2019c), 'Feasibility and implementation', in Malcolm Torry (ed.), *The Palgrave International Handbook of Basic Income*, Cham: Palgrave Macmillan, pp. 157–73.

Torry, Malcolm (2020a), *A Modern Guide to Citizen's Basic Income: A multidisciplinary approach*, Cheltenham, UK and Northampton, MA, USA: Edward Elgar Publishing.

Torry, Malcolm (2020b), *Evaluation of a Recovery Basic Income, and of a Sustainable Revenue Neutral Citizen's Basic Income, with an Appendix Relating to Different Universal Credit Roll-out Scenarios*, EUROMOD Working Paper EM7/20, Colchester: Institute for Social and Economic Research, accessed 10 January 2021 at https://www.iser.essex.ac.uk/research/publications/working-papers/euromod/em7-20.pdf.

Torry, Malcolm (2020c), 'Research and education in the UK Basic Income debate', in Richard Caputo and Larry Liu (eds), *Political Activism and Basic Income Guarantee*, Cham: Palgrave Macmillan, pp. 185–208.

Torry, Malcolm (2020d), 'Minimum Income Standards in the Basic Income debate', in Chris Deeming (ed.), *Minimum Income Standards and Social Protection Research: International and Comparative Perspectives*, Bristol: Policy Press, pp. 319–29.

Torry, Malcolm (2020e), 'The role of research in the Basic Income Debate in the UK', *LSE Public Policy Review*, 1 (2): 4, 1–10, accessed 10 January 2021 at https://doi.org/10.31389/lseppr.11.

Townsend, Peter (1979), *Poverty in the United Kingdom*, Harmondsworth: Penguin.

UBI Lab Network (2020), accessed 27 December 2020 at https://www.ubilabnetwork.org/.

Unite Research (2019), *Universal Credit Not Fit for Purpose: Unite Universal Credit survey report*, London: Unite the Union, accessed 10 January 2021 at https://unitetheunion.org/media/2631/8869_universal-credit-report_a4_finaldigital.pdf.

USBIG Network, accessed 21 November 2019 at https://usbig.net/about-big/.

van Berkel, Rik (1994a), 'Basic Income as trade union policy', *Citizen's Income Bulletin*, no. 17, January 1994, pp. 18–21.

van Berkel, Rik (1994b), 'Basic Income as a debatable utopia: The political and social feasibility of a basic income in the Netherlands', paper presented at the fifth BIEN conference, London, 1994.

Vanderborght, Yannick (2000), 'The VIVANT experiment in Belgium', in Robert van der Veen and Loek Groot (eds), *Basic Income on the Agenda: Policy objectives and political chances*, Amsterdam: Amsterdam University Press, pp. 276–84.

Vanderborght, Yannick and Toru Yamamori (eds) (2014), *Basic Income in Japan: Prospects for a radical idea in a transforming welfare state*, New York: Palgrave Macmillan.

Van der Veen (1988), 'Basic Income: The debate in the Netherlands', in Anne Miller (ed.), *First International Conference on Basic Income: Proceedings, 1986*, Antwerp: Basic Income European Network, pp. 296–306.

Van Oijen, Geert (1988), 'Basic Income and the Claimants Movement in Europe', in Anne Miller (ed.), *First International Conference on Basic Income: Proceedings, 1986*, Antwerp: Basic Income European Network, pp. 269–76.

Van Parijs, Philippe (1995), *Real Freedom for All: What (if anything) can justify capitalism?*, Oxford: Oxford University Press.

Van Parijs, Philippe (2009), 'Political ecology: From autonomous sphere to Basic Income', *Basic Income Studies*, **4** (2), 6, 1–9.

Van Parijs, Philippe (2020), correspondence with the author.

Van Parijs, Philippe and Yannick Vanderborght (2017), *Basic Income: A radical proposal for a free society and a sane economy*, Cambridge, MA: Harvard University Press.

Van Trier, Walter (1988), 'Basic Incomes in Belgium: The state of the political and academic debate', in Anne Miller (ed.), *First International Conference on Basic Income: Proceedings, 1986*, Antwerp: Basic Income European Network, pp. 279–87.

Van Trier, Walter (ed.) (1990), *Second International Conference on Basic Income: Basic Incomes and problems of implementation*, Antwerp: Basic Income European Network.

Van Trier, Walter (1995), *Every One a King*, Leuven: Departement Sociologie, Katholieke Universiteit Leuven.

Van Trier, Walter (2002), 'Who framed "Social Dividend"?', Paper presented at the first USBIG conference, New York, 8–10 March 2002.

Van Trier, Walter (2005), 'A.R. Orage and the reception of Douglas' Social Credit Theory', in Guido Erreygers and Geert Jacobs (eds), *Language, Communication and the Economy*, Amsterdam and Philadelphia: John Benjamins Publishing Company, pp. 199–229.

Van Trier, Walter (2018a), 'Scheme for a State Bonus and the early roots of the Basic Income idea in the UK', paper presented at the 'Basic Income: The Past and the Present' AEA-ASSA Conference, Philadelphia, 3–5 January 2018, accessed 10 January 2021 at https://www.aeaweb.org/conference/2018/preliminary/paper/YQEheHd4.

Van Trier, Walter (2018b), 'From James Meade's "Social Dividend" to "State Bonus": An intriguing chapter in the history of a concept', *Oeconomia*, **8** (4): 439–74, accessed 3 January 2021 at https://journals.openedition.org/oeconomia/4226#:~:text=An%20important%20feature%20of%20the,to%20each%20and%20every%20one.

Van Trier, Walter (2019), 'André Gorz's recantation of the "Second Cheque Strategy" and his adoption of Basic Income', paper presented at a conference in Cambridge, UK, 14 January 2019.

Van Trier, Walter (2020), correspondence with the author.

Vince, Philip (1983), *Tax Credit—the Liberal Plan for Tax and Social Security*, London: Women's Liberal Federation.

Vince, Philip (1986), 'Basic Incomes: Some practical considerations', in *BIRG Bulletin*, Spring 1986, London: Basic Income Research Group, pp. 5–8.

Vince, Philip (1990), 'Citizen's Income', *BIRG Bulletin*, no. 11, July 1990, pp. 20–21.

Vince, Philip (2011), correspondence with the author, dated 6 April 2011.

Vivant (2020), 'Vivant', accessed 10 January 2021 at http://www.vivant.org.

Voituron, Paul (1876), *Manuel du Libéralisme Belge*, Bruxelles: Librarie C. Muquardt. [Translation by Malcolm Torry.]

Voituron, Paul (2004), 'The right to labour and property', trans. John Cunliffe and Guido Erreygers, in John Cunliffe and Guido Erreygers (eds), *The Origins of Universal Grants: An anthology of historical writings on Basic Capital and Basic Income*, Basingstoke: Palgrave Macmillan, pp. 48–55, first published in 1848.

Walley, John (1986), 'Public support for families with children: A study of British politics', *BIRG Bulletin*, no. 5, Spring 1986, pp. 8–11.

Walter, Tony (1985), *Faire Shares? An ethical guide to tax and social security*, Edinburgh: The Handsel Press.

Walter, Tony (1989), *Basic Income: Freedom from poverty, freedom to work*, London: Marion Boyars.

Werner, Götz W. and Adrienne Goehler (2010), *1.000 Euro für Jeden*, Berlin: Econ, Ullstein Buchverlage.

White, Stuart (2003), *The Civic Minimum: On the rights and obligations of economic citizenship*, Oxford: Oxford University Press.

Whittaker, Matthew (2019), *Follow the Money: Exploring the link between UK growth and workers' pay packets*, London: The Resolution Foundation, accessed 10 January 2021 at https://www.resolutionfoundation.org/publications/follow-the-money/.

Whitton, Tim (1993), 'Does "insertion" work? France's minimum income', *Citizen's Income Bulletin*, no. 16, July 1993, pp. 11–14.

Widerquist, Karl (2010a), 'Lessons of the Alaska Dividend', *Citizen's Income Newsletter*, issue 3 for 2010, pp. 13–15.

Widerquist, Karl (2010b), 'Lockean theories of property: Justifications for unilateral appropriation', *Public Reason*, **2** (3), 3–26, accessed 22 January 2021 at https://www.researchgate.net/publication/45515620_Lockean_Theories_of_Property_Justifications_for_Unilateral_Appropriation.

Widerquist, Karl (2013), *Independence, Propertylessness, and Basic Income: A theory of freedom as the power to say no*, New York: Palgrave Macmillan.

Widerquist, Karl (2015), 'Ancient Athens might have had a Basic Income', *Reddit*, accessed 10 January 2021 at https://www.reddit.com/r/BasicIncome/comments/3bqgex/ancient_athens_might_have_had_a_basic_income/.

Widerquist, Karl (2018), *A Critical Analysis of Basic Income Experiments for Researchers, Policymakers, and Citizens*, Cham: Palgrave Macmillan.

Widerquist, Karl (2019a), 'Three waves of Basic Income support', in Malcolm Torry (ed.), *The Palgrave International Handbook of Basic Income*, Cham: Palgrave Macmillan, pp. 31–44.

Widerquist, Karl (2019b), 'The Negative Income Tax experiments of the 1970s', in Malcolm Torry (ed.), *The Palgrave International Handbook of Basic Income*, Cham: Palgrave Macmillan, pp. 303–18.

Widerquist, Karl (2021), correspondence with the author.

Widerquist, Karl and Michael Howard (2012), *Alaska's Permanent Fund Dividend: Examining its suitability as a model*, New York: Palgrave Macmillan.

Widerquist, Karl, José A. Noguera, Yannick Vanderborght and Jurgen De Wispelaere (eds) (2013), *Basic Income: An anthology of contemporary research*, Chichester: Wiley Blackwell.

Widerquist, Karl and Allan Sheahen (2012), 'The United States: The Basic Income Guarantee—Past experience, current proposals', in Matthew C. Murray and Carole Pateman (eds), *Basic Income Worldwide: Horizons of reform*, Basingstoke and New York: Palgrave Macmillan, pp. 11–32.

Wintour, Patrick (2015), 'Green party's flagship economic policy would hit poorest hardest, say experts', *The Guardian*, 27 January 2015, accessed 10 January 2021 at https://www.theguardian.com/politics/2015/jan/27/green-party-citizens-income-policy-hits-poor.

Wittgenstein, Ludwig (2001), *Philosophische Untersuchungen/Philosophical Investigations*, the German text with a revised English translation, third edition, trans. G.E.M. Anscombe, Oxford: Basil Blackwell. The first edition was published in 1953. References record the paragraph number followed by the page number.

Wogaman, Philip (1968), *Guaranteed Annual Income: The moral issues*, Nashville and New York: Abingdon Press.

Work and Pensions Committee (2017), 'Citizen's Income not the Solution to Welfare State problems', accessed 10 January 2021 at https://old.parliament.uk/business/committees/committees-a-z/commons-select/work-and-pensions-committee/news-parliament-2015/citizens-income-report-published-16-17/.

World Basic Income (2020), 'A way to share the world's wealth', accessed 10 January 2021 at http://www.worldbasicincome.org.uk/.

Yanes, Pablo (2013), 'Targeting and conditionalities in Mexico: The end of a cash transfer model?', in Rubén Lo Vuolo (ed.), *Citizen's Income and Welfare Regimes in Latin America*, New York: Palgrave Macmillan, pp. 67–85.

Yanes, Pablo (2019), 'Appendix: From Local to National—Mexico City and Basic Income', in Malcolm Torry (ed.), *The Palgrave International Handbook of Basic Income*, Cham: Palgrave Macmillan, pp. 334–6.

Yi, Gunmin (2019), 'Korean experiments', in Malcolm Torry (ed.), *The Palgrave International Handbook of Basic Income*, Cham: Palgrave Macmillan, pp. 418–21.

Yi, Gunmin (2020), correspondence with the author.

Young, Charlie (2018), *Realising Basic Income Experiments in the UK: A typology and toolkit of Basic Income design and delivery*, London: Royal Society of Arts, accessed 10 January 2021 at https://www.thersa.org/discover/publications-and-articles/reports/realising-basic-income.

Zelleke, Almaz (2012), 'Basic Income and the Alaska model: Limits of the resource dividend model for the implementation of an Unconditional Basic Income', in Karl Widerquist and Michael W. Howard (eds), *Alaska's Permanent Fund Dividend*, New York: Palgrave Macmillan, pp. 141–68.

Zero Poverty (2020), 'Q: How much poverty should exist? A: Zero', Zero Poverty, accessed 10 January 2021 at http://www.zeropoverty.io.

Zúñiga Fajuri, Alejandra (2017), 'El ingreso Básico Universal como nuevo derecho social', *Inicio*, **70**, accessed 1 January 2021 at https://revistas.uv.cl/index.php/rcs/article/view/1047/1045.

Index of names

[Korean names are given in the same way as other names: 'family name, given name']

Index of subjects

Printed and bound by CPI Group (UK) Ltd, Croydon, CR0 4YY

16/04/2025

14658489-0004